Co-operative Organizations and Canadian Society:
Popular Institutions and the Dilemmas of Change

Co-operatives in Canada have millions of members and control billions of dollars in assets. Nevertheless, they are viewed as institutions outside the mainstream of economic life. This apparent conflict between the reality and the public perception relates in part to the dilemma central to most co-operatives' existence: while they attempt to follow a logic of democratic control and social development, they must also respond to the demands of a market economy that operates on a fundamentally different ethos.

The essays in this volume offer a multidisciplinary analysis of co-operatives. Incorporating the perspectives of economics, history, political science, marketing, law, sociology, and education, they explore how co-ops deal with this dilemma.

The authors identify a broad range of social needs served by co-ops, from building community identity to controlling key aspects of everyday life. Along with institutions such as non-profit organizations and trade unions, co-operatives are an organizational response to the undermining of community identity and control by the evolution of our economy. Like these other institutions, co-operatives originated and developed because they had their own particular strengths, one of the most important being their ability to supply goods and services, and meet social goals, in a way no conventional institution could.

However, as these essays demonstrate, most co-operatives are market-oriented organizations for whom open rejection of the demands of the economy can easily spell business disaster. Particularly in competitive markets where the need for collective action is less, co-operatives may have difficulty satisfying both their economic requirements and the social and political objectives of their members.

MURRAY E. FULTON is Associate Professor, Department of Agricultural Economics, and an associate of the Centre for the Study of Co-operatives, University of Saskatchewan.

Co-operative Organizations and Canadian Society:

Popular Institutions and the Dilemmas of Change

edited by Murray E. Fulton

UNIVERSITY OF TORONTO PRESS
Toronto Buffalo London

© University of Toronto Press 1990
Toronto Buffalo London
Printed in Canada

ISBN 0-8020-2673-7 (cloth)
ISBN 0-8020-6711-5 (paper)

Printed on acid-free paper

Canadian Cataloguing in Publication Data

Main entry under title:

Co-operative organizations and Canadian society

Includes bibliographical references.
ISBN 0-8020-2673-7 (bound) ISBN 0-8020-6711-5 (pbk.)

1. Cooperative societies – Canada. 2. Cooperation
Canada. I. Fulton, Murray E.

HD3448.C66 1990   334.0971   C90-094194-4

Contents

Acknowledgments

This book is truly the result of a co-operative effort and I would sincerely like to thank all the authors for their enthusiasm for this project and for making it a reality. I owe a debt in particular to those at the Centre for the Study of Co-operatives for the environment in which the book was conceived and developed, and to the sponsors of the Centre for the support that made this and other research possible.

For their excellent editorial assistance, I would like to thank Aina Kagis, Zandra MacEachern, and Diane Mew. I would also like to extend my appreciation to Lynn Murphy and Anne Duff for their assistance in typing and proof-reading the manuscript.

Thanks to Virgil Duff and Lorraine Ourom at the University of Toronto Press for their overall support and for their help in preparing the manuscript.

Grants in aid of publication were provided by the University of Saskatchewan Publications Fund and the Centre for the Study of Co-operatives.

Finally, I would like to thank my wife, Leona, for her support and encouragement.

M.F.

Preface

The impetus for this volume came from informal discussions at the Centre for the Study of Co-operatives in the summer of 1986, concerning problems faced by co-operatives in the 1980s and 1990s. We felt that the increasing competitiveness of the economy was having a substantial impact on the financial health of co-operatives and on their ability to supply goods and services. In the context of an increasingly individualistic society, this trend raised questions about relationships between co-operatives and their members, and about whether co-operatives could continue to offer both social and economic benefits to their members.

As a group, we believed that our consideration of these questions ought to go well beyond coffee-break conversation. Each of us felt that our research could be applied directly to these problems, although the precise implications of such investigations were not yet clear. We also became convinced that a multidisciplinary approach was necessary if the full complexity and diversity of co-operatives were to be encompassed. What emerged was not only this volume, but one of the most intellectually stimulating exercises in our careers.

The process that produced this volume was characterized by four underlying currents which help to explain its emphases, final shape, and intended audiences. The first was an appreciation of our responsibility to examine and address publicly basic questions facing the co-operative sector in Canada. We wished to address these questions academically, while still providing food for thought to those working in co-operative organizations. In our research, we found the co-operative sector open to academic investigation and willing to provide the necessary data.

A second current running through the book emerged early in our project. As we began group discussion of our papers, we discovered the importance of communicating across our artificially separated intellectual disciplines. Initially we found this difficult, given our various disciplines' specific languages and conceptual structures. To bridge this gap, we were all required to present our ideas in the simplest language possible.

Breaking down these barriers led us to challenge the basic assumptions and intellectual underpinnings in each others' disciplines. The lawyer in our group found things lacking in the historical and political approach; marketing, history, and political specialists found inadequacies in the economists' approach; and so on. As we responded to our colleagues' challenges we began to incorporate their perspectives into our individual analyses. While this has not been taken so far as to constitute a true interdisciplinary approach, it has enriched and provided common focus for our disciplinary studies.

As we expanded our disciplinary boundaries, we often discovered that we were asking the same questions about co-operatives, albeit in different academic languages. Consequently this book reveals a number of common themes in the study of co-operatives, and offers many illustrations of their likely impact and evolution. Not surprisingly, our collective research effort led us to believe that these themes are not unique to co-operatives, but also apply to other organizations that attempt to achieve both social and economic objectives.

A third current was the need to pull together literature on co-operation. As this volume was being written, four of us were teaching courses on co-operatives at the University of Saskatchewan. When we sought material from within our own disciplines that we could use in our courses we found that most of the literature on co-operatives remains scattered in journals or books, often in a language inaccessible to students. We saw that it was imperative to develop notes and summary articles.

Our appreciation that no single discipline can fully explain co-operatives serves as the basis for a fourth current underlying our project. In our teaching we began to see the importance of making students aware of what we were learning in our research – that there are necessarily other, complementary ways of looking at the questions surrounding co-operatives than those associated with our individual disciplines. For example, political, historical, educational, legal, and marketing vantage points are all required to study co-operatives from an economic perspective. We came to see this volume as an excellent vehicle for such intellectual cross-fertilization.

These four currents establish very clearly whom we believe to be our audience. Given the volume's genesis in questions about the present and future of co-operatives, we expect an interest from those in the co-operative sector whose jobs require ongoing, practical attention to the issues we confront. We also expect that the book will be used in university and college courses dealing with co-operatives. Finally, we hope that our efforts at integrating a scattered and multidisciplinary body of thought and literature will be stimulating to academics and other researchers studying co-operatives.

This last point deserves elaboration. While there are a number of common ideas running through the book, it should be stressed that our goal was not to spell out a general theory of co-operatives capable of replacing the disciplinary perspectives represented in the volume's chapters. This is not a source of disappointment to us, primarily because we do not believe that the empirical and theoretical research foundations for such a general theory exist in Canada. Moreover, by making our findings and perspectives accessible to several important audiences – the co-operative sector, undergraduates, and researchers – we offer a more appropriate contribution to the field of co-operative studies than we could by artificially reconstructing our disciplinary perspectives to produce a 'grand theory' of interest to only a small group of academics.

We do not believe, however, that we have merely summarized previous work. Instead, it is our view that we have provided a novel and multidisciplinary application of two valuable theoretical perspectives on co-operative organizational activity: the principal-agent problem, and the existence of competing logics of group activity and decision-making within economic organizations. Included in these perspectives is the dilemma that co-operatives have always faced of attempting to borrow from a liberal and individualistic society, while at the same time trying to change it. We examine these theoretical perspectives and some of their consequences in the Introduction. Their application in this volume represents a provisional beginning for a more comprehensive account of co-operatives in Canadian society.

Obviously, much remains to be done. While we have examined non-Canadian experiences in order to understand the origins and traditions of co-operation and to put Canadian co-operation into the context of the world-wide movement, more work is needed. For instance, we regret that our research seldom incorporated French-language literature on co-operatives in Quebec, and that consequently the scope of our discussions is not comprehensively Canadian. This is particularly unfortunate since the large co-operative sector in Quebec is organized differently than in the rest of Canada, thus providing a fertile ground for additional understanding of the forces and problems we have identified. For those interested in this substantial theoretical and empirical literature, an excellent place to begin is *Coopératives et développement: revue du CIRIEC* (Centre interuniversitaire de recherche, d'information et d'enseignement sur les coopératives), published in Montreal.

We look forward to using some of the lessons learned in our project as a basis for future work on more specific topics. In the spirit of the discussions that gave rise to this volume, we invite comments from all interested readers. Given the importance of co-operatives to Canadian society, and in view of their leaders' desire to ensure that their organizations promote members' interests, we dedicate this book to co-operative members and leaders throughout Canada.

Lars Apland, Christopher Axworthy, Brett Fairbairn, Murray Fulton,
Lou Hammond Ketilson, Skip Kutz, David Laycock
March 1990

PART ONE

Dilemmas of Popular Institutions in Modern Society

MURRAY FULTON AND DAVID LAYCOCK

1 Introduction

While co-operatives have millions of members, and control billions of dollars in assets,[1] they are nevertheless viewed as institutions outside the mainstream of economic life in most countries. The distinctiveness of co-operatives' organizational form and practice has often been the source of their major strengths and weaknesses. This distinctiveness is also clearly the outcome of what emerges as a general theme in this book: while co-operatives take a crucial part of their logic from outside the prevailing market economy, they must respond to the pressures and logic of that market.

Co-operatives have been animated by, and have served, a broad range of social needs – including community identity and control over key aspects of everyday life. Co-operatives, along with other institutions such as non-profit organizations and trade unions, are one organizational response to the undermining of this identity and control by the evolution of our market economy. Like these other institutions, co-operatives originated and developed because they have their own peculiar strengths, one of the most important being that they have supplied something that takes its logic from outside the market.

At the same time, however, and to a greater degree than most non-profit organizations, co-operatives are market-oriented organizations for whom open rejection of the market can easily spell business disaster. Particularly in competitive markets where the need for collective action is reduced, co-operatives may find themselves unable to meet both the economic requirements and the social needs.

This chapter provides an introduction to what we consider to be the central dilemma for Canadian co-operatives: the conflict between democratic control (as expressed in the relationships between individuals and social institutions) and market competitiveness. We delineate this conflict from two perspectives. One is internal to the co-operative and is discussed with reference to the principal-agent problem; the other addresses the external aspects of co-operatives' dilemmas in the context of a market economy.

The Principal-Agent Problem

As chapter 2 points out, co-operatives have a number of features that both define and distinguish them from other organizations in society. One of the most distinctive is democratic control, which goes well beyond the principle of one member, one vote. Democracy in co-operatives is manifested, for example, in local control by board members, managers, and employees who are in touch with the community, and whose participation is simultaneously an education in democratic practice.

Democratic control in co-operatives also implies a sensitivity to the needs and goals of the people affected by their actions – namely, the stakeholders. It assumes that in all communities co-operative members and other citizens are interdependent and have legitimate goals of self-realization that depend on the quality of relations within the community. This notion of stakeholders is explored in greater detail in the latter part of chapter 2.

Sensitivity to the needs of those who have a stake in the outcome, however, does not imply that those needs will be met. In all but the smallest co-operatives the people actually making decisions will not be those most directly affected by their consequences. This raises at least two questions. First, how do decision-makers balance the often divergent needs and goals of different groups in the community? Second, what guarantee do any of the stakeholders have that their goals and needs will actually be met?

Chapter 7 addresses the first question at length. The second question raises what is often called the principal-agent problem, the problem of the extent to which someone (the agent) hired or appointed to represent another (the principal) will undertake actions that are in the principal's best interests. This topic is explicitly addressed in chapter 3 and serves the basis for part of the analysis in chapter 16. Moreover, as will be argued, it serves as the basis for many of the chapters in this book.[2]

Implicit in this definition of the principal-agent problem is some sort of hierarchical control structure, which exists in virtually all organizations and institutions. To facilitate specialization and co-ordination, principals delegate the task of implementing decisions to agents. In this process the principals often find themselves far removed from the agents. The principal-agent problem questions whether this implementation fully reflects the wishes of the delegating principals. Put somewhat differently, the problem is one of how decisions are made in co-operatives, who benefits from them, and what the overall consequences of these processes are to co-operative organizations.

The problem is perhaps best explained in terms of a flow of signals. Within any organization, signals flow from level to level and within each level. These signals may be directives or requests for certain actions to be undertaken or certain information to be provided, or they may be the actual information that is routinely or specifically requested. These signals can be expected to flow both up and down the organization. For instance, a manager may request that a certain product be produced and that reports on its production and sale be provided.

Whenever signals are transmitted, however, filtering occurs. A manager's request may not be fully understood by those producing the product, either because of poor communication, or because it is in the interests of those receiving the request to misinterpret it. Similarly, the information passed up to the manager is likely to be filtered; decisions regarding which data to report and the form of the reporting all involve filtering. Consequently, the manager is unlikely to obtain precisely what he or she requested. The result is a manifestation of the principal-agent problem. Chapters 3 and 16 discuss this explicitly.

There are, of course, other elements to the problem. For instance, we can ask whether the agents really understand the needs of the principals. Pursuing this question in the context of co-operatives naturally leads into a discussion of co-operative education, which is normally posited as another of co-operatives' distinguishing features. Chapter 6 addresses this topic further.

The root of the principal-agent problem is that all of us have our own goals, objectives, and philosophical orientations. Inevitably, as we assume responsibilities to make decisions and implement plans, these guide our actions. As agents or representatives, our decisions reflect our personal needs and concerns as much as those of the principals we represent.

The problem of principals and agents has been examined in many contexts. For instance, political scientists examine how government policy is affected by civil servants and other groups who implement policy, or how policies advanced by organized interests or party leaders reflect (or fail to reflect) their members' desires. The larger question of legitimacy and meaningful representation of citizen interests in democratic politics is directly posed by this variant of the principal-agent problem.

Similar questions arise in other areas. Economists usually assume that firms maximize profits. The question raised by the principal-agent problem is whether this will indeed happen, since the managers and employees hired by the owners may have very different objectives than the owners. For instance, if managers and employees have goals such as job security, promotion, organizational expansion, or innovation, they are likely to promote these goals, and it is by no means evident that this will fulfil the owners' goal of maximizing profits.[3]

Co-operatives face similar problems of representation. At the first level are locally elected boards of directors, who often do not adequately understand the wants and needs of the members they represent. Boards, in turn, must select managers for the co-operative. Like their private sector counterparts, co-operatives will find principal-agent problems arising between their managers and their employees. The result is a series of principal-agent problems, each of which will have an effect on the manner in which the co-operative functions.

The agency problem is compounded in co-operatives, which are trying to provide something more than private sector firms – namely, a democratic responsiveness to communal and societal welfare. The agency problem arises when co-operatives' decision-makers, in their attempts to meet the apparent demands of the market, depart from (or fail to advance) community and social goals that transcend the logic of the market. In other words, the large number of stakeholders in a co-operative provide many signals to the co-operative, the majority of which are likely to get lost because of the principal-agent problem.

It is tempting to characterize this problem as one between members – the principals – and those they have elected or appointed as agents – the board, management, and employees. However, given the large number of principal-agent relationships in a co-operative, it is useful to consider that the problem can also arise between the board and management, and between the managers and employees.

Generally speaking the dilemma facing co-operatives is that while certain stakeholders (for instance, members) value co-operatives as co-operatives and may wish to see social goals take priority over market demands, there are others (for instance, managers) who believe the demands of competitive markets must take precedence.

While there is some accuracy to this characterization of intra-co-operative conflict, it fails to capture the essence of the problem. First, not all members feel that co-operatives should meet community needs, nor do all managers and employees believe that market demands are paramount in all circumstances. More important, however, attaching these views to specific groups obscures the problem. The principal-agent problem in co-operatives is more the consequence of two different views of the nature of co-operative business activity, or between 'two logics of collective action' (market versus non-market),[4] than it is between two or more distinguishable groups in the organization. Indeed, one could argue that the interpersonal dynamics and inevitably distorted communication underlying the principal-agent problem in co-operatives do a good deal to obscure the distinctive implications of the two logics to both the members and their agents, each of whom may express both logics in their own behaviour and decisions about their co-operatives' activities. One cannot appreciate the depth of the principal-agent problem without reference to the two logics dynamic, or vice versa.[5]

As chapters 5 and 11 make clear, albeit in the more traditional political language of representation and participation, conflicts over which of the two available logics of collective action ought to direct co-operatives' activities are indicative of the dilemmas inherent in the practice of co-operative democracy.

The principal-agent problem among members and their agents is further complicated if the motivations of co-operatives' founders and inheritors are at variance. Current members of co-operatives are inevitably removed from issues that were crucial when the co-operatives were formed forty to fifty years ago. Most of the co-operatives' founding members were well aware of the potential for conflict between community and market imperatives. In fact, as chapter 2 argues, it was precisely a need to enhance social relationships, albeit within the confines of existing markets and socio-political environments, that led to the formation of co-operatives. Today, however, many (if not most) members are unaware of the two logics. Instead, they regard the kinds of service provision enabled by existing market conditions as co-operatives' primary objective, without appreciating how this objective distorts legitimate social objectives that their co-operatives formally or implicitly endorse.

Co-operatives in a Competitive World

All co-operatives feel the pressures of market competition. Often this pressure comes from other firms in the industry. Credit unions and other co-operative financial institutions are now experiencing increased competition from banks and trust companies as the result of financial market deregulation. Competitive pressure may also result from a shift in co-operatives' economic environments. Grain marketing co-operatives, for instance, currently face pressure with the downturn in agricultural markets. Market upturns, however, do not relieve this competitive pressure, as co-operatives and other firms normally use these opportunities to expand their assets and sales.

In responding to these market pressures, co-operatives feel compelled to adopt the style and strategies of the market-oriented firms that dominate the economy. Co-operative leaders and managers often believe that failure to follow the lead set by their private competitors will lead to their co-operatives' demise. They reason that if their co-operatives do not provide the same services, have access to capital on the same terms, pay the same rate for labour and other supplies, adopt the same technology, and make decisions in the same manner as the market-oriented firms, they will be unable to compete.

The problem that often arises for contemporary Canadian co-operatives, however, is that as more market-oriented strategies are adopted, co-operatives' abilities to promote specifically co-operative objectives are subtly undermined. As a co-operative business emulates more of its competitors' behaviour, it becomes less distinguishable from these firms, and gradually loses the distinctive relation to community that justified its existence in the first place and has continued to give it a co-operative-specific market advantage. The short-term rationality of consistently choosing a market-oriented strategy can thus undermine many co-operatives' abilities to pursue organizational or social goals that 'market logic' deems irrational.

This trade-off in co-operatives has a number of facets. At times, the decisions co-operatives are asked to make are a matter of short-term survival. To remain competitive in the market, co-operatives often believe they must adopt certain tactics. In the long run, if these tactics lead to the demise of the co-operative as a co-operative, then the problem is really between incompatible short-term and long-term rationalities. The problem is exacerbated because co-operatives often must implement the market logic that their organizations had been established, at least in part, to undermine, if their institutions are to retain their present business success and market share. The shorter-term rationality or logic often leads co-operative decision-makers (elected and non-elected 'agents') to perceive co-operative principles as a competitive burden.

A typical example is in co-operative financing. Some co-operatives believe that if they could offer investors a return on equity invested based on the firm's profitability, the co-operative could attract new capital for expansion and growth. Such a provision, however, would violate the principle of limited return on equity, and could easily begin a rapid transformation of the co-operative into a relatively conventional investor-owned firm.

In short, co-operatives face a vexing dilemma. Co-operative leaders often feel that institutional survival demands adoption of operational styles and strategies that are closer to those of market-oriented firms. Yet adopting these strategies can undermine institutional survival, albeit for different reasons. A number of these reasons are explored in this volume. For instance, chapter 7 examines situations where pursuit of a goal may actually lead to its non-attainment, while chapter 15 explains how adopting conventional wholesaling strategies may reduce member support for co-operative stores.

We argued earlier that many current co-operative members may have particular trouble seeing the importance of social relationships. In a sense, established co-operatives are what might be called ideological 'price-takers.' Just as it is impossible for price-taking firms to charge a different price for their product than their competitors, so it is extremely difficult for institutions to promote community if prevailing social relationships and business practices inhibit widespread recognition of the value of community. The result is that democratic and social participation may not be sustainable. Chapters 5, 6, and 8 examine this question of co-operative ideology.

The argument above can be extended. At the time of their inception, co-operatives almost inevitably offered two things: economic benefits as a response to the monopoly or oligopoly power of existing firms; and community-based economic democracy and participation. Each played an important role in their success, since members would be attracted to the co-operative if either of these benefits appealed to them. In particular, the ability to realize an economic benefit was often a strong motivator, enabling the co-operative to grow and expand.

While the economic benefit may have been the most important reason influencing most members to join the co-operative, this does not mean that they were not interested in democratic participation. Democracy is a collective good, requiring collective action for its achievement. In most cases of collective action, individuals may perceive little incentive to participate, even though they might benefit greatly if the good were supplied by someone else. One of the ways to ensure participation is to provide another good along with the collective good. In the argument above, this other good is the economic benefit of co-operative membership.⁹

If a co-operative succeeds economically, it soon establishes a new set of standards – better service or a more competitive price – that its competitors must meet. In achieving this goal, however, the established co-operative may plant the seeds of the 'two logics' dilemma. While the co-operative can continue to supply goods and services, the increased competitiveness it introduces may remove some of the profitability that led to the emergence of a community of interest among those exploited by monopoly profits. In addition, however, a vision of community is difficult to promote in the absence of companion economic benefits – benefits which co-operatives may now be supplying, and which may be taken for granted by their members.

The extent of this difficulty is obviously conditioned by many factors formally external to co-operatives' behaviour, such as the degree of economic hardship among their memberships, the extent of citizen mobilization for social change by other social and political organizations, and the power of both compelling alternative ideologies and compelling establishment-entrenching ideologies within the regional or national community. Clearly, the evolution of perceptions regarding problems and possibilities within co-operative organizations is closely related to the social and political context within which co-operative firms operate, as well as to the institutional dynamics evolving within these co-operatives. Co-operatives' life-cycles are intimately related to the patterns of change within the societies giving them birth.

The problem co-operatives face in pursuing democratic participation in conjunction with their economic needs is not limited to co-operatives' role in the market-place. Co-operatives' relations with governments are increasingly important. The dilemma co-operatives face in this instance is similar to their market dilemma, in that it involves both democratic participation and competition. Co-operatives' democratic natures should make them well-suited to participate in public policy formation, since they can legitimately claim to represent their many members' wishes better than most organized economic interests. However, existing patterns of business-state relations and public policy development in Canada do not turn primarily on considerations of democratic legitimacy.[7] Consequently co-operative democracy yields major disadvantages in policy-development competitions with organized economic interests whose relations with governments are constrained by fewer conditions of democratic decision-making procedure. Chapters 10, 11, and 17 explore the relationship between governments and co-operatives, with chapter 10 focusing specifically on the dynamics and environmental factors that produce these disadvantages for co-operatives.

Thus, in their relations with government co-operatives are also faced with a dual logic. As in the strictly economic sphere, this dual logic can usefully be equated with the principal-agent question, for the essence of the problem is how co-operatives' members can have their interests represented to government bodies by their elected and hired agents (directors and management) in a way that is consistent with their commitment to economic democracy. A number of chapters touch on this relation between the dual logics and the principal-agent problem in the area of government relations, including chapters 9, 10, 11, 13, 14, and 17.

The dilemma inherent in pursuing market and non-market objectives is not peculiar to co-operatives. Any organization with goals distinct from maximization of profit in the market economy will encounter the same conflicts. For example, non-profit organizations often depend on funds from market-oriented events but pursue distinctly non-market goals and objectives. To the extent that survival requires continued 'philanthropic' support by market-oriented firms, non-profit organizations will increasingly be under pressure to provide services beneficial to their corporate benefactors. This often reduces a non-profit organization's ability to pursue its primary goals. In rather different ways, trade unions face the dilemma of identifying the most rational mix of market and non-market logics of collective action in their bargaining strategies, pursuit of social and political goals, and creation of 'corporatist' relations with policy development bodies of government.[8]

Co-operatives' dilemmas concerning the best mix of the 'two logics of collective action' will not go away. In fact, one can safely predict that in the absence of strong countervailing forces, the non-market logic of collective democratic action will appear increasingly less important to co-operative leaders and members. Co-operative democracy's *raison d'être* can all too easily be forgotten by co-operatives' members and leaders as markets become increasingly competitive and centralized bureaucratic control becomes more attractive to both managers and success-conscious board members. As mass-media culture provides people with fewer reasons to engage in organizational activity, and the structures of local communities become less supportive of the collective identity required by participatory economic democracy, the overshadowing of co-operative democracy appears more and more likely. Many of the chapters in this book, particularly chapter 5, examine this larger problem.

The challenge to co-operators is obviously to be realistic about the relative strengths and socio-cultural supports of the two logics at work in their organizations. They must see that the market logic will triumph if they are not conscious of its strength and rationality, and if they do not consider how countervailing forces can be activated to prevent the triumph of this logic in their organizations. Co-operative democracy must be given both purpose and operational viability by a new generation for whom the logic of the market is an inadequate guide to social relations. It is our hope that the chapters in this volume will contribute to this effort.

Outline of the Book

Part One of this volume presents a general introduction to the book. Chapter 2 presents five disciplinary 'windows' on modern Canadian co-operatives, viewed as institutions with specific dynamics which are nonetheless importantly shaped by Canadian society. Christopher Axworthy's chapter 3 challenges several traditional assumptions about decision-making in Canadian co-operatives. Once again, this raises important questions for readers, encouraging them to see the chapters that follow as attempts to come to grips with the problems and dilemmas inherent in the confrontation of co-operative myth with co-operative reality.

Brett Fairbairn introduces Part Two, 'Co-operatives in a Changing Social Context,' with a comparative look at the social bases of the co-operative business form. David Laycock continues with an examination of selected factors in Canadian society which promote or prevent a closer articulation of co-operative organizational activity and democratic public life. Skip Kutz then analyses difficulties co-operators face in bringing their institutional perspectives and values into the Canadian public education system. Murray Fulton's chapter addresses the tensions existing between individual and collective interests within co-operative businesses. Finally, Lou Hammond Ketilson examines the problematic situation faced by co-operative businesses in using member commitment to advantage in their marketing strategies.

Part Three begins with Fairbairn's historical introduction to the political dimensions of co-operative organizational activity. Fulton and Laycock then provide a combination of theoretical and sector-specific insights into the pattern of relations between co-operatives and governments in Canada. Laycock's next chapter explores the historical and contemporary bases of Canadian co-operatives' uneasy relations with the partisan vehicles of political representation in Canada, with comparative reference to the very different pattern of relations between co-operative organizations and partisan political life in Britain. Lars Apland reports general results of a major survey-based study of co-operative directors in Saskatchewan, Canada's most intensively co-operative province, with a focus on directors' attributes most relevant to the functioning of co-operative democracy. The section closes with Apland and Axworthy's examination of tensions between collective and individual rights in Canada, from the perspective of co-operatives' interaction with Canada's legal system.

The final section of the book, 'Co-operatives in the Economy,' begins with Fairbairn's historical and comparative review of co-operatives' experiences and dilemmas in the economic sphere. In this case, he considers co-operatives as institutions that have had to find distinctive roles in a political economy whose dynamics have been shaped by interaction between a capitalist market economy, powerful capitalist enterprises, and a powerful state. The remaining chapters in this section provide concrete indications of co-operatives' struggles to attain or retain these distinctive roles. Ketilson examines co-operative management techniques and their relation to marketing practices, Fulton considers the case of a Canadian co-operative fertilizer operation operating in the oligopolistic farm input sector, and Laycock sketches the range of government interventions in Canadian co-operative business activity.

BRETT FAIRBAIRN, CHRISTOPHER S. AXWORTHY, MURRAY FULTON,
LOU HAMMOND KETILSON, AND DAVID LAYCOCK

2 Co-operative Institutions:
Five Disciplinary Perspectives

This chapter views the question 'What are co-operatives?' through the windows provided
by five different social research disciplines: history, law, economics, management, and
political science. The common themes include the heterogeneity of co-operatives as
flexible institutions that can serve different social and political goals in different
contexts. In their development co-operatives both borrowed from and reacted against their
environments, creating a constant dilemma in their relations with society. Their unique
internal democracy and membership base make them complex organizations that cannot
be explained by monolithic models. Instead, to analyse co-operatives requires close
examination of their relationship with their members and their environment, of their
values and culture, and of their wide range of objectives and the pluralism of stakeholder
interests.

What are co-operatives? Idealistic counter-culture alternatives to mainstream
business, or hard-headed economic enterprises, differing from big businesses
only in details of their ownership and voting structure? Are they exotic fringe
phenomena, or prominent community institutions? Methods of correcting
monopoly abuses, or seeds of a new society? Agents of social progress, or
holdovers of pre-industrial values? Some have argued that they are for the
working classes, the poor, and the powerless; others that they are for small
producers. These are dilemmas buried in the popular conceptions and in the
self-perception of co-operatives. There are elements of truth in all these
generalizations, but the best generalization may be 'all of the above' –
depending on the exact context and the observer's point of view. Assumptions,
standards of comparison, the social environment, and the purpose of the

discussion shape our interpretations of co-operatives. We may well find, on closer inspection or on examination from a different point of view, that co-operatives are something other than what they appear or were assumed to be.

The purpose of this chapter is to examine the assumptions, the comparisons, and the contexts that help us analyse co-operatives and how they work. The chapter is organized in five sections. First, there is a brief overview of co-operatives' historical development, intended to highlight both their diversity and the patterns of their reactions to their environment. This is followed by an analysis of the legal framework within which co-operatives developed, and an argument that co-operatives have borrowed many features from corporate structures. The third section considers the extent to which co-operatives can be understood as economic firms according to various theories. Following from this, the fourth section assesses the applicability of standard theories of management and planning to co-operatives' internal processes. This section maintains that stakeholder models of decision-making are the most applicable to the complex structure of co-operatives. Finally, the last section argues that political values, broadly speaking, are embodied in co-operative institutions and need to be appreciated as part of their culture. This chapter, then, looks through five methodological windows at the diversity and internal complexity of co-operatives.

Historical Dimensions of the Movement: What Are Co-operatives?

It is only fitting that the question, What are co-operatives? should have a pluralistic answer. Quite different groups of people have turned in many countries and eras to roughly similar co-operative approaches to their problems. Generally, the founders of co-operative movements were responding to the needs, stresses, and opportunities that resulted from social and economic modernization. They responded, for example, to growing markets and new technology in agriculture, marketing, and retailing, and they did so explicitly within the context of a competitive economy and an open society. Co-operative movements have been influenced both positively and negatively by the models of private ownership and of corporate and associational structure prevalent around them, accepting many of the assumptions implicit in this environment but also developing self-conscious critiques of existing forms of organization. No simple 'business' or 'Utopian' character has dominated co-operatives. Instead they have been subject to a dilemma of attraction to and repulsion from other institutions. Co-operatives seen in a broad view thus reflect certain recurring perceptions of the deficiencies of prevalent economic and institutional structures, and constitute controlled and deliberate variations on existing organizational themes.

It is possible to define a movement in terms of its myths about itself. One myth of the co-operative movement is that the essence of 'co-operation' can be summed up in a few brief rules about how organizations operate. This myth has been expressed in a century and a half of model statutes and statements of principles intended to separate legitimate co-operatives from the rest.[1] According to this view, a co-operative is an organization fulfilling a checklist of operating procedures. But appearances can be deceptive. Instead of defining co-operatives solely by their internal rules, abstracted from their context, a fuller picture is gained by painting them, however sketchily, in their historical contexts, in their full breadth and depth.

Let us begin with a brief general description. Over the course of their history co-operatives have tended to be voluntarily created local associations, formed and sustained by individuals to provide themselves with services of an economic nature, and intended to be controlled by their members in a participatory and democratic fashion. The key has been that co-operatives have been owned and controlled by their users (customers or employees), rather than by investors. Democratic control structures in co-operatives were meant to serve an economic role – to ensure the co-operative served its members – but also a developmental one, for participation in co-operative democracy has been seen as a way for people to grow and to gain more power over their lives.

Co-operatives have claimed to combine free association, mutualism, and democracy in economic enterprise. They also embody egalitarianism in the sense that control is not supposed to depend on the amount of capital or number of shares owned by any individual; each member is to have one vote. To see why co-operatives can be said to have a strong participatory emphasis, consider that members typically have a triple interest in the organization: as co-owners, as clients (employees or customers of the co-operative), and as residents in the same community. Usually, no owner stands in relation to the co-operative merely as a financial investor. In conjunction with this communitarian approach, co-operatives typically have dissociated themselves from the ideas of 'profit' and of speculative interest or high dividends on share capital, but have emphasized limited interest and the distribution of operating surpluses among the member-owners on the basis of their use of the co-operative or some other 'fair' formula.

A description of this kind serves to distinguish co-operatives from non-economic organizations, from compulsory economic organizations such as collective farms, from joint-stock companies (where shareholders usually are investors only and may have unequal numbers of votes), from most profit-oriented sorts of partnerships, and from charitable or state enterprises. In emphasizing the local, individual, and participatory basis of co-operatives, the distinction from cartels, to which co-operatives otherwise bear a family resemblance in their economic function, is also apparent. Nevertheless, as the use of words like 'normally,' 'usually,' and 'typically' suggests, it is not possible to arrive at a rigorous and exact definition for all organizations in all countries that have been called or have called themselves 'co-operatives.'

In 1966 a special commission on co-operative principles made its report to the International Co-operative Alliance, an organization representing most of the world's large co-operative movements. This commission specified six 'principles' which it claimed were 'universal' and 'inseparable' for co-operatives. The first of these stated that 'membership of a co-operative society should be voluntary and available without artificial restriction or any social, political, religious or racial discrimination to all persons who can make use of its services and are willing to accept the responsibilities of membership.' The second principle was that 'co-operative societies are democratic organizations,' which was explained in terms of membership control and accountability of the administrators to the members on the basis of 'one member, one vote.' Third, it was held to be fundamental that 'share capital should only receive a strictly limited rate of interest, if any.' Fourth, instead of returns being made to members on the basis of capital contributed, operating surpluses in co-operatives were supposed to be distributed to members in other ways – the most usual being in proportion to their use of the co-operative's facilities (patronage). The two remaining ICA points were 'education of ... members, officers and employees and of the general public ... in the principles and techniques of co-operation,' and the requirement that co-operatives 'should actively co-operate ... with other co-operatives.'

The ICA's six points illuminate co-operators' perceptions of their own goals. They indicate, for example, that the co-operatives from many countries that participated in the ICA saw themselves as a single world-wide movement, and that they characterized them-selves by attributes of democracy, of anti-profit or anti-capital orientation, and of commitment to education and improvement of society and of their members.

However, a list of organizational features can only note surface similarities among co-operatives. It cannot put co-operatives into any social, economic, political, or historical framework, and therefore cannot fully assess how co-operatives and their members have incorporated or reacted against other ideas and models, or what special significance they may have attached to certain principles. Indeed, the rapporteur of the 1966 commission on co-operative principles has recently argued that the points listed by the commission were not 'principles' at all, but only organizational rules intended to give substance in particular times and places to the true principles of the movement. These ideal principles he lists as association (unity), economy, democracy, equity, liberty, responsibility, and education.[3] In considering such ideas and values we have already moved beyond any simple, 'objective' categorization of organizations.

Let us now put this description of rules and ideas into a historical context. Doing so leads us to one immediate conclusion: the diversity and scale of co-operative activity has rarely been appreciated. In part this is because co-operatives, in accordance with the participatory character they embody, tend to be local or regionalized, not multinational or cross-border institutions, and hence may be easy to overlook.[4] They also tend to be distributed among several kinds of industries and many particular sorts of roles and services, as well as many different countries. A systematic overview of the range of types and functions is impossible here, but as a rough generalization to provide background for the reader, four main lines of development may be noted.[5]

The first is the phenomenon of consumer co-operatives formed to sell food and other goods (especially staple goods) to their members. Such co-operatives emerged in Britain in the 1830s and 1840s as urban, working-class institutions, epitomized by the Rochdale Equitable Pioneers Society founded in 1844. In its economic functions the Rochdale initiative was intended to provide pure, unadulterated food at competitive rather than monopoly prices, and through the provision of a patronage rebate enable members to accumulate capital.[6] Seen in its historical context, a broad critique of existing institutions is implied by the Rochdale model. The Pioneers' co-operative principles provided for a full and equal franchise within the organization at a time when the working-class membership did not have such a franchise in society at large. Likewise, its fixed interest rate on capital was intended to give labour primacy over capital within the co-operative, unlike the situation the members perceived in the wider economy; and the important adult educational duties undertaken by the co-operative also bespoke expansive social-cultural aims in an age when deprivation was the norm for the working classes.

In Germany consumer co-operatives in the late nineteenth century also became important focal points for an independent, urban, working-class culture, which in this case stood in a relation of mutual hostility to the state and the higher echelons of society. Here, too, they served to provide both economic and social value to members who did not believe they could escape poverty or obtain dignity in society's established institutions.[7]

In the twentieth century consumer co-operatives became major retailing networks, with differing class and cultural overtones, in Scandinavia and in parts of Canada and the United States, and to a lesser degree in France, Italy, and other parts of western Europe.[8] In certain cases these later co-operatives developed in conjunction with the agrarian co-operative movements to be described below; Denmark and the North American plains provide examples of co-operative retailing systems that were founded by farmers rather than by workers, and to provide production inputs for farming just as much as to provide standard consumer goods. Unlike the Rochdale co-op, for example, western Canadian retail co-operatives developed their greatest business in the 1920s in commodities such as binder twine, barbed wire, and petroleum.[9]

The second main development began in Germany in the 1850s, when Hermann von Schulze-Delitzsch promoted credit co-operatives to help struggling artisans. Then in the 1860s Friedrich Wilhelm Raiffeisen, persuaded of the merits of mutual self-help after a decade of experimentation and of arguments with Schulze-Delitzsch, took a similar idea very effectively to the German peasantry.[10] Schulze-Delitzsch also inspired Luigi Luzzatti in Italy to begin the movement of *banche popolari* in the 1860s, which were joined in the 1880s by Leone Wollemborg's *casse rurali* patterned on the Raiffeisen model.[11] Between 1900 and 1939 agricultural credit co-operatives spread widely throughout central and eastern Europe, and in North America. The caisses populaires of francophone Canada – the first was founded under the leadership of Alphonse Desjardins in 1900 – and the credit unions of English Canada and the United States are part of this international development. It was no accident that these large, successful, and in many cases substantially rural co-operative movements were concerned with financial services, for they developed during a period of rapid change in agriculture. A key agrarian grievance at the time was the unresponsiveness of urban capital (in Quebec and in parts of central Europe this was reinforced by ethnic differences between the agrarian hinterland and the bankers of the monopole), and credit co-operatives provided a mechanism within the rural community to address the problems of agricultural credit and the need for technological improvement.[12]

In a third development, co-operatives have frequently been formed to assist with marketing of members' products, especially agricultural products, and the co-operatives that have done so have frequently also supplied their members with production inputs: tools, fertilizers, chemicals, and, in general, improved technology.[13] By 1900 the leading international models for this kind of rural co-operation were provided by the Raiffeisen movements, by Denmark, and by Ireland.[14] In Europe dairy associations have probably been the most common and important producer-marketing co-operatives since their emergence toward the end of the last century. In addition to dairy producers' organizations, North

America has seen more ambitious agricultural marketing efforts. The wheat pools of the Canadian plains were originally founded for this purpose in the 1920s, and now serve a major role as co-operative grain handlers and farm suppliers. In this case as in some others the co-operative movement was part of a larger, regional protest movement that sought to wrest control of regional policies from remote financial and political institutions. Thus the size and power of the movement was expressed in the parallel formation of credit and retailing chains and of sympathetic political parties.

Actual production or workers' co-operatives, as a fourth pattern, where the tools and premises for production are co-operatively owned, have not generally attained the status of widespread movements, but have surfaced repeatedly and are now actively promoted by some established co-operatives and by governments. The Mondragon co-operatives in the Basque region of Spain incorporate employee membership in a large and successful network of institutions. In Britain small worker co-operatives are now promoted by municipal governments as community-based solutions to unemployment.

In addition, co-operatives have arisen in all manner of service and life-style-orientated industries: house construction and housing complexes, health care, child care, funerals and burial plots, recreation clubs and facilities of all types, insurance, taxi service, and many more.

This brief overview suggests several points. Co-operatives have clearly not been limited to any one country, decade, economic sector, or commercial function. Co-operative movements emerged in several major forms and many environments beginning in the mid-nineteenth century. They represent a broad and flexible form for organizing activity which can be applied in many different contexts, frequently serving both economic and social-political goals. They have attained considerable scale in particular sectors of particular economies, especially in retailing, credit, marketing (especially agricultural marketing), and more recently in services of other types. The history of the world-wide co-operative movement also reveals important variations. While the consumer co-operatives of Britain and Germany functioned, at least for their first decades, as working-class institutions aimed at social emancipation (and in both cases eventually became affiliated with socialist political parties), many (but not all) credit and marketing co-operative movements were based on an independent farm population, and were politically neutral, or involved in regional protest movements, or indeed were conservative and nationalistic. The goals of the latter might, indeed, be better characterized as social preservation than as social emancipation; and their leaders might better be characterized as petit bourgeois than as proletarian. The ambiguity in the class and ideological character of co-operatives can also be seen in part as a contradiction between consumers' and producers' co-operatives. This is one historical dilemma of co-operation. There are also others, as becomes apparent when one turns to the legal models within which co-operatives evolved.

The Legal Framework: Models for Co-operative Structure in British and Canadian Law

Co-operatives have a tradition as democratic and participatory institutions, yet in law and frequently in fact their members have little real power. In legal form and internal decision-making structure, co-operatives adopted many elements evident in the legal and commercial systems that prevailed in the era of their formation. The aims of co-operative organizations and certain mechanisms within them (one member, one vote; dividends based on use rather than on capital) were considered important features distinguishing them from normal businesses, but there was no major attempt to develop or to insist on a radically different structure. Instead many features were copied from existing institutions with which the founders of co-operatives were familiar. Over time the borrowing from or imposition of organizational models continued, so that an elite democratic structure became dominant within co-operative institutions.

When the Rochdale Equitable Pioneers Society was founded in 1844 there was no legislation dealing specifically with co-operatives. Even corporate legislation was rudimentary, for limited liability was not available, and incorporation was expensive and uncommon.[15] The Rochdale Pioneers therefore registered under the Friendly Societies Acts of 1834 and of 1842. These acts were patterned after the original legislation of 1793, which had been intended to encourage working people to form charitable societies to benefit the sick and infirm and thereby to reduce the burden on public expenditures.[16]

The act of 1793 had established firm member control of friendly societies. It required general meetings of members from time to time 'to constitute such proper and wholesome rules, orders and regulations' as were required for the governance of the society. These rules were to be submitted to the justices at quarter sessions for approval, and once approved could only be amended by a three-quarters' majority at a general meeting, and then only if notice had been given at two previous general meetings. It was specifically permitted that societies could resolve internal disputes by arbitration.[17] With ultimate control vested in a general membership and with an official set of rules covering the activities of officers and other matters, early co-operatives chose a model based on the familiar patterns of voluntary associational life. The affinity with the friendly societies lay in open membership and participatory democratic decision making within the organization, and reflected the self-help and educational goals of co-operatives, goals that made it reasonable to register under a structure originally set up for charitable endeavours.

While the 1793 act had restricted friendly societies to charitable purposes, the 1834 amendment allowed them to be organized for any purpose which was not illegal.[18] This phrase apparently enabled trading societies to be registered under the act, but the general wording created uncertainty as to which activities were permitted. In 1846, therefore, as a result of lobbying by the Rochdale Pioneers and influential sympathizers, the act was further amended to permit: 'the frugal investment of the savings of the members for better enabling them to purchase food, firing, clothes, or other necessities, or the tools or implements of their trade or calling, or to provide for the education of their children or kindred ... Provided always, that the shares in any such investment society shall not be transferable, and that the investment of each member shall accumulate or be employed for the sole benefit of the member.'[19]

While this amendment went some way toward accommodating the self-help activities of co-operatives, registration under the Friendly Societies Act imposed restrictions on the commercial activities of co-operatives which they believed unnecessary. For example, the societies could hold personal property only through non-member trustees, they could not own land, reserves could only be invested with the National Debt Commissions, and there was no provision for federations of societies. Dissatisfaction with these restrictions contributed to the first statute specifically intended to provide for producer and consumer co-operation, the Industrial and Provident Societies Act of 1852.[20]

The title of the 1852 act still reflects the belief that working men's trading societies would serve an essentially charitable purpose. Trading surpluses were to be put 'to provident purposes,' and societies would continue to be regulated by the Registrar of Friendly Societies. Furthermore, by section seven of the act, 'all the provisions of the laws relating to Friendly Societies shall apply to every Society to be constituted under this Act.' As with friendly societies, capital was to be raised through voluntary subscriptions, and loans and dividends were restricted. While the act laid out many matters a society's rules had to regulate, it did not specify how these rules were to be adopted. This was likely not considered necessary since the Friendly Societies Act already provided for member control through democratic structures.[21]

The act did not provide limited liability for co-operative societies, a significant deterrent to working-class investors but one that could to some extent be circumvented by vesting property absolutely in the hands of trustees.[22] The lack of provision for limited liability is not surprising since limited liability was not extended to companies until the Joint Stock Companies Act of 1855, which became the model for corporation legislation in

England and Canada for over a hundred years. Numerous features of this latter act were incorporated into a revision of the Industrial and Provident Societies Act in 1862, notably stipulations regarding the minimum number of persons who could form a limited liability company, the purposes of the society, the limitation of shareholders' liability to the value of their shares, publicity requirements, penalties for non-compliance, and provisions for winding-up of societies. At the same time, the Friendly Societies Acts, previously applicable to societies *in toto*, were made applicable only with respect to tax exemptions, settlement of disputes, certain court powers, and the jurisdiction of the Registrar of Friendly Societies.[23] Other restrictions of the earlier legislation, such as the fixed interest rates on member subscriptions and loans, were dropped in favour of more general guidelines. The treatment of co-operatives as charitable institutions was thereby replaced by a more explicitly commercial model, gaining for co-operatives the benefits of limited liability and less restricted operations. Indeed, the 1862 law made even fewer stipulations about the internal operations of co-operatives than were made about companies. The 1862 act did not mention limited interest on capital, patronage dividends, or the principle of one member, one vote – all of which are features taken to be characteristic of co-operatives and which had been mentioned in earlier legislation. The purpose of the 1862 legislation appears to have been to regulate the interaction of co-operative societies with other businesses and with government, but to leave internal management (including co-operative principles) to the society and its members.

In the period of co-operatives' formation, then – the period that saw the emergence of the influential Rochdale example – corporate legislation was in its infancy. In spite of the limited liability legislation of the 1850s, it was not until the case of *Saloman* v. *Saloman & Co. Ltd.* in 1897 that the law finally decided that the formation of a corporation should be available as a right to anyone who desired it and could pay the required fees.[24] In legal terms the early English co-operative movement found its framework in the voluntary charitable association, a structure that was adapted to parallel the evolution of corporation law. The predominant business structure in the mid-nineteenth century was not in any case the corporation, but rather the partnership, a form which also clearly influenced the Rochdale Pioneers. Partnerships are formed by contractual arrangement and, unless the contract provides to the contrary, equal participation in decision-making and profits and losses by all the partners no matter what their contribution in terms of capital and work is assumed. The widespread example of the operation of partnerships likely explains why the Rochdale Pioneers did not mention democratic control in their original constitution; it was presumed.

As corporation law emerged, however, it assumed an elite democratic model for the internal operations of incorporated businesses, and this had an effect on the formulation and interpretation of co-operative law. Since the promoters of corporations often became the first directors, the power and importance of boards of directors were entrenched in the initial constitutions, and as shareholders cared about little except the return on their investments, they were content to leave many matters to the directors. The contractual understanding of corporations, which viewed their structure as an agreement to vest decision-making in a few, legitimated the concentration of power at the apex. Shareholders, according to the law, have no say in the management of a corporation, except as regards fundamental changes, such as a merger or a sale of all or essentially all assets, and the election or removal of directors. Co-operatives, too, have boards of directors responsible for their affairs, and the effect of practice and of judicial interpretation has been to vest more power in these boards and less in the general meetings of members.[25]

As in the extension of limited liability to British co-operatives in the 1862 act, the trend in more recent Canadian law has been to make co-operative law look as much like corporate law as possible. The Ontario Co-operative Associations Act of 1865, the first of its kind in Canada, closely followed the British Industrial and Provident Societies Act of 1862, and mentioned only two co-operative principles: one member, one vote, and trade solely on a cash basis.[26] Manitoba passed an act similar to Ontario's in 1887, and Saskatchewan's Agricultural Co-operative Associations Act of 1913 was similar except in requiring 75 per cent of the members of registered co-operatives to be 'agriculturalists.'[27] Co-operatives did succeed in having many of their basic operating principles, such as voting, limited interest, patronage dividends, legislated in these British and Canadian statutes. Further amendments to co-operative law, however, have reinforced the trend to de-emphasize specific co-operative principles and to put co-operatives more and more on the same footing as corporations.[28]

While legislation has incorporated some distinctive principles differentiating co-operatives from other enterprises, it has also incorporated corporations' decision-making structure: a board of directors (in British co-operatives, 'management committee'), the general assembly of members, and, by implication, the management. The participatory democratic model derived from the friendly societies, from the operation of partnerships, and more generally from the working-class movement of nineteenth-century Britain was grafted onto an elite democratic model which paralleled that developed in the evolution of modern corporations. The relevant point for the purposes of this chapter is that co-operatives absorbed structural models from the social-economic and legal milieu surrounding them. The membership-board-management structure, limited liability, and other organizational features were adopted for pragmatic reasons under the influence of commercial examples; the overall structure of co-operatives did not spring from an isolated theory or tradition. While some important structural differences between co-operatives and private companies were emphasized, and while there was a quantitative difference of stress in the co-operative tradition on membership participation and democracy, it was nevertheless generally true that co-operatives were distinguished from private companies more by their goals and by specific organizational mechanisms than by their general organizational structure.

The historical and legal development of the co-operative movement shows that co-operatives copied general associational and corporate developments and paralleled the evolution of private firms. Perhaps it is possible, then, to apply models for the behaviour and functioning of firms directly or in modified form to interpret the activities of co-operatives.

Co-operatives and Organizational Theory: The Co-operative as a Firm

In economics, a great deal of attention is devoted to the theory of the firm. The firm is usually described as a rational entity (it seeks to maximize something) that is subject to a number of constraints (such as the type of production process, the level of resources available, the markets for its inputs and outputs) in its attempt to achieve its goals. While the usual notion of a firm is an investor-owned organization that has as its goal profit-maximization, the view is taken that any institution that employs a peak co-ordinator or a top-level manager may be viewed as a firm, no matter who owns the firm or what its goals may be.

This characterization describes many institutions, including crown corporations and co-operatives.[29] In the case of co-operatives, it is recognized that ownership rests with members who do business with the organization. As an owner, the member is interested in the profits that can be obtained from the co-operative, while as one who does business with the co-operative, the member is interested in the benefits that can be derived in terms of service, the quality of the goods, and the price paid or received. In short, members are interested in the total level of welfare that can be derived from their dealings with the co-operative. In strict economic terms, this can be expressed as the sum of profits plus producer or consumer surplus.[30] At a broader level, however, this concern with member welfare can also accommodate such diverse items as co-operative ideals and co-operative philosophy.

A common methodology for analysing the behaviour of firms makes it possible to compare the kinds of decisions different types of firm will make regarding price and output, thereby making it possible to determine the impact each organization will have on the economy or industry in which it operates. For instance, neoclassical economic theory concludes that a profit-maximizing firm in a perfectly competitive economy will make decisions that result in resources being used in the most efficient manner possible. Departures from a perfectly competitive environment due to monopoly, oligopoly, or the presence of market externalities will, of course, result in inefficiencies. Co-operative theory, in contrast, suggests co-operatives may be able to allocate resources efficiently, not only in the perfectly competitive situation, but also in a monopoly situation. This difference in behaviour results from co-operatives being controlled by members who do business with the organization, that is, members who are interested in avoiding the higher prices associated with monopoly or oligopoly markets.

While this allocative efficiency is an important standard for measuring the behaviour of firms, others have asked different questions about their performance. For example, the basic assumption in examining allocative efficiency is that all inputs are purchased and used in the most technically efficient manner possible. One economist, however, has provided evidence that, in profit-maximizing firms, inputs are not always used in the most efficient manner; individuals and firms do not search for new techniques as effectively as they could. The resulting 'X-inefficiency' may be much greater than the allocative efficiency on which economists so often focus.[31]

Little work has been done on the question of whether the level of such technological inefficiency is greater or less in a co-operative than in a profit-maximizing firm, although one recent paper has suggested that co-operative electrical utilities in the United States are more efficient than their profit-maximizing counterparts at identifying and implementing improved techniques.[32] Evidence from the United Kingdom suggests that productivity is enhanced when workers can participate in decision-making through the board of directors.[33]

Other questions also arise from the standard neoclassical theory of the firm. One such question considers the assumption that a firm can be treated as a single agency with a unified and integrated set of motives. For instance, when a firm's managers are not its owners, there may be a divergence of interest between the two groups. Similarly, in a large firm with an extensive bureaucracy, the goals of managers in different parts of the firm may be in conflict.[34]

In co-operatives such problems are also likely to occur. Since in most co-operatives the members are not the managers, the possibility of differences in goals between these two groups exists. This may be particularly the case as co-operatives are increasingly hiring their managers from business schools or from investor-owned firms, environments which typically emphasize profit-maximization as an appropriate goal.[35] In addition, if members feel that they are not obtaining the quality or type of information needed to control their firm, they may become dissatisfied with the co-operative. While these feelings are obviously not unique to co-operative members, they may be of greater consequence in co-operatives because of their democratic nature and the correspondingly higher expectations on the part of the membership.

Conflict and differences in goals may also arise among members. For instance, in a farm supply co-operative, the large farmer may have very different needs than the smaller farmer. Similarly, the services required by grain farmers may differ dramatically from those required by livestock farmers. Divergences in goals among members make it difficult for management to meet all members' needs, and raise the possibility that if the goals of one group are not met, the co-operative may lose members as they go elsewhere to meet their needs.[36]

The recognition that there are numerous objectives within the firm suggests that it is both improper to view the firm as an organization with a single goal, and that other models of the firm may not only be more appropriate, but may be required if the firm's actions are to be understood. For instance, the differences in goals between members and managers is at the heart of the principal-agent problem. This topic has been examined extensively in the economic literature with respect to profit-maximizing firms, but its importance for co-operatives is just being realized.

Differences among members raise questions about bargaining among them, the manner in which co-operatives are formed, and the likelihood that co-operatives will continue to survive without changes in their membership structure. These topics have been analysed with the aid of co-operative game theory.

The view of the co-operative as a collection of individuals, as opposed to a single and unified organization, raises yet another problem. Even without the divergence of goals among members or between members and managers, the individual actions of members may result in a situation where their collective interests are not met. This problem is broadly known as the Prisoners' Dilemma, and is increasingly being used to understand the workings of co-operatives.[37]

To sum up this discussion, co-operatives may be modelled as firms, but more than with profit-maximizing firms, it is necessary to distinguish the differing elements within them and the relations among these elements. Indeed, it is the nature of the implicit and explicit contracts that exist in the co-operative that determines who has the power and the goals that are achieved.[38] The planning and decision-making process in co-operatives, who is involved and how, is fundamental to understanding their activities and their potential as firms.

A Managerial Perspective on Co-operative Institutions: Paradigms of Planning

Co-operative institutional structures have found expression in an immense variety of economic roles, and any model developed for co-operative institutions must account for this variety. In attempting to explain this diversity, co-operative theorists have categorized in terms of political ideology, the nature of the economic exchange, the individual's understanding of the purpose and assumptions of the co-operative movement, and, of course, according to the various forms of ownership – by suppliers, employees, or clients.[39] In trying to understand the nature of organizations of any kind it is useful to adopt a particular paradigm that expresses a set of assumptions about the nature of social science and of society. An examination of the paradigms that can be applied to management and planning in co-operatives suggests that the current functionalist paradigm, identified by Gareth Morgan as the paradigm most frequently used by management theorists, is not only *not* the most appropriate perspective, but may be entirely inappropriate. It further suggests that it is useful to study the management of co-operatives within the parameters of three other paradigms defined by Morgan.[40]

The Functionalist Paradigm
Traditionally, a functionalist paradigm has been used to understand how organizations operate. Studies adopting this perspective abound in the field of organization theory. Within the general paradigm a number of metaphors have been drawn: the organization as a machine, as an organism, as a social system. Theorists using such metaphors have contributed extensively to the development of theory regarding managerial activity. In turn, this body of theory, with its underlying assumptions about how the world is organized, has been accepted by many different types of organizations, commercial and non-commercial, with little question as to the underlying assumptions' relevance to the organization concerned.

The assumption involved in teaching and in adopting this approach was that managerial skills were generic and applicable to any form of organization. Managers working within co-operatives have, with few exceptions, adopted the 'corporate' style of management. This phenomenon can be linked to the increasing need for expert management during the expansion in many kinds of co-operatives in Canada after 1945. The experienced managers available had been trained in business schools where management theory developed largely out of the study of practices in privately owned corporations. Yet uncritical acceptance of a corporate management style begs the question of whether this style is consistent with co-operative values or organizational characteristics. It can be argued that the failure to provide managers with skills oriented toward the values and objectives of co-operative organizations may be a reflection of society's normative assumption that only private ownership is efficient.

The traditional view of organizations is epitomized in the metaphor of the organization as a machine.[41] The organization is conceptualized as a closed system in search of certainty and determinateness; its 'rationality' leads it to chose all components and actions specifically for their contribution toward a goal. Every structure implemented in this way helps the organization to attain maximum efficiency. At every level, technical, managerial, and institutional, rationality prevails. Since this 'Milton Friedman' view of the world recognizes only a very limited number of stakeholders in the company's decisions – stockholders, the company, the customer – it is possible for a single overriding goal (profit for the benefit of the shareholder) to direct the goal-setting and planning by the management.[42]

In this view planning plays the role of a central control system for the organization. Planning contributes to efficiency and control, and thus to profitability. It may be internally oriented ('reactive') to maintain the status quo, or externally oriented ('preactive') to provide a framework for generating new product or service ideas, but in either case it is management driven, although the reactive mode is based on planning from the bottom up after initiation from the top. This 'planning' mode of strategy-making is based on rational choice models and an accepted hierarchy of authority.[43]

Alternatives to the Functionalist Paradigm
There are logical alternatives to a functionalist perspective on planning. Gareth Morgan has identified four paradigms based on different sets of meta-theoretical assumptions about society and social science. What results are four broad and mutually exclusive views of the social world – Functionalist, Interpretive, Radical-Humanist, and Radical-Structuralist.

In one dimension, assumptions about the nature of social science range along a continuum from subjectivity to objectivity (from Interpretive to Functionalist, Radical-Humanist to Radical-Structuralist) as regards human understanding of the environment and of reality. In a second dimension, assumptions about the nature of society range along a continuum from order to conflict, with the Functionalist perspective concentrating on the status quo and the function elements play in sustaining it. Those concerned with conflict and radical change, conversely, examine what is possible rather than what is, and are concerned with human emancipation from restrictive structures (Radical-Humanist). The two dimensions of subjectivity-objectivity and concern for order–concern for change define the four paradigms mentioned above.

The orthodox Functionalist view of organization, already described as dominant in management analysis, assumes that society and human behaviour are premised on the concrete existence of organizations with goals they pursue in a rational fashion. The adherents of an Interpretive paradigm, on the other hand, do not accept that organizations are separate entities, but view them as a product of the subjective experience and interaction of individuals. Like Functionalists, they believe there is an underlying pattern in society, but do not agree it can be understood in an objective fashion. Similarly, the Radical-Humanist paradigm stresses that 'reality' is socially created, but argues that 'human beings become imprisoned within the bound of the reality that they create and sustain.'[44] For example, some contemporary Radical-Humanist thought deals with the alienating properties of capitalist modes of production, and seeks to discover how to link thought and action to transcend this alienation. Finally, the Radical-Structuralist paradigm also accepts society as a dominating force, but admits the existence of organizations independently of the way they are perceived. This paradigm sees organizations as instruments of social domination, emphasizes action as a way of transcending this domination, and seeks alternative models to break down existing gender, class, ethnic, and other divisions.

Managers' goals and actions will differ according to which of these four mutually exclusive world-views they hold. It is argued below that the Interpretive paradigm offers new insights into the functioning of co-operatives, as do the Radical-Humanist and Radical-Structuralist perspectives. These contributions must be identified and recognized. The danger in accepting the orthodox functionalist view as the sole basis for explaining the behaviour of co-operative organizations is that it does not place value on the aspects of co-operatives which contribute most to their strength and effectiveness.

Planning in Co-operatives

Innovative views of organization have seen it as an open system, subject to influence from the environment. Goals are not established by a single decision-making group within a hierarchy, since the organization is interdependent with its environment, but rather by coalition behaviour.[45] Russell Ackoff has introduced a new metaphor to deal with this characteristic, a metaphor incorporating aspects of the Interpretive paradigm by accounting for organizations as the product of the perceived needs of individuals and subgroups. Ackoff suggests that 'to conceptualize a corporation as an organization is to see it as its stakeholders do. Stakeholders are all those inside or outside an organization who are directly affected by what it does. Therefore, they include all those whom managers should take into account, including managers themselves.'[46] Understood in this way, organizations are coalitions of interacting interest groups, and the interest groups involved may be both inside and outside the organization in question. In responding to these diverse interests, the organization is likely to pursue a variety of goals which may be in conflict with each other. Because of these conflicts, the assessment of effectiveness of the organization is problematic, and will vary according to which interest group is doing the evaluation.[47]

Planning in such a context assumes a variety of roles. It is done to increase participation in organizational decision-making, which in turn increases internal motivation and commitment. In addition, planning is seen to facilitate the selection of paths offering maximum convergence of the interests of all parties. The stakeholders approach and the social responsibility approach[48] both emphasize a shift from the establishment of goals to the *assessment of consequences*. Planning is also considered to be part of the process of social change, and the development of 'the plan' is not the sole product of the activity but just one element in a wider program of organizational change affecting managers, structure, and management systems. The planner takes on the role of 'change agent'; the end product is not the plan itself but the development of the capacity to plan and the ability to learn from the planning process.[49]

Why are such 'Interpretive' models more applicable to co-operative organizations? While rational models of organization may be useful in explaining the earliest stages of a co-operative's development when decision-making is vested in one authoritative element, they cannot continue to be applicable as the organization grows in size and its task environment becomes more complex. The stakeholders and social responsibility models are better suited to the culture and the democratic nature of co-operative institutions.

It is true that co-operatives adopted the apparatus of corporations in vesting the powers of control in a board of directors. In fact, as we have seen, this in turn means much power is likely to rest with senior management – a separation of ownership from control. In the case of corporations this means that the interests of owners are only represented to the extent that they parallel the interests of those in control, or, if their interests differ, to the extent that there are checks on the exercise of power by those possessing it.[50] But a co-operative rests fundamentally on its utility to its members and depends on their participation. If the same processes of separation of ownership and control occur in a co-operative, the consequences are more serious. For co-operatives in particular it is critical to remember the tenuous nature of the organization as a discrete entity and the importance of satisfying numerous key interest groups to make it function effectively.

Within co-operatives the stakeholder approach to planning is the one most likely to fit with the real needs of the decision-making process. However, to accept this approach the manager of a co-operative must accept some of the premises of the Interpretive paradigm. An integral characteristic of the stakeholder approach is that planning and decision-making become much more complicated because there can be no assumed consensus about the nature of the problem under consideration. And just as there may be disagreement as to the nature of the problem, there is also a range of alternative solutions. The ultimate decision- makers in an enduring co-operative, whether board, management, or general membership, must attempt to incorporate the problem definitions and proposed solutions of a wide range of stakeholders.

The form of an organization, its goals, its management style, its measures of performance, and its indicators of success, are all linked to the context within which the organization operates and within which actions are taken. The assessment of effectiveness will vary depending on the interest group that conducts the evaluation, and the criteria it uses. Success will not always be measured in terms of longevity or profit. In some co-operative institutions – for instance the anarchist communes of the 1960s – adherence to certain goals took precedence even over the survival of the organization. That members could think this way is an outright contradiction of the claims of the Functionalist model that preservation of the organization is a measure of success. What is required, then, in modelling co-operatives is a broadening of the understanding of the organization to allow for the differing goals and standards of success of different stakeholders interested in it. A plurality of perceptions, ideas, and goals, and not the single-minded hierarchy of power associated with conventional models of organization, has stimulated and guided the evolution of co-operatives. The concluding section of this chapter considers some of these factors from an explicitly political perspective.

Rights, Power, and Self-Conception: Political Dimensions of Co-operative Institutional Development

The purpose of the following discussion is to consider how the development of co-operatives has internal and external political significance, and from this to assess the difficulty posed for co-operatives in their self-conception as their institutions converge with those of society at large. The heterogeneity of co-operatives, their blending of new ideas with models copied from private firms, their nature as coalitions, and the stakeholder model of pluralistic decision-making within them, all stress the dependence of co-operatives as institutions on factors outside themselves. In attempting to understand their institutional characteristics, then, it must not be forgotten that the significance of many co-operative structures and principles is related to the context in which co-operatives found themselves: to the environment of other organizations, other values, other principles.

The emergence of the early co-operative movement paralleled movements for the democratization of society at large, for greater and more effective involvement of the unpropertied classes in political, economic, and social institutions.[51] In the 1840s, when the Rochdale Pioneers was founded, and in fact well into the next century in both Britain and Canada, formal rights of democratic citizenship were denied to large segments of the working population. The Reform Bill of 1832 and even the further reform of 1867 did not extend the franchise to skilled non-propertied labourers, let alone to the female half of the population. With the failure of the Chartist movement in Britain and of petit-bourgeois radicalism in Canada to break this pattern by the 1840s, many of the former advocates of institutional and largely centralized political reform turned instead to local and decentralized efforts to build separate economic institutions responsive to the needs and control of working people. Numerous Chartists were among the founders of Rochdale and similar co-operatives. The birth of the co-operative movement stemmed from frustration with movements for political democracy, when workers disillusioned with society at large formed their own economic institutions to complement or even replace their 'political' efforts at social change. It is not too much to argue that co-operatives in the Anglo-American world were seen by their earliest proponents as microcosms of a society in which the rules governing the use of politically significant power would remove the privileges based on ownership of capital or inherited status, and give equal power to the common people in the business of organizing and benefiting from social life.[52]

Co-operative institutions did much to spread the gospel of egalitarian democracy, in both political and economic terms, among the British working classes, and provided important focal points for the increasing unity and politicization of those classes as the century progressed.[53] When leaders of the trade union movement banded together at the end of the nineteenth century to formulate a specifically working-class political platform, resulting ultimately in the formation of the Labour party, they brought a good deal of the co-operative movement's social agenda into the centre of political debate and, decades later, into public policy. The creation of a welfare state was another means, like the activities of co-operatives, to reduce the penalties associated with non-ownership of property. None of this would have been necessary if the founders of co-operatives and the leaders of working-class movements had not believed that the prevailing political economy was guided by principles inimical to democratic distribution of power. The principles of one member, one vote, of economic returns to patronage rather than capital, of open membership and of co-operative education, formed a conceptual whole which makes little sense except when seen as an alternative to economic and political institutions that sustained an undemocratic social order.

In Canada co-operatives never became integral to working-class political culture to the extent that they did in Britain. The concentration of urban labourers was lower, hindering their potential to become a major political force, and the social system was looser with more opportunities for advancement, resulting in a less straightforward polarization between property-owners and workers. Perhaps equally important, the development of a working-class movement came later than in Britain, at a time when the acquisition of formal citizenship rights was not so pressing an issue.[54] One consequence of this development in a more liberal and democratic political environment was that the Canadian working-class movement was never so effectively politicized as in Britain. But if co-operatives left less of a mark on the working classes in Canada, they left a major imprint on the Canadian agricultural community. The co-operative movement in Canada developed rapidly at the end of the nineteenth and the beginning of the twentieth century among farmers anxious to counteract the power of central Canadian financial and political elites. By the mid-1930s farmers' movements based substantially on co-operative networks and ideas had transformed the party politics of the three prairie provinces, and contributed much to the establishment of a viable social-democratic party at the national level. In the prairie region co-operatives symbolized a struggle for locally responsive 'economic democracy' analogous to the earlier British experience. Like their numerous British forbears, prairie co-operators did much to provide a meaningful and empowering form of civic education in democratic life.[55] Without the battle for basic political rights to legitimize their agenda of economic democratization to the public and broaden their claims into a universal democratic movement, prairie co-operators and their political movements did not succeed in translating their social visions into terms meaningful for urban Canada.

Another point should be made concerning the democratizing character and impact of early co-operative economic activity in the two countries. While such activity began as something distinctive in and for class and regional constituencies, and did much to forge an anti-establishment culture within these constituencies, their success in promoting civic education and economic interests contributed to the democratization of the wider society and to the increased integration of the dissenting constituencies into the social and political systems from which they had felt excluded. That is, the movement's success appeared to its participants to obviate much of the reason for the movement's politicization and, by improving the status quo (according to the movement's own criteria), also helped legitimize it. As the franchise was extended and the political system gradually became responsive to the more pressing material needs of working people (urban and rural), the radical democratizing tendencies of the early co-operative movements became less relevant. The formation of third or 'protest' parties also served to draw off much participatory democratic energy – that is, activists – from co-operatives.

As the twentieth century progressed, co-operatives ceased to be exceptional as promoters and practitioners of democratic action. By the 1930s open membership, one person, one vote, and claims to represent the common working person, were no longer distinctive, as political parties and many other organizations had adopted these principles. With democratization a less urgent issue, co-operatives on both sides of the Atlantic tended to lapse into relatively self-satisfied and uncreative attitudes toward their own practices of democracy.[56] Ideas of 'direct democracy' withered away, leaving few vestiges in large co-operative organizations, while the representative-democratic framework of elected policy-makers and watch-dogs functioned less energetically.[57] Contentment with the existing state of internal affairs and decreased antagonism toward outside institutions contributed to this decline of organizational activism. And, indeed, co-operative members with the time, energy, and inclination to pursue democratic participation had many more opportunities than previously to do so outside the co-operative, in political parties, pressure groups, and the mass consumer society.

This 'convergence' between the values and traditions of the co-operative movement and those of other large social institutions is manifested in a number of ways that have political significance. As large organizations, co-operatives have had to develop complex bureaucratic structures, supervised by professional and full-time managers. The average member cannot and does not wish to know how these structures operate, except in periods of crisis – and then the desire to know far exceeds the opportunity to know offered by the established structures. Directors are themselves in little better position to grasp their organizations' overall activities. Internal decision-making is thus left to managers, whose policies (according to the model provided by the corporate sector) are assumed not to be public or inherently political, but private and politically neutral. Most managers do not have to worry about the intense scrutiny of their decisions and recommendations that occurs, for example, in governments or interest groups.

Where member and board scrutiny of managerial decisions is difficult (or, perhaps, apparently even unnecessary, if the manager has earned the confidence of the organization), member participation in the direction of co-operatives' affairs does not appear urgent to those involved. This reinforces a number of parallel trends. First, co-operatives do not feel as obliged as they once did to be instruments of democratic education and training. They still perform this function with regard to their directors, but the members are not normally greatly affected by their leaders' brief training, and these leaders' experiences in large bureaucratic organizations tend in any case to promote 'safe' and conventional approaches to addressing problems in public life. Second, an attitude of resignation and cynicism develops among those members of co-operatives who could be democratically involved in their co-operatives, or in other public and more overtly political organizations.[58] Whether their negative assessment of their co-operatives is justified is almost beside the point, since the mere existence of the perception weakens the organization's democratic and participatory commitment.

Third, the combination of difficult economic competition with a lessened urgency of internal democratic vision puts pressure on co-operatives to adopt the same attitudes and policies as their private competitors. One consequence of this is in labour relations: co-operative institutions once associated with the working class and the common person follow strategies with respect to their employees that seem no better than those of private firms.[59] What is especially pernicious about this trend is that co-operatives feel compelled to adopt the dominant management strategies of the private sector, those used by head-on competitors, not even the most progressive and innovative private strategies pioneered in other sectors of the economy in which co-operatives are less involved. This failure to be truly innovative, to lead industry instead of following it, has a long-term cost in lowering the public legitimacy of co-operatives among social groups that have historically been among their strongest supporters. It also increases the public perception of the legitimacy of private corporate and government attacks on trade unions. This can have important political implications in provinces such as Saskatchewan with strong co-operative presences in the regional economy.

All of these factors are intimately related to the self-conception of those involved in the co-operative movement, to the place members and leaders feel their institutions have in the overall socio-political structure. The position taken publicly by Canada's major co-operative leaders has been that co-operatives should be viewed as an economic 'third sector' coexisting legitimately and with similar statutes alongside public or private enterprise.[60] Outside of the prairie provinces, however, this perception is not acknowledged by governments or by the brokers of economic power. Apart from a few federal co-operative statues, occasional joint ventures with co-operatives, and the occasional government subsidy, the federal government does not treat co-operatives as an organized 'third sector' of anything like comparable importance or influence to the corporate sector or to government itself.[61] Co-operatives, that is, have a higher opinion of their own degree of integration and influence than do other key actors in national decision-making. Indeed, given the diversity of the co-operative movement (and the fading of its common democratic principles) there are few occasions when all Canadian co-operatives can speak with a united voice and advance goals that other institutions must take seriously. The social and democratic reform agendas of co-operatives have, in general, been the main unifying features that compensated for their basic diversity.

The commitment to 'political neutrality' is also problematic. Rather than merely avoiding formal alignment with political parties, co-operatives have avoided discussing any elements of controversial public policy not directly affecting their short-run business interests. Anxious to avoid internal division, their leaders have tried to restrict their members' attention to narrow institutional goals. The low and indistinct profile that results makes co-operatives virtually invisible to the major interests that struggle to influence state policy. Consequently, co-operatives lack 'automatic' allies when they attempt to enhance or defend their own interests in the halls of power. In effect, leaders of the co-operative movement feel compelled to choose (as they were not in the nineteenth century) between achieving legitimacy in their business domains by adapting to the standards set by the competition, or achieving social legitimacy by following through on the wider implications of their claim to 'third sector' status. In the context of democratization being less urgent, members less active, and competition fierce, it is not surprising that almost all co-operative leaders and managers have opted for the safer, narrower, institution-building type of legitimacy. It seems to allow them to survive, even if it undermines the fulfilment of their historical goals.

Co-operative Enterprise in Institutional Perspective

Whether co-operatives are viewed from a historical, legal, economic, managerial, or political perspective, two main conclusions are clear. First, co-operatives both reacted against and borrowed from the economic, social, and political institutions around them, and not necessarily in a systematic way or one fully consistent with their founding principles. In certain matters – internal democracy, subordination of the rights of capital, education and improvement of members – early co-operators were clear in the principles they wished their organizations to embody and in how those principles differed from those of other institutions in society. Some of these principles have become less urgent over time. In other areas, however, such as legal structure, internal decision-making, and management style, co-operatives borrowed uncritically from the models presented mainly by private business, and adopted theories for organizing their own institutions that had little in common with co-operative objectives, and probably even contradicted them.

Second, with regard to interpreting the operations and activities of co-operatives, it is productive to consider them as 'firms,' especially given the many structural and attitudinal similarities to other economic institutions, provided only that we recognize two critical variations on the usual models. To begin with, co-operatives pursue a wider range of objectives than do profit-oriented businesses. To work well they must strive for their members' economic well-being rather than their own. In a broader sense, their purpose and strength is inseparably tied to goals that are by no means purely economic. Both characteristics imply the critical importance of active membership control in keeping the organization on course. The participatory and democratic rationale of the co-operative form of organization remains fundamental, even if its urgency is lessened within a society formally recognizing the same values. The second essential variation in a model for the functioning of co-operatives concerns the pluralism of interests that must be accounted for in their decision-making. More than most private corporations they rely on the legitimacy and commitment conferred by the support of many different stakeholder groups, including members whose involvement or non-involvement is far more crucial to the organization than the corresponding behaviour would be among shareholders in a private corporation, as well as the differing levels of officers, managers, and employees. A co-operative, that is to say, may be modelled as a firm, but it is not likely to be as simple as a simple firm; it requires complex models such as have been advanced for more complex private entities.

A final point is that co-operatives as institutions, even their internal structures, cannot be studied in isolation from their environment. Historically they have consciously reacted to and borrowed from that environment in a way that gave special meaning to some of their unique structures and features. To understand the organization requires understanding the values its founders, members, and leaders have perceived to be embodied in the framework they created and operated. The membership structure ties the co-operative closely to a defined and local group of (somehow) like-minded individuals and provides a link between the organization and its community, a two-way link that makes it counter-productive to view the co-operative as an isolated entity. In important respects it remains a group phenomenon, a political phenomenon, for as long as that characteristic community linkage exists.

CHRISTOPHER S. AXWORTHY

3 Myth and Reality in Co-operative Organizations: Members, Directors, Employees, and Managers

This chapter argues that there is a marked contrast between myth and reality in co-operative organizations. The myth is that co-operatives are democratic organizations run by their members. The reality is that the practical and legal constraints on co-operatives mean that members have little, if any, real power to make decisions. The chapter stresses that the democratic control structures of co-operatives must be re-examined if co-operatives wish to be truly democratic.

This chapter discusses principal-agent relationships in co-operative organizations in order to assess the character of democratic participation in co-operatives. It is often assumed that co-operatives are quintessentially democratic organizations run by their members and that this democratic participation by the members is both qualitatively and quantitatively superior to that in other kinds of business organizations. It is assumed, for example, that members of co-operatives participate more meaningfully and more often than do shareholders of a corporation. The purpose of this chapter is to show that these assumptions are more myth than reality. Practical and legal constraints on co-operatives combine to ensure that agents rather that principals – the members – make most of the important decisions and that the members' democratic participation in these decisions is either non-existent or very limited at best. The chapter discusses not only how structural constraints limit members' participation in decisions, but also the extent to which these constraints restrict members' ability to monitor the activities and decisions of their agents, the directors and managers of the co-operative.

The Structure of Co-operatives

Legislative fiat aside, the organizational form chosen for any economic activity will be the one deemed to be the most efficient.[1] Since co-operatives are avowedly economic *and* social institutions, non-economic considerations will come into play in selecting an organizational form. Because co-operatives have other objectives than maximizing profit, what is rational for them will depend on the mix of social and economic aims to be pursued. These different aims give rise to different interpretations of efficiency. It will not be seen in purely economic terms, but rather in terms of both the co-operative's social and its economic objectives.

As far as structure within the chosen form of organization is concerned, however, legislation leaves little choice.[2] An organization operating on a co-operative basis could be unincorporated, but this would have undesirable consequences: the organization could not use the word co-operative in its name, it would have no separate identity, and its members would not be protected by limited liability – these attributes are reserved for organizations incorporated under the various co-operative acts. Thus, if a group of people want to form a co-operative and do not want to be part of an unincorporated association, they have to comply with all the structural and other requirements of the relevant legislation.

Co-operatives will be bound by legislative definitions, some of which may be quite uncertain, and by legislative restrictions on activity and on the use of the property of the organization. They will be required to have a fixed minimum number of members, develop constitutions as prescribed by the Co-operatives Act, follow the legislation's guidelines on securities matters, capital structure, and member rights, keep the required kinds of records and make them available as and to whom stipulated, elect a board of directors, have meetings of directors and members as laid down in the legislation, appoint officers and auditors according to the act, distribute powers within the co-operative as directed by the act, and be subject to the supervisory powers of the appropriate government official.

Some of the prescriptions and proscriptions may be desired by the co-operative while others may not; some may be advantageous, but others may be disadvantageous. The relevant acts will not be suitable for all of the organizations incorporated under them. Nonetheless, a co-operative organization must either conform or leave itself open to the various civil and quasi-criminal consequences envisaged by the act.

An Elite Democratic Model for Participatory Democratic Organizations
Perhaps the main consequence of this legislated regime is the requirement that
co-operatives adopt an organizational and managerial structure based on elite
democratic theory even though they espouse participatory democratic ideals.
They are required to elect a board of directors and to appoint certain specified
officers, and they are required to develop formal hierarchies within the
co-operative. Essentially, the legal regime specifies that co-operatives must
elect representatives to manage the organization, rather than operate on the
basis of grass-roots, participatory decision-making. In large co-operatives this
might well be the regime chosen by the members, either because they have no
experience of any other method or because of actual preference. In the smallest
co-operatives such a regime may be more troublesome. In other words, the
structure dictated by the act is inconsistent with some of the participatory
democratic ideals of co-operatives. Co-operatives have always asserted the
abstract desirability of a participatory model. More recently these assertions
have generally been unaccompanied by substantive argument and have seldom
been presented along with concrete action or proposals for implementation.[3]
Observation indicates that such ideals are only rarely put into practice. The fact
remains that participatory democracy and the legal regime borrowed from
corporation law and practice do not fit together.

There is some scope for adopting a structure different from that laid down in
the legislation. It is possible for the co-operative's internal operating rules –
the by-laws – to prescribe a participatory democratic structure. These by-laws
cannot, however, dispense with the structure stipulated by the statute. This
would give rise to a situation in which the legal regime remains the formal
structure while the by-laws, prescribing a participatory democratic structure,
constitute the actual operating structure.

Co-operatives have addressed this matter indirectly by developing more
frequent structured meetings and education strategies. Both of these are
important elements of any truly democratic organization, but they do not go to
the root of the issue. They do not serve to affect the theoretical underpinnings
of the structure. It should be noted also that most co-operatives hold the
minimum number of meetings permitted by the relevant legislation and make
very little effort to develop sophisticated and effective member and other
education programs. It should be no surprise, then, that the nature, quantity,
and quality of democracy in co-operatives come in for considerable criticism.

Agents
Any organization which is too large and complex for one person to operate
must have agents to perform various functions. The structure adopted by all

organizations is similar. The owners, usually through an election process, appoint agents, usually called directors, to run the organization. The directors in turn hire employees. Invariably, some of the workers are hired to perform managerial functions, including supervising non-managerial employees.

Co-operatives use this traditional structure. Consequently, they have four distinct internal actors: members, directors, managers, and employees. In the smallest co-operatives, in which the members do everything, the functions performed by these actors are rolled into one. In all other co-operatives they are separate.

A discussion of the legal provisions affecting the functions of the various players in the structure of co-operatives will enable an assessment of the role of the law in determining the kind of democratic participation which is possible for co-operatives and an assessment of the kind of democracy actually at work. The laws' structural prescriptions are of considerable importance in the final design of an organization. As far as co-operatives are considered, these prescriptions are in need of major reconsideration, and must be tailored to a more appropriate model of co-operative organization.

Directors

While a good deal of research has been carried out on the duties of directors of corporations, very little has been written on the specific question of co-operative directors' duties. An issue arises as to whether this research on private corporation directors can be applied in the co-operative context. The conventional wisdom is that the duties are essentially the same.[4]

Basically, directors have all the legal power and all the notional responsibility for running the organization. A close look at how large corporations operate reveals that most directors have no real power; power resides with the executive directors who are in fact the senior managers. Meetings of boards of directors generally rubber-stamp decisions of these senior managers. Thus directors have only that amount of power permitted them by the senior managers. This is satisfactorily documented.[5] Theory suggests that the same phenomenon exists in large co-operatives and, though perhaps to some lesser degree, in small co-operatives.

Whatever directors of corporations and co-operatives may or may not do, their duties are generally classified into two types: duties of care, skill, and diligence; and fiduciary duties of utmost good faith and loyalty. This section on directors will serve two purposes. It will describe and examine these legal duties and will also assess the extent to which these duties, and the legal rules attached to them, reflect reality in the co-operative context.

Duty of Care, Skill, and Diligence

The duty of care, skill, and diligence refers to the standard of conduct a director must exhibit to avoid being negligent. There is some comfort in the lack of effective power located in boards of directors. After all, the statutory standard of care, skill, and diligence required of a director is low; that which a 'reasonably prudent person would exercise in comparable circumstances.'[6] Statutory definition of directors' duties is a contemporary phenomenon built on common law heritage, and must be interpreted in this context. The law's general approach to the duty of care expected of directors of corporations was laid down in *Re City Equitable Fire Insurance Company Limited* and the terminology is appropriate for co-operatives. In that case Mr Justice Romer proposed a variable assessment of duty that would be based on the degree of care and skill which might reasonably be expected from a person of the director's knowledge and experience.[7] Therefore, much could be expected of an experienced and skilled business person but little might be expected of someone unversed in the ways of business.

Specifically, Mr Justice Romer said that directors are not liable for 'mere errors of judgment,' that they need not give continuous attention to the affairs of their corporation, and that as long as there are no grounds for suspicion, duties can properly be left to others in the corporation hired to perform these duties.[8] In this context, the comments of Neville J. in *Re Brazilian Rubber Plantations and Estates Ltd.* are relevant. He stated that a director of a rubber company can 'undertake the management of a rubber company in complete ignorance of everything connected with rubber, without incurring responsibility for the mistakes which may result from such ignorance.'[9]

Modern legislation has changed all this but little. The likelihood that the duty of care and skill will constitute a risk to directors is minimal.[10] In addition, of course, corporations and co-operatives can and do indemnify directors for, and insure them against, losses sustained as a result of their conduct.[11]

As a result of what is expected of directors, the law seems 'content to ask of a director that he do only as much as one might fairly expect of someone as stupid and incompetent as the director happens to be, which one would have thought is not a standard at all.'[12] One would have thought to hear a clamour for intensifying the duties and responsibilities of directors, for they carry all the legal responsibility for seeing that their corporation or co-operative operates in the long-term best interests of the shareholders and members respectively.

The business world has made no such clamour for the obvious reason that many of those who might be expected to have concern for the economy and improving its performance are directors of corporations, business leaders or their advisers, or aspire to be part of this group. In fact, when the Lawrence Committee of the Ontario provincial government recommended that the standard of care and skill for corporate directors be raised to be equivalent to that of a reasonably prudent director rather than the reasonably prudent person,[13] lawyers were in an 'uproar'[14] over the proposal. Canadian statutes have not subjected directors of corporations and co-operatives to the same sort of scrutiny of professional standards and qualifications as they have to other professionals holding positions of trust. It seems unlikely that they will, at least in the foreseeable future.

The business world, then, appears content with the very low standard of care and skill required of ordinary directors. This cannot be useful for the economy in general. Surely every effort should be made to ensure that those responsible for directing the economic institutions of the country are the most able, and every incentive, legal, statutory, and otherwise, should be presented with this in mind. The choice is either to permit this unsatisfactory situation to continue or to reject it and pursue attempts to raise standards for directors.

The issue is a difficult one for co-operatives whose directors generally contribute their time voluntarily or for a small honorarium. The business acumen of directors of co-operatives will run the gamut from completely inexperienced to highly sophisticated. A high standard, for example a professional standard, would make it inadvisable for a large number of potential and actual directors to hold office.

Nevertheless it is clear that the standards of care, skill, and diligence required of directors in corporate law militate against, or at least do nothing to encourage, effective management of corporations and co-operatives at the directors' level.

Fiduciary Duties
The law places extra demands on people who occupy positions of trust. Directors are in this category because they control other people's property. They are referred to as fiduciaries. As such they must exhibit utmost good faith and loyalty to their co-operatives and sometimes, but not in many instances, to others too.[15] This strict exhortation is weakened considerably by mechanisms that permit directors to be relieved of responsibility. The problem is not an easy one. Business activities are speculative in nature and the position of a fiduciary in a speculative context is not always a comfortable one.[16] It is considered almost indisputable that if great fiduciary burdens were imposed on directors, fewer people would want to be directors, although the argument is not made about trustees in similar situations. The argument is also made with regard to the required level of care and skill. It should be discarded summarily.

First, there is no proof of such a tendency: people do become trustees, lawyers, and accountants despite the incumbent heavy professional standards. Second, it appears to rationalize, even to prescribe, mediocrity.

It has already been seen that directors are rarely found responsible for failing to meet the required level of care and skill. The same can be said for directors in breach of a fiduciary obligation. In addition, the process is a difficult and expensive one for the members.[17] Generally, and especially as regards co-operatives, it will not be a process that is embarked on as a rational economic choice.

A number of specific directors' duties – referred to as fiduciary duties – flow from the general requirement that directors must function in their relationship with their co-operatives with utmost good faith and loyalty. One is the duty to act in the best interests of the co-operative. This is generally taken to mean the long-term best interests of the members. In Canada and the United States, corporate law has begun to recognize that this does not preclude actions which benefit other groups such as employees, consumers, or the community (and thus permits giving away money which would otherwise go to the shareholders). Such actions are viewed as being in the long-term best interests of the corporation because they improve its image and thus conceivably its business prospects, or because they serve to improve labour-management relations. With regard to such actions, Mr Justice Berger in *Teck*[18] argued that as long as the directors do not disregard entirely the interests of the shareholders, such actions would be acceptable and would not constitute a breach of duty. Because co-operatives have avowed social and community objectives, in all likelihood the same analysis would prevail.

The fiduciary obligation of utmost good faith and loyalty precludes directors from making profits at the expense of their co-operatives. The use for profit by directors of information which comes to them in their capacity as directors also constitutes breach of their fiduciary duty.

In order to satisfy their fiduciary obligations to their co-operatives, directors are prohibited from competing with their co-operative and from using their positions as directors to make profits which should properly go to the co-operative. With the notable exception of *Peso Silver Mines Ltd. (N.P.L.)* v. *Cropper*,[19] courts have strictly enforced these obligations, but this does not tell the complete story. The reason is that corporate constitutional documents, statutes and the common law recognize the ability of co-operatives to sanction and waive breaches of fiduciary obligations by their directors. Thus, on the one hand there are strict legal rules to enforce fiduciary obligations of directors, but on the other hand there is a routine mechanism by which to render those obligations largely illusory.[20]

The law has taken the view that, because of the speculative nature of corporations and also because they are, in theory at least, controlled by their 'owners,' it should intervene as little as possible. This view extends to co-operatives, which are thus permitted to include in their constitutions mechanisms allowing directors to escape responsibility when they act contrary to the co-operative's best economic interests.

Co-operative Law and Effective Management

The question might be posed: Does co-operative law help ensure that co-operatives' directors are of a high calibre? A further question might be: Can it or even should it? It surely would not be argued that the Canadian economic scene does not need the best directors, the best co-operative policy-makers, and the best managers available. Every effort should be made to improve the quality of co-operative management.

It would be hard to argue that the legislation or jurisprudence imposes heavy burdens on directors. In *Pavlides* v. *Jensen*[21] Mr Justice Danckwerts was prepared to admit that a board of directors could be 'an amiable set of lunatics'[22] without giving rise to responsibility on their part, and in *Daniels* v. *Daniels* Mr Justice Templeman seems to say that as long as 'foolish directors' do not make a profit as the result of their foolishness, they will escape liability. Apparently, directors need have no qualifications at all, nor any knowledge of business, and they are only required to be as diligent as an ordinary person would be. They are supposed to be under strict fiduciary obligations, but they can excuse themselves, or be excused, from their scope.

In conclusion, then, the law with regard to the duties of directors makes but a small contribution to the effective management and operation of co-operatives. Indeed, as a result of its permissiveness, it may be said to have a detrimental effect.

Enforcement of Directors' Duties

As far as the duty of care is concerned, even if it can be shown that a director has not acted as a reasonable person would have acted in comparable circumstances, there remains the problem of showing that this action caused the loss – or, to put it another way, that had the director acted as a reasonable person would have acted in comparable circumstances the loss would have been prevented. This is a problem of causation; it will rarely be easy to show a causal link between the director's negligence and the loss because there are too many variables. *Barnes* v. *Andrewes*[23] is an example. In that case Mr Justice Learned Hand said: 'When the corporate funds have been illegally lent, it is a fair inference that a protest would have stopped the loan, and that the director's neglect caused the loss. But when a business fails from general mismanagement, business incapacity, or bad judgment, how is it possible to say that a single director could have made the company successful, or how much in dollars he could have saved.'[24]

It is equally difficult to discover that fiduciary duties have been neglected, and even if the breaches are discovered it is very difficult for members to do much about them.

Relevant Differences between Corporations and Co-operatives

As indicated, the law has not paid a great deal of attention to co-operative directors' duties. At issue, therefore, is the degree to which the laws regarding corporate directors' duties are applicable to co-operative directors.

The first distinction centres on ownership. A co-operative is an organization of users not of capitalists. It is thus an organization whose members are users to whom the directors 'owe' their duties. Second, there is some sense in which co-operatives are concerned about socially useful limitations on profit- or surplus-making. While the prospect of economic gain is an important component of decisions to form co-operatives, there are other, arguably more significant goals, such as independence from outside forces and working together for the betterment of all. These are the social goals to which directors must pay attention.

Different attitudes toward democratic decision-making must be borne in mind. Democracy, such as it exists in corporations, can permit one person to control a corporation. With the greater commitment to democracy and participation in co-operatives comes an expectation of member involvement in the decision-making process and the formulation of policy. Directors are expected to have a major role in addressing this particular distinction. Co-operative directors have a closer affinity to the members of the co-operative than corporation directors have to the consumers of their organization's products and services. This relationship of members to their co-operative, which is much more complex than the relationship of shareholders to their corporation, complicates the role of co-operative directors.

Finally, while corporations frequently have directors who are versed in business, perhaps the nature of co-operatives suggests that many directors, especially of small co-operatives, will be without any or much business experience; care must be taken to ensure that the obligations placed on them are realistic.

There are two possible implications of these observations. The difference in orientation and philosophy between co-operatives and corporations could give rise to different rules regarding directors' duties, or the rules could be the same but applied differently. Daniel Ish thinks the rules are the same, and that while profit maximization might not be the objective of co-operatives, loss minimization is.[25] He argues that there is not much difference between these two approaches from the point of view of directors' duties.

It is worth bearing in mind that the law of corporation directors' duties has moved to recognize the acceptability (and desirability) of corporate funds being used for non-pecuniary purposes such as charitable and political donations, expenditures on pollution control above and beyond what is required by law, and more favourable treatment of employees than the market dictates. Thus, while assuming that such expenditures will be for the benefit of the corporation, the law has recognized that corporations can pursue legitimate social as well as economic objectives, and that directors who order such payments are acting within the scope of their duties, provided they do not ignore the interests of shareholders altogether. In this sense, corporation purposes and law are moving closer to the concerns co-operatives hold dear – the barriers are not as distinct as they once were.

Members

Member Rights
There is considerable divergence between theory and practice with regard to the rights of co-operatives' members. Co-operatives are free to establish whatever control structures they like within the confines of the relevant legislation, but there is very little variation in the models they chose. Most member rights have been consolidated in statutes. Some, such as the right to attend meetings, and to speak and vote at meetings, flow from the common law. These rights can be classified into six categories:

1 Access to corporate records and lists of the directors and members;
2 The right to elect and remove the directors (however, the directors' duties are not owed to those who elected them but rather to the co-operative itself);
3 The power to change the internal structure of the co-operative by passing by-laws;
4 The requirement that they must approve any fundamental changes to the co-operative's constitution;
5 The right, under stipulated circumstances, to have matters placed on the agenda of a general meeting and to requisition a special general meeting; and,
6 Enforcement powers or remedies – they can call on the registrar to investigate the affairs of the co-operative, bring an action on its behalf if the directors refuse to do so (a derivative action), seek a court order requiring

the co-operative to comply with its constitution, and seek the court's intervention if the co-operative is being conducted in a manner which is oppressive to, unfairly prejudicial to, or which unfairly disregards the interests of anyone involved with the co-operative.

This list may seem to suggest that members have considerable power. Closer analysis proves otherwise.

Rights to Regular Meetings, to Information, and to Appoint an Auditor

Legislation requires co-operatives to hold annual general meetings with appropriate notice, and to present audited accounts. In addition, co-operatives must keep, and provide the members with access to, such important information as the constitution of the co-operative, minutes and resolutions of meetings, and lists of the directors and the members. This provision is designed to provide members with the basic information they need to play a meaningful monitoring role in their co-operative. It is also designed as a brake on mismanagement, the argument being that if managers and directors know their actions are open to scrutiny because of the disclosure requirements, they will not misbehave.

The information, however, is rather formal and may not give a flavour of the dynamics of the organization. It may also be presented in such a way as to make it difficult to ascertain whether any problems are on the horizon. It will generally take an astute and determined member to sift through the information, analyse it, and ask perceptive questions of the directors and the managers. Even then, the answers may not be forthcoming. In addition, as we shall see, possession of information is only one element of being an effective member; there must also be the means to ensure that the co-operative acts appropriately. In fact, the power of members is very limited.

Auditors are appointed by and answerable to the members in general meeting. In practice an auditor will be recommended by the management to the board and then to the members. Almost without exception the recommendation will be adopted by the members. The problem with this process is that, while the auditor's function is to monitor the co-operative's activities for the members, he or she really owes his or her appointment to the management. Consequently, within the bounds of their professional ethics, there will be an incentive for auditors to satisfy the managers. If auditors in the corporate sector are relieved of their appointment, it is generally as the result of a dispute between the senior management and the auditors about how certain aspects of the financial reports are to be presented. The right to appoint an auditor, then, also affords little control.

50 Christopher S. Axworthy

Election and Removal of Directors
The members elect the directors at annual general meetings on whatever basis
is defined in the by-laws. Vacancies occurring between annual general meetings
can be filled by the remaining board members. Directors can be removed in the
manner prescribed by the by-laws. Generally it is more difficult for members to
get rid of undesirable directors than it is to elect them. For removal a special
resolution is often required, while a simple majority is all that is necessary in
the election process.[26]

Although the members elect and remove the directors, the duties and
responsibilities of directors are owed not to the members but to the
co-operative itself. As a result, if the directors breach any of these duties,
subject to the exceptions discussed below, members cannot sue them; only the
co-operative itself can do so. It is a management decision whether or not to
sue, and this is under the ultimate control of the directors. Needless to say, the
directors will be hesitant to sue one of their number.

By-laws
The power to pass by-laws resides with the members. Except in rare
circumstances, proposals for by-laws will emanate from the management and
be sanctioned by the board of directors. They will represent changes in the
internal structure of the co-operative that are desired by the managers and
directors. Invariably they are passed by the members. Under normal
circumstances member-instigated by-law changes not sanctioned by the
directors will have much less chance of passing. In addition, in most
jurisdictions, by-laws are effective only after they have been filed with, and
approved by, the appropriate government official.

Fundamental Changes
While the law dictates that the power of management rests with the board of
directors, some issues are viewed as being too important for the directors to
control. These matters are usually seen as fundamental changes to the
co-operative. Changes to the articles of incorporation, such as changing the
capital structure or the authorized business activity of the co-operative, can
only be carried out after a special resolution to that effect has been passed by
the members in general meeting.

On other matters not even a unanimous resolution by the members in
general meeting will be binding on the directors. There are only two means by
which a dispute between the members and the directors can be resolved: the
members can remove the directors, or they can change the by-laws to give
effect to their wishes. Therefore, as far as the law is concerned, the directors can

ignore the members' wishes even when they are presented as a resolution at an annual meeting.

Member Proposals and the Requisition of Meetings

Members have certain statutory powers to propose agenda items for meetings and to have meetings called. Generally the legislation dealing with proposals requires the directors to place a matter on the agenda of a general meeting if a member so requests. Directors can legitimately refuse to comply with the member's wishes if the agenda item represents a personal grievance of the member, if it promotes general political, religious, or social causes, if was acceded to or discussed in the last two years, or if its purpose is publicity.[27]

As a rule the directors must call a general meeting when requested to do so by a significant number of members.[28] The approach the courts have taken to the rights of members is well illustrated by two Canadian cases on the matter of member-requisitioned meetings. It is worth bearing in mind the participatory democratic model espoused by co-operatives because it contrasts so markedly with the law's approach.

Both cases involve similar issues. In *Re Smythe et al. and Anderson et al.*[29] a 'Committee of Concerned Co-operators' of the Sherwood Co-operative asked the directors of the co-operative to call a meeting to hear the members' views on how to deal with labour strife at the co-operative. Even though the legislation at the time specified that the directors 'shall ... call' a meeting when requested to do so by a significant number of members, they refused to do so. This was a classic co-operative struggle. The directors and managers did not want to negotiate over the employees' concerns. A group of members did not agree with this approach and wanted a general meeting to discuss the matter. When directors refused, the members sought a court order requiring them to do so. Although the legislation appeared to make the matter a straightforward one, the Saskatchewan Court of Appeal, speaking through Hall J.A., refused to so order.

The directors argued that a meeting to discuss the situation in the middle of negotiations would be damaging to the co-operative. In particular, concerns were voiced about the cost of holding such a meeting. The Saskatchewan Court of Appeal took the view that labour-management relations were within the managerial functions of the directors and not within the mandate of the members, and that the 'members cannot overrule or control the actions of the directors in this area.' The court concluded that the 'only remedy of the members, if they are dissatisfied with the manner in which the directors are managing the business is to remove them from office and elect new directors.'[30] Mr Justice Hall argued that the purpose of the requisitioned meeting was not to transact any business 'which they, as shareholders or members, [were] empowered to transact. The purpose amounts to an attempt to interfere with the management of the Association by the directors.' It was pointed out, as is undoubtedly true, that the directors would not be compelled to act on any decision made at the meeting and that, as a consequence, the meeting would have been a 'vain and useless thing.' Mr Justice Hall commented that the complaint indicated neither that the approach of the directors was causing harm to the co-operative, nor that the benefit of the co-operative was the main concern of the 'concerned' members. He also said that refusing to order the directors to call the meeting would not cause any harm to the members involved, and that the matters at issue were not so important that they could not wait until the next annual general meeting. Further, he pointed out that less than two hundred members out of twenty-seven thousand signed the petition.

The court concluded that 'the expense and inconvenience of calling the meeting would outweigh any possible benefit or advantage that could be derived from holding it. The applicants have not satisfied the court of the propriety of their motives. The meeting is requested by a small fraction of the overall membership ... the writ should be refused.'[31]

There can be little doubt that this decision is wrong. It conflicts with the wording of the statute – the legislation did not require the applicants to prove the things the court concluded had to be proved. The act stated that the directors 'shall' call a meeting when the members requisition one. It did not limit the meeting to one which was to conduct business under the jurisdiction of the members. In legal terms it is wrong, and in co-operative or democratic terms it is clearly wrong also. It is a decision that makes sense in the context of an elite democratic model, whereas co-operatives purportedly function on a participatory democratic model which would permit much greater member input.

In *Fraser Valley Credit Union* v. *Union of Bank Employees, Local 2100 et al.*[32] essentially the same issue was raised. However, the reason for the special general meeting was not just to discuss the issue, but to introduce a procedure to resolve the labour dispute. The members' group also wanted to introduce a special resolution at the annual general meeting to remove all of the directors and to hold elections for a new board. This, of course, is a matter within the powers of the members. These members requisitioned the directors to call a special meeting, which they understandably refused to do. The members obtained a court order requiring the meeting to take place, and it was held. The directors refused to circulate the notice of motion regarding the removal of the directors, so the member group placed an advertisement in the local newspaper informing the members of what was intended.

At the special meeting a resolution was passed to send the labour dispute to arbitration and a member was elected as the arbitrator. After the meeting the directors met and voted to reject the resolutions from the meeting; soon after, the credit union locked out its employees. A few days later the annual general meeting took place; the resolution removing the directors was passed and new directors were elected. Two incumbents who supported the requisitioning group were elected and the remaining directors were defeated.

The day following the annual general meeting the old board, which refused to accept the decision, met and so did the new board. The issue came to court on an application by seven members of the old board to declare the election invalid. The crucial question concerned the validity of the special resolution dismissing the old directors. In the middle of the hearing the Credit Union Reserve Board of British Columbia appointed an administrator to manage the credit union.

The British Columbia Court of Appeal held that the special resolution dismissing the directors was invalid because it was not preceded by the requisite notice. Yet the reason notice was not given was because the directors, whose responsibility it was to give it and who were called on to give it, refused to do so. Further, the members had not obtained the approval of the appropriate government official for their resolution. The court assumed that even if the old board breached the act by refusing to circulate the notice, that in itself was not enough to validate the resolution. In the final outcome, however, the court doubted that the refusal to circulate the notice was an offence under the act. As a result of the members' intention that the proposed by-law be operational without the approval of the relevant government official, the court doubted that the board 'was obliged to circulate to the members a resolution which was so obviously and fundamentally defective.' Consequently the five old directors remained in office and new elections were required to fill the vacancies.

While most statutes give courts wide powers to rectify irregularities and to make whatever orders are deemed advisable, the British Columbia Court of Appeal took a restrictive approach and chose not to act on behalf of the petitioning members.

It is clear from these two cases that members who are opposed to the direction in which the co-operative or credit union is heading will be very hard pressed to do anything about it unless they can persuade the directors to support their actions. Clearly, then, members do not have much real power.

Member Remedies
Legislation has, to some extent, expanded the remedies available to members when they are dissatisfied with the activities of their co-operative. These so-

called statutory remedies offer more in promise than in substance. A member (or indeed almost anyone affected by the co-operative's actions) can bring an action in the name of the co-operative to pursue a remedy for the co-operative (a derivative action). The situation arises when the directors refuse to bring the action. To permit this derivative action to begin, the court must be satisfied that the directors are not diligently prosecuting the action, that they have been informed by the complainant of his or her decision to instigate the action, that the complainant is acting in good faith, and that the action is in the best interests of the co-operative.[33] Within or in addition to these constraints, there are some limitations remaining from the law prior to the enactment of contemporary statute law. Essentially these exceptions reflect a respect for majority rule and a reticence on the part of judges to become involved in corporate management. Unless the co-operative is being run in a manner which is oppressive to one or more members, or unless justice demands that the action be brought, the members will not be permitted to bring the derivative action.

There are also considerable economic disincentives to members bringing an action. The members bringing the action will be named as plaintiffs, and if the action is unsuccessful they, not the co-operative, will be responsible for paying the court costs. If the action is successful the proceeds belong to the co-operative, not to the members (although the value of the co-operative will be increased by the amount of the award). It can be seen that these two consequences will serve to deter most members.

Members can also seek what is referred to as an 'oppression' remedy. A member may register a complaint that the co-operative is being conducted in a way which is 'oppressive or unfairly prejudicial to or that unfairly disregards the interests of a member.'[34] At issue here is the type of behaviour covered by these words. *Harbin and McKone* v. *Lloydminster Co-operative Association Ltd.*[35] discussed the oppression remedy. A board of directors of a co-operative with six stores decided to close one that had been losing money for some time. After the decision was taken, but before it was implemented, the co-operative held its annual general meeting. It was attended by 202 of the co-operative's 10,252 members. A resolution was passed by 68 members, with 21 members opposed and 113 members abstaining, instructing the board of directors to reverse its decision. The board ignored this resolution.

As has been seen, the decision to close the store was within the board's power. As far as the law is concerned, it does not matter what the members think, say, or do in this context. Some members sought a court order that this conduct offended against the standard of behaviour required of the co-operative. Mr Justice Gerein, of the Saskatchewan Court of Queen's Bench, held the behaviour not to be oppressive, unfairly prejudicial to, or unfairly disregarding the members' interests. He found that, while some members would be inconvenienced by the closing, it would benefit most members because it would remove a financial drain on the co-operative. Basically, this decision was viewed as a management decision within the responsibility of the directors. It was not action which was intended to be 'oppressive' to any members, in particular to those who patronized the store in question.

In discussing the sort of behaviour which would be within the definition of oppressive, unfairly prejudicial to, or unfairly disregarding the interests of the members, Mr Justice Gerein referred to things done in a burdensome, harsh, or wrongful manner, where there is a lack of probity and fair dealing, and where injury is caused unfairly or unjustly. Of course, these words, and perhaps all descriptive words of this sort, are most unhelpful in predicting unacceptable behaviour. They give the sense that unfair actions will be proscribed, but that is all. In practice, the uncertainty of the words, and of what is expected of directors and managers, together with the economic disincentives to members instituting actions, all conspire to limit severely any meaningful control by members over the directors and managers.

The obstacles faced by dissident members is well reflected in Mr Justice Gerein's conclusion. He said: 'the will of the majority of the [co-operative] was that of the board of directors until a contrary will was expressed. It is absurd to say that the will of 68 people [the number of members which formed the majority in voting for the resolution calling upon the directors to reverse their decision to close the store] could replace the mandate given the directors and become the will of the majority of the 10,000 membership when the membership had no knowledge whatsoever of what the 68 proposed.'[36]

The decision refusing to find the requirements necessary for granting an oppression remedy was probably correct in this case. However, the statements of the court make it clear how difficult it will be for the members ever to be successful. Admittedly, in this case the members could have given notice of their intention to move such a motion, but they were acting completely within the rules of the co-operative in introducing their motion as they did. If the motion were spontaneous, is that reason to deny its importance? What of the court's concern at the small size of the majority as compared to the total membership? What could the dissident members do about that? Is not a majority a majority nonetheless? What size of majority is required to show serious intent by the members? It suffices to say that the court's reliance on the notion of majority rule and the law's refusal to intervene in management decisions serve to entrench the power of the directors and the managers and to point out how little effective power members really have.

The Impotence of Members

Co-operatives espouse participatory democratic values and it might be expected that this would be reflected in their governance structures. However, co-operatives and corporations share the same legislated structure, even though they espouse different models of democratic theory. The basic premise on which the law is based is that the members surrender virtually all of their management powers to the directors when they elect them. It should be disturbing to discover that members of co-operatives are essentially powerless to affect the direction of their co-operative. This says more about the practical dynamics of the co-operative-member relationship than anything else.

Although the law has been rather one-dimensional and unimaginative in its approach to participatory democracy, clarification of the procedural machinery for derivative actions is useful, as are requirements that co-operatives must provide their members with more information. It must always be asked, however, just what members can achieve with the information they possess or can obtain. As we have seen, when faced with a dispute between a member and his or her co-operative, the law invariably finds the co-operative the victor.

While there can be no doubting that the issues are difficult, the law has done nothing to deal with this kind of conflict. Indeed, in practical terms, insurmountable obstacles are placed in the way of members who feel their co-operative is being managed inadvisedly. In addition, the law has washed its hands of disputes over corporate decisions in which no wrongdoing takes place. It has done this partly because it is thought best not to become involved, but also as a recognition of majority rule.

All this is not to say that the importance of member democracy has not been recognized. However, the issues have not been addressed in effective ways. As has been seen, the problems are only partly legal. They have a great deal to do with the simple dynamics of running a business organization, where economic considerations play the largest role. Such practical, non-legal considerations have not been taken into account and this has led to predictable and not very useful legal responses.

The legislative response to the managerial revolution described by A.A. Berle and G.C. Means[37] has centred around the futile task of building up the infrastructure necessary for the effective exercise of member democracy. In an economic and co-operative and corporation law system based on ownership, this is an approach which is philosophically unthreatening. Because of the dynamics of the co-operative-member relationship and the inefficiency of member involvement in the co-operative, it is also ineffectual.

In corporations, shareholders generally will sell their shares rather than engage in a dispute over corporate policy, and they will be acting efficiently in so doing. In co-operatives, members will not have this option, but they will be able to choose to take their business elsewhere. As we have seen, any member-instigated action will be inefficient for the member and will generally be ineffective. It is clear, therefore, that attempting to address governance issues in co-operatives by facilitating member democracy will not bring about the desired effect – indeed it will not bring about much of a result at all.

The responses to the problem of member impotence have been of two types. The first is to require disclosure of more information. It is argued that if shareholders are adequately informed about the affairs of the corporation they will not be disadvantaged in any controversy over corporate policy. In addition, with the senior management knowing that disclosure of relevant information is required, it is felt that the opportunities for misbehaving will be fewer because the risk of being discovered increases. The second approach has been to attempt to expand the scope of member rights and to facilitate the exercise of those rights.

Neither of these approaches can be expected to provide members of co-operatives with any real power, nor can it be anticipated that they will provide any real incentives for members to exercise their rights. The simple conclusion is that although co-operatives represent themselves as participatory organizations, they are not and cannot be participatory without a major rethinking of their structure and the ways and means in which members can challenge the decisions made by the managers and directors of their co-operative.

There will always remain the difficulties posed by the inefficiency of member involvement. This can be overcome partly by member education and participation programs, and by generating an awareness among directors and managers that member participation in decision-making and frequent contacts with the membership are desirable and should be encouraged.

Managers

Research tells us that neither directors nor shareholders play managerial roles in corporations. Directors do not fulfil their legal responsibilities of directing or supervising the management of the corporation; neither do they set policy or establish corporate objectives. At best they monitor the activities of senior management.[38] The shareholders sell their shares if they do not like the direction the corporation is taking. Only very rarely do they exercise their shareholder rights or seek shareholder remedies. Managers constitute the only distinct group within the corporation with the incentive to exercise managerial functions. Efficiency constitutes the rationale for the managers to run corporations. The larger the corporation and the more diffuse its shareholding, the more likely is this phenomenon to prevail.

This is not to say that the shareholders are not best served by this structure. When they are not satisfied they usually respond, normally by selling their shares, but sometimes by exercising their statutory and common law shareholder rights. Assuming that shareholders act rationally, if the system of control within corporations were not efficient, one would expect them to react and to attempt to change it.

Does this reasoning apply to co-operatives? Assuming that members and directors respond in their own best economic interests, the answer would be yes. But a co-operative's membership is widely held, meetings are sparsely attended, and each member has only one vote. This makes it very difficult for the membership as a group to have any impact on management. Invariably members are not sufficiently well informed to challenge the management and, as discussed above, do not have much economic incentive to mobilize against the management.

Some members and directors are more concerned about how their co-operative is managed and about its impact on the community than strict profit considerations would dictate and tend to monitor the co-operative's managers more effectively. However, there will always be problems with information flow to, and its analysis by, directors and members. Managers have a strong incentive to sift out information that places them in a negative light, and as only the largest co-operatives have full-time elected officials, in most cases managers do not have to deal with directors who spend very much time requesting and analysing information. This gives managers even more power.

If the co-operative is a successful economic unit, the manager will invariably be left to run it unhindered by the directors and members. This may mean that little attention is paid to such matters as member relations and the social aspects of co-operation. Generally, no devices to measure managerial effectiveness in these areas are in place in a co-operative; success will be measured by reference to the 'bottom line.'

Employees

While laws dealing with worker co-operatives address employment relationships, most co-operative legislation omits any reference to employees. In practice, co-operatives have treated employees in the same way as have corporations – as an input to be paid for at the market rate, and with no decision-making power in the organization. Co-operatives in Canada and elsewhere have exhibited a strong anti–trade union bias and have resisted with almost total success the trend to involve employees in decision-making and ownership of economic institutions.[39] This is unfortunate for both economic and philosophical reasons.

Numerous studies have shown the positive economic benefits to an enterprise that involves employees in management or ownership of their workplace. Some countries, notably those of Scandinavia and the European Community, have taken major strides in response to the mounting evidence of the benefits of such approaches. Canada has shown few signs of following these European developments.

The reality of most workplaces is that those who know particular tasks best and who would be most able to envisage constructive ways to reorganize these tasks are the employees who actually carry them out. Yet the employees have no formal or legal role in management, and in most organizations no actual managerial role.

In addition to the economic advantages of greater employee participation, there are co-operative principles to consider. The basis for co-operative principles is surely social, human, and economic dignity. It is difficult to see principled reasons for denying these same dignities to co-operative employees. Why should these notions be essential to members of co-operatives but be kept from their employees? Bearing in mind the anti-capitalist and anti-exploitation origins of co-operation both in Europe and in North America, it is difficult to see ownership (the generally articulated reason) as a rational basis for this distinction.

Conclusion

This brief exposition of the marked contrasts between myth and reality in co-operative organizations should, if the analysis has merit, present grave cause for concern. Co-operatives take great pride in the democratic components of their organizational structure and compare themselves favourably to corporations. Yet what has been presented here is the argument that such favourable expositions and comparisons are better treated as myths.

One would be hard pressed to generate economic analyses to explain why co-operatives should respond any differently than corporations to issues about who should make decisions and how they should be made. It must generally be regarded as inefficient for directors and members to play much of a decision-making role in their co-operatives. This is not to say that none takes place, but it is not widespread.

The co-operative movement needs to reassess the ways in which its so-called democratic control structures work or do not work. Consideration needs to be given to instituting mechanisms to reinvigorate the democratic aspects of co-operation. Such ventures may fly in the face of cultural values and economic principles, in which case the co-operative movement faces a major challenge to its identity and purpose. If we value democracy, then we will pursue it energetically whatever the economic considerations. The costs must be met out of the efficiencies generated through greater member commitment to co-operatives and to the social and community values they represent. It remains to be seen whether co-operatives are up to this challenge, or whether they will continue merely to talk about but not to practise a different, more participatory decision-making structure. Will form continue to prevail over substance, or will co-operatives return to their roots to meet the challenge of democracy?

PART TWO

Co-operatives in a
Changing Social Context

4 Social Bases of Co-operation: Historical Examples and Contemporary Questions

Co-operatives, properly defined, are modern institutions born in the wake of the industrial revolution and in an environment of economic liberalism and individualism. It was not the most impoverished or deprived who formed them, but those in more stable circumstances who possessed a common social outlook. Where co-operative movements flourished it was because they represented some sort of group identity or articulate collective aspirations among those who felt excluded by the predominant economic structures, and who had the necessary material and intellectual resources to attempt to set up an alternative. Co-operative movements, the chapter concludes, have developed most strongly where economic and socio-cultural interests overlap.

Who forms co-operatives, and under what circumstances? That (empirical) question, the thought behind this chapter, implies some more difficult questions: Why do people form co-operatives? What are the motivations, the concerns, the psychology, that create and sustain such institutions? To address these points, the following discussion will look selectively at some of the larger co-operative movements of the last century and a half, in order to see what common patterns and what differing tendencies may lie behind co-operative approaches to modern problems. The history of co-operatives has usually been written within institutional or national frameworks, but it is important to realize the universal aspects of the co-operative phenomenon in industrialized and industrializing societies. One conclusion that comes from such a perspective is that large co-operative movements have, historically, been intimately bound up with some particular social environments. Their function as expressions of social needs, values, and structures has made them instruments of social goals and at the same time institutions uniquely sensitive to social conditions and processes – agents of change, and vulnerable to change.

It is possible to adopt a broad definition of 'co-operation' comprising all ideas and social structures that emphasize mutual roles and responsibilities. Such a universal concept, which can be taken as a logical counterweight to equally universal concepts of individualism and centralism, can then be applied to any human society in any era. For present purposes, however, this is too blunt an intellectual tool. What is needed is an understanding of modern co-operatives that permits study of their specific relationship to the dynamics of their own times – that is to say, a historical definition, one relating the given phenomenon to its context.

Any successful social institution springs not only from abstract ideas but also from the dynamic realities of its own time. The questions posed at the start of this chapter require consideration of chronology and contingency, the relation of one event to others before and after. Co-operatives, as products of the industrial age, are very different from communal structures of earlier eras. There is no meaningful similarity, for example, between a modern co-operative dairy and a medieval estate worked by hereditary serfs and ruled by an aristocrat. There is very little in common between a worker co-operative and a medieval guild, especially considering the latter's role in society as a compulsory, hierarchical unit of town government. As one historian of the co-operative movement has put it, 'modern co-operation is not, except perhaps in idea, a continuation of these ancient forms. On the contrary, it arose just at that point in history when the ideas of mutual aid and of an ordered, regulated economy ... were at their weakest.'[1]

'Individualism' as a philosophy and a principle of economic organization has been a pervasive force in western societies for only a century or two. In most of Europe the corporatist and communal structures of medieval society persisted in significant respects – in village government, in artisans' guilds – well into the nineteenth century, being only gradually eroded and undermined. This happened earlier and more quickly in Britain, the first country to industrialize, but in continental Europe artisan and peasant populations were numerically dominant even three-quarters of the way through the century.[2] They were, however, in decline and in crisis, with much of their authority, vitality, and prosperity eroded in the face of newer ideas and industries. Modern co-operation is not a continuation of these pre-industrial traditions, but a product of the conditions of their demise, an immediate and conscious reaction to the victory of liberal economics and modern industrialism. The origins of co-operation lie in the victory of individualism.

This is not to say that co-operatives may not perform a social function in their societies analogous to that performed by guilds in earlier eras; indeed, an argument for this will be made below. But the point here is that there is no linear historical connection between the two. Where medieval corporatism was pre-liberal, modern co-operativism is in some senses liberal or even 'post-liberal': a deliberate response to the conditions created by nineteenth-century liberalism and industrialization. The dynamics of that response are where we must look for the answers to the questions of who forms co-operatives, and why.

The social problems of the industrial revolution are popularly conceived in terms of smoke-belching factories, but this telescopes what actually happened. The role of small business, of artisanal manufacture and small traders, in many of the stages of industrialization has been greatly underestimated. Large-scale, capital-intensive production was present and growing from an early stage; coalmines and steel mills, steam-power and railroads were highly visible and central to economic change. But until a comparatively late date most of the population was not directly involved in such heavy-industrial enterprises. Instead, the revolution that had, initially, the greatest effect was a revolution of 'soft' technology – of law and commerce, company organization and market size and rules, investment and credit. New legal principles like freedom of movement and occupation destroyed the old guild and peasant economies. The exchange of monetary currency and bills of credit, instead of transactions in kind, instead of pay partly in terms of room and board, dissolved tightly knit local structures and gave individuals a mechanism for independent participation in a broader economy. Peasants who had lived from subsistence agriculture and barter sent their children to the cities to live off wages. The trend of liberal economics to remove the granting of monopolies, to eliminate tariff and other trade barriers within markets, to promote new credit institutions and forms of share investment, all created larger and more flexible markets. In the process the social structures of the old society were slowly dissolved.

When the first co-operative organizers, 'Utopian' social reformers such as Robert Owen in Britain or Charles Fourier and others in France, set out in the first few decades of the nineteenth century to address the social problems of their time, it was not only poverty that they were concerned about.[3] Poverty had always existed, though perhaps the material claims of the new age made poverty more visible and objectionable. It was the particular form of poverty that prompted these reformers, a form that resulted from the dissolution of traditional bonds in society, and from uncontrolled growth. Instead of secure poverty within the reassuringly stable and ostensibly charitable structures of the old society, the urban poor of the industrial revolution were insecure, living off wages that were both low and unpredictable. They crowded into squalid urban environments that were far beyond the experience of town governments to regulate or of charitable institutions to mitigate. Their lives lacked structure, stability, and dignity; as a result, they were seen as both materially and spiritually deprived. Owen, a factory owner, commented that he found his workers 'idle, intemperate, dishonest, devoid of truth and pretenders to religion,' and he concluded from his experience that 'there can be no superior character formed under this thoroughly selfish system.'[4] It was this combination of material and moral problems resulting from the competitive economy that impelled Owen and others like him to consider co-operative solutions.

The efforts of Utopian reformers were directed mainly toward the creation of self-sufficient model communities, normally with a strong agricultural emphasis. For present purposes, three features of these initiatives are noteworthy. First, these co-operative communities were organized from the top down by benevolent industrialists and wealthy patrons. The high cost of the land required for setting up an entire community was part of the reason for this. But in addition, Owen and reformers like him did not actually believe the lower classes were capable of running their own co-operatives, not to begin with. The whole point of such communities was to take the morally deprived poor and educate them, by way of a strict regime, to the level at which they could in fact take charge of their own affairs. Until such a time, the Owenite co-operatives remained heavily dependent on their wealthy sponsors and on a tiny handful of self-appointed leaders.[5]

The second point about these communities that is relevant to the present discussion is that they sought to 'save' the poor of the industrial revolution by removing those people altogether from the industrial economy. The model communities were to be as self-sufficient as possible, many of them having restricted contacts with the outside world. Some went so far as to set up their own systems of currency for internal exchange of goods and services, based on units of labour. All of them restricted or in large measure forbade private property among their members. These efforts to remove the members of the co-operative from the legal and economic environment of the industrial world were complemented by policies such as temperance, which was to protect them from the immoral behaviour that was common on the outside. To a significant degree, therefore, such model communities represented negative reactions against the whole of industrial society and efforts to escape from it into a harmonious community embodying traditional pre-industrial ideals. One historian has called one of these communities 'a variant, albeit in a more efficient and improving form, of agrarian feudalism.'[6]

The third point to be made here about such communities is that they failed, both in the sense that individual communities broke up after a few years (generally because of internal problems of motivation, leadership, or finance) and in the sense that the numbers of such communities and their advocates did not grow to become a self-sustaining movement. It seems likely that the 'top-down' organizational approach and the effort to escape from the larger economic environment, both in contrast to later co-operative movements, were important factors in these failures. Owenite co-operative communities were dependent on too few key personnel, rather than on a broad and active membership, and this made them vulnerable to collapse. Likewise, their ideal of community was out of tune with the realities of the industrial age. The self-sufficient, all-encompassing, harmonious entity envisaged by the reformers was too difficult to create by artificial means out of the material available in the emerging liberal-industrial society.

Most of the large co-operative movements in western countries today look back not so much at the Owenite communities of the 1820s and 1830s as their predecessors, but at later co-operatives of a model epitomized by the Rochdale Society of Equitable Pioneers of 1844. These later co-operatives differed in fundamental respects from their Owenite predecessors. First, they did not form all-encompassing communities to govern every aspect of their members' lives; they attempted only, at first, to form specialized economic institutions functioning within the existing market framework of the urban economy, mainly in retailing. The goal of improving members was still strongly present; co-operation had lost none of its strong moral overtones. But the co-operative itself, instead of embodying ideal social relations, was to be a mechanism within industrial society for developing such relations among its members. The co-operative was redefined from being the embodiment of the social ideal to being a tool for working toward such an ideal. In economic terms, it aimed immediately only at performing a limited set of functions that would allow its members to live better and accumulate capital, not, like an Owenite co-operative, to be both employer and supplier to all of its members in all of their capacities.[7]

With this said, it is necessary to add that the transition from one orientation to the other was gradual. The statutes of the Rochdale Society, for example, stated that its purpose was to enable the accumulation of capital so that an Owenite community could be established. The difference, in the minds of the founding members, was not the ultimate goal – they still hoped to found a Utopian community – but the means, which were gradual, evolutionary, and enabled members of the working classes to run their own co-operative and accumulate the necessary capital out of their own resources and expertise. They owed this evolutionary idea not to Owen, but to Dr William King of Brighton.

Once they began to trade with this intent, however, co-operative retailing justified itself by the co-operative principles and economic advantages it entailed, and the ideal of founding self-sufficient communities was gradually forgotten by the British consumer movement. Instead, co-operatives were to spread *within* the capitalist economy and within urban society, and transform the competitive system itself to the benefit of the working-class members.

Post-Rochdale consumer co-operatives in Britain and in parts of continental Europe also exhibited another important characteristic. They were operated by working-class labourers, for working-class interests, in existing working-class neighbourhoods. Unlike grand Owenite projects, they could therefore start with very little capital and without the patronage of the powerful, springing instead out of the skills, the needs, and the daily experience of an existing community. The shift of emphasis in the British co-operative movement from the Owenite to the Rochdale model parallels the emergence of autonomous working-class culture and of more mature and self-sufficient working-class organizations.

Although a great many co-operatives were founded *for* the working classes, it was not always true (as it was not in Owen's communities) that they were founded *by* the working classes. The German co-operative movement mainly owed its origins, in terms of practical organizational activity, to Hermann von Schulze-Delitzsch, a left liberal judge and politician in Saxony. Impressed by the distress of artisans in the 1848 revolutions, and removed from office by the Prussian authorities because of his political activities, he turned shortly after the revolutions to organizing credit and supply co-operatives to help artisans. Co-operation was, to Schulze-Delitzsch, a way to solve the social question without either revolution or state intervention; by forming co-operatives artisans would be given a stake in society and accorded a viable place in the competitive economy. For Schulze-Delitzsch this was the perfect social liberalism, preserving the existing liberal economy and social structure, while helping the working classes by making them cease to be working class.[8]

Friedrich Wilhelm Raiffeisen, who popularized agricultural credit unions in Germany in the 1860s, also wanted to stabilize society, if not precisely in a liberal sense. Raiffeisen was a retired Prussian officer and small-town mayor. It is revealing that Raiffeisen's first initiatives in the 1850s were charitable rather than co-operative in nature, designed to mobilize the strong and wealthy, rather than the weak, to solve social problems in the countryside. Like Owen, Raiffeisen started as a paternalistic reformer. He arrived at the mutual self-help doctrine of co-operation only by trial and error – as the only solution that worked.[9] Similar patterns are repeated elsewhere. In Italy, for example, Luigi Luzzatti and Leone Wollemborg, founders of the Italian credit union movement, were also middle-class reformers.[10] Luzzatti, in fact, was a liberal jurist and politician like Schulze, and met Schulze while studying in Berlin.

Neither the artisans Schulze-Delitzsch hoped to help, nor the peasants in the Rhineland addressed by Raiffeisen, were 'working-class.' Although pressed increasingly into dependency during the course of economic change in the nineteenth century, artisans, like peasants, preserved attitudes about their role and status in society that were perhaps more middle class than working class. Thus one historian of the German co-operative movement has argued that, unlike in England, 'the first German attempts at co-operation were made by farmers, peasants and artisans whose outlook was typically middle-class and whose main concern ... was the *defence of their independent middle-class existence* against the overpowering competition of large-scale capitalist enterprises.'[11] Seen in this way these co-operatives were an effort to preserve a vanishing middle-class reality, rather than an attempt to uplift labourers as labourers.

The subsequent development of the German co-operative movement tells another story, however, for in the five decades up to the end of the nineteenth century, Schulze-Delitzsch's movement developed in ways he sometimes did not intend or approve of. Among urban artisans credit and supply co-operatives developed fitfully, while consumer co-operatives, of which Schulze-Delitzsch increasingly disapproved as their working-class and radical tendencies became clearer, developed more and more powerfully. In the 1860s Dr Eduard Pfeiffer, an idealistic banker's son, decided after visiting the Rochdale co-operative that he should promote similar ventures among the working classes in his native Stuttgart. This first blossoming of urban consumer co-operation in Germany was, as events turned out, premature; the economy and the working class at that date did not have the qualities necessary (without aid from the state or other groups) to build a genuine co-operative movement.[12] The boom in consumer co-operation in Germany developed among the working classes in the period from 1890 to 1914, as real factory wages rose, urbanization and concentration of industry progressed, and a vital and autonomous working-class culture emerged. And as this occurred, most consumer co-operatives shed their middle-class and liberal sponsors, split from the Schulze-Delitzsch movement, and affiliated themselves with the working-class socialist movement. In spite of their beginnings in liberal attempts to prop up declining artisans, German urban co-operatives became socialist institutions of a self-conscious and increasingly prosperous working class.[13]

The real distress of the nineteenth-century urban poor was among the unemployed and occasionally employed, or, on the continent, among the struggling artisans and independent small manufacturers up to the turn of the century. Yet these were not the people who formed co-operatives, and it was not in the decades of their greatest distress that co-operatives spread and developed. It is revealing for our understanding of modern co-operatives that it was not the 'dangerous poor' of London, the extremely insecure seasonal and occasional labourers of the capital, but the working poor of the industrial north who founded co-operatives such as Rochdale.[14] The better wages and more secure employment of the factory economy, plus the greater concentrations it created of working people with similar interests and outlook, provided a favourable social climate for the development of a large consumer co-operative movement in Britain over the last half of the nineteenth century. Urban co-operation was not the philosophy of destitute classes, but of those materially and psychologically capable of mutual self-help; and it was not the philosophy of declining or fragmenting classes, in spite of the artisans' long traditions of 'co-operation' in guilds. It was a modern idea associated with the new working classes, and expressive of their growing aspirations and sense of identity.

In considering European agricultural co-operatives one may draw parallel conclusions. In Germany, which with its extensive system of credit co-operatives became an international leader in this area, the social basis of co-operation was not initially the landless rural labourers of the Prussian northeast, nor the uneconomic 'dwarf' peasantry of certain areas of the southwest, but the prosperous middling peasantry of Raiffeisen's Rhineland. Co-operatives in such regions went together with agricultural modernization and improvement – greater investment, new techniques, a more business- and credit-conscious mentality. The Raiffeisen co-operatives actively encouraged such a mentality. And, once again, this large and important co-operative movement was based on close integration with local society. Raiffeisen co-operatives emphasized on-the-spot knowledge of their debtors, and it was a fundamental principle of the movement to keep their co-operatives small and decentralized in rural villages.The intimate relation of co-operation and social-economic structure is borne out by European rural co-operation as well.

In Denmark the remarkable success of the dairy and bacon co-operatives made that country an international model for agricultural co-operation; and this success was based on a smallholding peasantry which was protected, given legal rights, and provided with credit by the state, and which enjoyed a superior level of education. This strong legal, financial, and educational position enabled Danish farmers to undertake a systematic technological improvement and reorientation of their industry. Formation of co-operatives was one part of a thorough, scientific modernization, clearly illustrating that co-operation in this case was the philosophy of the innovators and the 'winners' in the competitive economy. This Danish example was one inspiration for Sir Horace Plunkett's advocacy of co-operation in Ireland, beginning in 1888, which produced another international model.[15]

There were, to be sure, efforts to organize co-operative movements other than among the working classes and the peasantry. In central Europe, where the artisanal and shopkeeping economies persisted until the last decades of the nineteenth century, then to be confronted (in Germany) with rapid and intense industrialization, these groups turned on occasion to co-operative solutions to their economic problems. Grocers were a notable example of one group that attempted, through co-operative purchasing, to maintain the viability of their small enterprises in the face of massive competition from chain stores, department stores, and the working-class consumer co-ops. By and large, however, such lower-middle-class urban co-operatives failed to attain any significant breadth or depth of activity. They were restricted by several factors, chief among which was the precarious and declining position of many of their potential members. In the sequence of industrialization, the artisanal economy was the first to be badly affected by economic 'progress,' so that by the latter part of the nineteenth century its remaining members were too financially precarious, too fragmented, and too differentiated to sustain any serious collective economic action. Shopkeepers endured better, but here, too, the process of differentiation undermined their unity. Large shopkeepers who could make a go of it on their own refused to join co-operative projects, leaving the latter to rely on capital-starved and inefficient small retailers. If economic trends conspired to make the working classes more and more united, the same trends made the lower middle classes more and more fragmented. Their respective co-operative movements reflected this.[16]

On the basis of the nineteenth-century origins of co-operation, the argument therefore seems strong that co-operative movements flourished where they represented some sort of group identity or articulate collective aspirations among those who felt excluded by normal commercial and industrial organization, and who had the material and intellectual resources to take their own initiatives. Where they were organized from above and aimed at separating their members from the rest of society, as in the Owenite examples, they failed. Where co-operatives attempted to organize groups whose economic situation and psychology made them undisposed to collective solutions, they also failed. Where they emerged instead from the daily realities of life in industrial society, from the psychology and skills and needs of cohesive groups, they developed to the status of movements.

The same arguments apply to the more recent co-operative movements of the new world, especially to the farmers' co-operatives of the North American west. Here grain farmers were united by a single economic interest, the production of grain, and had common economic adversaries – the big-business institutions of transport, marketing, credit, and exchange. They were in a growing and developing economy, with plenty to gain from taking the economic offensive, and were not subject to the sorts of processes of rationalization and differentiation that set German artisans and shopkeepers against each other. They were independent, highly motivated, and capable of self-help. As in the other cases we have considered of successful large-scale co-operative movements, their co-operativeness sprang out of their daily economic needs, their social-economic unity and sense of common identity, and their reservoir of skills, education, confidence, and leadership qualities.

In North America large-scale co-operation originated in farmers' experiences in the last decades of the nineteenth century with the business institutions that supplied them and handled their products. In the Canadian plains perhaps the farmers' greatest grievance was with the railroads that were their lifeline to suppliers and markets. Out of their frustrations with availability of rail cars, with procedures for assessment of the quality and value of their crops, with fees for storage and transportation, came the first efforts at co-operative grain elevators and shipping. As with all other successful co-operative movements, this one began with local initiatives to solve immediate local problems. It grew, however, particularly in the 1920s as farmers' interest in co-operative selling increased. Grain farmers in the geographic and climatic conditions of the Canadian and American plains generally harvested only once a year and sold their crop to far-off markets, rather than within their region. They competed, therefore, not only with each other, but with farmers in other regions, and suffered the consequences of fluctuating and seasonally variable prices. There was a logical economic reason to band together and control sales so that farmers (not 'speculators') got the higher prices. The 'pooling' campaigns of the 1920s on the Canadian prairies illustrate the populist appeal of the idea, its breadth of support as well as the reserves of dedication and leadership on which it could draw in the farming population.[17]

Co-operatives, however, became more than a logical economic expedient; as a result of such campaigns co-operativism became embedded as an aspect of regional culture. Farmers in western Canada (also separately inspired by Rochdale principles and led by old-country consumer co-operators) founded co-operative stores to supply their farm inputs, groceries, clothing, and hardware, and later wholesalers to serve these stores; became involved in co-operative feed, lumber, coal, and petroleum production, in chemical supplies and farm equipment; supported credit unions and co-operative insurance; welcomed co-operative dairy and poultry marketing; and even turned to co-operative recreation facilities for their leisure, co-operative health clinics for their illnesses, and co-operative funeral societies for their burials. They thereby created an interlocking family of co-operative institutions. While the grain economy provided the original incentives to co-operation (and dominated the regional economy), co-operativism quickly became not just economics, but ideology. This ideology was an ideology of loyalty and shared membership, a sort of 'organization patriotism' (to apply a concept used for the German working-class socialist movement) that inspired the committed co-operator to find a co-operative means of meeting every economic need. The values and attitudes of the farming community reflected their basic social unity and common economic interests.

The examples considered above emphasize the class and economic bases of successful co-operative movements as the source of a certain identity or cohesiveness that sustains the movement as a whole. Large co-operative economic structures have been built on independent and pre-existing patterns of co-operation that arise from the daily experience of people at work and in society at large. But the significance of this basis of co-operation in social identity is made even clearer when we consider examples of successful co-operative movements not based on class, or not directly, and instead organized on other principles of social solidarity. A primary and recurrent motivation for forming co-operatives has been the political or cultural goal of solidifying a minority culture or nationality. Such examples of economic institutions defined on a cultural basis merit special attention.

It is surprising how frequently, in the last century or so, minority status in a multicultural environment has been a basis of separate co-operative institutions. The German empire of 1871-1918 included large areas of what had once been Poland and whose rural population retained Polish language and culture and Catholic religion, in contrast to the aggressive German nationalism and Lutheran religion promoted in the state of Prussia. The Prussian government, aided and egged on by radical nationalist pressure groups, turned in the last decades of the nineteenth century to more and more overt repression of the Polish population. Its language was forbidden in public meetings and in schools; communal self-government was withheld from areas with Polish majorities; Polish political parties were fought with official influence; and a concerted effort was made to encourage and subsidize German settlers to decrease the Polish domination. This last activity, the product of a population policy motivated by geopolitical strategy and state security, made economics and land ownership into a field of national struggle.

Besides using what political avenues were open to resist these efforts and preserve their culture, the Polish population turned to economic countermeasures, specifically to rural co-operatives intended to prop up the Polish population. The entire region was experiencing a flight from the land, as farms failed or were unable to absorb farmers' children and the population moved to the industrial and mining centres of Silesia and the Ruhr for better wages. It was felt that the nationality best able to support a large peasantry would win, and co-operatives therefore acquired a socio-cultural purpose. The Polish co-operatives of eastern Prussia did not, therefore, necessarily represent coherent economic classes. They included aristocratic magnates alongside impoverished cottagers, skilled master craftsmen alongside manual labourers. And they excluded, of course, most of these people's German counterparts. The common interest and social identity represented by such organizations was therefore cultural, not strongly economic – except in the aspect of the shared interest to preserve a declining rural economy.[18]

These co-operatives appear to have been fairly numerous in some regions and, considering the impoverishment of much of the Polish population, comparatively successful. It is hard to judge exactly how successful, however, because the calamities of the period from 1914 to 1945 in central Europe cut off any chance of stable development. The same is true of other comparable co-operative movements, such as those across the border in the Czech regions of the Habsburg empire. Here, too, a small ethnic minority deprived of self-government and language rights resorted to co-operatives as socio-economic tools for their cultural community's goals. This line of thinking reached a new stage in the inter-war period, when the new governments of the central European successor states found in the co-operative idea a means both to stabilize and modernize their new national economies and identities. Throughout central and eastern Europe after 1918 co-operatives retained an importance as state tools for implementing land reform and stabilizing rural society and, accordingly, the interests of the nation as a whole.

It is not, however, necessary to look only to Europe for examples of this phenomenon, because the same has occurred in North America. The caisses populaires of the francophone regions of Canada represent one of the strongest and most successful credit co-operative movements in the world, and developed in a way that was intimately bound up with language and culture. In rural Quebec they represented a socially desirable, local community alternative to the 'English' banks of the large, 'alien' cities, while in the rest of Canada, in areas where francophones are in a minority, they serve as important focal points of franco-Canadian culture. The movement, despite its success, does not by and large cross cultural lines. Once again, we are led to conclude that the milieu represented by a co-operative movement may be more than an economic one.

Likewise, immigrants from northern, central, eastern, and southern Europe who arrived in Canada and the United States began, after 1900, to set up co-operative movements as vehicles for their social and economic advancement and simultaneously as institutional expressions of their cultural identity. Powerful components of the American urban consumer co-operative movement were set up by Slovenians in Chicago, Bohemian miners in Ohio, Italians in the eastern states, Scandinavians in the north, and above all by Finnish immigrants who brought with them co-operative traditions and a socialist philosophy from their home country. They did so in part because they found that their actual opportunities for advancement in an alien culture were less than their expectations. Americans long established in the new world and those of the majoritarian anglophone background, by contrast, only began to turn to this kind of co-operative in large numbers during the depression of the 1930s, and then it was largely a white-collar, middle-class movement.[19] The same was true in Canada. Ukrainians, Germans, Mennonites, and, once again, the Finns, all supported and sustained consumer co-operatives as means to advance themselves in socio-economic terms while preserving their minority culture.[20]

Are co-operatives social institutions, then, rather than economic ones? The answer, perhaps, is that they are necessarily both, forming where the two sorts of interests, the social-cultural and the economic, are congruent.

Many people formed co-operatives out of a pre-existing sense of shared interests and identity. That sense might have developed in many ways, whether out of common practical economic interests, a shared experience of separateness or discrimination in society, or cultural and political awareness. All of these elements apparently contributed to making groups in society capable of sustaining co-operative institutions. These considerations were not, in the final analysis, separate from economic ones, but bound up together with economics. Strong social ties influenced how each group perceived and developed its economic interests. European workers would have found no common interests with their employers in the period when they founded their co-operative movements, yet in the same period Polish labourers in German territory considered it suitable to sit alongside their aristocratic employers in credit co-operatives, because of the common bond provided by nationality. Likewise, the existence of some integrating social, cultural, or political ties helped make co-operatives economically successful, since they defined and held a loyal and committed membership. Co-operatives, presumably, cannot exist if economically unviable, and seem often to work best with prosperous, advancing, and improving economic groups. Yet, the strength of the social and cultural ties that bind together the membership seems to be part of what makes them economically viable, part of what makes a co-operative the logical expression of that community's economic interests rather than a private business.

These observations about the co-operative movement's origins and past have interesting implications for its future. For one thing, what will happen to existing co-operatives if social changes undermine the conditions that promoted co-operation among their members in the first place? What if prairie farmers become subject to the extreme processes of differentiation that made the European urban lower middle classes stony ground for co-operation? One would expect to see, and may well now be seeing, a lessening of grass-roots co-operative energy. That is not to say the viability of existing co-operatives is necessarily threatened, because the observations in this paper have more to do with what creates co-operatives than what is necessary to preserve them. As modern institutions, co-operatives have not yet had to live through many social changes. Still, one can detect a certain lack of vitality in some of the older co-operative networks, such as the British and German consumer co-operatives. Here, the changing awareness of the working classes, their better integration into society, and their lesser sense of isolation correspond to co-op stores stagnating or losing out in the market, cutting back and retrenching. If such problems do arise, historical experience suggests the co-operative must redefine its constituency in order once again to represent the psychology and needs of a cohesive group – and maybe a smaller and more tightly knit group.

More interesting still are the implications concerning where co-operatives will form in the future. The record suggests the impracticality of forming co-operatives from above, and the unlikelihood of their emerging from fragmented or declining communities. Much more attention could be paid in future to the purely social and cultural bonds, the shared values and life-styles that have contributed to co-operatives' emergence and endurance. Unlike the nineteenth century, it is now possible that governments, as well as existing co-operatives, may as a matter of general policy encourage (or out of inaction tacitly discourage) new forms of co-operatives. It is important that in so doing they be guided by the lessons of the past, and above all what seems to be the chief lesson, that the formula of success will differ in each period and in each environment.

DAVID LAYCOCK

5 Democracy and Co-operative Practice

This chapter examines obstacles to and opportunities for democratic practice in Canadian public life from the perspective of co-operatives' commitment to popular democratic control of basic economic and social institutions. Conflicts between prevailing ideologies and economic institutional logics, on the one hand, and co-operative democracy, on the other, are given special attention.

For close to a century Canadian co-operators have contended that their primary long-term objective is to extend democratic control into all institutions that shape people's lives. This contention is less frequently prominent in co-operative leaders' public pronouncements today than it was several generations ago, but co-operative activists still take it seriously.[1] In this chapter, I will examine some obstacles to and opportunities for democratic practice in Canadian economic and social life. With the presumption that co-operatives are important vehicles for such democratic practice, I will simultaneously inquire into the prospects for co-operative practice.

In this discussion, I will emphasize cultural obstacles to and opportunities for democratic and co-operative practice. I am using the word 'cultural' in its broadest sense, to include mass culture, socialization, and political or civic culture. These aspects of contemporary culture are of special importance to my analysis, since they illuminate public orientations to social relations, and thus do much to shape member participation in co-operative organizations.

This chapter is dedicated to the memory of C. Brough Macpherson, who passed away in July 1987. All students of democracy will profoundly miss this great teacher, thinker, and humanitarian.

Minor alterations in political culture, and the relative strength and strategic modification of political ideologies, can have a major impact on co-operatives and other forms of collective action. It is also true that co-operatives can be 'packaged' to appear consistent with many variants of socialist, liberal, and even conservative ideology. In this chapter, I will consider how recent changes in Canadian political culture and ideology have posed serious challenges to co-operative democratic practice, and how co-operatives might respond by altering their self-presentation to prospective co-operative constituencies.

Alterations to Canadian social structure and social relations in the past generation, or even the past decade, have been too vast to summarize here. I will only comment on the changes that seem particularly threatening or promising to the future of co-operative and democratic practice, including those in the workplace and employment market, in social and geographical mobility in Canada, and in the changing character of community in Canada.

A final word of warning is in order. It is easier to see obstacles to democratic social and economic practice than it is to see opportunities for their advancement, especially with our recent experience of an ascendant conservatism. But we should remember that, over the last two centuries at least, conservative actions have tended to beget widespread frustration and opposition sooner or later. The technologies and techniques of producing popular acquiescence in elite advantage are more powerful now than ever before. However, popular opposition can still be harnessed by institutions and movements that offer a demonstrably better life to the victims of elite power. People do seek and achieve the means of their own freedom, and co-operatives can continue to be important in this regard. It is with this in mind that I conduct the remainder of this discussion in a spirit of critical optimism.

A Word on Democracy

Identifying the essence of co-operative goals and future prospects with democratic economic and social relations, as I have already done, requires some clarification of the general character of democracy. For our purposes, the key elements of democratic practice are as follows:

1 Freedom, understood as self-determination in pursuit of individually chosen objectives, protected and advanced by ...
2 positive, enforceable, and equal rights of access to employment, goods and services which constitute the effective 'means of freedom.'[2] These make freedom a realistic and concrete possibility, not just an abstract condition.
3 As an important corollary of 2, these equal rights of access must entail equal

rights to, and socio-cultural promotion of, participation in the making of decisions that affect individuals' lives, whether in social or political organizations, or in their working lives. These equal and effective rights of access and participation empower individuals to be citizens in a meaningful sense.[3]

4 Institutions allowing for the representation of public opinion and interests which simultaneously promote translation of majority wills into public policy consistent with these wills, via the election of governments, *and* a complementary participation by average people in local institutions that direct important aspects of community life. In other words, what is needed is a combination of indirect or representative democracy and participatory democracy.

5 Socio-cultural, economic, and political institutions that simultaneously facilitate expression of community and group interests and identities and promote a larger recognition of the public interest within national boundaries. An effective pluralism in the organization of civil society provides concrete opportunities for developing diverse human capacities, as well as channels for political representation. It also provides a dynamic structure capable of contesting gratuitous, bureaucratically expansionist, or economic elite–backed attempts by the state to dominate civil society and public life.

6 Institutional and cultural safeguards against exploitation of some citizens by others, to prevent the exercise of certain individual rights – especially property rights – from inhibiting the exercise of other democratic rights.

7 Legal rules and mechanisms that provide for:
a) disinterested resolution of conflicts between groups and individuals, and enforcement of such decisions, and
b) protection of citizens' freedoms from the unlawful or arbitrary use of state power.

Most readers will quickly see ambiguities, sources of fundamental ideological debate, and shortcomings in this seven-point account of democracy. But in simplified terms it does reflect a broad consensus among non-conservatives as to what the democratic ideal in principle requires. Most disputes with this account originate in the concerns of traditional liberalism for the threat posed by state or collective group power to individual liberty. At issue would be the practicality of certain democratic principles incorporated in the above. Can things like 'equal access to the means of freedom,' 'participation in decision-making,' and 'safeguards against exploitation' be integrated into public life without seriously reducing individual freedom?[4]

These fundamental disputes cannot be decisively resolved, here or elsewhere. Rather, I intend to use elements of the definition to illuminate obstacles to and opportunities for co-operative democratic practice. By doing so, I will also illustrate how maximizing these abstract conditions of democracy promotes development of co-operative institutions.

As limited a democrat as seventeenth-century philosopher Thomas Hobbes felt it crucial to contend that co-operation among atomistic, egoistic men was the key initial and continuing condition of human freedom. The co-operation he had in mind was agreement to the terms of a 'social contract': a minimum set of basic laws governing social relations, plus agreement as to who or what constituted the sovereign power to enforce and supplement these laws. Without this, he argued, a comfortable and peaceful existence amongst egoists pursuing individualized freedom would be impossible. Since Hobbes's time freedom in some sense has always been posited as the primary goal of democracy, even by those who thoroughly reject liberal individualism as the best means of enhancing freedom and welfare across a population.

Co-operators break with classical liberal individualism in their assertion that co-operative human endeavour promotes the realization of a fuller freedom and human personality than isolated, competitive pursuit of individual goals. In this sense, they are in agreement with the normative perspective on participatory democracy central to post-1950s debates on democratic politics, succinctly expressed by Alan Wolfe in these terms: 'A democracy is authentic to the degree that the choices it offers its citizens allow them to realize self-fulfillment through social co-operation.'[5] Co-operative institutions are to be valued, consequently, as vehicles for the achievement of a more complete freedom for more people, with more positive contributions to aggregate social welfare, than would be possible in the absence of such institutions. Achieving better quality or cheaper services or consumer goods for their members is, from this perspective, best understood as enhancing the means of freedom which co-operative membership and activity make possible.

However, the efficacy of co-operative institutions in promoting this fuller freedom cannot be simply a function of the efforts made by their members. With very few and rather insignificant exceptions, individuals cannot 'live inside' their co-operatives in modern industrial societies. Their attitudes, belief structures, and the social experiences that shape these are largely creations of the world exterior to co-operative institutions. In crucial ways, then, the extent to which co-operatives can perform a freedom-enhancing function is determined by social and cultural factors over which co-operatives have little control. This is true so long as we do not live within what utopian co-operative thinkers have called the co-operative commonwealth.

**Social and Cultural Determinants of
Co-operative Democratic Practice**

Mass Culture
If we must look primarily outside co-operatives for the forces that structure
their members' attitudes and activity, where do we look? A good place to start
is the world of North American mass culture. To what extent are the prevailing
messages of contemporary mass culture consistent with co-operative and
democratic values? At first glance it would appear that the astounding diversity
of cultural offerings, and the relative freedom afforded their expression, would
promote a widespread appreciation of individuality and the importance of the
means of its free and full development.

How accurate is this widely held perception? At one level it is accurate,
simply because North Americans have access to a far larger number of cultural
products and experiences than did people of any previous civilization. To
achieve a more critical perspective, we should ask: (a) do the social values and
themes projected in the most influential of these products promote co-operative
social activity? and (b) does the primary fashion in which individuals relate to
these products, as they consume them, either orient these individuals
favourably to, or give them practical experience in, co-operative social practice?

To the first question, we must respond that most popular entertainment
emphasizes the virtues of heroic individual attainment whether it is in pursuit
of criminals (i.e., 'justice'), love, sex, money, power, freedom, or status. This
is as one would expect in a liberal, capitalist, and commercialized civilization.
On prime time television and in Hollywood films the individual is most often
struggling against a corrupt or uncaring or oppressive or just plain stupid
collective entity. This antagonist may be the state, some large organization, or
some personification of society at large. Collective action appears almost
irrational and illegitimate in the overwhelming bulk of television programs,
and in many of the human interest news stories of the major networks.[6] To the
extent that orientations to group action are presented more positively by the
other media of Canadian culture, they must fight an uphill battle against
negative presentations of the same on Canadian television screens.

Unlike print media, television's products are passively received. The
possibility of collective action is decreased in a culture that takes television as
the model for acquisition of knowledge. Television culture is not actively
experienced as is a local culture that people take responsibility for making
themselves, interdependently and consciously as collective action. Passively
experienced culture almost unavoidably produces greater acceptance of elite
dominance, depoliticization of public life (in the sense that the issues affecting

individuals are perceived to be beyond their control), and a reciprocal decline in meaningful community. One could even go so far as to argue that television has remade political discourse in the image of its commodity-adulating commercials. Opportunities for intelligent discussion of public issues are no longer even expected by the vast majority of the population.

This is true even in those regions of the country where distinctive community-based cultures have survived until relatively recently. To take an illustrative case: one generation ago, the average farm family in Saskatchewan took many of its cultural bearings from locally produced and distinctive organizations and events. Now that family will far more likely depend on American programming relayed by satellite, and frequent visits to commercially homogenized urban centres, for their cultural cues. Their local culture of one to three generations ago was profoundly shaped by experiences in and values of co-operative organizations, while today such organizations could not have a fraction of this impact even if they wished to.

The culture produced by a viable community is far more likely to assist and be assisted by co-operative and democratic values. The cultural homogenization that television has effected unavoidably undermines viable communities within which participation in co-operatives and other forms of public life becomes meaningful. In important ways, then, mass culture dominated by television undermines freedom as self-determination, which we identified earlier as a basic condition of democratic – and hence co-operative – life.

The passive character of television culture extends the anti–co-operative impact of its products' content, as does its operation as a medium of general life-style socialization into a political culture of 'possessive individualism.'[7] This process is antithetical to the development of autonomy and the skills of social participation that co-operatives and other democratic organizations require from their members.

It is pointless to yearn for the return of a television-less culture, or the wholesale substitution of mass culture by thousands of distinctive local cultures. But it is important to recognize that elite manipulation of public needs and concerns, or political neutralization of popular dissatisfactions with the power exercised by elites, is considerably easier when people lack the participatory and developmental experience of local culture. Television-based mass culture does much to trivialize and politically defuse the powerlessness, exploitation, and unfulfilled capacities experienced by so many people, and to stunt the growth of the social capacities that allow individuals to participate in co-operatives and other democratic organizations. If these organizations are crucial instruments of a more individually and socially valuable freedom, this is an unfortunate development for more than just co-operatives.

Social Mobility and Changing Co-operative Constituencies

Like all community-based institutions, co-operatives have had to adapt to the rapid transformation of their local constituencies. Such adaptation is especially difficult if the organization in question has successfully adapted its values to its constituencies' characteristic needs. This kind of success can breed complacency about the real difficulties in continuing to achieve this fit between values and needs, and is rather easily followed by imitating the values and methods of private competitors. This imitation is particularly likely if the old constituencies are discovered to be disloyal, or if new constituencies are not attracted by the way in which the older, founding values are presented. The constituencies that a co-operative must now attract are being shaped by a mass culture inhospitable to co-operative and even some democratic values. In such a context, it is clear that the social and economic changes responsible for relocating and reorienting members of these constituencies will have profound effects on co-operative and democratic practice.

In a period of rapidly declining attachment to communities and their distinctive values, community institutions relying on active participation and conscious application of community-based values operate at a clear disadvantage. If group participation in pursuit of social rather than strictly personal objectives is viewed as a dis-utility, as it is in modern North American culture, community institutions whose success depends on the opposite perception face additional difficulties. These are increased when the composition of interests within their constituencies undergoes rapid change. Generational change within a previously solid source of membership, or loss of members leaving in search of more opportunities, poses a substantial challenge to most Canadian co-operatives. This is strikingly true in the case of agricultural co-operatives; the descendants of the pioneers of agricultural co-operatives may not have moved far geographically, but are far from their parents and grandparents in cultural terms. It is also true for co-operative retail stores; their members' geographical relocation severs the link between the community and its co-operative membership, which cannot be easily reconstituted in a new town or city.

From another perspective, however, it can be argued that co-operative organizations should view this situation as an opportunity to build creatively on one of their most basic and enduring strengths. Co-operatives are not just dependent on community; where they are responsive to current and specific social needs, they can also do much to create community. In this sense, co-operatives can perform an important part of the necessary democratization function we identified earlier in the chapter, in which the creation or maintenance of independent and self-governing institutions in civil society acts as a foundation for expanded democratic practices and relations in political life. This has been the accomplishment of co-operative marketing organizations, credit unions, and co-operative retails in the past, and may be increasingly true of housing, worker, health, and fishing co-operatives in the near future.[8]

People value community because it meets basic human needs, especially the need for active involvement in shaping immediate life circumstances. Television and other distractions of mass culture may disguise the nature of this need, but they do not eliminate it. Older, established co-operatives can undertake initiatives that make use of residual or potential sources of community feeling, possibly by promoting newer co-operative forms that meet specific needs (meaningful employment, adequate and affordable housing, or locally controlled and high-quality health care). They can demonstrate concern for problems or challenges facing their existing and potential constituencies in ways that go beyond transparent public relations exercises.[9]

For such initiatives to be undertaken on a meaningful scale, Canadian co-operative leaders must reject the narrow interpretation of political neutrality that they currently accept. These leaders now use the doctrine of political neutrality as an excuse to disengage co-operatives from public debate over issues that profoundly affect co-operators' lives. Re-engagement would inevitably involve confrontation of political and economic elites' definition of the legitimate range of responses to these issues. It would mean 'naming the enemy', which in many cases is well represented by large co-operatives' major market competitors, and then presenting critiques of state policy, and of social and economic interests that promote the more exploitive and anti–co-operative results of capitalist enterprise.[10] In one sense it would mean a politicization of co-operative institutional activities in ways that incorporate the spirit of the old co-operative movement.

This strategy will incur short-run economic and social costs. Co-operatives' competitors and conservative political allies will strike back if accused of promoting socially regressive policies. Nonetheless, economic costs stemming from this repoliticization strategy will have to be borne if co-operatives are to succeed in attracting old and new constituencies as institutions that meet human needs for community and democratic control. Co-operatives cannot be all things to all people if they are to meet these needs. Their strength. as democratic institutions lies in their relationship and contribution to community. Co-operatives must choose between competing with the private sector exclusively on its own terms and setting the terms of their social value and success with some substantial autonomy from corporate capitalist standards.

Moving in this direction to enhance the complementarity of co-operative and democratic practice may well require smaller co-operative organizations and constituencies for a time. The alternative, however, may be to retain democratic form and rhetoric but to abandon their substance in all save trivial ways. Co-operative values and the lives enriched thereby would be the losers in such a trade-off.

Working Life

The changing nature of working life, and the expectations people have of it, are now on the co-operative and democratic agenda. Dramatically increased job insecurity caused by recent technological change and world-wide economic recession has been responsible for much of the social and geographical mobility of the past several decades, as has dissatisfaction with the authoritarian, unfulfilling character of much workplace activity. While the resulting alienation and widespread disillusionment – or even resignation – have negatively affected co-operatives along with other public institutions, such changes have also presented opportunities for creative co-operative practice.

As democratic institutions, co-operatives – particularly worker co-operatives[11] – can reduce negative work experiences far more easily than private capitalist firms. The conflict between democratic rights and property rights that has hobbled the progress of the former in western liberal capitalist societies is not inherent in co-operative enterprise. This is due primarily to the democratically accountable and potential socially integrative character of co-operative property.[12] Imitative forms of co-operative management, adopted uncritically from the private sector, are obviously obstacles to minimizing employee dissatisfaction, as are the competitive contexts within which most co-operatives operate, the potential conflicts between member interests and employee interests,[13] and the limited experience with democratic work relations in North America to date. While these are considerable problems, they are far from being as serious as the anti-democratic logic of capitalist property rights operating in corporate contexts.

Co-operatives thus have a distinct advantage as institutions that can offer positive alternatives to the workplace experiences of most Canadians. Recent studies have shown that levels of frustration with this experience, and vague but powerful popular desire for democratized social relations, are at a significant level in Canada.[14] They can be expected to increase as long as consumer satisfaction from relatively high wage levels is unable to hide workplace dissatisfaction. According to social philosopher Charles Taylor, this consumer satisfaction has been the effective palliative for undemocratic workplace life, substantial poverty, and inequality in North America.[15] Co-operatives' opportunities to demonstrate their distinctive utility to average citizens will expand as long as this trend continues.

However, most Canadians do not see co-operatives as transformative and accessible democratic institutions.[16] To use C.B. Macpherson's terminology, co-operatives tend not to project a strong enough image of themselves as 'developmental,' as opposed to 'possessive,' groups or associations.[17] The cultural and economic predominance of corporate capitalist activity and the absence of consistently and insistently anti-capitalist, participatory practice within large Canadian co-operatives are responsible for this to a large degree. As well, Canadians have rather minimal experience in and expectations for participatory or economic democracy.

Beyond these factors, however, we must note the role played by technocratic and/or partisan decision-making in the various agencies, departments, crown corporations, and other arms of Canadian government. The technocratic, gratuitous or 'inefficient' interventions of the state in public and private life and the transparent venality of many politicians have recently done much to put all actions of the state in a negative light. This includes those measures of resource redistribution that provide disadvantaged people with some minimum access to the 'means of freedom.' These aspects of government and political action have also bred increased public disillusionment with the representative and democratic processes which legitimize the state – welfare state, or otherwise – in the first place.[18] For many North Americans politics has become simply another – albeit unattractive – product to be consumed through the media of mass culture. Disillusionment with politics has hastened the retreat from all forms of public life, including co-operative economic activity, into individualistic experiences that stunt the capacity for democratic citizenship and leave people susceptible to authoritarian and anti-egalitarian appeals.

The Challenge of Neo-conservatism

Neo-conservatives have exploited this disillusionment very effectively over the past decade, and re-legitimized the virtues of decision-making by 'the market' to a degree many thought impossible after Keynes. They have also contended, in a variety of subtle or bluntly anti-democratic ways, that western democracies face the problem of 'ungovernability' and economic decline because too many minority groups and organized beneficiaries of the welfare state have successfully made claims on the budgets of regional and national governments.[19] By denying that the pluralism of democratic politics was ever intended to 'entitle' so many groups in our political economies, neo-conservatives are insisting that advances in participatory democracy and opportunities achieved since the Second World War should be rolled back. This is the practical political agenda of everyone from Ronald Reagan and Margaret Thatcher to Bill Vander Zalm and Grant Devine, even though they lack a legitimate electoral mandate to pursue these sweeping reforms.

Opponents of this resurrected religion of pre-Depression capitalism are now forced to defend the welfare state, regulation of private sector activity, public enterprises, and any redistributive, egalitarian, or democratic intentions that may underlie them. This defensiveness regarding the objectives and methods of the welfare state is as much in evidence in academia as in public debate. It suggests that there has been a major reordering of ideological power relations in North America. It also demonstrates the dependence of democratic and egalitarian values on this continent on the experience of ever-increasing aggregate prosperity. Defensiveness regarding the limited redistributive gains of the welfare state also shows the remarkable cultural and social strength of capitalist property rights, as against and prior to democratic rights and equality.[20]

To the extent that market forces are successfully presented as the principal facilitators of freedom and democracy, Canadians will continue to have only isolated, inconsistent, and educationally inadequate experiences with democratic relationships in the workplace and elsewhere. As deployed by contemporary conservatives, market forces are code words for the priority of corporate property rights over almost all other rights, including those to democratic control over the character of community life. Market forces are presented as the instruments of individual rights against the power of the state and its economically irresponsible clients.

Average citizens' disillusionment with the ability of the state to deal with economic crises, or to administer social welfare programs equitably and efficiently, provides conservatives with an audience hungry for viable alternatives. This is especially understandable given the inability of social democrats to assess the shortcomings of a bureaucratized welfare state, and to propose participatory and socially equitable alternatives.[21] This disillusionment also prevents many for whom the neo-conservative 'cures' would be disastrous from seeing that the contraposition of property rights and market forces with state intervention is a clever ideological smoke-screen for an anti-democratic and anti-egalitarian big business agenda.

Like all effective ideological campaigns, the neo-conservatives' is aided by a set of striking and annoying facts of everyday life. The state does, among other things, limit and intervene massively in the lives of most citizens, and dispense public funds to many undeserving recipients (although corporate beneficiaries in this category are noticeably absent from the neo-conservative litany). State agencies also regulate many economic activities poorly or inappropriately, and shape the character of much social interaction between individuals and groups in clumsy, ill-conceived, or gratuitously authoritarian ways. Removing different types of this state intervention in the ways advocated by the 'New Right' would not, however, open many avenues for the autonomous pursuit of average citizens' goals. The alterations to state/civil society relations championed by conservatives and business spokespersons would, on the contrary, subject average citizens even more to the publicly unaccountable and inegalitarian power and interests of large bureaucratic organizations. The difference in kind would be the far larger role played by corporate capital in directly controlling the publicly significant consequences of bureaucratic action.

Neo-conservatives are able to appeal to a negative image of the state that has deep roots in North American society. This is not the place to summarize the history of the image of the state in Canada. Suffice it to say here that our society has primarily liberal ideological bearings, with traces of European pre-revolutionary toryism, and a significant element of moderate socialism, competing with this liberalism.[22] Liberalism originated in Europe and continued in North America with powerful anti-statist and anti-collectivist impulses and directions. Its predominance in Canada is thus bound to involve strong suspicion of the state as an arbitrary and generally freedom-limiting force.

Contemporary social scientists have learned how to measure some aspects of citizens' orientations to the state. The two most commonly employed measures are of 'political trust' and 'political efficacy.' Since the early 1960s Canadians have trusted government officials and politicians less and less, and have felt decreasingly able to affect government decisions or public life generally.[23] These perceptions, it must be said, are grounded in the reality that most people cannot influence government on significant matters, and that politicians are making good on a decreasing proportion of their policy commitments.

Neo-conservatives have exploited public cynicism regarding governments' inability to deal with social problems, economic crises, and the opportunism of political parties in power, as well as feelings of political and social helplessness. Public cynicism regarding democratic decision-making in public life, and a pervasive distrust of the state, are clear prerequisites of the more elitist and inegalitarian society neo-conservatives wish to usher in. The market is presented as a magically democratic instrument, or at least as one that will distribute rewards efficiently to those who truly merit them. The social world promoted by neo-conservatives is truly Hobbesian: to all but those with the reigning tokens of power (i.e. dollars), life is quite deservedly 'solitary, poor, nasty, brutish, and short.' This vision of society cannot be reconciled with co-operative philosophy.

Co-operatives often originated as the defensive institutions of empowerment for exploited people. If co-operatives do not wish to undermine their ability to empower ordinary people, their leaders must identify the character and *modus operandi* of their economic and political antagonists. This is not to deny the need for some form of peaceful coexistence with economic and political forces which will remain pre-eminent in our lifetime. But this practical accomodation need not be extended to the point of passivity toward the democratic deficiencies of dominant institutions and values.[34]

If significant numbers of Canadians are to see co-operatives as democratic alternatives to state and corporate institutions, co-operative leaders must appreciate the anti-democratic and anti-co-operative implications of the neo-conservative campaign. This appreciation does not come easily to Canadians in the current ideological, cultural, and economic context, partly because our social and political relations have not suffered from an excess of democracy.

One indication of this is that the positive alternative of workplace and economic democracy is still foreign to the private mass media and most educational institutions. Voices speaking in favour of workplace democracy tend to have meagre resources or to be contemptuously dismissed as utopian by the business and media elite. The cynical manner in which the major business lobby groups and private sector media dismissed the Catholic bishops' recent *Economic Reflections* is a case in point. In a period of economic uncertainty, it is apparently unacceptable to bring moral considerations to bear on the priority of profits over human needs.

More than at any time since the late 1950s, the public now accepts the argument that stimulation of business confidence and profits are naturally in the public interest, while extended employee rights, power, and welfare must be contrary to it. This is despite the increase in job dissatisfaction and employee interest in elements of workplace democracy. Ubiquitous job insecurity, which is one of the tools used by conservatives to 'discipline' labour and to minimize expectations for a more democratic and egalitarian social order, is responsible for much of this apparent contradiction.

Neo-conservative public talk and policy pose serious obstacles to the advance of economic democracy. Clearly, co-operatives require an increase in public interest in economic democracy if their own fortunes are to improve. Co-operative leaders need to speak out against the more pernicious elements and expressions of neo-conservatism. It remains to be seen whether they will take such initiatives, either on their own or as a consequence of membership pressure to do so.

Co-operative Opportunities

Most Canadians do not recognize the inadequacy of the dominant institutions of our political economy. A whole range of agencies of socialization work to assure us, from childhood onwards, that the present social order and distribution of power is natural, and is a reasonable approximation of the best order that people can collectively construct. Educational institutions, family life, and increasingly the mass media, play crucial roles in developing this image of the 'natural' character of our experiences and expectations in social relations. To the extent that people accept this image, we can say that the dominant ideologies are doing their job well.

However, the incorporative power of these institutions and processes is never complete. Peoples' experiences inevitably show them that our society's promises of free, full, and democratic life are not met to the extent that we sense is possible. As long as this intuition is not completely lost in the bread and circuses of consumer culture, co-operatives as distinct institutions and expressions of democratic social values will have significant opportunities for growth. Obviously, much here depends on the extent to which co-operative leaders recognize and act on these kinds of opportunities. To do so, they must give prominence to the democratic values of access, participation, and community discussed earlier in this chapter, rather than focusing exclusively on market expansion[25] or bottom line growth.[26]

One of the more promising avenues for democratic and co-operative advance in Canada is in the area of 'rights talk.' In the modern Anglo-American tradition, group claims for increased power – whether made by the already powerful or the relatively powerless – have most successfully been made in terms of their rights as individuals who share certain characteristics that merit greater recognition or resources from society and the state. This has been as true of the extension of property rights to individuals and corporate entities as it has been of the extension of voting and office-holding rights to women and native people. With the attention and strength given to rights claims as a result of the 1982 constitutional entrenchment of the Charter of Rights and Freedoms, this avenue is in fact now sanctioned as the most legitimate way to contend for additional social power in Canada.

There are clear difficulties involved in applying the strategy of an individualistic tradition of political and social action to the promotion of group interests and institutions. This is especially true if we recall our culture's bias against collective action. On a philosophical plane, the argument for group rights is weakened if one concedes the superiority of individualistic perspectives on group or social welfare, as has been occurring in most judicial decisions on Charter cases in the past five years. This need not be conceded. Rather, it may simply be noted that the cultural strength of individual rights claims makes them a necessary, albeit not definitive, part of any viable reform action aimed at a democratic redistribution of power and opportunity in North America. On the positive side, it can be argued that co-operative modes of economic activity are superior to corporate and most other forms of private enterprise, as well as to much state enterprise. More than their private and public sector counterparts, co-operative businesses are able to deliver the human developmental benefits claimed for private property in the liberal tradition.[28]

In the case of co-operatives as democratic reform institutions, group rights and power can be advanced by claims for citizens' rights to participate in decisions affecting their community and personal lives. To translate this belief into something that serves co-operative–specific purposes, it is necessary to employ the old social democratic argument about the moral and practical interdependence of political and economic democracy. Economic life and relations have to be presented as political arenas, involving unavoidably public consequences of power. Imposition of democratic values, procedures, and relations on this economic arena must, therefore, be presented as a matter of individual citizens' rights, whose exercise has positive social consequences.[29]

The other crucial cultural support on which this case can rest is the widespread popular predisposition in favour of participatory behaviour. Even if much in North American culture inclines its consumers to passive experience, there is at least rhetorical support given to, and often subtle life-style pressure to engage in, public organizational activity. Co-operatives may have trouble presenting themselves as attractively as aerobics classes in this regard, but the largely novel opportunity of participating in directing economic activity should be marketable.

While it can be argued that the decline of meaningful community deprives most people of a comprehensible context for co-operative participation in organizations,[30] this decline may also prove to be part of co-operatives' competitive advantage. For all but the most competitive souls, it is natural to seek meaningful community relations and experiences. If co-operatives begin to take distinctive and systematic initiatives in this regard, they can be seen as important means to community experience, as vehicles that enhance people's ability to achieve a fuller freedom. It is also worth stressing that the democratic experience of co-operative participation can be transferred to the more traditional realm of competitive politics, thus strengthening individuals seeking means of freedom. If the possibility of this transference can be demonstrated in concrete ways, co-operative participation will offer heightened cultural and political credibility to attempts to reduce the veto power of property rights over other human rights.

Co-operatives operating in this fashion can advance key aspects of the democratic experience, thus taking advantage of some of the most positive aspects of Anglo-American culture. Success is by no means assured, but if co-operatives do not attempt such a democratic campaign, they will be left even more susceptible to subversion by the social and cultural forces sketched here.

K.J. (SKIP) KUTZ

6 Canadian Co-operatives and Public Education

In order to survive in the future, co-operatives will need to do more than simply emulate the practices of their private-sector counterparts. To combat a trend towards a less engaged membership, co-operatives have to renew their commitment to co-operative education. This means more than just educating students and society about co-operatives; it also involves developing a co-operative, rather than a competitive, attitude among people. The challenge of preserving the values of co-operation will require significant human and financial resources.

Conventional wisdom has it that co-operatives are at a turning point in their long history in Canada. Having survived the economic downturn of the late seventies and early eighties, it seems that co-operatives have entered the recovery phase with a new optimism.

The question remains, recovery to what? Craig and Carden suggest co-operatives will need to do more than simply return to past practices.[1] They go on to say that unless co-operatives change, they will become increasingly peripheral in the Canadian economy and will not be viewed as a viable alternative to the private and public sectors. Certainly, the idealism and vision that attracted thousands of Canadians to co-operatives in former years cannot be recaptured by re-creating the co-operatives of the mid-1970s. Co-operatives in that period were victims to the period's affluence; because of their size and relative power, almost everything they attempted seemed to be successful. Co-operatives began to emulate the private sector, vying for an ever-increasing share of an expanding market.

A consequence of this emulation, which blurred the distinction between co-operatives and their private sector counterparts, was a less-committed membership. An omnibus study partly commissioned by Credit Union Central of Saskatchewan mirrored an uncertain future when it indicated that the Saskatchewan credit union movement was not getting its share of financial institution recognition by young first-time service users.[2] The provincial credit union system was charged with the dilemma of how to attract and maintain a new generation of committed co-operative members and leaders.

The affluence of the 1970s was to pave the way for a new challenge in the hard-pressed economy of the 1980s. A failing economy in many parts of the country left co-operatives grappling with their private sector counterparts to maintain their share in a shrinking market. In many cases they did not. The member profile of co-operatives became evident at this time as well. The Co-operative Future Directions Project in its comprehensive movement overview, *Patterns and Trends*, observed that co-operative members, especially in the agricultural sector, are generally older than non-members, and that fewer farmers are joining co-operatives.[3] The situation was and is the same in many parts of the country, especially in long-established co-operatives. For example, Gene Creelman, marketing manager with Credit Union Central of Saskatchewan, observes that while 25 per cent of the province's population is under the age of twenty years, only 12 per cent of credit union membership is in that demographic group. 'While some of the shortfall may be attributed to young people not having an account at a financial institution,' he adds, 'we're concerned about that situation.[4]

Many views have been posited about the increasing age of co-operative members in Canada. They may be summarized into several categories that, either individually or in tandem, offer a general explanation of the phenomenon. The following is a non-exhaustive and rather arbitrary grouping of those views:

1. Co-operatives have moved from a philosophical/social mandate to an economic one, making them almost indistinguishable from their private sector counterparts. The latter, especially in the case of multi- or transnational competitors, generally have the economic wherewithal and self-interest necessary to capture the younger market. And because co-operatives have a relatively aging membership base, the goods and services they offer reflect the needs of those members. This is in concert with the democratic functioning and organizational responsiveness implicit in this business form. However, this democratic responsiveness may make it even more difficult for co-operatives to market goods and services to a potential demographic grouping, such as young people, while maintaining their obligation to the established membership.

2. The economic downturn, the 'me generation' (partly a media creation), and

a new generation of better-informed consumers, coupled with a perception that some co-operatives are not price competitive, have militated against younger people being involved in co-operatives.

3. School systems and their bureaucracies, which many observers describe as always being 'out of sync' with contemporary trends, have ironically caught up and become congruent with the individualist generation. Through their emphasis on individualism and competition they may have reinforced the attitudes of a generation of young people who believe they have little or no reason to understand co-operatives.

All of these factors may affect co-operatives' ability to revitalize the movement by involving young people. However, in the rest of this chapter, I will focus on the third point – that is, on the ways the co-operative movement's future prospects may be damaged by the attitudes fostered in our education system. Throughout the chapter I assume that the movement does need to perpetuate itself.

Children and Co-operation: What School Teaches

Co-operators and other Canadians should be concerned about what school teaches our children. The situation in Canadian classrooms is, in part, a microcosm of those societal forces that co-operative philosophy maintains encourage anti-social values and, to some extent, anti-democratic values. At best, most schools perform a stabilizing role for society by teaching children early that school will ready them for a not-so-rosy world outside the classroom doors. Giroux paints schools as institutions which transmit a 'common' culture and skills to assist students to function effectively in society.[5] An important part of that process is an effective system of sorting, marking and labelling of children that begins when they enter kindergarten and continues with increasing vigour until they graduate from (or drop out of) secondary or technical schools and universities. Children are trained to be individualistic and competitive; the training is rooted in the belief that the educational system must, at any cost, teach children to compete so they may take their rightful place in a social Darwinist world. The tariff for this process, as is being discovered by more educators, may be a shortfall in the potential achievement of children at school, less than adequate preparation for a democratic environment, and, perhaps most important, a subordination of the intrinsic value of knowledge to what schools have defined as the most important outcome of education: grades.

The noted American educator Jules Henry states: 'The function of the high school, then, is not so much to communicate knowledge as to oblige children finally to accept the grading system as a measure of their inner excellence. And a function of the self-destructive process in American children is to make them willing to accept not their own but a variety of other standards, like a grading system, for measuring themselves.'[6]

While noting that grading, as a logical outgrowth of a pedagogy based on competition, is not implicitly a negative phenomenon, co-operative learning proponent Robert E. Slavin observes that competition need not be a negative if it exists in an appropriate context, although competition in classrooms typically results in a less than effective learning environment.[7] An examination of competition, individualism, and grading yields insight into the shortfall in education experienced by many youngsters in our school systems.

What is competition, and why is it of a 'less positive' nature than many of our schools would have us believe? Henry describes it as 'the wringing of success from somebody's failure.'[8] In commenting on the competitive nature of schools, David Campbell argues that 'winning and losing are what our schools are all about.'[9] There appears to be little evidence to support the assumption that individuals are highly motivated to learn through competition. Perhaps more important, critics argue that the very nature of the competitive process undermines education itself and negatively affects (individual) performance. From the learner's point of view this can be devastating.

Parents have wondered why youthful enthusiasm for inquiry dissipates as children ascend the formal education ladder. As the emphasis on grading and other forms of competition increases throughout children's education, most of them derive less satisfaction from the 'learning process.' They are surrounded by competition, both inside the classroom and beyond. From the sports field to the spelling-bee, children are constantly evaluated, ranked, and sorted. Music and annual drama competitions reinforce the notion that participation and learning simply have no value, except when they are adjudicated, scored, or ranked by so-called experts.

The system, whether intentionally or not, 'engenders feelings of inferiority or worthlessness.'[10] The role of the school extends to helping children adjust to their rank – as is determined by 'experts' – and to fulfilling the education system's economic duty by steering 'non-achievers' into technical or other non-academic streams. Campbell characterizes schools as 'nothing more than bargain-basement personnel screening agencies for business and government.'[11]

The more traditional justification of education as a process to liberate the mind and foster the individual's ability to reason and adapt to a changing world has all but been abandoned in schools. Similarly, the individual's fundamental need to be valued and feel worthwhile has been relegated to a status far below the institution's need to categorize and standardize students in an attempt to mesh them with the logic and supposed needs of the economic sector in society.

Certainly, people are less than satisfied with their own education and that of their children. A Gallup poll conducted throughout Canada in 1977 indicated that among six public services, the general public ranked their satisfaction with the school system sixth, well below other services including medicare, garbage collection, fire protection, the police and the post office.[12]

Could the undue emphasis on classroom competition and the subordination of the joy of learning and the inquiring spirit be at the root of dissatisfaction with the educational status quo?

Making the Case for a Co-operative Approach to Learning

The case against competition as the foundation of learning strategy is persuasive, and the most compelling evidence has been gathered by Professors David and Roger Johnson and their associates at the University of Minnesota. Their meta-analysis, which reviewed 122 studies 'comparing the relative effects of co-operation with intergroup competition, inter-personal competition, and individualistic goal structures on achievement and productivity of North American samples,'[13] revealed that: (a) co-operation is considerably more effective than are interpersonal competition and individualistic efforts in promoting achievement and productivity; (b) co-operation with intergroup competition is also superior to interpersonal competition and individualistic efforts in promoting achievement and productivity.[14]

Alfie Kohn characterizes the essential differences in the competitive and co-operative process by stating: 'Co-operation takes advantage of all the skills represented in a group as well as the mysterious process by which that group becomes more than the sum of its parts. By contrast, competition makes people suspicious and hostile toward one another and actively discourages this process.'[15]

If competition results in less than satisfactory achievement in the classroom, why is it the dominant pedagogical technique in Canadian classrooms? Certainly, breaking out of the mould that society has tacitly endorsed as the only one appropriate to prepare children for a competitive world is an overwhelming task. The traditional classroom is a prototype of the traditional workplace, and schools have attempted, with generally good intentions, to ready students for the reality of that work world. The system has been shaped for the convenience of the administration and teaching staff as well. Power and control in the traditional classroom have been vested in the teacher, while children have, to a great extent, been the passive receivers of 'knowledge.' Within this context, grading, evaluating, tracking, and other competitive activities are germane to the philosophy of learning. But just as North American industry has realized that there is a serious productivity problem in traditional hierarchical workplaces (as witnessed in the marked decline of real economic growth in the North American economy),[16] schools must realize that teaching methodology must reflect a society that is rethinking the competitive ethic as the best and only way to get things done. Both educators and industrialists should assess the realities of competition as seen by Alfie Kohn: 'Success often depends on sharing resources efficiently, and this is nearly impossible when people have to work against one another ... competition makes people suspicious and hostile toward one another and actively discourages (co-operation) ... competition generally does not promote excellence because trying to do well and trying to beat others simply are two different things.'[17]

Educators must reflect on the status quo with special attention to the extent that emphasis on competition is resulting in a lack of student productivity and achievement, a subordination of the love of learning as a worthwhile and humane pursuit, and, perhaps most important, the societal alienation of young people whose sense of personal failure is defined by a variety of extrinsic standards that are generally irrelevant to their own lives. This perusal may afford educators a unique opportunity to explore co-operative learning models as an alternative to contemporary pedagogic practice, as well as a chance to make the school experience more relevant to the needs of society in the 1980s and 1990s.

At the heart of co-operative learning models are notions of collaboration and community, and these are logical extensions of the reality of individuals' interdependence and their need to co-operate at all stages of development. By definition, pedagogy focuses on the notion of 'group' as a teaching/learning unit and supports not only the rights of individuals to learn, but also the responsibility of educators to ensure that group members acquire skills and information that contributes, to the common good. In practice, it is a student-centred model as contrasted to the traditional teacher-centred classroom.

Traditional notions of power are also redefined in a process in which students acquire power to enhance the group learning; the teacher must share his or her authority, empowering the groups to take collective responsibility for the task at hand. Implicit in this process is the transition from traditional notions of individual responsibility (i.e., taking responsibility for one's life; acting 'responsibly,' whatever that means) to one of group responsibility, where the mutuality of the group dictates that individuals assume a collective responsibility for each other's achievement. Co-operative learning proponents Ted and Nancy Graves have succinctly described the philosophical and practical underpinnings of co-operative learning methods:

Students collaborate with one another, help one another, share ideas and information with others in the group in order to achieve the goal that the group sets for itself. Co-operative learning also gives students an active role in deciding about, planning, directing and controlling the content and pace of their learning activities. It changes the students' role from recipients of information to seekers, analysers and synthesizers of information ... Co-operative learning transforms school learning into work which is meaningful instead of it being labour which is drudgery ... It is under such conditions that pupils will know that school is for them and not only for their teachers.[18]

In practice, co-operation in the classroom manifests itself in the sharing of ideas and materials within the learning groups. Children are often given a task in which the various components can be divided among group members. Social psychologist Elliot Aronson, for example, has devised the 'jigsaw' method in which certain periods of a well-known person's life are assigned to group members for investigation. This process fosters the interdependence of group members in the 'reporting back' phases, and supports group cohesion by assigning a group mark, rather than an individual score. In all co-operative learning techniques, students take responsibility for the learning process, the mastery of skills, and the performance of their fellow group members. Kohn also notes that, while working collaboratively has yielded improvements in achievement and productivity for low- and middle-ability students, gifted children may also improve their performance.[19]

Co-operatives and Co-operative Learning

The National Task Force on Co-operative Development stated in its 1984 report that education concerning co-operatives and co-operation will be necessary in public school systems if future generations of Canadians are to reap the benefits of co-operative enterprise.[20]

For generations prior to that report, co-operative and credit union annual meetings had been passing resolutions in support of increased emphasis on education about co-operation and co-operatives. Even in provinces such as Saskatchewan and Quebec where there was a strong co-operative presence, provincial curricula dictated hardly more than passing mention of co-operatives and did not recommend co-operation as a viable learning process. Pioneer co-operators became anxious that the organizations and their intrinsic democratic base, which they had struggled so long to build, were at risk of being neglected by a more affluent contemporary generation. Consequently much of the movement's effort in this public education endeavour centred on the need for curriculum development in the area of history, with less emphasis on development of business education materials on the topic of co-operative enterprise and how it differs from the private and public sectors.

Only recently has the apparent need for re-examining teaching methodology in schools surfaced as a potentially vital issue for co-operatives. Studies such as the omnibus survey commissioned in part by the Credit Union Central of Saskatchewan have alerted the organization to the fact that credit unions are not getting what they would define as their share of young Saskatchewan people's business, and that like their counterpart co-operatives in the retail and grain handling sectors, their membership base is aging. Organizational response to this and similar situations in other Canadian co-operatives has been to reshape marketing strategies to focus on the provision of goods and services more compatible with young people's needs. Assuming that member co-operatives will redirect their practice and policy to make it easier for those members and potential members to patronize the co-operative, many organizations have continued to support (or increased their commitment to) inter-co-operative programs directed toward co-operative education of young people through sponsorship of programs such as provincial co-operative youth programs, young couples' seminars, and dissemination of information about co-operatives/co-operation to elementary and high school students. Much of this has been useful in maintaining and solidifying the young-member base of co-operative organizations; in some cases continued emphasis on co-operative public education and its apparent results has confirmed Doug Holland's findings that commitment, involvement, and patronage loyalty are directly related to knowledge about co-operatives.[21]

Although there has been little investigation into attitudes toward co-operative enterprise of young adults leaving school, the gap between the traditional pedagogy based on individualistic and competitive models and Craig's characterization of the essence of co-operative principles – equity, equality, and mutual self-help – appears to be large. Indeed, many people move through the school system and into the workplace without any experience of sustained collaborative or co-operative processes.

Ethan Phillips of the Worker Ownership Development Foundation of Toronto suggests that most people bring a 'suspicion of, and a frustration to, the collectivist approach' when contemplating working together, out of necessity or choice, to accomplish a task. He concludes that many workers who have not had the benefit of union involvement, which may be their only lifetime experience in a democratic organization, 'take refuge in private action.'[22]

These remarks would seem to indicate that co-operatives will continue to have problems in recruiting a new generation of members and leaders if the concept and practice of co-operation are unfamiliar to them. Taken with Craig's and Carden's assertion that co-operatives may 'remain marginal ... serving a declining constituency,' and an unstated feeling among many co-operative leaders that co-operatives cannot compete with their larger, private sector counterparts, especially on the latter's terms, co-operatives must carefully consider how the message and practice of co-operation may be communicated to the potential memberships and leaders of the 1990s.

In planning for continued or new involvement in co-operative education directed toward the school system, co-operatives must be cognizant of the well-funded initiatives undertaken by the private sector to provide high-quality materials to school systems with the implicit purpose of shaping views on consumer goods and services, promoting the value of individual initiatives, and trying to shape attitudes toward controversial business interests such as nuclear power. In his 1986 paper 'Economic Education Funded by the Private Sector,' Matthew Sanger asserts that 50 per cent of US teachers surveyed in the late 1970s used industry-sponsored materials in the classroom: 'Considerable amounts of money have been spent on producing and distributing materials which, to varying degrees, reflect the interest of the private sector but are presented as "neutral" or "objective" treatments of current issues ... Individual competition is portrayed as consistent with human nature, while co-operative forms of organization are not considered.' Sanger estimates that industry in the United States alone spent $120 million on public education in 1980. Further, multinationals have used the downturn in the economy and subsequent shortfall in public funding to schools as an entrée to supplying badly needed materials to schools at no charge.

In light of the realities of the contemporary school system and the increased emphasis on individualistic and competitive influence-peddling by the private sector in those same schools, co-operators are faced with a dilemma in the ongoing support and funding of multifaceted co-operative education materials for Canadian schools. The National Task Force on Co-operative Development concluded that 'co-operatives have been dismayed by the reluctance of public school officials to provide for co-operative curricula within the general public education system.' That being the case, and irrespective of the inequity of the current situation, co-operatives have been, and should continue to be, filling the void of co-operative education in the public system.[23] Youth-targeted marketing of goods and services is simply not enough – there are literally thousands of interests competing for the patronage of young people who develop lifelong consumer habits during their teenage years. More important, the social mandate of co-operatives to create communities and societies based on mutual self-help, dignity, and the respect for others is rooted in a more fundamental understanding of and appreciation for collective and collaborative values. Contemporary education systems do not provide many experiences for young people to explore and experience those values.

Co-operatives have played a prominent leadership role in empowering ordinary people to create meaningful and peaceful lives through social and economic democracy. The challenge of preserving the values of co-operation for a new generation of people who are facing a set of economic circumstances disturbingly familiar to those the co-operative pioneers confronted in the early part of this century will require significant human and financial resources, as well as the political will to address this important task.

MURRAY FULTON

7 Individual and Collective Interests in Co-operatives

Co-operatives are a form of collective action in which members participate in order to achieve personal as well as group goals. Diversity among the membership can have considerable consequences for the management and growth of these organizations. One of the implications of diversity is that conflicts among members will exist, even when group decisions are made in a democratic fashion. If the conflicts among members become too large some members may decide to leave the co-operative. In general, the greater the differences among members, the greater the likelihood that the co-operatives which reform or remain will be small in size. This chapter also discusses the notion that while there are benefits to be had from collective action, these benefits are often only forthcoming if all members participate. If individuals believe that they can do better by behaving independently, and act accordingly, then the benefits from collective action will vanish.

The increasing diversity in society and the economy has important implications for the formation, growth, and stability of co-operatives, since it suggests that members of a co-operative may not be, nor perceive themselves to be, as similar as they perhaps once were.[1] An implication of this diversity is that the benefits of co-operation may differ from member to member, with the result that some members may find it in their best interest to take their business elsewhere. In addition, the lack of a common interest may actually cause people to pursue more individual goals, which in turn, makes it less likely that any common interest is served.

The basis of this chapter is the idea that co-operatives are a form of collective action in which individuals participate in order to achieve personal as well as group goals. In particular, this chapter examines the complex relationships between the individual and the group. It begins with a discussion of voting in co-operative organizations. One of the conclusions of that discussion is that conflict in a co-operative where members are different is commonplace and that the goals of all members can rarely be met – that is, the notion of a common good may be impossible to formulate. The discussion further implies that if a group of members find themselves outvoted on most issues, the likelihood of this group leaving the co-operative increases. To understand the bargaining inherent in such action, the chapter reviews co-operative bargaining theory which stresses the notion that if people join (or remain in) a co-operative, they will join (or remain in) the one that makes them 'best off.' The analysis suggests that as the diversity of the total population grows, the likelihood increases that the co-operatives formed will be smaller and more numerous.

Co-operative bargaining theory is based on the view that members form a 'contract' with each other; the question naturally arises as to whether members will honour this contract – in other words, will they act for the 'common good'? This leads directly into a discussion of the Prisoners' Dilemma, a theoretical construct that describes succinctly one of the problems of co-operation and collective action.

Voting in Co-operative Organizations

One of the salient features of co-operatives is their democratic nature which is epitomized in the co-operative principle of one member, one vote. As Zusman points out, 'the basic co-operative decisions, therefore, are group choices, and whenever members are not identical, conflicts among them are likely to arise.'[2]

Although differences do exist among co-operatives, the usual way of making decisions in these organizations is through majority rule, by which the co-operative undertakes a particular action if a majority of the members in the co-operative prefer that action over other alternatives. Interestingly, however, if members are even the least bit different, the possibility arises that the decisions made are not in the best interests of the 'group.' Indeed, as will be seen, even the notion of what is the best interest of the group has little, if any, meaning. This will be true no matter what voting rule is used; any method of making a group decision, with the exception of requiring complete unanimity on all issues, has the potential of giving rise to a conflict among members.

A classic example of the conflict to which diversity in membership gives rise is illustrated in the following. Suppose there are three members (1, 2, and 3) in a co-operative and that three alternatives (A, B, and C) are being proposed.

Suppose individual 1 prefers A to B and B to C (and thus A to C), that individual 2 prefers B to C and C to A (and thus B to A) and that individual 3 prefers C to A and A to B (and thus C to B). Since a majority prefers A to B and a majority prefers B to C, it might be thought that a majority prefers A to C. However, as can easily be determined, a majority actually prefers C to A.

Another way of describing this conflict is that the method of majority rule fails to aggregate individual preferences (the preferences of the three members) into a preference for the group, making it impossible to say that the *group* has a preference as to the choice to make. Furthermore, it has been proved for the general case that there *does not exist* a single method (majority rule, two-thirds majority, or any other) by which the preference of a group can be aggregated or determined from examining the preferences of the individuals in the group.[3] Any time the members of a group are different the potential exists, no matter what method of decision-making is in place, for the decision that is made to be in conflict with at least one of the member's preferences.

The above analysis suggests that co-operatives, with their emphasis on democracy and member involvement, are more likely to suffer from internal dissatisfaction than are other organizations that do not attempt to take account of their members' wishes. As well, it suggests that since the 'good' of the co-operative may not be definable, various groups may form within the co-operative in an attempt to ensure that their particular preferences are reflected in the decisions being made. Thus, political lobbies and pressure groups are likely to form in the co-operative as a result. Finally, it suggests that if a large enough group of members are dissatisfied with the decisions being made, they may organize and threaten to leave. In such a situation, the various groups within the co-operative are likely to bargain.[4] In that case, the final 'look' and 'feel' of the co-operative will depend on the outcome of the bargaining process.

Co-operative Bargaining Theory

The question posed in this section concerns the conditions under which potential co-operative members will agree to form a co-operative and, if they form a co-operative, how large it will be. The 'co-operative game' captures this notion in a theoretical model. In this game, the players (members and/or potential members of the co-operative) are allowed to communicate, bargain, and make binding commitments with one another. The game is called a co-operative game, not because it is solely concerned with the formation of a co-operative, but rather because the game concerns the conditions under which any group of people will voluntarily decide to work or join together, that is, to co-operate. Co-operatives per se are a special instance of this game.[5]

To model the question formally, consider a group of N potential co-operative members (players) who are each interested in maximizing their own gain from joining the co-operative. While in economic theory this gain is usually measured in dollar terms, this does not have to be the case. Instead, the gain may be in terms of power, prestige, class consciousness, or other intangibles. Intuitively, it is clear that a player will join a co-operative consisting of all N members if the satisfaction from doing so is greater than either of two alternatives: the satisfaction from acting alone; or the satisfaction from joining an alternative co-operative consisting of some subgroup made up of S of the N members $(S < N)$. For the co-operative of the whole to form, all players must be able to do better in that co-operative than they could either by themselves or in a co-operative with a smaller group of people.

An analogy might be useful at this point to illustrate the concept. Consider a group of children who have gathered at a playground and are attempting to decide what game to play. In making the decision, each child will have to consider whether he or she would get more pleasure out of playing a game that includes all the children, a game that includes only a portion of the children or sitting out of the game altogether. Leaving aside considerations such as personality conflicts, a child will decide which option to choose based on the rules that are being proposed for each game and how his or her skills in the games compares to those of the other children.

It is clear that if the children are relatively similar in terms of skills and the game is better if played by more people, then a single game will form. If, however, the game's quality deteriorates when more than a certain number of children play, it is likely that multiple games will form, each with roughly the same set of rules.

What happens if the children possess widely different levels of skill? The children may form a number of different groups, each of which will play a game that may have very different rules from the others. The number of groups may be still larger if the quality of the game decreases when the number of players increases. In addition, a number of the children may actually sit out, preferring none of the options being offered. Of course, a single game with all the children playing may develop, but this will only happen if each individual derives little satisfaction from either sitting out or playing one of the other games proposed.

In this example, three elements are crucial to the final outcome: the relationship between the number of players and the quality of the game; the relative skill of the players; and the rules to which the players agree. Since the situation described is nothing more than a co-operative bargaining game, three similar elements will determine the outcome of any bargaining situation.

Consider, for example, a group of N people who are thinking about forming a co-operative to improve their economic situation. A necessary condition for all N people to join the co-operative is for such a co-operative to provide more total economic benefits than would a co-operative of any other size. This is the counterpart to the first element listed above.

It is crucial to note that this is a necessary but not sufficient condition. If this total benefit cannot be divided up in a way that makes all members better off than they would be if they were going it alone or were in some other, smaller-sized co-operative, then the co-operative of all N members will not form. In other words, if the 'rules' of the co-operative are such that potential members do not obtain enough of the total benefits to make them better off than under some alternative, the large co-operative will not be formed. This is the counterpart to the third element described above. Elements two and three are inextricably linked – the 'rules' or method of division of the total benefit of the co-operative cannot be separated from the type of person each potential member is. As an example, a rule that is agreeable to a member doing only a small amount of business with the co-operative may not be agreeable to a member doing a large amount of business. This might be the case, for instance, if a co-operative decides to allocate benefits on the basis of patronage rather than equally to each person; a member who does a lot of business with the co-operative will prefer the former, while those who patronize the co-op less will prefer the latter.

The first element can also interact with the other two. In the same example, the members who do little business with the co-operative will only consider forming a separate co-operative if they could obtain more benefits from the new co-operative under what might be new rules of allocation than they did in the old co-operative. If the total benefits are strongly influenced by the size of the co-operative, then a small co-operative may not be able to generate enough benefits to make it worthwhile for the members to leave the larger co-operative. In this type of situation, despite the diversity among members, one or two large co-operatives may nevertheless form.

In the playground example, the children's skill was introduced to denote differences between the players. While it is clear from the discussion that the question of differences between members can never be completed isolated from other characteristics of the game, it is possible to draw some conclusions about the effect of heterogeneity of members on the formation of co-operatives.

The main conclusion is that the greater the differences between the potential members of a co-operative, the greater is the likelihood that two or more co-operatives will form, each with a membership that is relatively homogeneous. In terms of a 'common good,' the members still join a co-operative to achieve this, but the 'good' is now 'common' to a much smaller group of people and there may be not one but many 'common goods.'

The second point is that the failure to form one large co-operative may not be 'bad.' If potential members of a co-operative decide to go elsewhere, it is because they find themselves better off by doing so. The members who remain should also be better off than they would be in one large co-operative, since if they are not, they should have offered the members who left some concessions in order to make them stay, thereby increasing the total benefits that could be distributed. Of course, this is conditional on the co-operative being able to alter the rules sufficiently to encourage members to remain. This will not always be possible. Indeed, a third conclusion that can be drawn is that fixed and invariable rules of distribution may lead to situations where more co-operatives are formed than would be the case under ideal circumstances.

On this point a number of comments are in order. The first is that in most co-operatives the rules of distribution *are* fixed: patronage is the usual method. This has led some authors to suggest that co-operatives might have to reconsider the patronage rule in order to attract more members and to make the co-operative more stable.[6] While this point has some validity, it does not consider a number of additional factors. The first is that in a co-operative where there is a *positive* total benefit to distribute among the members, it will generally be the large-volume members who prefer patronage to other methods and the smaller-volume members who might wish to leave. This was illustrated in the case discussed above. In such a situation, however, the smaller-volume members alone may not do enough business among themselves to warrant starting a new co-operative. This suggests that the patronage method of payment may indeed be a relatively stable method of allocating any benefits of co-operation. As well, the patronage method with its inherent appearance of fairness may provide other benefits to the co-operative, benefits not described by co-operative game theory. In particular, the bargaining that must take place in order to set up a co-operative may be greatly facilitated if all the potential members know there is a method of allocating costs and benefits that is perceived to be fair by all those that are joining.[7] The discussion of the Prisoners' Dilemma will consider other factors.

I pointed out initially that society is becoming increasingly diverse, and that we must ask what impact this might have on co-operatives. While in many cases the impact might be minimal, this is unlikely to be true for all co-operatives. For those co-operatives that are affected, the impact is likely to be twofold: tensions within the co-operative and between members are likely to intensify; and membership may begin to decline or fail to grow as quickly as it once did.

In the short run, both of these possibilities will place considerable strain on the co-operative. Increased conflict between members may divert the co-operative's human and economic resources from such areas as marketing and strategic planning, with the result that the co-operative may be weakened. Declining membership or slower growth in membership may leave co-operatives with facilities that are not being used to capacity, thereby raising the average cost of providing goods and services and having a detrimental effect on the financial health of the co-operative and on the remaining members' benefits.

The Prisoners' Dilemma

The assumption in the foregoing discussion was that the members made a binding commitment to each other, and that all members would behave precisely as they said they would. But is that assumption accurate? Why, for instance, might not a member join a co-operative and, instead of playing by the established rules, decide to act independently to benefit himself or herself at the expense of the others? In the context of the playground example, why might not one of the children decide to cheat (providing that everyone else did not) to be more likely to win?

The costs and benefits of reneging on agreements can be analysed with a theoretical construct known as the Prisoners' Dilemma. In the Prisoners' Dilemma there are two players, X and Y, each with two possible ways of acting. They may co-operate with each other or they may compete. In an economic context, the co-operative strategy might be to agree to cut back output of the good both produce so that the price could be raised, thereby making both of them better off; the competitive counterpart is that both would continue producing at their normal levels, keeping price and profits low. Of course, if one of them should decide to keep producing while the other one cut back, the one that kept producing would gain at the expense of the one that cut back.

The Prisoners' Dilemma may be illustrated graphically (Figure 1). The choices available to X are listed along the side, while those available to Y are listed along the top. In all, there are four possible combinations of choices that can be made. If both X and Y decide to co-operate, both are relatively well off, each receiving a level of profit equal to 3. If both compete, however, the level of profit for each is 1. If X co-operates while Y competes, the result is that X receives nothing, while Y receives a profit of 5. However, if Y co-operates while X competes, the result is that X receives a profit of 5 while Y receives nothing.

Figure 1. Prisoners' Dilemma

	Y	
	Co-operate	Compete
Co-operate	(3, 3)	(0, 5)
Compete	(5, 0)	(1, 1)

X (to the left of the rows)

What choice do the two players make? Clearly, if X co-operates, the best thing for Y to do is to compete, since this gives Y a profit of 5 versus a profit of 1. If X competes however, the best thing for Y to do is compete, since this results in a profit of 1 versus a profit of nothing. Thus, if Y is rational, the choice will be to compete. Of course, since both players have the same pay-offs, X will come to the same conclusion. Thus, the outcome of the Prisoners' Dilemma will be that both X and Y will compete.[8]

What is interesting, however, is that by both acting to maximize the profits they receive, the players actually end up receiving lower profits than had they co-operated. This, in fact, is the Prisoners' Dilemma. There are gains from co-operation, but only if both parties/players co-operate. Yet there is no incentive to co-operate, since no matter what strategy the other player chooses, the best thing for any player to do is compete.

Another way of saying this is that the group can be made better off if the players co-operate. However, the 'common good' may never be achieved, since each person, acting in his or her own rational best interest, will not undertake the behaviour needed for such a solution. While the question 'What is the best thing for the group to do?' might be answered in theory, it should not be expected that the group will actually undertake such action. Arguing that the group will in fact do what is in its best interests is to commit the fallacy of composition. As the philosopher Mackie notes, 'this, or a similar, fallacy, is committed whenever we assume, without adequate reason, that we can speak about groups in the same ways in which we can speak about their members.'[9] The Prisoners' Dilemma illustrates this fallacy clearly.

While the discussion above centred on two players, the notion of an N-person Prisoners' Dilemma is easy to envisage. Suppose that it is possible for all N members of a potential co-operative to provide a good more cheaply than a private firm could. Thus, all members would be better off if they all patronized the co-operative. But what will ensure that all members actually purchase their supplies at the co-operative? If all patronize the co-operative, all will be better off, but if only one or two do, they will have to pay the entire cost and will be much worse off.[10]

Thus, the Prisoners' Dilemma suggests that potential members of a co-operative may not actually co-operate, even though it would be in their collective interests to do so; bargains entered into may well be broken if individuals perceive a benefit from doing so. Merely establishing that members of a society or community would be better off if they formed a co-operative does not imply that such a co-operative will be formed or, if formed, that it will succeed.

Thus, bargaining theory must be discussed in the context of the Prisoners' Dilemma. To develop a successful co-operative, it must not only be established that those who join can be made better off; the question of ensuring that the members actually patronize their co-operative, even when it would appear that it might be cheaper or 'more rational' to go elsewhere, must also be addressed. In other words, there are two sets of questions: (1) What is the optimal size of a co-operative, what are the rules under which it will function, and what are the benefits that individual members will receive? (2) Will the co-operative members actually patronize the co-operative? The first derives from the discussion of bargaining theory, while the second derives from the Prisoners' Dilemma.

It is in the relationship between the potential benefits of a co-operative and the actual running of it that co-operative principles play a potentially important role. It was noted in the section on bargaining theory that the rules on which co-operative members might agree would influence the size of co-operative formed. The Prisoners' Dilemma discussion suggests that these same rules might also influence the degree to which co-operative members support their co-operative. In particular, rules like dividends on the basis of patronage and one member, one vote might convey the notion to members that everyone will be treated fairly and that members can be trusted to co-operate, rather than to compete. In this atmosphere, co-operation among the members might well become the norm.

The need to establish a norm of behaviour is extremely important, since the compete-compete solution to the Prisoners' Dilemma is not hard and fast. As Hardin argues, to reason thus is to commit another fallacy, in which what is good in a static situation is believed to be good in a dynamic setting as well.

In trying to understand dynamic social relationships, we generalize from our understanding of static relationships. Again, an analysis of Prisoners' Dilemma shows why the generalization can be wrong. The prisoners [players] in the story above face their dilemma once only, and they face it in isolation from other aspects of their relationship with one another. You and I, however, may repeatedly face a smaller version of their dilemma. We may therefore quickly realize that our self-interest now dictates that we cooperate rather than defect (which, in the case of the prisoners, would be not to confess rather than to confess). Since your cooperation tomorrow may depend upon my cooperation today, I have incentive to cooperate today.[11]

Thus, in a dynamic framework people may actually co-operate since they recognize that by co-operating today they may make it more likely that others will co-operate in the future, which will in turn make themselves better off. Hardin, in fact, argues that when the problem is examined in a dynamic setting – that is, one in which the two players meet each other time and time again – there actually is an incentive for people to co-operate and this action becomes the rational solution to the problem.

Other writers have come to similar conclusions. Axelrod presents the results of a computer tournament in which different strategies for playing iterative Prisoners' Dilemma games are squared off with each other. In an iterative Prisoners' Dilemma game, a game like that shown above is played period after period. In deciding what to do at any time, each player can base his or her decision on any knowledge that has been gained about the manner in which the other player has behaved in the past. The rules a player uses in making this decision are known as his or her strategy.[12]

The winner of Axelrod's tournament was a strategy called 'Tit for Tat.' The strategy was very simple: in the first period, co-operate; from then on do whatever the other player did the period before. Not only did this strategy emerge as the clear winner when pitted against strategies that attempted to profit every once in a while by cheating, it is clear that if everyone were to follow this course of action, the result would be co-operation for all periods.

Runge presents still another solution to the Prisoners' Dilemma. In the discussion above, the assumption was that each player had particular preferences for the various strategies and their outcomes. Specifically, player X had the following preferences: (compete, co-operate) > (co-operate, co-operate) > (compete, compete) > (co-operate, compete). With this preference ordering, the rational thing for player X to do was to compete. Runge suggests, however, that in many cases the preferences of player X may be somewhat different, namely: (co-operate, co-operate) > (compete, compete) > (compete, co-operate) = (co-operate, compete). In this situation, the rational strategy may well be to co-operate.[13]

The idea behind the second preference ordering is that, all other things being equal, players prefer a strategy that has them doing the same thing as the other players. In other words, if everyone else is co-operating, then a player prefers to co-operate as well. However, if all the players are competing, a player would prefer to compete as well. In short, to be the odd person out with a strategy is a bad thing from a personal point of view.

In this situation, each player is looking for assurances from the other players regarding which type of strategy to undertake. If player X can be assured that player Y will co-operate, then player X will co-operate as well. Of course, if player X is assured that player Y will compete, then player X will also compete. Thus, providing the assurance problem can be solved, the rational strategy choice for the players will be to co-operate.

This, of course, brings up the notion of the norms of behaviour alluded to above. If co-operation can be established behavioural norm, then all members might well be expected to follow this norm, since doing so will assure them that they will be adopting the same strategy as others in the group. The fact that such behaviour is likely to promote further co-operation as the result of the dynamic aspect of the game further increases the chance that co-operation will become the dominant strategy for everyone.

Conclusion

Diversity among members in co-operatives is not only a well-established fact, but can be expected to have considerable consequences for the management and growth of these organizations. In particular, the combination of member differences and a democratic structure implies that conflicts will invariably develop within the co-operative. Indeed, conflict is a direct result of there being no way to determine the goal or objective of the group as a whole. While conflict can be healthy in terms of ensuring a vibrant organization, it can, if serious enough, lead to pressures by groups within the co-operative to seek a better arrangement through bargaining.

The bargaining theory literature generally concludes that the greater the differences among members, the greater the likelihood that the co-operatives which form or remain will be small in size. In fact, the general rule appears to be that members will join a co-operative that has as members people more or less similar to themselves. As a result, and in spite of the conclusion of the section on voting behaviour, the notion of the common good may have some relevance. This also suggests that the fragmentation of larger co-operatives into smaller ones may not necessarily be a bad thing, since it may be possible for all the groups involved actually to be better off. Note, however, that such a conclusion does not hold every time a co-operative splits (or fails to come together), since the reason for such action may be that the co-operative members did not fully explore the ways in which a large group could exist and fulfil all the members' goals.

A further reason for such behaviour may reside in the Prisoners' Dilemma, which indicates that in many situations the pursuit of what appears to be each member's self-interest actually ends up making all members worse off. Thus, while there are gains to be had from collective action, each member may believe that he or she can do better by behaving independently; the result, however, is that the benefits of collective action vanish. The gains from collective action should not be assumed to be automatically forthcoming.

Instead, an environment must be nurtured within the co-operative that promotes trust and assurance that all members will act in a co-operative, as opposed to a competitive, manner if the potential gains from collective action are to be realized. This is particularly important when the membership is diverse, since the gains to particular groups from adopting independent actions are even greater than when the membership is more homogeneous. Co-operative principles, in addition to other factors, are likely to have an influence in promoting this atmosphere.

8 Marketing Member Commitment: Potentials and Pitfalls

Co-operatives have held a historical aversion to marketing, narrowly defined as selling. A review of the marketing process reveals, however, that the marketing of ideas and issues, as well as a societal marketing approach, has been integral to co-operatives since their inception. This chapter considers employing marketing techniques to develop co-operative member involvement and commitment as one possible solution to the problems associated with a declining membership base.

The problems associated with a declining membership base plague almost all types of co-operatives in Canada, giving rise to a number of perplexing issues. One is the apparent inability of co-operatives to expand their active membership, especially among younger consumers; another is co-operatives' failure to involve large numbers of members in the co-operatives' decision-making process. Related to both of these are the difficulties encountered in attracting new leaders. As is often the case with issues of this magnitude, co-operators spend a great deal of time discussing how the problems have evolved, but not nearly as much time considering ways of solving them. This chapter considers employing marketing techniques to develop co-operative member involvement and commitment as one possible solution.

The term 'marketing' elicits different responses from people, some positive, many negative. Negative views originate from narrow definitions of marketing as selling, and from criticisms that advertising influences the formation of values and attitudes in today's society. Leiss, Kline, and Jhally argue that advertising is now a 'privileged form of discourse,' replacing the former prominence of church sermons, political oratory, and the precepts of family elders in providing the 'guideposts for personal and social identity.'[1] The current source of influence – consumption practices – depends on advertising as a medium to provide messages about products and their possible meanings when employed as representations of an individual's concept of self-image. As a consequence of our 'consumer culture,' individuals send signals to others about their life-styles through patterns of preferences for consumer goods.

Whether one agrees with the contention that the essential evil of advertising is its creation of false needs,[2] or the view that it appeals to deep-rooted human needs in unscrupulous ways, advertising bears the brunt of the attack. A further criticism is that advertising's main cultural function is not to sell us particular goods but rather to persuade us that we find satisfaction and happiness only through consumption.

There can be no doubt that advertising and the mass media have had a profound impact on the lives of Canadians. This chapter argues that advertising, as a part of the greater marketing process, has a positive role to play in attracting and keeping members in their co-operative organizations.

Marketing as Something More

Marketing is more than advertising. Taken all together, the components of the marketing mix – product, distribution, price, and promotion – have the potential to contribute to positive outcomes.[3] Throughout the remainder of this article marketing will be considered as an orientation which can be adopted by an organization in its interaction with its various constituencies. It can result in the organization delivering products or services truly needed or desired by the consumer, rather than 'selling' what it thinks the consumer wants or needs. Since the distinctions can be clearly drawn, but seldom are by critics, one must devote some time to identifying how the distinctions can be made. 'The difference between marketing and selling is more than semantic. Selling focuses on the needs of the seller, marketing on the needs of the buyer. Selling is preoccupied with the seller's need to convert his product into cash; marketing with the idea of satisfying needs of the customer by means of the product and the whole cluster of things associated with creating, delivering, and finally consuming it.'[4]

Kotler further clarifies the distinctions by identifying five basic orientations that any organization may adopt when interacting with its publics.[5] The *production* orientation assumes an internal focus, with the emphasis on achieving efficiency in production and distribution; the *product* orientation focuses on putting out products and services that the organization thinks would be good for the public; the *sales* orientation focuses on stimulating demand in potential consumers for existing goods and services. The *marketing* orientation focuses on the needs and wants of targeted markets, and satisfies these needs through design, communication, pricing, and delivery of appropriate products and services. The *societal marketing* orientation includes the organization adapting to delivering 'satisfactions' that preserve or enhance the consumer's and society's well-being. I shall argue that the latter two are the preferred orientations for co-operatives.

The marketing orientation was first advocated in the early 1950s within the marketing community. Many organizations actively sought to change from an internal 'production' orientation to an external 'consumer' one. The latter emphasized the position of the consumer in the economic process and the responsibility of the organization to satisfy the needs of the market, rather than those of the business or of the product. Although much of the early change in orientation resulted from increased competition in the market-place, the concern with more socially responsible marketing that evolved through the 1960s and 1970s reflected a growing feeling that business organizations should develop their social responsibilities beyond those implied by the pursuit of profit. It would, however, be incorrect to attribute completely altruistic motives to business. Large legal settlements with customers made business people more aware of the need to be attentive to consumer needs than did the activism of consumer advocates.[6] In addition, organizations adopted this approach because they recognized that the ultimate consequence of the consumer orientation was the profitability and survival of the organization.[7]

The range of orientations to marketing within different types of organizations is associated with divergent views regarding the proper role of marketing as a discipline. Much of the debate in the marketing literature of the 1970s focused on this issue. Participants in the debate advocated definitions which included a rather narrow definition of marketing as solely a distributive activity (the Distribution System Perspective), an identification of marketing as a generic activity appropriate for all organizations (the Organizational System Perspective), and one which attributed to marketing the responsibility for all consequences of the organization's actions on the rest of society (the Social System Perspective).[8] It is from this social system perspective that the societal marketing orientation and associated social marketing techniques have evolved.

Two important assumptions underlie the societal marketing orientation. First, customers may have wants that are not proper to satisfy because, for example, they go against either the consumer's or society's interests. Second, they may have needs which they do not recognize, such as a need for a quality education or a healthier life-style. Thus Kotler argues that marketers must take into account not only consumers' needs, wants, and interests, but also society's interests.[9] In doing so, marketers have shifted their focus from marketing products and services to marketing ideas and social issues to influence attitudes and behaviour – in other words, social marketing.[10]

Social marketing has generally been associated with the advocacy of socially beneficial ideas or causes.[11] The approach was adopted quickly, primarily by organizations concerned with influencing the adoption of family planning practices. It has also been used with varying levels of success by organizations promoting energy conservation, improved nutrition, smoke-free workplaces, safe driving, seat-belt use, and fitter life-styles, to name just a few.[12] Although there are questions to be raised about the ethics of applying commercial marketing techniques to the objective of social change,[13] most advocates of this market-oriented approach have adopted it out of a genuine belief that it is a technique which, if coupled with others, can contribute to social problem-solving. Theorists examining the historical success rate of social marketing have concluded that organizations have acquired a better understanding of the need to address issues proactively.[14]

This broadened understanding of marketing as a process has occasioned considerable debate. The following discussion provides a brief overview of how the marketing process has been conceptualized, evolving from a very narrow approach with an emphasis on the economic market transaction, to the much broader approach of social marketing, which considers all human activity to be engaged in a form of marketing. Such a broadened understanding of the marketing process is required for an appreciation of its role in developing member commitment to co-operatives. It is through such an understanding that one can address the issues associated with the harnessing of 'popular opposition' to which Laycock refers.

The Marketing Process

One of the primary objectives of marketing activity is to influence individual purchase behaviour. Historically, this behaviour has been linked to economic transactions where the objective of marketing activity has been the exchange of goods and services for money or other resources. Only recently has the marketing literature suggested that the concept of marketing be broadened to incorporate the marketing of organizations, ideas, social issues, and social causes.

Kotler has provided a theoretical framework for this generic concept of marketing by identifying three stages of marketing consciousness:[15]

Consciousness One: marketing is viewed solely as a business subject. The core concept is the market transaction, consisting of the exchange of economic goods and services for some form of payment. Non-market transactions are distinguished by the lack of the payment element and are usually ignored.

Consciousness Two: the concept of marketing is broadened to include organizational marketing. The core concept is now the organization – client transaction, and the payment element is no longer necessary. Marketing becomes relevant in all situations where one can identify an organization, a client group, and products (broadly defined).

Consciousness Three: marketing moves beyond the narrow approach of marketing to a client, to encompass marketing to all publics.[16] The core concept is the transaction, which consists of an exchange of 'values' between two parties. 'Things of value' would not be limited to goods, services, and money, but would include other resources, such as time, energy, and feelings. In addition, an individual's purchase behaviour would be expanded to include the adoption of new ideas or behaviour.

Introducing the idea that marketing could be broadened to incorporate the marketing of services, persons, and ideas, Philip Kotler and Sidney Levy argued that, 'the modern marketing concept serves very naturally to describe an important facet of all organizational activity. All organizations must develop appropriate products to serve their sundry consuming groups and must use modern tools of communication to reach their consuming publics. The business heritage of marketing provides a useful set of concepts for guiding all organizations.'[17]

The proposition that ideas and issues, as well as products and services, can be packaged, positioned, promoted, priced, and distributed has been thoroughly discussed in the marketing literature. The more pressing question for the purposes of this discussion is the applicability of a societal marketing orientation and techniques to promotion of co-operative beliefs and practices. As will be demonstrated in the following section, neither of these two concepts is inconsistent with the intent or the practice of co-operation. Indeed, both have been integral to co-operatives since their inception, albeit under different names. The following discussion provides a review of current and historical attitudes within the co-operative community toward marketing in general, with subsequent sections devoted to examining the appropriateness of adopting a societal marketing orientation and implementing social marketing techniques.

The Attitudes of Co-operative Members toward Marketing

Historically, individuals within the co-operative movement have had an aversion to marketing. This aversion has been rooted in an understanding of the relationship between the co-operative and the member which is substantively different from the way in which that relationship is conceptualized within privately owned organizations.

The essential difference stems from the transactional perspective inherent in co-operatives. As Thompson and Jones state, 'even though co-operatives perform functions similar to those of traditional business firms, they have unique differences in their relationship to their owners. The co-operative organization does not buy, process and sell to make a profit as a separate entity; instead, it procures services for the benefit of its members - who hope to increase their savings if it is a consumer co-operative, or to increase the profits of their own separate business if it is a farmer or business co-operative.'[18]

This perspective, rooted in a consumer-oriented transactional base, resulted in an attitude which dismissed the importance of any marketing activity by the co-operative. In fact, marketing – narrowly defined as selling – was seen to be manipulative and exploitive, particularly through the medium of advertising, or through the hard sell when personified by the salesperson. Co-operatives only accepted advertising, if at all, if it was considered to be 'educational.'

Much of the research which has been conducted regarding the marketing activities of co-operatives has been done by economists examining the behaviour of consumer co-operatives and commodity marketing co-operatives. Researchers have tended to focus on these organizations as distributive agencies, and thus have limited their examination to the activities of selling and advertising.

Bakken and Schaars examined the marketing of farm products, and suggested that advertising in co-operatives serves two functions in making sales.[19] One is an *educational* function, which serves to apprise prospective customers publicly of the wares on the market, and is of value from a social standpoint. The second is a *non-educational* function, which serves to persuade a potential buyer that one brand is preferable to another but has no social value and 'cannot be justified as a means of increasing social capital.'[20]

More recently LeVay has provided a comprehensive review of articles on advertising policies in agricultural co-operatives.[21] In the past others have asserted that both requisite and marketing co-operatives will spend less than a conventional firm on socially wasteful advertising (such as advertising designed to promote brand switching) because members form a loyal group with a 'sense of proprietary interests in their own shop.'[22] But LeVay argues that this claim is difficult to justify, since all organizations attempt to stimulate demand, either through encouraging current members to increase purchases, or by convincing non-members to purchase.

Aversion to adopting marketing as a managerial tool due to its ostensibly exploitive nature is a recurring theme throughout the literature on co-operatives. Burley states this perspective succinctly: 'although the Consumer Co-operative movement has accepted the appellation of a distributors' organization, it has not yet recognised that it is a marketing institution. Marketing implies selling, and selling of a high pressure, "puffing" type. The Co-operator has always felt that such methods were out of place (as, indeed, they are) in the field of consumer co-operation where the society is selling to its owners.'[23] The co-operative writer of the day assumed, however, that this was a tool commonly adopted by the agricultural commodity marketing co-operatives, which cast doubt on the purity of their co-operative nature: 'to the usual consumers' co-operative member there is little or no difference between private business enterprise and the capitalistic "marketing" co-operative.'[24]

In describing the performance of the marketing function within a consumers' co-operative, Burley began by stating that marketing in co-operatives, as opposed to private organizations, is 'characterized by a different mental and philosophical attitude.'[25] He described the selling function as 'demand fulfillment,' a state in which careful product selection by a co-operative would ensure that members' needs would be met without having to sell them on the virtues of the available products.[26] Educational advertising was appropriate, but advertising which promoted brand switching was misleading and wasteful, and hence out of place in a co-operative society.

We should not be surprised that this negative view of marketing activity is held by so many, both inside and outside of the co-operative movement. As consumers, we are continually on the receiving end of advertising and personal selling efforts. However, as was discussed previously, there is more to marketing than just selling. A genuine effort to implement the marketing concept can result in a consumer-oriented approach to product and service development and delivery, ultimately resulting in benefits to both member and co-operative organization.

What is most ironic about this historic aversion to marketing activity is that co-operative organizations are the most appropriate advocates of the societal marketing orientation, having institutionalized the marketing concept since their inception. Boisvert discusses this point.[27] He suggests that co-operative marketing incorporates two models, an economic and a social model. By virtue of its unique nature, the co-operative sector potentially can provide the ultimate in consumer satisfaction, with social and economic considerations being given equal importance. Boisvert argues that product selection should be based primarily on consumer satisfaction, rather than on sales (an approach similar to

Burley's 'demand fulfillment'), with decisions at the local level based on the social objectives of the co-operative, and decisions at the co-operative sector level based on a product/services-needs portfolio. In addition, consistent with proposals made by Burley, Boisvert suggests that the objectives of commercial promotion should not be distinguished from the objectives of member education.

Although the marketing concept has had various names within the co-operative sector, it has always existed as a *raison d'être* for the co-operative movement. Indeed, if we look closely at Levitt's description of the differences between selling and marketing, and compare that to Thompson's and Jones's description of the unique transactional nature of co-operatives, we find striking similarities.

In addition, if we consider some of the characteristics of the social system perspective, and its offspring, the societal marketing orientation, it becomes apparent that they share a good deal with the transactional nature of co-operatives and the attendant social as well as economic imperative. As agents for providing collective consumption goods,[28] supplementing the public provision, and providing an alternative to the private provision, co-operatives are involved in marketing activity which is quite consistent with a social system perspective. This perspective 'suggests that marketing decisions cannot be justified on [the basis of] economic costs and profits alone. It indicates that some products and services should be marketed where there is little or no economic profit. It holds that marketing has dimensions that extend beyond the profit motive. It maintains that management know-how must be applied to the solution of society's problems.'[29]

Social responsibility is therefore not an obligation imposed on the organization, but a reason for the marketing activity. In this view, marketing is an instrument of the consuming groups associated with the organization, or in the co-operative context, the members. Since there should be no perceived difference between the organization's goals and values and the members', this marketing activity need not be seen as exploitive. An implication of this is that managers will need to develop new means for assessing marketing performance, one which moves beyond economic audits to include social audits. In the process, much richer and more consistent criteria will be created for evaluating marketing effectiveness. The criteria used are not derived from the organization, but from the value systems of the organization's publics, once more quite consistent with co-operative activity.

Today, organizations engaged in marketing activities are being challenged by the industry to accept the marketing orientation, at a minimum, and ideally, the societal marketing orientation as a basic part of their organizational philosophy. Having already institutionalized the approach, albeit without any reference to marketing, co-operatives should be utilizing their inherent capability to their competitive advantage.

Merely accepting the importance of such an orientation and recognizing its compatibility with co-operative practices does not ensure that it will be applied. No change will occur if the individuals within the co-operative do not understand where their respective realm of activities fits, whether it be as president of the board or chair of the member relations committee, within the context of adopting a societal marketing orientation. A necessary starting point is conceptualizing the member education program and the role it plays in advocating democratic ideals and practices in marketing terms.

Member Education as Social Marketing

From the moment that Kotler first proposed a generic concept of marketing, advocates of this broadened definition have argued that it allowed for the application of marketing principles to non-profit organizations and other public institutions which choose – or are mandated – to bring about socially desirable attitudes and behaviour. Implicit in this is the recognition that these organizations will be marketing ideas with the intent of creating planned social change.

Given this implied purpose, it would appear that social marketing is quite consistent with the practice of co-operative member education. A review of historical approaches within the co-operative movement again illustrates this point.[30]

It is interesting to note that the advertising of co-operative commodities or services was typically not differentiated in the budget from educational expenses. Co-operators believed that sales training consisted of preparation for a dual task – selling the product, and selling co-operation, or, more correctly, marketing the co-operative philosophy. This did not mean high-pressure selling, but 'intelligent selling under the peculiar relationship which exists between the co-operative and its members.'[31] If we place this activity in a marketing context we see that the tangible product/service sold by the co-operative is associated with another core product, the ideals of co-operation.

It can thus be argued that ideas have been treated as products in co-operatives since their inception, under the guise of member education. Most co-operators, however, would not recognize member education as an essential social marketing activity. The denial of the marketing aspect of education can be linked to the distinction drawn between educational and non-educational advertising, again indicating the extremely narrow definition of marketing within the co-operative sector. More recently there has been increasing interest in the application of social marketing methods to disseminating co-operative ideas. Examinations of co-operative marketing practices have targeted the marketing function to assume primary responsibility for advancing the values of co-operation, and for increasing member participation and commitment.[32]

Some have related the past failure of the marketing function to the unquestioning use of private sector models, the focus on economic purposes, and the failure to recognize the potential of marketing for furthering co-operative values. It has been suggested that values should form the basis for the identification of market segments and underlie the development of the marketing mix strategy. An additional suggestion is that more attention should be paid to identifying the specific values common to members of the co-operative market, and more specialized submarkets within this larger market, as a starting point for defining that which is unique about co-operatives. These values would then serve to differentiate the products and services the organization offers.[33]

There have been some practical applications of the social marketing approach. A most recent example is the formation of the CU Financial Information Centre, a subsidiary of Saskatchewan's Credit Union Central. The Financial Information Centre has a rather broad mandate, part of which is the difficult task of designing a strategy to redirect the activities of the credit union system toward a more consumer-oriented approach. The centre has adopted an innovative approach to the development of products and services which focuses entirely on deriving policies from member needs. It is still too early to assess the outcome of this approach; however, the precedent has been established and, if successful, will have a positive impact on member satisfaction and utilization of the services, attracting new members into the credit union system.[34]

Despite the possibilities associated with adopting a social marketing approach to product and service development and delivery, there are other issues which must be considered. Concerns have been raised by both marketers and non-marketers regarding the use of social marketing techniques. Laczniak, Lusch, and Murphy argue that there may be both positive and negative societal effects: 'on the plus side, examples abound which illustrate how marketing thinking has improved the saleability of useful social programs. However, on the negative side, it is quite possible that the widespread involvement of marketing professionals in the marketing of social ideas may raise severe ethical problems and further turn public opinion against marketers and the marketing field.'[35]

Those outside the marketing profession associate the main area of concern with the problem of power. There is a fear that 'social marketing could ultimately operate as a form of thought control by the economically powerful'[36] and that those who possess power might communicate socially detrimental ideas. An associated and even more complicated issue involves determining what is socially beneficial or detrimental, and whose values should prevail in applying social marketing techniques to the solution of social problems.

These issues are not easily resolved. But, how are we to address the impact that the current use of these tools has on the perpetuation of a culture of individualism, supported by the legal system, which strikes at the collective premises of co-operatives, if we do not accept their validity for achieving positive outcomes as well? It is with this thought in mind that the remainder of this discussion is conducted.

The Importance of Marketing to Co-operatives

Marketing, as an orientation, is always important for an organization concerned with providing needed products or services to its consuming publics. However, marketing as an activity is almost always identified as an act of final recourse when competition within the market-place becomes severe. One has only to examine the changes introduced to a marketing strategy as a product and, indeed, an organization moves through its life-cycle, to witness the increasing importance of such techniques. Institutions such as universities, schools, unions, non-government organizations, and many non-profit and not-for-profit[37] organizations have found themselves in competition with each other for government funding, and for monetary and voluntary support from private individuals. Workshops on the merits of developing a marketing orientation abound, and organizations struggle to come up with innovative means for attracting and retaining an active and committed membership.

Researchers writing from an organization theory perspective link the sudden interest in marketing to the organization's response to attitudinal and cognitive complexity among its stakeholders. Efforts are made by the organization's leaders to shape the attitudes of participants and potential participants toward the organization and its outputs, thus 'legitimizing' the activities of the organization to ensure support and access to needed resources.[38]

The unfortunate outcome of many of the final recourse attempts at introducing a marketing orientation to the organization is the over-reliance on advertising as the means for strengthening market positions. Institutional advertising has become increasingly attractive to profit and non-profit organizations alike. This has only served to add advocacy messages of many kinds to the already cluttered media, exacerbating currently strong criticisms of this particular component of the marketing process.[39]

Co-operative ideals and practices cannot be perpetuated by the use of a slick advertising campaign, but member education alone will not strengthen the membership base. In a society where ideology is overshadowed by economic imperatives, there must be more to draw and keep the member. Co-operative values and differences can, however, be presented, accentuated, and used as a means for increasing awareness about the organization. This must be done in concert with a greater marketing process, a process which incorporates all aspects of the marketing mix, and recognizes the importance of conducting thorough research on member needs. Also critical is a clear understanding of what is attitudinally and organizationally required of members involved in a social marketing orientation. Such an orientation constitutes a world-view within an organization – a holistic approach to the planning, production, and delivery of products and services, which throws the responsibility for marketing into the laps of all members, directors, and staff. As Foxall contends, simple change in orientation is not an end in itself, but rather is necessary to facilitate planning of marketing action and implementation of marketing plans, policies, and strategies.[40]

Can we market member commitment? The answer is necessarily equivocal. We cannot sell or advertise the values of co-operation to secure member commitment. To suggest that this approach in itself would be sufficient would be to put the solution of a complex problem into extremely simplistic and unwarrantedly optimistic terms. What we can do is utilize the precepts of a societal marketing orientation, and recognize the value of such an orientation in placing the activities of co-operatives into a broader social context. Marketing as a process can be utilized to assist co-operatives to become more responsive to their membership, in turn providing an attractive alternative which in itself should strengthen member support. Advertising and promotion play an essential role in this process, both in identifying the character of co-operative institutions, and in identifying what co-operatives have to offer as participants in the 'democratic campaign.'

PART THREE

Co-operatives and
the Political Environment

9 Co-operation as Politics: Membership, Citizenship, and Democracy

In spite of their claim to be politically neutral – a claim which has had quite a variety of definitions in different times and places – the circumstances in which co-operatives arose often forced co-operation to have political implications and even partisan affiliations. Co-operatives imply ownership and participation in economic power by the groups they represent, and where the participation of those groups is a political issue, co-operative activity is itself politicized. More broadly, co-operatives are forced by context to be agents of democratic political values – those who form them are by definition those who are disadvantaged by the status quo and who desire reform – and must support extended democratic values for their own good as well as for that of their members.

Many leaders of co-operatives have claimed that political neutrality is one of the basic principles of co-operation and that any violation of such a principle is divisive and threatening. They argue that co-operatives require unity and cannot afford to alienate members by taking political stances, and that they are economic and self-help associations and politics is none of their business. While this is undoubtedly true in many instances, history suggests that the relationship between co-operation and politics is much more complex than such generalizations allow.

A sort of 'neutrality' was for a long time a principle of the British co-operative movement, originating in its declaration of its independence from Robert Owen, its spiritual figurehead, and from the more controversial of the ideas he and his followers promoted. In a well-known resolution the London Co-operative Congress of 1832 stated: 'Whereas the co-operative world contains persons of every religious sect and of every political party, it is resolved that co-operators as such, jointly and severally, are not pledged to any political, religious or irreligious tenets whatsoever; neither those of Mr. Owen, nor of any other individual.'

Although this was only a reactive resolution whose purpose was to dissociate the movement from Owen's provocative anti-clerical and socialistic utterances, it was considered important enough to be made the standing motto on all congress publications. Co-operators at this stage clearly felt Owen's views on subjects other than co-operation were an impediment to the growth of their movement.[1] The Rochdale Pioneers, considered a model of consumer co-operation, did not, however, include the principle of neutrality in their statutes. In a motion concerning free speech at a meeting in 1850, and in a letter to the press in 1861, the Pioneers did advocate neutrality, but it appears that they meant neutrality only in questions that divided the working-class movement at the time.[2] Nevertheless, when the International Co-operative Alliance struck a special committee on co-operative principles in 1934-7, that committee reported that 'neutrality in politics and religion' was one of seven principles that were 'undoubtedly part of the Rochdale system.'[3] Political neutrality remains the position of many large co-operatives in North America and elsewhere.

Yet there are also many who would argue that their co-operatives are in fact political. One thinks of the small 'counter-culture' co-operatives of the 1960s, or of large working-class or agrarian co-operative movements, especially in Europe, that have had a long formal affiliation with a particular political direction. Even the British co-operative movement, long associated with the principle of neutrality, eventually sponsored its own political party, and then permitted it to ally with the Labour party.[4] There are many revealing examples of situations in which co-operators did, indeed, become involved in politics, and several of these will be considered below in an attempt to understand how and why they did so.

The differences among co-operators over neutrality are both revealing and important. They are revealing because of what they tell us about co-operatives' conception of their own role in society, their relations to broader groups and movements, and their self-interpretation of their own experience. Clearly, for such disagreements to exist there must be major differences among co-operators in their motivations and experiences. These differences are important also because opinions on this subject govern how co-operatives participate in public decision-making and how they achieve their objectives with respect to governments and other institutions in society. In other words, it makes practical differences in how co-operatives act and how others act towards them.

It is not an exaggeration to say that what is involved in one's view of politics is a conception of one's own relationship to everyone else in society.

One immediate problem is the definition of the word 'politics,' a word that has had unsavoury connotations in many eras, and perhaps rarely more so than today. Indeed, the prevailing cynicism about political processes, parties, and politicians may help explain the continuing reluctance of many large co-operatives to become involved in such affairs. But in a broad perspective, politics comprises the entire realm in which people living in a society make collective decisions about collective and compulsory actions. In this sense politics is inescapable and of importance to every individual and institution. Parties, politicians, voting, and bureaucracy (what most people mean by politics) are merely the chief twentieth-century mechanisms by which society pursues a function which must be carried out everywhere and in all times. In complaining about politics, however, what is usually meant is 'party politics,' and it is in this particular sphere that co-operatives have had great differences of opinion. One reason for this is that the nature of party politics has varied from time to time and place to place. In other words, it may not be a case of 'politics, good or bad'; there may be no one answer precisely because co-operatives have never dealt with politics as an abstract societal process, but instead with specific conjunctures of historical circumstances.

In the early nineteenth century, when Robert Owen formulated the idea of co-operation as an alternative to the prevailing competitive system, party politics in the modern sense barely existed. In many respects parliamentary parties had to do with patronage, personal connections, 'influence,' and family allegiance, rather than with ideology, activists, or propaganda. The French Revolution of 1789-99 had helped introduce questions of party philosophy and ideology into political discussion, but (at least in terms of those who governed, those who made decisions, and those who collaborated with them) this penetration was gradual. As a result, Owen's Utopian experiments in self-sufficient co-operative communities were not, at first, necessarily recognized as 'left' or 'right' (terms deriving from the French Revolution) or as 'liberal' or 'conservative.' They were the imaginative private projects of a reforming industrialist, intended to deal with a social problem recognized by many: the material and moral deprivation of the lower classes. In fact, in important respects social reform schemes of the sort advocated by Owen and others after him were deliberately meant to avoid the polarization between revolution and the status quo that was apparent to some at the time. Co-operation was seen as a non-revolutionary solution to the social questions posed by social and industrial change, and was advocated in part as a means of forestalling revolution. As in other examples from the history of the co-operative movement, however, events gave a distinctly radical and working-class colouring to something that started as a patriarchal or middle-class initiative. The British consumer co-operative movement – like, as we shall see below, the German consumer co-operative movement – evolved from liberal sponsorship to labour socialist alliance.

It was in the late 1830s and 1840s, the great mid-century period of political ferment, that the word 'socialist' became widely spoken, and became identified with Owen and with the co-operation he advocated. British Tories began to perceive Owen's experiments as dangerous; they agitated for the government to suppress them, demanded inquiries, and cried out in indignation when Owen was received by Queen Victoria herself. A Tory pamphlet literature sprang up condemning the co-operative movement in unmistakably ideological fashion. Co-operativism had been made political, and party political at that, and not necessarily because co-operators desired it.[5]

The political circumstances of the day imparted a highly political character to what had been eccentric experiments. Why should this have been so? A large part of the answer is Owen's extreme and provocatively expressed opinions, particularly on religion; but though this made him a convenient bogey for Tory pamphleteers, it does not entirely explain the sudden vehemence of the latter. It was precisely Owen's attempt to create working-class organizations that was, as the Tories saw it, the problem.

The 1840s was the decade when the 'social question' was redefined, becoming no longer a matter of charity or private initiatives to help the morally deprived, but now instead a question of political rights and political representation. The Chartist movement, demanding universal male suffrage in its People's Charter of 1836, saw the active participation of the working classes in the nation as the ultimate remedy for their distress. Some of the founders of the Rochdale Pioneers of 1844 were former Chartists, for Rochdale had been a major centre of working-class radicalism, and their idea of an independent organization of and for the working classes was partly a product of the Chartist tradition.[6] The social question was now not so much a question of charity but of power, and the participation of the working classes in co-operatives was a model for their participation in society as a whole. Co-operatives were political because, in the context, mass participation itself was inherently politicized. British labourers adopted their roles as members in democratically organized co-operatives in parallel to claiming a role as citizens in their country.

One of Europe's other large working-class co-operative movements, in Germany, developed several decades later, and gravitated more quickly and more decisively still toward the political left. Here, as in Britain, the working classes were shut out of effective participation in society, and developed in their own separate organizations substitutes for their non-existent or impaired roles as full citizens. Unlike in England, the co-operative movement in Germany owed its origins not to concern about the industrial working classes, but to concern about the middle classes: Hermann von Schulze-Delitzsch and Friedrich Wilhelm Raiffeisen, a left liberal politician and a non-partisan social conservative respectively, set out to assist artisans and peasants, not wage labourers.[7] Yet consumer co-operatives grew to become what a German scholar has called one of 'the three great pillars of the socialist working-class movement,' standing alongside the Social Democratic party and the free trade unions in a tightly knit web of working-class institutions.[8] As in Britain, this was not the result of a planned development, but a reaction to the rest of German society.

German working-class co-operatives developed separately from the socialist political movement, but shared with the latter a mainly urban and working-class environment. The Social Democratic party (or SPD after its German initials), founded in the 1860s and radicalized by government repression between 1878 and 1890, did not until its massive growth starting in the 1890s, have to think formally about its relations with the co-operative movement.[9] If anything, party theorists had a bias against consumer co-operatives because of the heritage of the party's founder, Ferdinand Lassalle, who had instead favoured production co-operatives. When, however, both the SPD and the consumer co-operative movement had grown strong among the same working-class constituents by the end of the 1890s, the common interests of the two were found to be so great that an association between them developed. In particular, trade union leaders in the SPD caucus had strong ties with the working-class co-operative movement. When in 1903 the socialist-oriented co-operatives split from the more middle-class Schulze-Delitzsch co-operative federation, the way was cleared for the close alliance of the socialist party with the co-operatives.[10] The shared experience of working-class culture and frustrations, of repression and social exclusion, made the growing together of the two movements perfectly natural. Feeling excluded from the state proper, the German working classes developed an alternative citizenship in their state-within-a-state, in their trade unions, co-operatives, and clubs.

Across Europe and across the world, consumer co-operatives, in particular, tended toward reform socialism when they visualized their doctrine in relation to the rest of society, and when they imagined its continued spread. The reason this was particularly true of consumer co-operation was that consumption was recognized as a universal interest of all people. Producer-oriented co-operation could only ever mobilize people separately within each branch of industry, and might, moreover, mobilize them in self-interested ways; but there was no necessary or logical boundary to the spread of consumer co-operation, nor did the interests of one consumer conflict with the interests of another in the same way that producers' various interests divided them. Especially from the 1920s to the 1940s, ideologues of the consumer movement spoke of eventually forming a 'Co-operative Commonwealth' or a 'Co-operative Republic,' in which co-operatives would have taken over the entire private economy and perhaps the state itself.[11] A similar idea survives in modern European traditions which see co-operation as one part of a socialist sector of public, trade union, co-operative, and mutualist economics – a 'commonweal' economy or *Gemeinwirtschaft*.[12] Old world working-class consumer co-operatives drifted to the left initially as a result of the real daily experiences of their members, and because their members' claims to participation in society were politicized by a system that was afraid of them. When they formulated ideals for the kinds of societies they wished to produce, these ideals resembled socialist ideals.

Many European agricultural and credit co-operatives evolved politically in the opposite direction for equivalent but opposite reasons, moving inexorably from liberalism to conservatism in the period before the First World War. This current of co-operation flowed from the pioneering work of Schulze-Delitzsch with artisans and of Raiffeisen with peasants in the decades following the mid-century. To begin with, these co-operatives reflected the liberal or reform conservative political persuasions of their founders: uplifting of the hard-working poor through self-help and independence from government, solving the social question without government intervention by giving workers, artisans and peasants a stake in society.[13] But this changed over time.

The hard-pressed artisanal sector of the German economy, which in the course of the nineteenth century was gradually undermined by modern commerce and industry, proved to be comparatively barren ground for co-operatives. Many politicized artisans turned instead to efforts to regain their past, demanding that the government intervene to re-create closed and compulsory guilds. This line of thought, which became more and more pronounced by the 1890s, resulted in some intervention by a sympathetic regime, notably in legislation in 1897 enabling voluntary guilds.[14] Peasants, too, facing long-term falls in grain prices associated with competition from the Americas, proved willing to turn to a variety of solutions to the late nineteenth-century agricultural crisis, including both credit co-operatives and, increasingly, political demands for state intervention. Many rural co-operatives moved, with the peasants, to political conservatism. As with the artisans, peasants' abandonment of liberalism was exhibited in demands for government intervention in the 1890s: tariff protectionism, changes in inheritance laws, and other forms of state-sponsored social protectionism.[15]

Once again the political implications of co-operation were determined by the political overtones of participatory citizenship roles. Village structures, village patronage, and the peasantry as a whole were interpreted by the German government and by conservatives as the reliable pillars of traditional society, counterpoised to the dangerous urban classes. Conservative aristocrats headed Raiffeisen federations in eastern territories dominated by large estates. National Liberal (which is to say right-wing liberal) politicians such as Wilhelm Haas led their own co-operative federations, which pressed for and received assistance from conservative state governments like that of Prussia, which created a Central Co-operative Bank in 1895 to subsidize rural co-operatives. Conservatives looked to rural society for stability, and found and exerted their influence among the rural classes. Farmers themselves, sensing declining power and prestige, looked to the conservative nationalism of the state to save them from social change. In the atmosphere of conflict between agriculture and industry, between cities and the countryside, between perceived threats of social revolution and perceived sources of stability and time-honoured values, the political role of the peasantry could hardly have been otherwise. Throughout central Europe it was not socialists who sponsored rural co-operation, but conservatives, nationalists, and particularists – all those who attached a positive political importance to the preservation of the old rural society.[16]

In more recent times and in North America, too, advocacy of co-operatives has appeared in surprising political circles. Once again, where conservatives advocated co-operation, it was generally because of its links with the rural community and its role in providing social stability. Raymond W. Miller, a self-styled conservative and friend of Herbert Hoover, argued that 'farmer cooperatives are a natural business development within a democracy, because they are democratic in form, practice, and principle.' 'Cooperatives,' he also claimed, 'are conservative organizations dedicated to individual ownership and to the principles of efficient and enlightened operation.' Because of this, he wrote (during an especially cold part of the cold war), co-operatives were America's 'answer to Communism' – 'where cooperatives are strong, Communism cannot exist.'[17]

Nor were socialists and conservatives the only modern, political advocates of co-operation. Like Schulze-Delitzsch, Luzzatti, and other nineteenth-century liberals, the republican regime in France (1876-1940) also tried to stake a claim to the principles of co-operation. Here, the French Radicals (progressive liberals) elevated the idea of co-operation in various forms to become part of their official state philosophy. Particularly with the development of a socialist challenge from the 1890s onward, and the need for a new republican synthesis, co-operation and mutualism were presented as answers to the social question and as means of ensuring harmonious relations in society. Leading statesmen, politicians, educators, and intellectuals praised the virtues of *solidarité*. On the practical level of building co-operative and mutualist structures in the countryside, less was accomplished than in some other countries, and what was accomplished was, like French party politics and patronage in general in this period, highly localized. In certain areas co-operatives became vehicles for the political influence of republican deputies. By and large they were associated with the peasantry – which was the segment of the population on which the republicans liked to consider themselves to be based.[18]

These examples seem to demonstrate clearly enough that co-operatives can, at least in certain circumstances, fall into any party political camp whatsoever. The key determinants seem to be the overall political environment and the nature of the co-operatives' membership base, which together can impart a highly political significance to the economic activity of organizing a co-operative. Where a particular group's participation in society is given political overtones, that group's co-operative activity may acquire the same overtones. Where the working classes were excluded from control of the state, their co-operatives were leftist; where the rural population was courted as a pillar of a set of established values, its co-operatives tended toward the conservative (or perhaps, in France, republican) political colouring of that set of values.

Co-operation in general, then, is not party political, in the sense that only one political philosophy mates with it. But according to political and social conditions, circumstances can arise in which it is inevitable that a given group's co-operation acquires political overtones, and the nature of those overtones depends on the group and its role in society. Recalling, however, the distinction between 'politics' and 'party politics,' there is more to be said about what political elements are common to all co-operative endeavours. There remains a universal element in co-operative activity which is highly political, even though this is manifested only under certain circumstances as party political affiliation.

Co-operatives have always been intended by their founders as solutions to social questions. Another way of saying this is that they address themselves to perceived inadequacies in the prevailing system of organizing the economy: if the prevailing system worked perfectly, no one would be impelled to form a co-operative. Another aspect of this is that co-operatives are by nature mass-oriented institutions, concerning themselves (even if, as with early middle-class reformers, in a paternalistic way) with the problems of ordinary people and absorbing the energies of those people, their desires for participation, and their desires to find solutions to their problems. The purpose of forming a co-operative is to satisfy a need that the founders do not believe can be met by a standard form of organization; so it is not surprising that the supporters of co-operative movements, over the long term, are those not bound up in standard institutions, but instead those with less power in the other structures of society, and particularly those lacking economic power.

For these contextual reasons (more, perhaps, than because of innate organizational characteristics) co-operation is 'democratic,' in the broad sense of furthering the participation of ordinary people in the affairs and decisions of their society. Democratic principles and co-operative principles are inseparably connected, as, correspondingly, are the roles of people as co-op members and their roles as citizens. Co-operation is one aspect of the emergence of mass society in the nineteenth- and twentieth-century world. It is one expression of the participatory impetus that also lies behind modern ideas of citizenship and democracy. Where these ideas are themselves politicized, as in the cases of European workers whose participation was seen by others as a threat to society, or European peasants whose participation was seen as essential to its stability, the ideas of co-operation are also politicized. Co-operative ideas then acquire a universal social-reforming or social-stabilizing significance, an ideological significance.

Conflict, in the last analysis, is what produces politics and causes people to line up on different sides. It is no different for co-operatives, and may explain the various attitudes toward politics among different co-operatives. The European situation in the nineteenth and early twentieth centuries was characterized by the stresses and strains put on old societies as they struggled to adapt to the transforming power of industrial technology. These were comparatively small and densely populated nations (in contrast to Canada and the United States), with many occupational categories of greatly different economic interest intermixed in limited geographic and cultural environments – accentuating the aspects of conflict among competing and opposing interests. By contrast, the farmer co-operatives of the North American plains developed within a more homogeneous regional culture, which was, largely because of its newness, dominated by a single occupational group, farmer-proprietors, who as settlers mostly started out from similar beginnings. Within this comparatively homogeneous regional environment, the participatory impulse of co-operation does not seem to have been politicized in the same partisan way.

Farmers' political organizations, like the early Progressives in Canada, were moulded by non-partisan activism. A characteristic idea of such movements was to create an independent political force to represent farmers first, rather than one aligned with any existing political philosophy. This was an explicitly *anti*-partisan politicism. And, characteristically, it was a kind of politicism closely associated with advocacy of co-operatives, the mutual self-help solution for farmers banding together to fight their enemies.[19]

The 'agrarian socialism' of the Co-operative Commonwealth Federation in Saskatchewan is another illuminating example. CCF strength was strongly based on activists, members, and voters who received organizational experience and exerted influence within the province's co-operative movement. There was an explicit attempt by the political movement to appeal to symbols and social goals that were associated with the co-operative movement. In many ways farmers' co-operatives were the basis for the mass rural strength the movement developed, and yet in spite of this the co-operatives themselves were able to continue without making an overt partisan commitment.[20] As in the case of the German working classes a few decades before, prairie farmers gave rise to both a political socialist movement and a co-operative movement; yet in the Saskatchewan case the two remained distinct, two separate plants in the same soil. It is easy to explain the difference. German labourers experienced repression and isolation, forcing all of their participatory organizations together into one conglomeration fighting the same foes. Prairie farmers faced no equally intense politicizing conflict within their local society. Not faced by such inveterate party political foes, farmers' co-operatives did not so desperately need exclusive party political friends.

Yet even North American co-operatives, when faced by organized challenges in the political arena to their essential interests, have turned to political solutions. The biggest realm in which this has occurred is in the area of income tax policy, where the taxation of co-operatives' surpluses has raised the question of whether such surpluses are to be considered income by the co-operative and taxed like corporate profits, or whether the user-owned nature of the co-operative and the practice of paying patronage rebates means the surplus is to be accounted to the members. Organized business lobbies claimed the former, and pressed repeatedly for heavier taxation of co-operatives. This led co-operatives to form counter-lobbies. In Canada the largest of these was likely the nation-wide campaign by the Co-operative Union of Canada in response to the 1944-5 royal commission on co-operatives and taxation – a campaign which saw the co-operatives convert the royal commission to their views, only to see the commission's findings overturned by the government in its first legislative proposal. Renewed lobbying led to an eventual compromise.[21] In the United States, farm co-operatives helped ensure the election of Hubert

Humphrey to the Senate in order to safeguard their interests in a similar income tax dispute.[22]

The nature and origins of co-operative movements give them both advantages and disadvantages when it comes to promoting their interests in the general political arena, in convincing legislators to take account of the needs and objectives of co-operatives. The chief advantage and the chief disadvantage reside in the same feature: the participatory and mass-democratic character of co-operatives' origins and activity. This feature makes it possible, on the one hand, for co-operatives and federations of co-operatives accurately to represent the informed opinions of large groups of committed and active individuals. On the other hand, it makes it nearly impossible for co-operatives to act as a lobby in the normal sense, exerting sustained influence by direct input into governments. By virtue of their (partisan or non-partisan) association with the political realm of democratic participation, they are compelled to involve large groups of members in major decisions, and hence expose their deliberations and their divisions to intense public scrutiny. They have difficulty taking strong positions except where their members are overwhelmingly in agreement. Private businesses and their federations, responsible in practice to fewer individuals and with more tactical flexibility, will always be better than co-operatives at the particular kinds of influence in which they excel.[23]

It is inherent in the nature of co-operatives that they will have a problematic relation to society's decision-making structures, because co-operatives owe their origins to attempts to find economic solutions outside of those structures. Co-operatives define their philosophy and find their niche in society where neither private capital nor government planning is optimal; they are 'autonomous.' The principle of self-help practised by members of co-operatives corresponds to a self-help attitude of the co-operative movement as a whole, which looks inward for solutions rather than outward to society's most powerful institutions. Yet this historical attitude sits uneasily with the need of co-operatives for a suitable legal basis, for a fair position in taxation, and for reasonable consideration in private and government economic planning. The framework in which co-operatives operate can only be created, and must be continuously preserved, by a political presence of some kind. The examples quoted above illustrate that where these essential interests meet strong opposition, co-operatives learn to be party political. This is not a danger to co-operatives in such circumstances, but a survival strategy.

Co-operative movements, therefore, must reflect carefully on their political strategy and ensure that it remains in tune with the times, for if history shows anything, it shows that the political role of co-operatives must vary with circumstances. The least common denominator is that co-operatives must stand always for democratic values and for the principle of participation in public life and in society, for co-operatives are very much part of the mass-participatory impulse of modern society. In particular they need to promote such values continuously among their own members and potential members, and to link the responsibility of members with the responsibility of citizens. More than private businesses and more even than many voluntary organizations, co-operatives are part of society at large, intimately bound up with its character and its changes. They cannot, in a broad view and over the long term, afford a policy of virtuous isolation from political processes.

10 Co-operatives and Government

Co-operatives encounter special advantages and difficulties in their attempts to influence Canadian public policy. Their major advantage is support by a large and heterogeneous membership. While this support places limits on the strategies co-operatives can undertake, it should accord co-operatives a prima facie legitimacy which few policy contestants can match. In an era when politicians and the public are suspicious of attempts to influence public policy, economic enterprises that elect leaders and advertise open membership should have an advantage in influencing public policy. Whether they do, and why, are the subject of this paper.

Introduction

The major difficulties co-operatives face in relating to government are a function of the special internal dynamics of democratic organizations, the ways these dynamics fail to 'fit' with the structures and processes of policy development in Canada, and the inevitable disadvantages faced by non-capitalist firms competing in a predominantly capitalist economy. We focus on the first two dimensions in this chapter; other chapters address the third.

The remainder of this section identifies the importance of two variables in the overall environment of co-operative–government relations in Canada: Canadian federalism, and the historical character of Canadian co-operators' attitudes towards the state.The second section identifies two basic modes of pressure group policy influence: policy advocacy and policy participation. The third section identifies the theoretical conflicts between these two roles. The fourth section examines the emergence of policy conflicts among co-operatives within the national organization of anglophone co-operatives, and among agricultural co-operatives. The chapter concludes with a discussion of current and future patterns of co-operative-government relations in English-speaking Canada.

Federalism

Canadian federalism has complicated life for most economic interest groups in Canada.[1] In some cases the complication benefits a group, while in other cases the division of legislative powers between provincial and federal governments impedes presentation of interests to government officials. Classic instances of federalism's advantage to particular interests can be found in large-scale private sector investments in regional economies, where provincial governments and federal cabinet ministers are played off against each other to extract the largest state subsides and other concessions.[2] In terms of disadvantages, it is often argued that provincial jurisdiction over labour has stifled the development of a strong and politically influential national labour movement.[3]

It is impossible to generalize about federalism's distinctive impact on the welfare of co-operative enterprise. The competitive and bureaucratic logic of federalism has spawned numerous regulatory agencies, boards, and commissions at each level of government. This decentralization of power has dramatically increased the work of co-operative lobbyists.

At the same time the existence of provincial jurisdiction has done a good deal to structure co-operative business, particularly in the agricultural and financial sectors. At some level, provincial legislative and/or economic support has always been instrumental to the growth of successful co-operative enterprise in Canada.[4] By contrast, federal support has seldom been a decisive factor in co-operative development.[5] Instead, the federal government's impact on co-operative enterprise has primarily been a function of policy applied to particular sectors or sub-sectors within which co-operatives operate.

Co-operatives' concerns with federal policy and its administration usually result from federal policy-makers' failure to recognize or care about the peculiar impact their sectoral policies have on co-operatives, rather than from co-operatives being singled out for special treatment. Thus co-operatives are faced with the challenge of ensuring that federal and provincial policies affecting their operations will be complementary and positive.

Co-operators' Attitudes toward the State[6]

Canadian co-operatives have generally been led by people suspicious of close relations between co-operatives and the state.[7] This suspicion has been expressed in two forms: a disinclination to become involved in broad-ranging public policy discussions, and an opposition to expansion of state enterprise except where it directly promotes co-operatives' institutional interests. Traditionally, the strategic basis of this position has been the belief that an interventionist state might take up the economic and social space within which co-operatives had discovered a market niche. At a very practical level, co-operators' antipathy toward the state emerged from their frustrations with governments that facilitated domination of average citizens by distant economic elites.

When anglophone co-operative leaders abided by or even promoted particular forms of state enterprise, such as subsidy of firms, or other forms of 'state intervention,' they did so because their communities or organizations were faced with economic crises. Thus they promoted federal control over grain marketing after grain prices dropped precipitously following the First World War; during the Depression, they supported the Wheat Board, the Bank of Canada, and the Prairie Farm Rehabilitation Act; in the mid-1940s, and again in 1969-70, they lobbied against tax changes that threatened their viability. Elimination of the Crow benefit for prairie grain producers, abandonment of branch rail lines, and low world grain prices have recently posed threats to communities represented by prairie wheat pools. Their pleas for expanded state assistance should be seen in this context.

The other basic problem co-operators have with either increased participation in policy development or with more broadly focused and high-profile political activity is that these seem to contravene the Rochdale principle of political neutrality, interpreted by most Canadian co-operative leaders to proscribe not just partisan commitments by co-operatives, but also commitments to social reform agendas. Mixed with anti-statist feelings, this concern with political neutrality has produced a profound yet unarticulated uneasiness about co-operative-state relations.

Pressure Groups and Policy Influence

Paul Pross defines pressure groups as 'organizations whose members act together to influence public policy in order to promote their common interest.'[8] Within this broad category, the activities of pressure groups fall into two main areas: traditional lobbying or policy advocacy; and actual policy-making and implementation. These two areas are discussed below. Pressure groups also communicate group needs to policy-makers, the public, political parties, and contending interests; they legitimize or endorse government policy, and perform regulatory and administrative functions in areas of their special knowledge and judgment.[9]

Is it appropriate to consider co-operative organizations as pressure groups, given that most co-operatives' primary purpose is to provide services or goods on more reasonable terms, rather than to participate in the world of power politics? Does the non-capitalist character of co-operative enterprise not rule out applying the same theoretical framework to them as to capitalist firms?

To the first question, it must be sympathetically replied that so long as co-operatives (and their second- or third-tier organizations) deal with governments to assert or protect their members' interests, they will be compelled to act as pressure groups. In fact, to be successful in representing their members' interests to governments and other interests, co-operatives must increasingly use some of their competitors' techniques, and respond effectively to a good number of the state's needs. The world of politics is not one that major organizations can avoid, except at their own peril, even if the processes and results appear objectionable.

Organizations can place limits on the extent of their involvement in politics, but because survival requires understanding and occasional favours from the state, the politics of interest representation are unavoidable. All large co-operatives recognize this, so their actions are appropriate subjects of analyses designed to understand relations between the state and conventional business groups. Co-operatives are nowhere nearly powerful enough to design a framework and an agenda for their relations with the state. They enter an environment that is shaped by the interaction between large capitalist firms and a powerful state. While it is crucial to identify the specific dynamics that characterize co-operative-state relations in Canada, this in no way allows us to ignore the fact that many co-operatives' actions are a function of the environment they enter and not of their 'co-operative difference.'

Lobbying or Policy Advocacy
Pressure groups lobby or influence government either to obtain or to defend benefits for the constituencies they represent, competing with each other for a say in how the power of the state is articulated.[10] Policy advocacy refers to attempts by pressure groups to influence the state's decisions so as to improve the welfare of their groups vis-à-vis that of other groups.

The word 'influence' suggests that groups which lobby are outside the policy process. It also suggests that the relationship between the groups and the state (and other interest groups) is one of conflict and competition. The pressure group is attempting to influence policy in one direction, while other actors, including the state at times, attempt to push in another.[11]

To be effective in distributing benefits to their members, pressure groups must collect information regarding (1) the political process and the bureaucracy, and (2) the likely benefits and disadvantages of particular policies. In addition, groups must be able to mobilize support for policies they advocate, among either their members or the public.

Gathering information and obtaining member support requires member cohesion; members must believe the group truly represents their interests. In Coleman's words, the group 'strives precisely to be the mouthpiece of the members.'[12] Such cohesion is necessary not only because it increases member support, but also because it signals to government that the pressure group is indeed speaking for its members.

Thus, an interest group is granted legitimacy as a player in the public policy process on the assumption that it represents the interests of its members. By accepting or endorsing the policies put forward by government, a pressure group provides reciprocal legitimacy for the government and its policies. To retain its legitimacy and support of its members, however, an organization must constantly ensure that its policy positions are indeed those of its members.[13]

Groups adopting primarily a policy advocacy role are likely to be narrowly focused, since this allows them both to present the views of membership and to make statements and decisions for them. Given a society that is economically and geographically diverse, this further implies that industry and/or regionally specific groups will be the most successful. Furthermore, since pressure groups' lobbying resources are limited, they can be most effective if they act to influence the decision-making or power centres in government. In a federalist state such as Canada, pressure groups would presumably be organized so that they could lobby both the provincial and federal levels of government. This tendency will be further strengthened in those cases where both levels of government have concurrent jurisdiction in policy formation.[14]

Policy-making
In addition to policy advocacy, pressure groups in Canada are also involved in policy-making and implementation, activities quite distinct from lobbying. Pressure groups involved in policy-making need to be able to do two things: order and co-ordinate a large amount of detailed and technical information, and remain relatively autonomous from both their members and the government.[15]

The question of autonomy is particularly important, since group negotiation and compromise with both the state and other groups in the economy are fundamental to policy participation. Salisbury makes the point well. In contrasting membership groups and institutions, he notes that institutions possess a number of advantages in proposing policy changes.[16] First, the interests of an institution engaged in lobbying are not necessarily those of its members (e.g., employees). To the extent that the institution has political power, this power does not depend on a legitimization process. Second, the decision to influence public policy is a management decision and gives managers a great deal of independence in the decisions they make. Third, because institutions often have greater financial resources than member organizations, they have more freedom to exert pressure on the policy process. In short, institutions have autonomy to act as policy-makers and to make policy choices.

To be most effective in policy-making, a pressure group should ideally be part of a policy system in which other interest groups representing different regions, economic sectors, and/or different levels in the same economic sector are present. At the top of this system is a peak organization which integrates the demands and interests of the various groups below it. To bargain effectively with government and other pressure groups in the economy, the peak organization must persuasively represent a significant portion of the economy, and make binding its decisions for its members. Without such authority, the peak association is unable to speak for, and promise government the support of, all players to be affected by policy being formulated. In Canada, such a system might include pressure groups representing the country's major regions and commodity producers, as well as a set of peak organizations representing these groups' views to governments.

Pressure Groups in the Policy Process
The two modes of pressure group activity suggest two aspects of the policy process in Canada. Following Pross, the process of policy formation can be described as revolving around a policy community, or that part of a political system which acquires the dominant voice in determining government decisions. There are two major parts to the community: the sub-government and the attentive public. The former is a small, tightly knit group of people who make or influence the day-to-day decisions; the latter is neither, but instead engages in continuous policy review. Unlike the attentive public, the sub-government segment of the policy community is not usually interested in making or reformulating policy; rather, the people in this group prefer to keep policy-making routine and technical through a process that Pross describes as 'consensus management.'

Utilizing the distinction between policy advocacy and policy-making, it would appear that policy-advocacy interest groups would likely be part of the attentive public, while those groups that emphasize policy-making or implementation would be members of, or have greater access to, the sub-government. The same pressure group, at different times or on different issues, may engage in both policy-making and policy advocacy – that is, be part of the sub-government and the attentive public.

To gain access to the sub-government, pressure groups must adopt bureaucratic structures and views of the policy-making process similar to those of the sub-government. As a result, what Pross defines as institutional groups will likely be much more effective in obtaining power than will other organizations. Institutional groups have stable memberships, organizational continuity, and cohesion. They have extensive knowledge of the government sectors important to their membership. Their specific objectives are amenable to pragmatic negotiation and compromise. As well, they see organizational continuation as much more important than any particular policy they might press on the government. The result is that the leaders of the groups adhere to 'rules' that govern their behaviour toward the government, for example, the non-condemnation of civil servants. An institutional group's major goal is a place in the policy process.

At the opposite end of the spectrum are issue-oriented groups, which combine limited organizational continuity, minimal knowledge of government, extremely fluid membership, difficulty in formulating and adhering to short-run objectives, and a low regard for their organizational continuation. These groups show less concern for involvement in the policy process and a greater interest in major policy changes.

While this type of group is often quite effective in influencing policy during times of dramatic policy shifts, it is unlikely to play much of a role in the day-to-day evolution of policy. The ideological base of the majority of such groups places them among those that Coleman identifies as being restricted to policy advocacy.

Conflicts between Policy-making and Policy Advocacy

For a pressure group, the roles of policy advocacy and policy-making are often in conflict. Policy advocacy requires a group to focus its energy on generating information regarding who will gain and who will lose from particular policy alternatives. This is quite different from the detailed technical information required by policy-making groups. With limited resources at their disposal, pressure groups can usually not afford to undertake both tasks. More telling, however, is that policy-advocacy groups require member cohesion. To achieve this, the group must appear to represent its members' interests continually, since only this can confer legitimacy on both the group and, occasionally, the government. In contrast, a pressure group involved in policy-making must be relatively autonomous from its members, so as to maximize the group's ability to negotiate and compromise with the state and other policy-making groups in the economy.

Policy-making groups with organizational structures similar to government will be most successful in gaining access to government, all else being equal. This means that successful organizations will be geographically organized in a manner that corresponds to the federal structure of Canadian politics. It also means a similar bureaucratic style, which keeps policy-making routine and technical. All issues will be negotiable, and continued access to government remains more important than winning or losing any particular policy round.

For lobby groups, however, adopting the bureaucratic, policy-making style invariably leads to a seriously reduced ability to speak for their members, and a decline in the member support so vital to their success. In attempting to retain members' support, these groups remain outside the policy process, promoting significant policy changes as opposed to minor policy realignments.

The Dual Nature of Co-operatives

The logic sketched above for pressure groups or business associations can be applied equally well to co-operatives. As will be seen, specific co-operatives can be viewed as members of a co-operative business association, an approach which can be used to examine the role of the Co-operative Union of Canada (CUC) and its successor, the Canadian Co-operative Association (CCA), in public policy formation.[17] Individual co-operative members, however, can also be viewed as members of co-operative pressure groups. This approach is useful for a discussion of agricultural policy in which specific co-operatives (e.g., the Saskatchewan Wheat Pool) act as pressure groups for their individual farmer members.

There are a number of reasons that co-operatives may be successful as pressure groups. First, as quintessential membership groups co-operatives should be well poised for policy advocacy. Members join voluntarily, albeit not always for political reasons, and a democratic structure allows members to register their views. The member commitment and support accompanying such representative processes are crucial in policy advocacy.

A co-operative is also an institution, however. In the larger co-operatives there is a bureaucratic hierarchy consisting of members, directors, upper, middle, and lower-level management, and other employees. Within this structure, directors and management often take independent action (i.e., without formal membership approval) on both the commercial and policy fronts.

As a business concern, a larger co-operative (e.g., the Saskatchewan Wheat Pool, United Grain Growers, Federated Co-operatives Limited, Co-op Atlantic) may have as much access to funds for policy development as the usual membership groups. Related to this, the directors and management will often have the time and the technical resources (e.g., lawyers, a research department) to monitor the policy environment if they so wish. As well, these officers may also have the bureaucratic mind-set necessary to deal with the sub-government portion of the policy community and to accept small policy changes.

While the dual nature of co-operatives has the potential to make them effective in their dealings with government, it also poses conflicts between policy advocacy and policy participation. As a membership group the co-operative has to speak for its members continually. This implies not only a constant dialogue with the members, but also a style of lobbying that is often issue-oriented and conflict-ridden. At the same time, the co-operative may also wish to bargain, to accept small changes and compromises in policy for the right to remain in the game.

An ordinary pressure group will likely decide which path to take – policy advocacy or policy-making – early in its existence. Most pressure groups are relatively secure in the role they have chosen, and while they are unable to alter that role fundamentally, they usually face little debate about that being the correct role to adopt.

For co-operatives, such security may be more elusive, and the conflict between policy advocacy and policy participation can be much more divisive. In part, this stems from the relationship between the membership and management of the co-operative. Co-operative members will often want their co-operative to adopt a policy-advocacy role, since this provides members with the opportunity to see their co-operative in action. Management, however, generally prefers a policy-making role, wishing to negotiate and compromise with government in much the same way it negotiates a business deal. Management finds the bureaucratic world of the sub-government much more comfortable than the advocacy world of the attentive public.

This basic tension between membership and management increases when management takes policy stands opposed by significant elements of the membership. If these elements feel that democratic control has been contravened, they are likely to speak out against management's view. Member cohesion will then almost certainly be weakened, as will the co-operative's ability to pursue either a policy-advocacy role or policy-making functions.

This is not to suggest that co-operatives have not enjoyed successes in their chosen policy roles. The following sections illustrate some of the successes co-operatives have had in influencing government policy, while acknowledging the conflicts identified above.

Co-operative and Government Relations

Strategic Conflicts in National Co-operative Association Relations with Government

The CUC/CCA is a third-tier co-operative dominated by the major co-operatives in anglophone Canada.[18] These forty-three organizations include memberships of almost nine million Canadians. Member organizations are active in grain marketing, farm supply, consumer retail, resource production, secondary processing and manufacturing, housing, and financial service sectors of the economy. While their strength is not geographically even across the country, all regions of Canada have a co-operative presence of some significance. When the CCA assumed the role of the former CUC, it inherited an institutional membership whose short- to medium-term interests and economic needs are almost as diverse as members of the Canadian Chamber of Commerce.

This organizational portrait suggests some of the potential difficulties that such a peak association of businesses will encounter when it attempts to achieve consensus on matters that affect all or even most of its members. It is easy to predict that consensus will seldom emerge, and often not be attempted, on matters affecting CCA organizations' members in ways tangential to their business success. However, there are other reasons to suggest that the policy clout of CCA will be limited.

For example, if CCA member organizations are simultaneously members of sector-specific trade associations, the state will likely prefer to hear their voices in this more specialized context. This results because the government correctly perceives that more definitive and legitimating information will be forthcoming from these sources. As we will see, the major agricultural co-operatives have joined sectoral and sub-sectoral trade associations, often dominated by private firms, to increase their policy clout for precisely this reason.

With co-operative business concerns being regularly represented in this fashion, government officials do not automatically look to the CCA when reviewing policy incidentally affecting co-operatives. That government officials rarely think of co-operatives as distinctly affected by most policy decisions reduces the CCA's profile even more. This in turn exacerbates the CCA's tendency to approach government officials defensively and with a focus on informing them that co-operatives' distinctive operational styles require different treatment than given to private sector firms.

We noted earlier that co-operatives should possess a substantial advantage over private competitors in their dealings with government agencies and officials by virtue of their democratic organizational and operational character.

Whatever reservations one might have about the vitality of democratic practice in the larger co-operatives, there is no doubt that their control structures function far more democratically than their private sector equivalents.[19] Should not the congruence of co-operative 'representative democracy' with the norms of our political system ensure that co-operative voices are accorded special legitimacy in the halls of bureaucratic and legislative power?

The reasons for answering a sobering 'no' to this question illustrate the value of Coleman's account of business association–state relations, the necessity of understanding co-operatives as pressure groups, and the need to see co-operative–state relationships in the context of Canada's capitalist political economy. We can only skim the surface of these reasons here.[20]

The first and least controversial part of the answer has to do with the needs of the state for rapid and effectively legitimated decisions on matters of public policy. Governments have political and bureaucratic needs to resolve many policy matters at particular times in legislative or program life-cycles with a minimum of public controversy. Governments thus come to rely on players in the various policy communities that can make informed and consensual contributions to policy development on very short notice. These contributions must come at times convenient to the government's legislative and policy agenda, and in terms which fit with the ideological messages and the political debts of the ruling party.

Given these needs of the state, the democratic and member-responsive character of the CCA puts it at a comparative disadvantage as either a policy advocate or a policy participant. State officials and legislators often value groups' positions when they are clearly representative of broadly based member opinion. There are many occasions, however, when the 'policy machine' cannot wait for an organization to resolve its internal disputes sufficiently to produce useful contributions on particular policy questions.

Group participation within policy communities requires a level of political autonomy for the business association which is simply incompatible with the democratic character of a third-tier co-operative organization. In the long run this autonomy would generate so much member antipathy and distrust, and reduced institutional appreciation of member concerns, that the CCA would lose much of the legitimacy it had acquired in the policy communities. Such autonomous action would also cost the co-operative peak organization some major institutional members and reduce its currently modest abilities to sustain cohesion in a 'co-operative system' or to retain support for a co-operative 'movement.'

The CCA clearly has enjoyed a certain degree of autonomy from its institutional members. Examples include the administration of its overseas development projects, its representations to recent royal commissions and parliamentary committee hearings, and of course its role in the 1984 Report of the National Task Force on Co-operative Development. The CCA has always taken some responsibility for co-ordinating efforts to help define the longer-term, common interests of co-operatives in Canada, and to translate such efforts into a broader strategy for action. But it would be quite illegitimate for the CCA to negotiate privately with the state and other organized interests on comprehensive programs that had not been democratically reviewed by its member organizations. Legitimacy and the ability to carry its membership would be lost if the CCA ventured much beyond the role of proxy negotiator for members on well-defined policy issues. These constraints do much to limit the CCA's value to the state in its policy development processes.

It is against this background that we must assess the probable value of the federal Co-operative Secretariat to the Canadian co-operative system generally, and the status of the CCA more specifically. This secretariat was established in May 1987 'to simplify and strengthen government relations with co-operatives,' and 'in recognition of the social and economic importance of Canadian co-operatives.'[21] The secretariat reports to Charles Mayer, minister of state responsible for the Canadian Wheat Board and liaison with co-operatives, and has chosen an executive director from the co-operative sector. It is to work in conjunction with an Interdepartmental Co-operatives Committee, a federal committee of 'senior policy personnel from concerned federal departments.' Most of the secretariat's personnel and mandate have been transferred from the Co-operatives Unit in the Department of Agriculture. Since 1975 this small enclave of bureaucratic support for Canadian co-operatives has provided marketing information for co-operatives and briefed federal bureaucrats whose paths cross with particular co-operatives.

The Co-operative Secretariat can be considered as a response to the 1984 National Task Force's request for a minister of state for co-operatives 'with a small supporting secretariat.'[22] This proposal had its origins in the mid- to late-1970s when it was raised in a CUC brief to the federal cabinet in response to the 1977 white paper, 'The Way Ahead.' The proposal for a secretariat has since then become one of Canadian co-operative leaders' clearest expressions of intent to establish closer and formal ties to the state. It seems a logical extension of the heavy dependence on state funding implied in the task force's other proposals,[23] and may in fact be required by the reduction in political autonomy demanded of policy participants by the state.

Such a proposal is a major departure from the Canadian co-operative tradition of anti-statist political neutrality. It also carries the potential of reducing the democratic character of inter-co-operative and intra-co-operative activity in

Canada to dangerously low levels. But even if co-operatives do sacrifice crucial amounts of autonomy, democratic responsiveness, and their movement's grander social objectives, the secretariat may still not significantly increase co-operatives' collective policy clout in Ottawa. We will consider these last two issues in greater detail.

The recent reliance of Canadian co-operatives on the federal government for joint financing or loan guarantees in two major energy projects,[24] and bail-out financing for co-operatives in financial distress,[25] are arguably anomalous instances of co-operative dependence on state assistance. When taken in conjunction with the implicit and explicit suggestion of federal government financial responsibility for most of the major elements in the co-operative system's chosen development agenda, however, these joint ventures and loan guarantees indicate a historical break with co-operatives' past. In what must be seen as a curious paradox, co-operatives are asking the Canadian state to play the principal role in assisting co-operatives to provide an alternative to what the task force describes as the unresponsive, bureaucratic institutions of the state.[26] The state is to help co-operatives save Canadians from the state.

It is misleading, however, to pose the paradox of co-operative development in such simple terms. For one thing, the same paradox exists in the area of human rights protection, but we do not shrink from calling on the state to be interventionist in this area. This is because we recognize that only the state has the power and the institutional capabilities to ensure that its own bureaucrats, and other individuals operating under the cover of laws which the state enforces, do not deprive citizens of their rights.

The simple structure of the paradox does have the virtue, however, of forcing us to admit something that the report and most co-operative leaders do not publicly acknowledge: that state-assisted co-operative development is most effectively rationalized as a way of making up for the unfairness and other shortcomings of a capitalist market economy, which include massive state financial assistance to private sector firms for economic development. It can be argued that state assistance to co-operatives in the short run will reduce community and individuals' dependence on state assistance in the long run. But this claim acquires legitimacy only in the context of a critique of the dominant alternative presented to people in most Canadian communities: that is, reliance on the private sector to create jobs, and reliance on the state to provide subsistence incomes for those the market has determined are 'surplus labour.'

Ultimately it is the state's reliance on the workings of the market, and the reliance of Canadian society for its economic health on this state-assisted market, which place Canadian co-operatives in the midst of the paradox noted above. This same reliance can also be credited for the cruel fact that, from a

lobbying perspective, Canadian co-operatives are now generally worse off for
having internalized the legitimizing democratic logic of our political system.
Canadian co-operatives are forced by the dynamics of the capitalist political
economy to play pressure group politics if they are even to hold their own as
firms in competitive markets. This context also helps to explain why Canadian
co-operatives lobbied for a Co-operative Secretariat in the federal government,
in an attempt to offset disadvantages arising from governments and the public
viewing the private firm as the paradigmatic producer of jobs and prosperity. In
our conclusion we ask whether this new institutional mediation between the
federal government and co-operatives will significantly increase their clout in
the policy communities of their choice.

Agricultural Policy
Co-operatives play a significant role in Canadian agriculture. For instance, the
grain handling co-operatives in western Canada market approximately 76 per
cent of the grain and oilseeds on the prairies, while in Quebec, co-operatives
process roughly two-thirds of milk produced in the province.[27] As might be
expected, co-operatives are extensively involved in forming agricultural policy
and programs. Through their joint policy organization, Prairie Pools, the three
prairie wheat pools are members of the Canadian Federation of Agriculture
(CFA), the major farm interest group in Canada. Prairie Pools also works
directly on policy matters, as does United Grain Growers (UGG), the other
major prairie grain handling co-operative. In Quebec, Coop Fédérée du Québec,
both alone and in conjunction with l'union de producteurs agricoles (UPA),
plays a major policy role.

Few studies have dealt specifically with the question of co-operatives' role in
the formation of public policy,[28] but a number of observations from agriculture
show that at least in this sector co-operatives are effective. Our discussion
focuses primarily on agriculture outside of Quebec. The situation in Quebec is
quite different; where co-operatives' close involvement with supply
management marketing boards and the UPA ensures them a policy role that is
far greater than that of co-operatives in the other provinces.[29]

The prairie wheat pools have been among the more successful co-operatives
in agricultural policy, both individually and in concert through their joint
organization, Prairie Pools. Prairie Pools' membership in the Canadian
Federation of Agriculture gives the prairie grain co-operatives an additional
mechanism for presenting their views. The Alberta Wheat Pool is a member of
Unifarm, which is also a member of CFA. In Quebec, Coop Fédérée, along
with UPA and the Quebec Farmers' Association, is a member of CFA. As an
indication of the role they play in policy formation, Forbes lists the CFA, the

Saskatchewan Wheat Pool (SWP), UGG, and UPA as examples of institutional groups.

Of these, the CFA is viewed as being the most effective and influential of the farm interest groups.[30] While a major role of the CFA is undoubtedly lobbying, with officials of the federation carefully cultivating government officials and key politicians, Forbes also points out that an important aspect of the CFA's activities is involvement by member organizations in federal advisory and regulatory bodies. In these activities, the CFA is engaged in the policy-making and implementation role.

In addition to being members of the CFA, co-operatives have also played important policy roles on their own. Perhaps the best example is from the Crow debate, in which both the SWP and Coop Fédérée du Québec (in alliance with UPA) were able to persuade the federal government that the Crow benefit payment should be made to the railways and not to farmers. While such efforts in the latter stages of the Crow debate by the SWP were clear instances of policy advocacy, the pool's willingness to discuss Crow abolition illustrates that it had some policy formulation interest and capability. Opposition near the end of the Crow debate was equally strong in Quebec, with the UPA joining forces with the Quebec government and Coop Fédérée to lobby Quebec MPs intensively.

The Crow debate is also a good example of the perils of becoming active in the policy arena. While the SWP was successful in modifying the legislation (i.e., the method of payment) to meet some of its members' needs, it was nevertheless forced to compromise on the fundamental point, the removal of the Crow. While to some this would seem like a reasonably good trade-off, the SWP may have lost on both counts. Its stand on the Crow caused considerable member discontent, some open and hostile. The end result was that many members believed their views were being ignored, while the policy-makers in Ottawa may have concluded that the SWP could not be counted on to deliver the kind of support needed to legitimize the legislation.[31]

To the extent that compromising on the Crow can be described as undertaking a policy-making role, the SWP directly experienced the effect of adopting such a policy strategy. To engage continually in policy determination, a co-operative must be willing to bargain and compromise, attend to small details, and avoid criticizing public officials or particular policies. Such an approach, however, may not accord with the needs of members, since they usually demand some sort of public involvement and recognition of their organization in the policy debate.

While co-operatives may be able to chart both courses at different times and on different issues, our earlier conclusion regarding policy role conflicts still holds – on a specific issue and over time generally, organizations like co-operatives have to choose and retain one policy role. If policy debates like the Crow are any indication, co-operatives in Canada must opt more for policy advocacy than policy-making. This is the same conclusion arrived at in the discussion of the CCA, implying that with regard to both inter- and intra-sectoral questions, co-operatives usually have to chose the policy-advocacy role.

This conclusion, however, appears to neglect co-operatives' roles in policy-making through farm organizations such as the CFA. As noted above, the CFA and its member organizations are heavily involved in federal advisory and regulatory bodies. Does this not constitute a policy-making role?

There are a number of reasons to suggest that the CFA's role is not policy-making in its truest sense. For instance, the activities referred to above are concerned more with the day-to-day operation of agricultural boards and commissions than with formulation of broad policy. While Coleman argues that the interest group and business association system in agriculture is the most policy-capable of any in Canada,[32] the strength of this system to actually propose policy must be strongly questioned. Although there are many regional and commodity-specific groups in the system, thus satisfying one key condition of a policy system, it is also true that no method exists for aggregating and developing compromises among these interests.

Most interest groups in the agricultural policy system have characteristics associated with policy advocacy rather than policy-making. Groups such as the Canadian Cattlemen's Association, UGG, Western Canadian Wheat Growers' Association (WCWGA), and Canadian Canola Growers' Association (CCGA) in western Canada are narrowly defined commodity groups, often unwilling to compromise on issues affecting their members. Groups representing more regional interests such as Prairie Pools and UPA would generally fit this description as well.

In addition, there is no peak association that aggregates agricultural interests from across Canada and across commodity groups. Since Coleman contended that the CFA has played this role, the UGG has dropped out of the organization, the Saskatchewan Federation of Agriculture and the Manitoba Farm Bureau have disbanded, and Unifarm faces reduced membership and weak finances.[33] The CFA continually provides a presence in Ottawa on many issues important to agriculture, but it is usually unable to play a role in policy matters that involve trade-offs between commodities or regions of the country. The Crow debate is an excellent case in point. As Forbes points out, the CFA remained silent on the debate, realizing it could neither speak for the industry nor help negotiate a compromise.[34]

The overall picture in Canadian agricultural policy, then, is one of competing and specialized commodity groups and regional interests. On the major policy issues requiring resolution (in the past the Crow; currently transportation, livestock production, and support for grain producers), the various groups adopt a policy-advocacy role, and attempts at compromise rarely occur.

Seen against this background, it is clear that agricultural co-operatives must be primarily involved in policy advocacy. At this they have been reasonably successful. English-speaking co-operatives' inability to play a policy-making role is neither surprising nor any different than the experience of other major players in the agricultural policy arena. Compared to their policy competitors, however, agricultural co-operatives suffer from internal discontent. Since co-operatives are democratic, they deal publicly with topics that remain hidden in ordinary pressure groups. In part, the internal discontent results from the greater heterogeneity of co-operative memberships, which in turn results from agricultural producers joining the co-operative for economic reasons as well as for its stands on policy issues.

Discussion and Conclusion

The theme of this chapter is that co-operatives encounter special difficulties and advantages in their attempts to influence the nature of public policy in Canada. When it comes to assessing their net impact, however, we encounter problems. In agriculture, for instance, co-operatives have at times played a critical role in policy formation. But how much of the co-operatives' power is due to their being co-operatives, and how much to their being large firms with many farmer members? Outside of agriculture, is the CCA's pattern of defensive reactions to policy changes the result of it being a co-operative, or the result of it representing a sector that is simply too small and too heterogeneous to have much political clout?

The answer to this last question is both. Canadian co-operatives are, at least for the foreseeable future, destined to obtain less than their fair share of policy influence because they are non-capitalist entities in a capitalist political economy. This means that their distinctive needs and virtues will continue to remain obscure to members of most policy communities they wish to influence. There is little that co-operatives can do about this; it is not easy to reverse the political-economic socialization of current bureaucrats, and Canadian co-operatives have in any case not been interested in emphasizing their non-capitalist character.

While this informal logic of discrimination against non-capitalist entities limits co-operatives' effectiveness, there is a formal logic of state decision-making which does so as well. As we have noted, economic policy-making occurs primarily with reference to intra-sectoral matters; inter-sectoral decision-making tends to occur only at the level of cabinet and its central agencies. Co-operatives are very unlikely to be given special access to these higher levels of policy-making, and can thus only work to ensure that co-operative voices are regularly heard at the intra-sectoral level. But this happens with reference to individual co-operative firms, not the co-operative sector as a whole. Indeed, as we have shown, the co-operative sector is often too divided or politically cautious to generate consensus on inter-sectoral policy issues. As our discussion of agriculture pointed out, co-operatives are often divided even on intra-sectoral issues. Where the sector itself does not go, the CCA or the new Co-operative Secretariat will not venture. Only if co-operatives as a group become oriented to policy-making could the CCA and the secretariat begin to co-ordinate and focus different federal departments' attention on the needs and virtues of co-operatives as co-operatives.

Interestingly, the answer to the question concerning co-operatives' power *qua* co-operatives is also both. A good deal of the influence co-operatives have in the agricultural sector is due to their large and responsive memberships. As we saw above, these features are important for legitimizing government policies. While having these particular characteristics increases the likelihood that the interest organization is a co-operative, the point to recognize is that co-operatives in agriculture have their influence not because they are co-operatives, but because they have these characteristics. Another way of putting this is to say that co-operatives have no culturally sanctioned advantage; their ideologically determined democratic structure is perceived to be valuable by federal policy-makers principally because it guarantees representation of a large and important economic interest.

Nevertheless, being a co-operative has not lessened the power of such agricultural organizations, as our discussion of the capitalist political economy might suggest. Within agriculture, co-operatives are not seen as a marginal force. Their size requires that they be listened to and legitimizes their particular form of organization. As well, the historical links between co-operatives and the development of Canadian agriculture have given them support that co-operatives in other sectors of the economy do not possess.

Finally, since policy communities deal with intra-sectoral policy, agricultural co-operatives are in a much better position to influence policy than co-operatives in other sectors. Their narrow interests allow them more room for consensus on policy decisions, and a much greater chance of government adopting their position. However, when a particular co-operative is unable to arrive at a consensus position, the problem it faces is not much different than those faced by the CCA on inter-sectoral issues.

It is difficult to make any generalizations about the nature of co-operative influence on public policy formation, although certain patterns do appear. For instance, we saw that both on their own and through the Canadian Federation of Agriculture, agricultural co-operatives sometimes do play a policy-making role. However, in most cases co-operatives have been policy advocates.

This mixed bag of results should not be taken as an indication that co-operatives are ineffectual; their private enterprise counterparts are often less 'policy-capable.' What it does indicate, however, is the degree to which co-operatives suffer from the inherent conflicts that Coleman has identified in pressure groups' contributions to policy formation. Coleman shows that policy-making and policy advocacy are often mutually exclusive activities.[35] For business associations, this implies that once they have chosen a certain role, they will rarely be able – or want – to exchange their strategy for another.

For co-operatives the situation may be different. Their democratic structures make it almost certain that in their policy activities they will adopt a policy-advocacy role. At the same time the institutional nature of their organizations will often result in co-operative managers and leaders wishing to engage in policy participation. This desire may be heightened by co-operatives' historical isolation from the policy development process. Yet, as we have seen, co-operative organizations, at least as they are now constituted, do not have sufficient autonomy from their members to undertake a policy-making role regularly. With large and heterogeneous memberships, co-operatives cannot allow a peak policy organization to determine their stands on particular policy issues. The ensuing member discontent would soon weaken the co-operatives politically and economically.

In addition, the pressures of the 'political market' will tend to encourage co-operatives to adopt a policy-advocacy role. It may be advantageous for all economic interests to be represented by peak associations that can undertake an autonomous policy-making role on behalf of their members,[36] so that the various groups' objectives can be truly weighed and negotiated against each other. But until each group is actually represented by such a peak association and, at the same time, has confidence that the peak association will bargain effectively for it, it is likely that individual groups will see more advantage in direct policy advocacy. Indeed, in such a political climate, surrendering political power to a peak association may easily make the group doing so worse off.

In this regard co-operatives encounter the same strategic dilemmas as other groups in the economy. If all adopt policy-making roles, all are likely to be better off. Yet there is always an incentive for a co-operative to be more advocacy-oriented, to gain a little bit more for its membership. Co-operatives face an additional dilemma. For most groups, adopting a policy-making rather than a policy-advocacy approach means giving up short-term gains for long-run benefits. By contrast, for co-operatives the choice between the two strategies strikes at the heart of their democratic nature. Not only must the members make the trade-off the members of other groups make, they must also give up some of their autonomy – by letting the peak association make decisions for them.

It is of course possible that organizational means of giving the members democratic control can be developed and implemented, while ensuring that the negotiating body has the autonomy it requires. This would require a major shift in the direction of corporatist relations between organized interests and the state in Canada, along with a simultaneous commitment of all major organized interests to a democratic and responsive relationship with their constituencies.[37] For co-operatives there would have to be a restructuring of decision-making processes, and some key changes in the orientations towards participation in group politics held by average co-operative members. A move towards a greater policy making role would also involve a collective act of faith by co-operative members; they would like, but could not get, assurances that these changes would guarantee them more clout in national 'policy communities.'

The difficulties associated with making such changes decrease the likelihood that co-operatives will become seriously involved in policy-making with governments. They will be encouraged to remain policy advocates rather than lose more ground to private sector groups which lobby extensively. At times co-operative organizations will wish to engage in policy discussions with the government in the belief that by doing so they will ultimately become more effective – in formal terms, that they can become part of the policy sub-government. Emphasis on the latter strategy will probably lead to member dissatisfaction, the result of which is likely to be even less political power for Canadian co-operatives.

DAVID LAYCOCK

11 Political Neutrality and the Problem of Interest Representation: Co-operatives and Partisan Politics in Canada

This chapter examines the problematic relations between Canadian co-operatives and the political party system, so as to illuminate the difficulties of interest representation faced by a movement that is committed to partisan and political neutrality. Comparison with British co-operatives' experience of engagement in the party system reveals some of the factors that have inclined the Canadian co-operative movement to retain the stance of political neutrality throughout the twentieth century, and suggests several difficulties Canadian co-operatives will encounter in any approach to representation of their interests in our political system.

Major Canadian co-operatives have scrupulously avoided formal alliances with political parties. To the extent that achieving short- to medium-term goals and objectives has required involvement in the political process, they have chosen other methods to represent their interests. Not just partisan neutrality, but increasingly even public silence on contentious issues of social and economic policy affecting co-operatives' members, have become entrenched as part of the creed of Canadian co-operative organizations.

For Canadian co-operative members and activists this may not seem odd. After all, with the exception of organized labour, few organized interests have sought to create and maintain such formal linkages. The International Co-operative Alliance principle of political neutrality also appears to sanction this distance from partisan politics philosophically and historically.

But to most British co-operative leaders, many in Scandinavia, and most in the third world, the absence of partisan ties immediately raises several questions. How are the interests of co-operators represented in public life, if not

162 David Laycock

at least partly through the most obvious vehicle of such representation, the political party system? What has happened to co-operatives and the political system to prevent representation of co-operative interests and values by a party sympathetic to these interests and values? What, if anything, might alter this situation?

These questions are appropriate because they force us to think of the present situation as contingent rather than natural. This in turn facilitates critical assessment of Canadian co-operatives' relations to competitive political life. We may well discover that the current arrangement is comprehensible in historical terms, and easily defended in terms of the inescapable realities of Canadian co-operatives and their environment. If this is so, we may still wonder whether the relationship between political parties and co-operatives in Canada might change in the future.

In the next section, we will consider the problem of co-operatives' representation in the political system to see some of its broader implications. This will set the stage for brief historical accounts of the factors that have kept Canadian co-operative organizations formally detached from the fortunes of partisan politics, and of those which have entwined the two in Britain. Discussion of the British experience is designed to help set up the fourth section, which offers an overview of the factors that will reinforce political neutrality for Canadian co-operatives for the foreseeable future.

Co-operatives and Political Representation

The concept of representation raises some of the more difficult questions in political and social theory. At a very basic level, one encounters Jean-Jacques Rousseau's serious question as to whether one citizen's interests can really be represented by another, or the later arguments along these lines by G.D.H. Cole. Representation is not the easy process implied by the glib assurances of vote-soliciting politicians.

Representation of group interests in public institutions assumes at least provisional resolution of many thorny problems. These include criteria for determining which common characteristics are most significant for patterning political representation: occupations, religions, opinions on major issues, geographic locations? How and why do groups come into being? How should public authorities decide that enough groups' interests have been either directly canvassed, or (another thing altogether) indirectly considered, on particular issues?

The trickiest practical question at any given time concerns how group interests are reconciled in the process of determining the public interest. The overarching problem implicit in these last two questions is choosing appropriate standards for allowing certain groups' interests to take precedence over others on basic matters of social choice and resource allocation. This takes us into the realm of distributive justice and the general principles of political society, and suggests how crucial the presuppositions of representational political theory are to life in a democracy.[1]

The problem of common interest as a basis for group organization, and perhaps then political representation, is provisionally solved for co-operatives' members by their voluntary membership in organizations offering specific goods and services. But the perceived common interests of co-operative members seldom extend beyond a rather narrow range of matters. Co-operative leaders commonly recognize this when they reject co-operative organizational support for a particular political party. The reasons for rejecting this move tell us a good deal about the representation of interests within the Canadian co-operative movement, and their reception within the Canadian political system. In practical terms, a co-operative group's interests are assumed to be those identified by internally elected leaders, and in resolutions at general meetings. However, it is important for us to appreciate that many issues are intentionally avoided by directors, managers, and active members because they are too political, which is to say too divisive. The characteristic Canadian co-operative fear about many public issues is that their consideration will put the co-operative on the slippery slope away from political neutrality. For most co-operative leaders, this slope moves in the direction of business-threatening positions on non-mandated issues, and toward representation of only minority interests within co-operative organizations' memberships.

Contemporary Canadian co-operative leaders have recently shown that they view public awareness of internal co-operative conflict as anathema to their co-operatives' welfare. This sensitivity exceeds that of many other large organizations, and should be considered unusual for organizations taking pride in their democratic practices. Clearly, there must be interesting historical and organizational reasons for co-operatives' sensitivity about interest representation.

The last basic question about representation – that regarding the standards of distributive justice operative in the state's treatment of organized and other interests within the Canadian polity – has historically been resolved by forces beyond the control of co-operatives. Nonetheless, co-operators' perceptions of how this question is addressed within the Canadian political system are crucial to their decisions on representation of co-operative interests. If co-operators find prevailing standards of distributive justice to be seriously deficient, we might reasonably expect that social movement activities such as political activism would characterize their organizations. This may or may not find an outlet in links with reformist political parties, but would certainly involve high-profile attempts to represent a distinctively co-operative voice in public institutions shaping public policy. In the absence of a strong movement orientation, these signs of political activism are far less likely to be in evidence.

At the same time it is crucial to recognize that all organized interests must assess the efficacy of different means of policy influence. Resources and opportunities for effective representation are limited for all organized groups. Co-operatives must develop political strategy with a clear vision of how the game is played and won, including an appreciation that following a strategy can eventually change the character of the goals being pursued.[2]

To hypothesize why organized interests prefer certain kinds of representation, some discussion of basic types of representation is necessary. Traditional debates over the nature of representation have focused on the distinction between mandated and independent representation. The first prescribes direct control over representatives' actions in legislatures and other public bodies by the constituency(s) of those represented. The second advocates substantial freedom for elected representatives to resolve issues on the basis of their personal judgment. Intermediate positions combining the two approaches are most common in political life.[3]

Nonetheless, this distinction draws our attention to co-operative organizations' probable expectations regarding representation of their interests in the political system. The organization would presumably wish to ensure that its representatives were accountable to its members. Representatives should also accept active member participation in shaping policy and in assessing the value of the representational efforts they had mandated.[4]

However, co-operative members must often be willing to trust representatives' judgment regarding issues and practical alternatives. This is what happens when members of a co-operative elect their board of directors. Why should this same logic not extend to representation of co-operative interests in the political realm? It does, but selectively. As we have seen in previous chapters, the logic is extended to regional and national organizations of co-operative business, but not beyond the boundaries of relatively traditional pressure group strategies to the more public world of party competition.

It is important to note here that independent representation of co-operative interests by their officials involves a much wider range of activities than might be inferred from the above. Co-operative organizational officials are entrusted with the majority of decisions about how to present co-operatives' business interests to public bodies (i.e., agencies and arms of the state). But it is not generally appreciated that this includes the *de facto* power to decide which issues in the public realm are to be treated as relevant to co-operative members. These officials thus have much power to determine the scope and character of co-operative politics, including the extent to which societal influences on co-operatives – and vice versa – should be politicized.

This means that co-operative officials have the power to make what have been called 'non-decisions,'[5] which restrict member control over matters that might affect the operation of the co-operative. In this sense these officials exercise a degree of independent representational power which presupposes widespread agreement about the social character and purposes of co-operatives. This activity also tends to reduce the significance of mandated representation in co-operatives' connections to the political realm. This pattern of informal extension of independent representation, at the expense of mandated representation, is common within large bureaucratic organizations and their relations with complex processes of state decision-making.[6]

Is there anything one can say about the types of representation appropriate to particular kinds of organizations seeking political representation? Or is everything so dependent on the peculiarities of the party system, socio-economic structure, policy-making patterns, and governmental form in a polity that no conceptual generalization is worth while?

Superficial historical and international comparisons among co-operative economic activities suggest one correlation. One might expect a positive correlation between the degree of social transformative commitment within a co-operative movement and the likelihood that mandated representation through partisan political avenues will be chosen to represent group interests. Political parties are not always the most effective vehicles of social change, but they almost always play a crucial role in such change.[7]

A corollary to the above hypothesis suggests that co-operatives with mildly reformist objectives will adopt less strictly mandated forms of representation. In modern democratic polities, this implies pressure group activities seeking incremental advantage for group members in a competition whose rules are not fundamentally opposed by the group members.

Do these correlations have enough plausibility to justify their use as investigative hypotheses? The early-twentieth-century experience of the Co-operative Union of Canada suggests an obvious contrary case. It was led by people who clearly thought of themselves as pioneers in a social movement, but refused to allow formal partisan alignment. By contrast, the British co-operative movement today has lost the character of a socially transformative force while still maintaining a partisan connection as a key part of its political representational activity.

But the origins of the movement, and of its decision to enter politics, may lend support to the hypotheses. We know, for example, that there has been a strong relationship between third-world co-operative and political movements since the Second World War. The politicization of the American great plains co-operative movement into the People's party just after the Civil War also lends the correlation plausibility.[8] Finally, we must not forget the experience of organized farmers and their co-operatives in partisan competition in Alberta (1921-35) and Saskatchewan (1935-60).

We can also ask whether any correlation exists between the degree of homogeneity within a co-operative movement (or sector) and its establishment of close links with a political party. If a mildly reformist 'sector' is less likely to seek party avenues of representation than a more radical movement, is this tied to the member composition of either? And how might the question of composition be linked to a co-operative movement's acceptance of a mandated or an independent style of political representation?

With these hypotheses in mind, we can consider some of the historical contingencies which placed Canadian co-operatives on their non-partisan path, the different path taken by British co-operatives, and finally whether Canadian co-operatives are likely to change their representational politics in the future.

The Character and Causes of Co-operative Political Neutrality in Canada

Several accidents of history do much to explain the Canadian co-operative movement's strict interpretation of the Rochdale principle regarding political neutrality.[9] One set of accidents involves the experiences and ideological perspectives of major Co-operative Union of Canada (CUC) leaders from 1900 to 1930. A second set relates to the absence of a viable social democratic party in Canadian political life until the early years of the Great Depression. Another factor is the heterogeneity of co-operative enterprise across Canada, and the CUC's consequent difficulties in speaking effectively to and for these co-operatives. Relative prosperity of the regional economies since the Second World War, and the growth of an extensive welfare state during the same period, are also important. Finally, evolution of some major co-operatives into bureaucratic and management-dominated institutions has depoliticized many issues once deemed crucial by co-operative members. The cumulative effect of these factors is that co-operative leaders have rejected partisan representation or alliances, since they have not seen such representation as essential to defending co-operative enterprise and their members' communities.

Early Canadian co-operative leaders' experiences provided an initial and perhaps decisive bias against direct co-operative participation in partisan politics.[10] George Keen was involved with the Liberal party and then briefly with a local branch of the Independent Labour Party in southern Ontario before the First World War. W.C. Good's experience was with the United Farmers of Ontario from 1910 to 1933, and on the margins of the early CCF. Early in their public lives these senior statesmen of the fledgling CUC developed a very low opinion of the value of partisan political activity to the co-operative cause.[11] This opinion was communicated with considerable force to all CUC affiliates.

In Keen's case, the disillusionment started with the federal Liberals' unwillingness from 1906 to 1911 to deliver on a campaign promise to enact distinct legislation for co-operative societies. Shortly after the 1911 election Keen told readers of the *Canadian Co-operator* that 'Canada is bankrupt in political principles, and the policy of both parties is one of opportunism only.'[12] His disillusionment with political life deepened with mounting evidence that even promising local third-party activity was being dominated by shallow, careerist politicians, and thus appeared unable to provide a principled alternative to competitive politics.[13] Keen's alienation from party political activities came to a head from 1926 to 1931, with the struggle between the CUC and warring factions of the Communist party over the political activities and autonomy of several prominent and successful co-operatives in northern Ontario.[14]

In Good's case, experience as a United Farmer MP from 1921 to 1925 accentuated his already low opinion of conventional party politics. It convinced him that participation in any party-structured competition or legislative forum was a waste of time. He felt that this was true whether one was trying to promote either the co-operative cause or other 'rational' alternatives to the established political economy. Good gradually refined a purist's critique of Canadian party politics, which retained some of the principles but also rather too much of the naivety of the non-partisan perspective within Canadian agrarian politics from 1917 to 1935.[15] For both Keen and Good, 'politics increasingly became an unimportant arena: torn by personal rivalries, perplexed by ideological hair-splitting, characterized by pandering to the masses, politics was incapable of ultimately changing society.'[16] The preferred instrument of reform was 'co-operativism,' which politicians could only contaminate.

The early CUC leaders' anti-partisan conclusions about political life are reminiscent of those drawn by contemporary populist politicians and farmers' movement leaders in the prairie West. The conjunction of anti-party and pro-co-operative sentiment was most striking and theoretically advanced within the United Farmers of Alberta, particularly Henry Wise Wood and William Irvine. They eventually developed distinctive strategies to advance their common goals, and both approaches differed significantly from those of the CUC leadership. Wood was more narrowly devoted to co-operation as a superior alternative to all other forms of economic activity. Irvine's advocacy of co-operation in economic and political life was more a strategic decision regarding creation of an anti-capitalist, social democratic political movement than a commitment to co-operation per se.

Yet even Wood's co-operativist theory of social evolution required political action by the combined forces of democratic co-operation to defeat the forces of competition and Mammon. Thus while he was essentially pushed into agreeing to have his organization enter the partisan political fray as early as 1920, he never gave up on politics as did Good. Wood's organization held government office from 1921 to 1935 in Alberta, without apparent damage to its co-operative promotional activities, and he never directly participated in legislative debate.

William Irvine became disgusted with the policies and practices of the old-line political parties immediately following his 1907 arrival in western Canada. Surveying the range of progressive forces in the region, he quickly recognized the potential of organized farmers and their co-operatives. When no social democratic party emerged in the war's aftermath to coalesce progressive forces, he became an advocate of occupational political representation. Irvine married the rationale of functional representation and workers' control in G.D.H. Cole's 'guild socialism' to the United Farmers' forms of delegate democracy and Wood's vision of group government.

By the late 1920s the group government proposal had not attracted support outside some provincial farmers' organizations. Irvine returned to a search for the most viable vehicles of social democratic reform in the Canadian context. He continued to support co-operatives, but could see no hope for their success in the absence of partisan political activity. Politically detached anti-capitalism was not enough for him; co-operatives could only benefit society if they supported socialist parties, whose legislation would ensure the success of co-operative business and values. By themselves co-operative enterprises could not reform society, since only socialism would ensure the removal of capitalism. Unlike Good,[17] Irvine saw socialism as almost a sufficient condition of democracy.

It is worth imagining what might have happened if a message like Irvine's had found a larger receptive audience within co-operative circles. Would the eventual result have been either a greater co-operative lobby within at least one of the national parties, or a separate party which maintained close ties with another party whose support for co-ops was most dependable? Might there have been a greater degree of ideological homogeneity among co-operative leaders and members as a result of the self-selection that would occur within a more clearly politicized set of economic organizations? And would such ideological bearings have remained more to the left over time?

The second historical factor to consider is the failure of social democratic party politics at the national level in Canada, at least relative to western European experience. We are not primarily interested here in why no Canadian third party has displaced the party of moderate liberal reform as one of the two major political forces in their polities, as social democratic parties have done in much of western Europe.[18] The major question is, rather, what might have happened to the co-operative movement's stance on party politics if the CCF had experienced a breakthrough nationally, or even beyond Saskatchewan in regions of co-operative strength?

Co-operative leaders were generally disillusioned with the national Liberal and Conservative parties as instruments of reform. However, they saw dangers in alignments with the sectarian and parochial socialist parties existing before 1932, and also perceived dangers in similar alignments with a perennially third-place party after the CCF became such a party. Co-operatives had enough trouble getting the ear of government officials and ministers; why should they make things worse by antagonizing these people with red flags of partisan opposition to their governments? It would be different if these ministers and officials believed that they might well be replaced by or serve under CCF politicians after the next election, but this threat never seemed plausible outside of Saskatchewan. (In that province, of course, the networks of friendship and organizational association between CCF politicians and co-operative leaders provided the basis of an unofficial yet mutually advantageous alliance from at least 1938 to 1960.) The plausibility of such an occurrence was a strong factor in British co-operative leaders' decision to establish a mutually beneficial electoral alliance that has lasted from 1927 to the present.

If a social movement sees no point in taking risks by directly entering political competition, its leaders will feel much less challenge to define its preferred form of representation. The stakes involved in moving more in the direction of either mandated or independent representation of group interests are smaller if representation does not take place in public forums through partisan vehicles. Such groups are then less likely to come to terms with what their members need and want, and to determine what might be their most appropriate long-term contribution to social reform. Choices among forms of representation inevitably raise many issues which sharpen a group's understanding of its relations with the rest of society. As we will note later, these same questions can also be very divisive, and it would not be surprising if some leaders within any movement did not wish to risk major internal debates for the sake of ideological clarity and long-term reform.

But if these questions are not addressed at a relatively early stage of co-operative organizational and movement development, they will soon take a back seat to operational and business considerations. They are then in danger of becoming little more than a source of bad conscience to the organizations which originated as vehicles of reform. Although partisan activity has deflected its participants from these questions on many occasions, it still remains one of the few means of coalescing the reform activities of heterogeneous interests, since it is only through partisan activity that social movements can share control over the state's policy agenda.

There are many other considerations concerning the effect that alignment with a nationally competitive CCF/NDP might have had on Canadian co-operatives.[19] This question might have arisen for debate within the Canadian movement, and perhaps even have been resolved in favour of such alignment, if the question had been forcefully put between 1940 and 1949. Before 1940 the CCF had not shown much potential as a national party. From 1949 until the present, the cold war, the success of liberal reform and 'welfare capitalism,' the success of the major co-operatives within their respective markets, and the alignment of organized labour with the NDP have all reduced co-operators' attraction to alignment with partisan social democracy.

Had some alliance between the CCF and the co-operative movement been arranged, what might have been the eventual effect on the movement's leadership and public image? If the British and Scandinavian cases are anything to go by, we can guess that Canadian co-operatives would have been led by a more ideologically committed and left-wing group than has emerged since the Second World War. This presumes, of course, that the CCF/NDP would have emerged as one of the two major parties, and that both the political culture and state-promoted range of business opportunities would thus have favoured co-operative expansion in ways that were more directly linked to the social philosophy and values of the earlier co-operative movement.

As it was, Canadian national politics were never defined by a partisan political cleavage over the question of support for or opposition to capitalism and private corporate power, as occurred in Britain and Scandinavia between 1918 and 1935.[20] Canadian co-operators' views of political life and their strategic political options were thus differently constructed than their European fellows'. They never felt forced to choose between partisan forces that would continue to threaten co-operatives' viability and those that could be most relied on to enhance this viability. Our co-operative traditions and leaders became comfortable with partisan political neutrality well before a viable social democratic contender entered public life. These leaders have never, as a group, felt comfortable about the CCF's attempt to redefine political debate along the lines of the 'capitalism question.' Leader acceptance of partisan neutrality then reinforced the power of other forces militating against co-operatives' entrance into the partisan fray and thus contributed to the general perception among political parties that there were no obvious electoral returns to be gained from appeals to the 'co-operativism' in co-operative membership constituencies.

With a general idea of the factors that prevented a formal alliance between the national co-operative movement and a political party, we can now consider what produced the opposite result in Britain. When we return to the Canadian case, we will examine how the gulf between co-operative organizations and social democratic forces has deepened since the Second World War.

Co-operatives and Partisan Politics in Britain

It can be argued that the adoption of partisan activities and alliances by the British co-operative movement just after the First World War was almost as accidental as the political neutrality of the Canadian movement. Indeed, a perceptive historian of the British movement has contended that 'the essential point to observe is that what brought the Co-operative Movement into politics was not a conscious will to unite on a common political programme or to form a new party in any ordinary sense, but a feeling of acute grievance and a disbelief that co-operation could ever look for fair treatment from Governments unless it took matters actively into its own hands.'[21]

But the circumstances surrounding the 1917 decision to take as yet undefined political action were considerably more supportive of longer-term partisan alliances than ever existed in Canada. In the first place, the British co-operative movement had been overwhelmingly dominated by retail co-operatives affiliated to the Co-operative Wholesale Society since before the turn of the century. Secondly, the membership of these retail societies had been predominantly working class since the middle of the nineteenth century. Defending co-operators' interests against those of 'private traders' and their political allies in the Conservative party thus always meant defending the interests of working-class consumers. The Labour party has always recognized that appealing to this consumer interest is an important part of its overall political appeal, and hence has little trouble attending to the general concerns of co-operators as consumers.

With the co-operative movement's business objectives and membership base so homogeneous, functional and mandated representation are much more viable options. The Co-operative Union in Britain has experienced internal political opposition over the question of alliance to the Labour party by its own

Co-operative party, and over the question of whether any co-operative 'party' need exist; but this opposition to partisan activity pales in comparison to that within the Canadian co-operative sector.

The emergence of the Labour party as the major opposition to the Conservatives after the First World War was also essential to partisan activity by the British co-operative movement. It is true that most senior leaders and local activists within the movement were socialists by the war, and were often privately active in Labour politics.[22] But had they not seen the recent rapid rise of Labour and the corresponding decline of the Liberal party, they would likely have avoided adopting the Labour party as one of two main vehicles of political representation – even though they believed that only Labour would ultimately care about or be able to serve their members' interests.

Britain's unitary political system also favoured an alliance of Co-operative and Labour parties. Once the Labour party developed a policy on a particular issue, whether in annual convention, parliamentary caucus, or cabinet, that policy applied throughout Britain. Unlike the Canadian movement, the British movement did not have to worry about twelve party organizations responding to twelve distinct party systems, policy environments, and political cultures. National government legislation was of the greatest importance to co-operators, even though local municipal councils might contribute to small co-operative development projects from region to region. In the Canadian case, of course, provincial legislation and economic development policy have generally been much more important to co-operatives, with several notable exceptions such as the federal Wheat Board. In short, the British co-operative movement was lucky to have one party as organizational and legislative target on which to focus the bulk of its representational energies. This situation gave British co-operators greater confidence that their attempts to influence Labour policy would be successful. This is true even though there have always been conflicts between the two personalities of their working-class constituency: the consumer and the organized trade unionist.

We should backtrack now to outline the process by which the British movement developed an official partisan extension and alliance, and the practical arrangements that made this alliance useful to both parties. The Independent Labour party was founded in 1892, and the more broadly based Labour party was created in 1906. During this period sympathetic co-operative leaders made several attempts to establish electoral and reform alliances between co-operators and working-class political representatives. Co-operative activists successfully promoted resolutions supportive of such action at several Co-operative Union congresses before the First World War. They initiated negotiations between the Union's Parliamentary Committee, the Trades Union

Congress, and Labour party officials, but could not muster support by a majority of local co-operative societies.

The matter was left unresolved until the pro-partisan activists found issues favourable to their cause. In 1917 disgust with wartime abuses in food control procedures, and inequitable subjection of co-operative societies to an excess profits duty, allowed activists to crystallize rank-and-file opposition to the government and the Tory party–private sector nexus.[23] At a special national emergency conference in 1917, the Co-operative Congress resolved that 'in view of the persistent attacks and misrepresentations made by the opponents of the Co-operative Movement in Parliament and on local administrative bodies, this Congress is of the opinion that the time has arrived when Co-operators should secure direct representation in Parliament and on all local administrative bodies. It therefore calls upon the Central Board of the Co-operative Union to take such steps as may be necessary to put into operation the terms of the above resolution.'[24]

This resolution committed the union to some form of direct representation, which did not necessarily entail the creation of a distinct political party, and certainly required no alliance with Labour. By the standards of the movement it was a large step to suspend temporarily the fear that organized political activity would cost local societies customers and money, especially since many co-operators had been voting Liberal until the war. Between 1917 and 1919 the issues of independent party formation and subsequent alliance were raised more explicitly. Reform of the Labour party constitution in 1918 opened it up to constituencies beyond the trade unions, as did publication of its *Labour and the New Social Order* manifesto, with its proposals for social and economic reform.

These developments made the direct representational strategy of the co-operative movement at once more complicated and more obvious. It was more complicated because for direct representation of co-operative interests in Parliament, a Co-operative party or its equivalent would have to arrange some mutually beneficial electoral alliance with the Labour party. After all, both groups had essentially the same electoral base, and the Labour party had already established itself as the primary contender against the Conservative party. The strategy was obvious, however, because any direct representation would have to involve such electoral alliances; there were simply no other practical alternatives, once the decision to proceed with direct political action had been made.[25]

In 1919 the Co-operative Representation Committee became the Co-operative party. The Co-operative Union's annual congress instructed the new party to begin negotiating with the Labour party and the Trades Union

Congress for an electoral federation, 'with the ultimate aim of a United People's or Democratic Party.'[26] At the 1920 congress proponents of this strategy proposed a joint body to take instruction from all three organizations' congresses, to prevent policy clashes in public debate when possible, and to co-ordinate mutual endorsement of local candidates.

Co-operative Union congress delegates defeated this proposal by a four-vote margin. But in the 1923 general election four of six successful Co-operative party candidates became either Parliamentary secretaries to ministers, or ministers in a Labour government. The others also caucused with the parliamentary Labour party, both before and after its defeat a year later. These harmonious and mutually advantageous relations between Co-operative and Labour party MPs paved the way for a more formal alliance. Local co-operative party organizations could affiliate with local Labour party organizations, paying affiliation fees and receiving delegate representation in local and national Labour party meetings. This proposal barely passed the 1927 Co-operative congress, since it entailed a decline in the Co-operative party's independence. Nonetheless, its victory signalled a majority recognition of the futility of dividing working-class efforts in the political realm.

Since 1927 interest in the activities of the Co-operative party within the co-operative movement has waxed and waned, usually in response to perceived threats to the retail co-operative sector from Conservative governments' policies, or to Labour party attempts to dominate within the joint local organizations. Labour party policy positions which appear to diminish the role of co-operative distribution, to the advantage of state industries or state regulatory bodies, have also intermittently raised the question of the two-party alliance among co-operative leaders and activists.

For many years the Co-operative party was a creature of the annual co-operative congresses, kept alive in several dozen constituencies where active alliances between Labour and Co-operative organizations have been sustained. The question of responsibility in representation has been further complicated by the *de facto* requirement that Labour-Co-operative MPs accept the Labour party's constitution and changing program. As Cole contended presciently in 1944, the 'impetus towards political activity comes from quite a small fraction of the total membership' of the British co-operative movement.[27] In the last general election only nineteen candidates contested seats under the Labour/Co-operative banner, with nine successful. However, despite continuing disputes over joint organizational matters, there have been surprisingly few fundamental differences between the two parties on policy matters. Even the question of the appropriate mix of public and co-operative enterprise in different sectors of the economy has not raised much serious debate since the Second

World War outside relatively isolated, academic forums.[28]

In the absence of basic policy disputes that can excite either co-operative or labour rank and file, the obvious question for co-operators to address regarding their political activity is strategic. Is there still a need for a separate Co-operative party, when it has become little more than an adjunct of the Labour party in less than 5 per cent of British constituencies? What would be lost if the co-operative movement sought close ties with individual MPs from any party who have shown some sympathy for co-operatives? Could a strategy of 'retained MPs' working in conjunction with the lobbying efforts of the Co-operative Union (or Co-operative Wholesale Society) not achieve better results for smaller costs in both autonomy and finance?

Intermittently one can witness considerable debate on such questions within British co-operative circles. The Liberal party has a vested interest in stirring the pot. Liberals argue that Labour party statism is falling out of favour with the public, and that the Labour/Co-operative electoral alliance is damaging the co-operative movement's image. To their credit, Liberals have played a modest role in promoting worker co-operatives in Britain, although the major practical work has been done by agencies funded by Labour-dominated municipal councils.

In spite of the scale of the Labour defeat in the 1987 national election, most senior co-operative leaders wish to continue the current arrangement. They generally accept the argument that the co-operative movement needs a political focus in its own party to provide it with some greater impetus to think strategically about its place in British society. In practical terms, they see the Co-operative party as a representative mechanism which exerts influence within the councils of a political organization that is sympathetic to the long-term goals of 'the co-operative commonwealth.'[29] Retained MPs seem unlikely to do this as effectively, and their choice by the annual congress could raise the issue of partisan affiliation and political strategy in a destructively divisive way. Representation of co-operative interests in Parliament by Labour MPs will continue as long as Labour is the major alternative to the Conservative party, joint MPs act diplomatically toward both their constituencies, and the co-operative movement remains predominantly working-class.[30]

Contemporary Canadian Co-operatives and Political Representation

We have seen that there are many historical reasons for the rejection of partisan representation by the Canadian co-operative movement and its acceptance in the British case. In this section we will bring the Canadian story up to date to determine the likelihood that the Canadian movement will adopt the British approach. This will involve assessing the hypotheses ventured earlier concerning possible relationships between the character of co-operative movements and the adoption of partisan political alignment as an avenue of political representation.

In the previous chapter we detailed the relationship between the logic of national policy-making and problems in co-operative associational decision-making on policy matters. In recalling the economic and sociological heterogeneity of the Co-operative Union of Canada's membership, we can appreciate that large co-operative organizations face delicate situations when different member interests are to be served through political representation. This problem is magnified in regional or national associations of co-operative business.

If these problems are daunting in the relatively unpublicized activities of policy advocacy and policy participation, then how much more difficult would be reconciliation and representation of interest through the public forums and processes of party activity? This problem lurked in the background of all efforts by early Co-operative Union leaders to broaden its co-operative organizational membership. In practical terms, the question was whether co-operative leaders would have wished to confront their membership with partisan affiliation as the first political 'price' of belonging to a national co-operative association. Only seldom was the answer positive, and agreement on the party with which the movement should align itself was lacking even within this group. The CUC's leaders knew this, and cannot be blamed for thinking that the growth of an inclusive national organization was more important to the movement's success than partisan affiliation. In Albert Hirchman's terminology, they recognized that forcing decisions on partisan affiliation would lead many of their co-operatives' members to choose the 'exit' option for influencing organizational behaviour.[31]

Even if there had been agreement among most co-operative leaders that party X was most likely to promote co-operative growth and values, the problem of representation still stood between such agreement and a decision to affiliate to that party. Keen and Good had personally witnessed the unreliability of the Liberal party on matters close to co-operators' hearts. Good correctly saw that the early CCF, with its ample supply of centralist, technocratic socialists, was by no means an ideal vehicle for co-operative policy representation.[32] What guarantees were there that a CUC link to the CCF would not be treated as a simple marriage of convenience by this element in the party, to be compromised when circumstances required? In the absence of national office control over provincial CCF groups, what good would even these guarantees be if several provincial CCF organizations dealt with local co-operatives in ways that damaged the national co-operative movement's public image? Most provincial co-operative leaders might also have wondered why their movements should suffer slower growth as a function of affiliation to a regionally unpopular party.

The problems posed by organizational heterogeneity among co-operatives begin to seem rather modest after we consider the volatility of their mixture with the problems of policy continuity, competitive success, and inter-regional cultural compatibility within a federal party. And we should also raise the problems entailed in political representation through party. Identifying the interests and positions that would be given voice in a complicated process of mandated representation would be difficult enough. The divisive effects likely to emerge from more independent representatives in any political party could easily scare many co-operative leaders.

We must also consider the perspective of vote-maximizing party leaders and strategists. Would any party be well advised to treat co-operative memberships as a special constituency? This would mean crafting a special appeal, and perhaps allocating a special place and set of perquisites in the party organization. Even the CCF in Saskatchewan never saw the strategic value of concessions going beyond policy commitments, while in Alberta the subject has not been raised since 1935.

The increasing ideological vagueness of most major co-operative business since the Second World War sends a message to all party strategists: co-operative memberships are not sufficiently distinctive to be worth targeting in high-profile public appeals. Party strategists know that people of many socio-economic types join co-operatives, for largely pragmatic rather than ideological reasons. This reinforces parties' inclination to treat co-operative members as subsets of their other support bases. Co-operative leaders have done little to encourage anything else. Their recent election packages do not describe co-operative members as people with significantly different needs, interests, or social perspectives, opting instead for requests for distinctive treatment of co-operatives as businesses.[33]

There is no partisan advantage in offering co-operatives' representatives special status within a party organization if co-operatives do not insist on special treatment that complements current party policy goals and agendas. This combination occurred in Britain from 1917 until at least the Second World War. It has not occurred in Canada, partly because the primary cleavage in partisan competition has never been that of economic class. There has never been consensus among Canadian co-operative leaders and members that the 'co-operative commonwealth,' or even co-operative business success, ultimately requires the supersession of capitalism.

Another obvious obstacle to the success of a co-operative request for special status within a Canadian party organization is the federal character of such organizations. Suppose that the Saskatchewan NDP were to receive such a request from major provincial co-operatives (which is not likely), and see some electoral advantage in accommodating it. It would still be constrained by the need for federal party convention or council agreement to such an arrangement, which would not come easily. Other provincial NDP organizations could see such an alliance as an electoral liability, or as pressure to endorse economic development policies that they would not otherwise. Faced with this situation, provincial co-operative organizations would likely withdraw their request, recalling the conventional wisdom as to why these alliances were more trouble than they are worth.

Another barrier to official co-operative representation through partisan channels also presents a daunting logic. The major co-operatives are all well into a phase of their organizational life-cycles characterized by extensive bureaucratization and increasing power of management in relation to members and elected directors. This process has reinforced the sector-wide disinclination for partisan alliances, and has effectively withdrawn most major co-operatives from all but the most co-op–centric public policy debates. From the perspective of career bureaucrats and managers increasingly schooled to private sector specifications, the risk presented to 'their' corporate welfare by partisan affiliation is simply too great. This risk can always be portrayed as outweighing intangible longer-term benefits in the areas of social reform to which co-operatives have been historically committed. In any case, many of these managers have little sympathy for the co-operative project of meaningful economic democracy. They can thus see no good reason why perfectly good businesses should start messing with 'anti-business' politicians.[34]

Even those managers and bureaucrats who do share their directors' commitments, however, wish to depoliticize issues. For people in bureaucratic work environments, issues and processes would be needlessly complicated by concerns about party interference in business organizational life. The politics of promoting policy through both business associations (co-operative and other) and a political party could easily appear nightmarish.

The question of who really represents co-operatives would awkwardly arise when affiliated party and co-operative business associations took incompatible positions on policy questions. Historically, the national co-operative association has avoided public statements on divisive issues, the number and sensitivity of which has increased in direct proportion to the heterogeneity of co-operatives' memberships and markets. Past CUC leaders, and current leaders of the Canadian Co-operative Association, have recognized that some member firms' interests are incompatible in the short run, or that their reconciliation is not worth the trouble for the national organization. In short, they abdicate the representative function to their organizational juniors, or bury these potentially divisive issues below the surface of issues over which inter–co-operative conflict is unlikely to arise.

But political parties are loath to do this, since their success hinges on their ability to speak for as many interests as possible, in ways that superficially reconcile conflicting interests. It is thus difficult to convince a party to step out of a policy debate, especially when there are other supportive or attractable groups with whom the same policy position will score valuable points. In any case, under the glare of media attention it is difficult for a political party to side-step issues completely.

Fifteen years ago Ian MacPherson commented that 'the turn away from politics ... contributed to the rather limited impact co-operativism ... had on Canada after 1930'; in this country, 'a reform movement operating outside of politics has little chance of gaining widespread support.'[35] There seems to be little reason for believing that forces within the party system or Canada's co-operative sector will alter this situation in the foreseeable future. With even provincial New Democratic parties ignoring specific co-operative constituencies for which appeals can be crafted, it is not surprising that co-operative leaders have seen no great incentive to remove co-operatives from the margins of political life.

The Future of Co-operative Political Representation in Canada

We can now return to the hypotheses advanced in the first section, to see whether they have any value in relating the character of co-operative economic activity and organization to their patterns of representation in the political realm. The first hypothesis concerned the relationship between the commitment of a national co-operative movement to substantial social transformation, and its tendency to seek largely mandated political representation through partisan political channels.

The Canadian movement's early leadership began with a clearly anti-capitalist commitment to social change. However, the coincidence of immaturity and organizational complexity in both Canadian co-operatives and social democratic parties presented almost insuperable barriers to an alliance between the two reform forces. This coincidence heightened, but was by no means responsible for, the leaderships' suspicion about political parties as vehicles of representation. They were understandably concerned that they would cede too much representational independence to existing political parties, and reduce the impact of their preferred mandated representation, if they established formal ties to a political party.

Co-operative leaders' personal experiences reflected this coincidence and amplified the mythology of Rochdale political neutrality to the point where only Alberta and Saskatchewan third parties managed to make practical arrangements for mutual benefit with indigenous co-operative movements. Only in these cases were co-operative business interests perceived to complement widespread third-party support within co-operative constituencies. Such complementarity seems to be the minimum condition of co-operative alliances with parties in Canada. In each case the political reform organizations presented an image something like the 'People's or Democratic Party' that British co-operators originally hoped would result from their alliance with the Labour party.

Where this condition is not met, the other obstacles discussed earlier will prevent alliances and representation through partisan channels. A perception that the most appropriate partisan ally is a perennially third-place finisher in national and most provincial competitions will scuttle such alliances. An increasingly decentralized party system across the country will make commitment to any one party increasingly risky. The complications of economic policy development processes make another level of representation of co-operative interests (through parties) unattractive to those now dominating co-operatives. Management and bureaucratically oriented decision-makers will balk at such prospects more than co-operative leaders, since the leaders still often see representation partially in terms of larger agendas of social change.

Socio-demographic diversification within co-operative memberships is growing so rapidly in Canada that no political party can hope to represent more than vocal minorities within most co-operative organizations. This fact is usually seen by most senior co-operative managers and elected leaders as a sufficient argument not only against partisan alignments, but also against co-operatives' statements on contentious issues of public policy. Recent evidence from a survey of elected officials in Saskatchewan tends to reinforce the argument that co-operatives and politics do not mix because members and elected local leaders wish this to be the case.

With all of these complicating variables, the Canadian case does not provide a very good test of the hypothesis linking the character of the co-operative movement to the choice between partisan and mandated representation. Nonetheless, in tentatively rejecting the hypothesis, we have had to consider other important factors that channelled co-operative political representation into pressure group policy advocacy. There are too many intervening variables for us to say that the early Canadian co-operative movement's gradualist character guaranteed its political neutrality and incrementalist, pressure group approach to representation later on. Co-operative movements in all countries have appeared gradualist in comparison with contemporary radical political forces.

Nonetheless, it is probably fair to say that a gradualist orientation by movement leaders will incline them to be cautious about partisan attachments, and to prefer forms of representation which leave movement institutions and leaders space for flexible manoeuvering. This would mean *prima facie* opposition to partisan alliances, and to mandated representation in either parties or state decision-making bodies, since both means of representation limit the range of options open to leaders regarding both public policy and internal affairs of the movement.

Thus the corollary to our first hypothesis is partly substantiated by the British and Canadian cases. As both movements have become more interested in business success than social change, political influence through relatively conventional channels of interest representation has become the only alternative taken seriously. In the British case, Co-operative party relations to the Labour party have taken the *de facto* character of interest group activity through an established party. Most co-operative leaders and members have ceased thinking of this alliance as a prelude to a 'Co-operative Commonwealth.' Functional representation of the consumer interest happens through the Labour party on the one hand, and through the lobbying activities of the Co-operative Union and CWS on the other. With a co-operative business sector overwhelmingly concerned with retail activities, such a complementarity of representational efforts is possible. Unitary political and party systems are also important in this regard; the British co-operative movement would eliminate formal partisan alignments if its leaders felt that these threatened its lobbying activities.[36]

In the Canadian case the absence of partisan alliances has done a good deal to reinforce the tendency of the co-operative sector to lose more and more of its character as a movement. Its leaders now perceive both their private competitors and the prevailing socio-cultural system in less antagonistic terms than one would expect of a democratic reform movement in capitalist society. Individual co-operatives have generally promoted their business interests through the pragmatic mechanisms described in chapter 17.

It is also important to recognize that the policy-making logic of the federal policy process pushes individual co-operatives further in this direction. Development of policy consensus on most reform-related issues necessarily diverts attention and effort away from particular business concerns of particular co-operatives, and is largely avoided. Thus the policy process which co-operatives must penetrate undermines the conditions of movement-maintenance. Opportunities to integrate business concerns with broader reform orientations do not often arise in this policy process. When they do, as in the advocacy of new forms of co-operative development, it is still difficult to produce consensus on strategies for movement-bolstering activity among co-operative business enterprises.[37]

Perhaps the easiest of our earlier hypotheses to evaluate here concerns the relationship between the degree of business and member homogeneity within the co-operative movement, and the inclination of leaders to seek partisan affiliations. The contrast between the British and the Canadian cases suggests that member and organizational similarity is the *sine qua non* of partisan affiliation by co-operative movements. One might argue that the dependent variable in this relation is the strength of the social democratic party in the national political scene. But it is clear that this, too, is dependent on cultural and sociological homogeneity of a working-class population that loses faith in 'bourgeois' parties.

Since the degree of cultural and sociological homogeneity in the Canadian working-class and farmer populations was never high nationally, partisan affiliation was always a difficult proposition. Now that the larger Canadian co-operatives have memberships with diverse class and other characteristics, partisan affiliation would alienate those members who see nothing political in their co-operative memberships. Informal partisan affiliation, like that between the co-operatives and the CCF in the 1935-60 period in Saskatchewan, was possible because a high degree of socio-cultural homogeneity within co-operative memberships was complemented by a CCF party and government commitment to co-operatives as a form of 'social ownership.'

Co-operatives easily contain the largest number of citizens involved in Canadian democratic organizations. Given their avoidance of direct involvement in the world of partisan politics, they are also the Canadian organizations with perhaps the trickiest set of problems in representing their concerns to the political realm. In this and the previous chapter we have seen a good number of historical and structural reasons for these difficulties. In the previous chapter we saw that the most likely future departures in the area of co-operative political representation will build on tentative moves toward the establishment of weak, quasi-corporatist relations between the major co-operatives and the federal government. This approach will remove co-operatives further from their traditions of mandated representation and autonomy from the agendas of particular governments, two of the co-operative democratic virtues supposedly threatened by any form of partisan affiliation.

If Canadian co-operatives continue to emphasize business success much more than the reformist thrust of community economic democracy, continued partisan neutrality and increased involvement in 'policy participation' may be

.the only viable alternatives for representation of co-operative interests in Canadian national politics. Individual co-operatives may take activist stances on matters of public debate related to the larger campaign for economic democracy. In doing so, they can still stop well short of formal alignment with a political party, although they will understand that co-operative and other politically sensitive publics will nonetheless believe that an informal alignment exists. There are business expansionary costs to be paid for elevating democratic reform objectives above the level that most public officials, politicians and businessmen in Canada deem appropriate.[38] As long as some co-operative leaders are willing to pay these costs, the issues of political neutrality and interest representation are unlikely to be settled in Canadian co-operatives.

LARS APLAND

12 Election of Directors in Saskatchewan Co-operatives: Some Attributes of Success

This chapter argues that it is inappropriate to focus on democratic processes or mechanisms as the sole means by which to assess the co-operative sector's democratic health. An assessment of the democratic process must include an analysis of the results of that process. Accordingly, the chapter provides an analysis of electoral results of directors of Saskatchewan co-operatives, based on findings from a survey conducted by the Centre for the Study of Co-operatives. Of necessity, the discussion of survey results is somewhat descriptive, since there is little information with which to compare it.

Introduction: Assessing Democratic Health

Democracy and its implicit notion of member control are features which help define co-operatives and distinguish them from most other organizations. For co-operative organizations to maintain their distinctiveness, their democratic process must be healthy and effective. Clearly, the democratic principle of one member, one vote has little value unless it translates into member control. Accordingly, an assessment of the processes and results of co-operative democracy will, to some extent, be an assessment of the health of the co-operative sector as a whole.

There are various criteria by which the democratic processes of any organization may be measured. A primary consideration, of course, is whether elections are held; democracy cannot exist without opportunities for popular participation. The existence of electoral structures is often considered to be conclusive evidence of the presence of democracy, while the more important question of whether that democracy is healthy is often forgotten or ignored. To address this question, it is necessary to assess the results of the democratic process.

For a healthy democracy, it is essential that voters have real choices available to them, and that there be prospects for their decisions to result in change. That an informed choice between real options is made and implemented is as important as the process by which that decision is reached. If, for instance, there consistently is no competition for board positions and, hence, no choices for voters to make, the electoral process, while perhaps functional, cannot be described as democratically healthy. If voters are uninformed, elections may become virtual coronations for some directors, and while an uninformed decision may be made democratically, once again, it is not necessarily indicative of democratic health. Indeed, Åke Linden and Roland Norman of the Co-operative Union and Wholesale Society of Stockholm, Sweden, have argued that democracy in co-operatives should be given a more normative interpretation to reflect ideological content more than form.[1] Results are just as important as democratic structure and process.

The results of a formal democratic process cannot fully be assessed or understood without some consideration of issues such as the equality of voters, the opportunities for individuals to become involved in the democratic process, the electoral system used, and the qualities and characteristics of individual candidates. Furthermore, while change in itself cannot be the definitive indicator, its presence clearly suggests some democratic health. Simply on this basis, it would be improper to suggest an appropriate rate of electoral change (i.e., rate of incumbency) among directors of co-operatives. But the comparison of these rates will provide a point of reference from which the electoral performance of various co-operative organizations and of particular individuals may be compared and assessed.

Examining characteristics of the directors who have been elected is likely to indicate the character of particular co-operative organizations and, perhaps, of the sector as a whole. There are many reasons that some individuals are elected and re-elected and others are rejected, but if a higher rate of electoral success can be attributed to particular social, political, or economic attributes and views of those who are elected, this should provide some insight into the nature of parts or of the whole of the co-operative sector. Accordingly, an examination of democratic processes in the co-operative sector also requires a critical assessment of the nature and characteristics of those who are elected through it.

With these and other considerations to the fore, the Centre for the Study of Co-operatives conducted a self-administered mail survey of directors of Saskatchewan co-operatives. From 26 January to 12 February 1986, questionnaires were mailed to the directors of every known co-operative in the province. The survey sought factual and statistical information on directors and the co-operatives in which they were involved. It also attempted to elicit the directors' views on a number of concerns and issues faced by co-operatives and by the whole of society. Information gathered from the survey provided the basis for this analysis and the discussion of these issues.[2]

Rates of Incumbency

For the purposes of this study, rate of incumbency was defined as the percentage of respondent directors serving in their second or higher consecutive term of office. On this basis, the average rate of incumbency for directors in Saskatchewan's co-operative sector was found to be 63.1 per cent. This figure provided a focal point from which incumbency rates attributed to particular groupings of directors could be compared and assessed.

While a complete understanding of all the factors that affect rates of director incumbency is unlikely, numerous valid assumptions can be made about the kind and extent of various influences. Organizational characteristics, such as the kind of co-operative,[3] its age, and its membership size, as well as directors' personal attributes, will undoubtedly influence the rate of director incumbency. Although the ways these factors affected incumbency rates may not be easy to ascertain, analysis of them may reveal results that are incongruent with co-operative philosophy but have stemmed from members' acceptance of the co-operative sector's ostensibly inherent democratic processes.

This point is illustrated by considering the sex of directors who responded to the survey (Table 1). The figures in the table do not accurately reflect the demographic reality of society. Accordingly, it would appear that the co-operative sector may have failed to recognize women as a co-operative constituency and that its democratic processes have not represented fairly the female population. In addition, when rate of director incumbency is examined on the basis of the individual's sex, it is apparent that women, once again, are treated differently than men (see Table 2). It can be argued that these results are the natural end of a healthy democratic process. At the same time, however, it is apparent that they are incongruous with the basic principles of member equality and fair representation implicit in co-operative theory. Furthermore, the results may suggest that action should be taken, through member education, electoral measures, or by other means, to promote and encourage more active involvement by women in the affairs and administration of their co-operatives.

When rates of incumbency are determined on the basis of directors' age, it appears that these two factors are positively correlated (see Table 3). This

TABLE 1: Sex of respondents*

Type	Male	Female	No response
	(%)	(%)	(%)
Credit union	91.2 (563)	8.3 (51)	0.5 (3)
Retail	82.6 (347)	16.9 (71)	0.5 (2)
Agicultural implement	85.7 (6)	0.0 (0)	14.3 (1)
Health care	31.8 (7)	68.2 (15)	0.0 (0)
Housing	46.2 (24)	53.8 (28)	0.0 (0)
Wheat pool	100.0 (14)	0.0 (0)	0.0 (0)
Day care	11.1 (19)	85.4 (146)	3.5 (6)
Recreational	64.9 (233)	32.9 (118)	2.2 (8)
Agricultural	86.5 (166)	12.0 (23)	1.6 (3)
Other	80.0 (64)	17.5 (14)	2.5 (2)
Totals†	74.6 (1,443)	24.1 (466)	1.3 (25)

*Total figures for each category are indicated in parentheses.
†21 observations are missing because of incomplete questionnaires.

seems logical since the older an individual, the more opportunity he or she will have had for involvement in the sector. The table indicates, as well, that there is a slight decline in incumbency after age sixty-five, reflecting a natural reduction in involvement following retirement.

Table 4 indicates the level of education achieved by directors in the sector. It shows that over 54 per cent of responding directors were without any post-secondary education. It is likely that these education levels stem from and reflect the demographic and social realities of rural Saskatchewan.

Given the lengthy history of co-operative development in Saskatchewan, it is not surprising that older individuals with lower levels of education constitute a substantial proportion of co-operative directors. And, in many cases, higher levels of education may be unnecessary for director competence. Indeed, there are demographic reasons and, in some organizations, justification for the presence of directors who have not been educated beyond high school. The relatively low percentage of more highly educated directors from professionally directed retail co-operatives and credit unions, however, may come as some surprise and may be a factor in the health of the co-operative sector.

If level of education is taken as the basis for comparison of incumbency rates, those directors in the 'Grade 9 or less' category enjoy the highest rate of re-election: 75.9 per cent (see Table 5). The relationship between incumbency and level of education is inverse. Given that the vast majority of co-operatives in the sector have existed for more than ten years, it is likely that re-election rates based on education reflect an older population that, again for reasons of

TABLE 2: Incumbency according to sex of directors

Sex of director	Consecutive terms served						Incumbency rate
	1	2	3	4	5 or more	No response	
	(%)	(%)	(%)	(%)	(%)	(%)	(%)
Female	55.1 (254)	20.8 (96)	8.0 (37)	2.8 (13)	8.9 (41)	4.3 (20)	40.6
Male	28.0 (401)	23.2 (333)	16.2 (232)	8.0 (114)	23.0 (330)	1.6 (23)	70.4
No response	36.0 (9)	24.0 (6)	8.0 (2)	8.0 (2)	8.0 (2)	16.0 (4)	48.0
Totals*	34.6 (664)	22.7 (435)	14.1 (271)	6.7 (129)	19.4 (373)	2.4 (47)	63.1

*36 observations are missing because of incomplete questionnaires.

TABLE 3: Incumbency according to directors' age

Directors' age (years)	Consecutive terms served						Incumbency rate
	1	2	3	4	5 or more	No response	
	(%)	(%)	(%)	(%)	(%)	(%)	(%)
18-25	81.6 (40)	10.2 (5)	2.0 (1)	0.0 (0)	2.0 (1)	4.1 (2)	14.3
26-35	53.8 (266)	24.9 (123)	11.7 (58)	3.0 (15)	4.7 (23)	1.8 (9)	44.4
36-45	37.5 (173)	28.0 (129)	15.2 (70)	7.2 (33)	9.8 (45)	2.4 (11)	60.1
46-55	24.5 (98)	21.8 (87)	20.0 (80)	9.3 (37)	23.8 (95)	0.8 (3)	74.7
56-65	15.9 (50)	18.8 (59)	12.4 (39)	7.6 (24)	42.4 (133)	2.9 (9)	81.2
Over 65	16.5 (30)	15.4 (28)	11.5 (21)	10.4 (19)	40.7 (74)	5.5 (10)	78.0
No response	36.8 (7)	21.1 (4)	10.5 (2)	5.3 (1)	10.5 (2)	15.8 (3)	47.4
Totals*	34.6 (664)	22.7 (435)	14.1 (271)	6.7 (129)	19.4 (373)	2.4 (47)	63.1

*36 observations are missing because of incomplete questionnaires.

TABLE 4: Education of directors

Type	Level of education					No response
	Grade 9 or less	High school	College/ technical	Some university	University degree	
	(%)	(%)	(%)	(%)	(%)	(%)
Credit union	21.9 (135)	29.0 (179)	13.5 (83)	15.7 (97)	19.4 (120)	0.5 (3)
Retail	17.6 (74)	33.8 (142)	14.3 (60)	17.4 (73)	15.0 (63)	1.9 (8)
Agricultural Implement	0.0 (0)	28.6 (2)	0.0 (0)	28.6 (2)	28.6 (2)	14.3 (1)
Health care	18.2 (4)	13.6 (3)	4.5 (1)	36.4 (8)	27.3 (6)	0.0 (0)
Housing	9.6 (5)	26.9 (14)	21.2 (11)	19.2 (10)	19.2 (10)	3.8 (2)
Wheat pool	14.3 (2)	28.6 (4)	7.1 (1)	50.0 (7)	0.0 (0)	0.0 (0)
Day care	3.5 (6)	33.9 (58)	23.4 (40)	16.4 (28)	19.3 (33)	3.5 (6)
Recreational	29.0 (104)	41.5 (149)	12.8 (46)	7.2 (26)	5.6 (20	3.9 (14)
Agricultural	30.2 (58)	38.5 (74)	10.4 (20)	9.9 (19)	7.8 (15)	3.1 (6)
Other	20.0 (16)	32.5 (26)	11.3 (9)	12.5 (10)	18.8 (15)	5.0 (4)
Totals*	20.9 (404)	33.7 (651)	14.0 (271)	14.5 (280)	14.7 (284)	2.3 (44)

*21 observations are missing because of incomplete questionnaires.

TABLE 5: Incumbency according to directors' education

Level of education	Consecutive terms served					No response	Incumbency rate
	1	2	3	4	5 or more		
	(%)	(%)	(%)	(%)	(%)	(%)	(%)
Grade 9 or less	21.1 (84)	20.6 (82)	14.8 (59)	9.5 (38)	31.1 (124)	3.0 (12)	75.9
High school	37.2 (239)	19.9 (128)	15.1 (97)	5.3 (34)	20.5 (132)	2.0 (13)	60.8
College/Technical	39.3 (106)	23.3 (63)	13.7 (37)	5.9 (16)	14.1 (38)	3.7 (10)	57.0
Some university	37.5 (105)	25.0 (70)	14.3 (40)	5.7 (16)	16.1 (45)	1.4 (4)	61.1
University degree	40.5 (115)	28.5 (81)	12.7 (36)	8.5 (24)	9.2 (26)	0.7 (2)	58.8
No response	34.9 (15)	25.6 (11)	4.7 (2)	2.3 (1)	18.6 (8)	14.0 (6)	51.1
Totals*	34.6 (664)	22.7 (435)	14.1 (271)	6.7 (129)	19.4 (373)	2.4 (47)	63.1

*36 observations are missing because of incomplete questionnaires.

historical development, did not have access to or opportunity for advanced education. At the same time, however, these rates seem to suggest that a higher level of education is a handicap to director incumbency.

As seen earlier, the average rate of incumbency for directors in Saskatchewan's co-operative sector was found to be 63.1 per cent. Table 6 provides a breakdown of this figure, from the standpoint of the different kinds of organizations in the sector and the consecutive terms served by their respective directors. The table indicates that day-care co-operatives had the lowest rate of incumbency in the sector while agricultural co-operatives had the highest rate of re-election on an organizational basis.

In some instances, incumbency rates can be attributed to characteristics of particular kinds of co-operatives. The high rate of director incumbency for agricultural co-operatives, for example, may be attributable at least in part to many of these organizations having been small and informal and, accordingly, conferring directorships on all who joined them. When asked to indicate the length of time they had served, these member-directors often responded '5 or more' consecutive terms and commented in writing that no elections were held. Day-care co-operatives have a relatively transient membership and board of directors because, by their nature, these organizations are of utility to individuals, for a limited time. It may well be that these organizations are useful to particular individuals directoral term. Finally, day-care co-operatives are a relatively recent phenomenon in the province; many of them have not existed long enough for more than one or two terms to have expired. All these factors may contribute to a low rate of incumbency for day-care organizations. A similar assessment might be made of incumbency rates for directors of housing co-operatives, since these have only recently developed in Saskatchewan.

The data in Table 7 suggest that rates of incumbency increase with organizational age. If this is the case, it is consistent with Robert Michels's 'Iron Law of Oligarchy,' according to which leadership and control in any democratic entity tend to become concentrated among a few individuals over time.[4]

While the sample size for organizations in the 'over 25,000' membership category is quite small, directors of these co-operatives were found to have the lowest rates of re-election when incumbency is determined on the basis of organizational size. This is an interesting point for several reasons. Although charges of democratic unresponsiveness have most often been levelled at these larger organizations, a low rate of incumbency may indicate that they are actually democratically responsive, since electoral change is not hindered. But it also may suggest that members of these organizations are dissatisfied with their

TABLE 6: Incumbency among co-operative directors

Type	Consecutive terms served					No response	Incumbency rate
	1	2	3	4	5 or more		
	(%)	(%)	(%)	(%)	(%)	(%)	(%)
Credit union	27.6 (170)	25.8 (159)	17.2 (106)	7.6 (47)	21.1 (130)	0.8 (5)	71.6
Retail	34.6 (146)	24.2 (102)	13.5 (57)	6.9 (29)	19.9 (84)	0.9 (4)	64.5
Agricultural implement	28.6 (2)	14.3 (1)	0.0 (0)	14.3 (1)	28.6 (2)	14.3 (1)	57.1
Health care	36.4 (8)	18.2 (4)	18.2 (4)	4.5 (1)	9.1 (2)	13.6 (3)	50.0
Housing	61.5 (32)	28.8 (15)	1.9 (1)	0.0 (0)	5.8 (3)	1.9 (1)	36.6
Wheat Pool	35.7 (5)	7.1 (1)	21.4 (3)	0.0 (0)	35.7 (5)	0.0 (0)	64.3
Daycare	70.2 (120)	17.5 (30)	3.5 (6)	2.3 (4)	1.8 (3)	4.7 (8)	25.1
Recreational	32.6 (115)	22.7 (80)	15.3 (54)	8.2 (29)	17.6 (62)	3.7 (13)	63.7
Agricultural	23.1 (43)	15.1 (28)	14.0 (26)	7.5 (14)	37.6 (70)	2.7 (5)	74.2
Other	29.5 (23)	19.2 (15)	17.9 (14)	6.4 (5)	17.9 (14)	9.0 (7)	61.5
Totals*	34.5 (664)	22.6 (435)	14.1 (271)	6.8 (130)	19.5 (375)	2.4 (47)	63.1

*33 observations are missing because of incomplete questionnaires.

TABLE 7: Incumbency according to age of co-operative

Age of co-operative	Consecutive terms served					No response	Incumbency rate
	1	2	3	4	5 or more		
	(%)	(%)	(%)	(%)	(%)	(%)	(%)
Less than 2 years	83.7 (82)	10.2 (10)	0.0 (0)	0.0 (0)	0.0 (0)	6.1 (6)	10.2
2-5 years	59.6 (81)	25.7 (35)	7.4 (10)	1.5 (2)	2.2 (3)	3.7 (5)	36.7
6-10 years	40.1 (61)	21.1 (32)	15.8 (24)	2.0 (3)	17.1 (26)	3.9 (6)	56.0
10 years or more	28.7 (438)	23.3 (356)	15.4 (236)	8.2 (125)	22.6 (345)	1.8 (28)	69.5
No response	28.6 (2)	14.3 (1)	14.3 (1)	0.0 (0)	14.3 (1)	28.6 (2)	42.8
Totals*	34.6 (664)	22.6 (434)	14.1 (271)	6.8 (130)	19.5 (375)	2.4 (47)	63.1

*34 observations are missing because of incomplete questionnaires.

TABLE 8: Incumbency based on organizations' size

Number of members	Consecutive terms served					No response	Incumbency rate
	1	2	3	4	5 or more		
	(%)	(%)	(%)	(%)	(%)	(%)	(%)
Under 500	36.9 (391)	21.4 (227)	12.9 (137)	5.8 (62)	19.6 (208)	3.3 (35)	59.8
501-2000	32.5 (164)	25.0 (126)	15.4 (78)	6.7 (34)	20.0 (101)	0.4 (2)	67.1
2001-5000	25.8 (42)	25.2 (41)	18.4 (30)	9.8 (16)	19.6 (32)	1.2 (2)	73.0
5001-10,000	30.5 (18)	25.4 (15)	16.9 (10)	10.2 (6)	15.3 (9)	1.7 (1)	67.8
10,001-25,000	36.0 (27)	21.3 (16)	10.7 (8)	13.3 (10)	17.3 (13)	1.3 (1)	62.7
Over 25,000	44.7 (17)	7.9 (3)	18.4 (7)	5.3 (2)	23.7 (9)	0.0 (0)	55.3
No response	23.8 (5)	28.6 (6)	4.8 (1)	0.0 (0)	14.3 (3)	28.6 (6)	47.6
Totals*	34.6 (664)	22.6 (434)	14.1 (271)	6.8 (130)	19.5 (375)	2.4 (47)	63.1

*34 observations are missing because of incomplete questionnaires.

directors' performance – in other words, the directors are not responsive to member concerns. Nonetheless, it indicates that at least part of the democratic process in these organizations, the electoral system, is responsive to member involvement.

A perusal of the by-laws governing Saskatchewan co-operatives indicates that these larger organizations are the only ones in the sector which might legitimately be characterized by their use of a majority run-off electoral system (as described in section 14(2) of the Co-operative Associations Act of 1963). The lower rates of incumbency attributed to these organizations, therefore, might be an indication that a majority run-off system is more democratically responsive than are other standardized electoral systems in the co-operative sector. However, these larger organizations tend to use systems of representation based on electoral districts which, J.W. Still argued, have the most potential to undermine the democratic process and voter equality.[5] Because population sizes of electoral districts are seldom equal, the democratic process may provide low-population districts with power and influence equal to that of districts with larger populations.

The district system, however, allows for a certain amount of power delegation and decentralization not possible in more structurally unified systems. Its apparent responsiveness to pressures for change may give credence to Alexander Laidlaw's claim that people's involvement needs to be 'decentralized in order to be meaningful and real.'[6]

Finally, while general incumbency was lowest in this size category, the percentage of directors having served five or more consecutive terms was highest in this group as well. Thus, while there has been a relatively high turnover rate on these organizations' boards, it seems that the turnover tends to be among less experienced, newly elected directors. Despite the relatively low rate of incumbency for directors from organizations in this large size category, Table 8 indicates that the rate of re-election tends to be higher among directors who had served the most time on the boards of these co-operatives. Once again, the co-operative experience suggests some consistency with Michels's 'Iron Law of Oligarchy.'

The Analysis of Incumbency: Regression Results

To this point, this analysis has been largely a descriptive and correlative account of information gathered through the survey of Saskatchewan co-operative directors. While some anomalies and electoral tendencies have been illuminated, a clearer understanding of the apparent relationships among various factors requires more sophisticated statistical analysis. The identification of correlations between independent variables such as sex or director age and rates of re-election cannot account for the relationships that may exist among these independent variables. For instance, although director age and incumbency were positively related, in order to state that director age is a determining factor in rate of incumbency, other factors such as the nature and age of the co-operative must also be taken into account. Suppose, for example, that director age had no effect on incumbency while the age of the co-operative did, and that director age and co-operative age were highly correlated. While this would mean that incumbency and director age were highly correlated, it would be wrong to conclude that director age was a factor influencing incumbency. It must be recognized that factors that influence incumbency do not act in isolation from one another and, hence, must be examined together. Regression models are designed to take this into consideration; they approximate the relationship between the independent variable (i.e., rate of incumbency) and a set of independent variables (i.e., directors' age, co-operatives' age, and so on), while accounting for relationships among these independent variables. Accordingly, a model for regression analysis was constructed, with pertinent data from the survey, to explore these relationships in more depth.

In the multivariate analysis shown in Table 9, 'Consecutive terms served' was used as the dependent variable since it reflects the electoral performance of directors and, to some extent, it can provide a basis from which to assess the democratic health of various organizations. The independent variables have been divided into four general categories. These describe the characteristics of the co-operative for which the respondent is/was a director, the attributes and characteristics of the respondents, and directors' beliefs about co-operatives and about problems in the economy. Organizational characteristics represented as variables in the regression model include the kind of co-operative, its membership size, and its age. Directors' personal characteristics represented included age, sex, and level of education. Also included were variables representing respondents' involvement in their co-operatives and in the political realm. Political involvement was included since at least one other study noted a strong tendency for those involved in the co-operative sector to be involved politically as well.[7]

The regression model has an adjusted R^2 value of .328 indicating that the independent variables explain approximately one-third of the dependent variable, a value that compares favourably with other cross-sectional data series.

Type of Co-operative
The coefficients for retail, agricultural implement and day care co-operatives were not statistically significant. Statistically significant at approximately the

TABLE 9: Regression results: consecutive terms served

Variable	Coefficient	t value
Characteristics of Co-operative		
Kind of co-operative[a]		
Retail	−0.0786	−0.876
Ag. implement	0.5106	0.897
Health care	−0.5304	−1.459
Housing	−0.7654	−2.792
Sask. Wheat Pool	0.6727	1.615
Day care	0.2395	1.191
Recreational	−0.2632	−2.312
Agricultural	0.3673	2.621
Other	0.3787	1.708
Age of co-operative	0.0641	7.375
Membership of co-operative	−1.283E−05	−2.014
Attributes and Characteristics of Directors		
Age	0.0637	3.222
Age (squared)	−1.929E−04	−0.942
Sex	−0.2188	−2.191
Education[b]		
High school	−0.0765	−0.767
College/technical	−0.1189	−0.974
Some university	−0.1063	−0.891
University degree	−0.2280	−1.842
Experience as member	−0.0415	−8.530
Involvement as member[c]		
Medium	0.1280	1.581
High	0.2523	2.811
Committee memberships	0.0511	1.128
Total directorships held	0.1020	1.312
Attempts at co-operative office	0.0817	1.308
Other directors from same family	−0.2191	−2.799
Political attempts[d]		
Municipal	0.0292	0.075
Provincial	−0.2343	−0.481
Federal	1.689	1.294
Municipal and provincial	−0.6120	−0.634
Municipal and federal	−0.4150	−0.318
Political success[e]	−0.0130	−0.269
Municipal	−0.1049	−0.438
Provincial	1.210	1.253
Federal	*	*
Municipal and provincial	1.328	1.166
Municipal and federal	*	*

Table 9 (continued)

Variable	Coefficient	t value
Director Beliefs re Co-operatives		
Co-ops have community responsibility	–0.0493	–1.460
Co-ops are theoretically different from private enterprise	–0.0519	–1.213
Co-ops, in practice, are different from private enterprise	0.0794	2.192
Co-ops are part of a social movement	–0.0451	–1.102
Director Beliefs re Economy		
Government intervention disrupts the natural forces of the marketplace.	0.0375	1.213
Problems due to government reinforcement of corporate power	0.0666	1.883

Number of observations: 1414
R^2: 0.328

[a]Credit unions are excluded.
[b]The education category 'Grade 9 or less' is excluded.
[c]The 'Low' involvement category is excluded.
[d]The category for 'No attempts' at political office is excluded.
[e]The category for 'No political success' is excluded.
*Since there were no respondents in this category, no coefficients were estimated.

6 per cent level, however, was the coefficient for housing co-operatives (–.7654), indicating that, on average, directors of these organizations served .765 *fewer* consecutive terms than credit union directors. Directors of health care (–.5304) and recreational (–.2632) co-operatives also served fewer consecutive terms than to those of credit unions. These were statistically significant at approximately the 14 and 2 per cent level, respectively.

A factor contributing to the negative coefficient on recreational co-operatives, in particular, might be the tendency for a directorship to be viewed as a burden and an obligation rather than as a position of prestige, as perhaps is the case in some other kinds of organizations.[8] Accordingly, in recreational co-operatives there may be a greater tendency for incumbents to feel their time has been served and to pass the responsibilities (and burden) of directorship to others. That health care co-operatives may be more apt to attract individuals philosophically or ideologically committed to co-operative principles may be part of the explanation for the negative coefficients obtained for these organizations. The negative influence on incumbency results from a healthy democratic process and from the more rigorous democratic activity that is apt to accompany commitment to co-operative philosophy. The positive coefficient on agricultural co-operatives (.3673) is consistent with earlier postulations that incumbency rates in these organizations will be relatively high at least in part because of the informal electoral procedures many of them follow. The figure determined for the Saskatchewan Wheat Pool (.6727) was the highest positive coefficient attributed to a co-operative organization and was statistically significant at the 11 per cent level. This suggests that Wheat Pool directors enjoy significantly more success in their re-election bids than directors of credit unions. Finally, the coefficient associated with the 'other' category (.3787) was significant at approximately the 9 per cent level. Because of the variety of organizations included in this category, however, an explanation of the coefficient is not without difficulties.

Age of Organization
The coefficient for the organizational age variable .0641 was significant at the 1 per cent level. This suggests, for instance, that a director of a co-operative that is ten years older than another is likely to serve .641 terms more than the director of the younger organization. Earlier hypotheses about age of a co-operative being influential in director re-election are supported by the regression results.

Membership Size
The coefficient estimated for membership size (−.00001283) suggests that consecutive terms served will be influenced negatively by substantial increases in the variable. It is unlikely, however, that the relationship is constant as here described; large changes in membership in smaller co-operatives likely will have more of an impact on re-election than large changes in the membership of larger co-operatives. A linear equation does not seem to describe the true relationship between organizational size and the re-election of directors. This is an item for investigation in future research. Nonetheless, the coefficient appears to support earlier results outlined in this chapter that indicated a tendency for directors from larger co-operatives to serve fewer consecutive terms. Again, while this does not necessarily mean that they are more democratic than smaller organizations, it does indicate that there is high potential for change to be effected through their democratic processes.

Age of Directors
The resulting coefficient (.0637) suggests, as was earlier intimated, that this variable is a significant positive influence in re-election bids. The coefficient

for the square of directors' ages is negative, but not significant statistically. This suggests that, after some point, age has a negative influence on the number of consecutive terms served, but that the relationship between these two items is probably best approximated by a simple linear equation.

Sex of Directors

The coefficient for directors' sex (–.2188) suggests that, compared to male directors, women board members were at a disadvantage in their bids for re-election. The fact that this coefficient was significant at approximately the 3 per cent level supports earlier analyses suggesting that women face electoral disadvantages when seeking directorships. At the same time it may be an indication that women actually seek re-election less often than men. Neither hypothesis, however, changes the fact that women are underrepresented in these organizations.

Directors' Education Levels

The coefficients for education and their respective t values suggest that, for the most part, level of education is not a factor in consecutive terms served by directors of co-operatives. According to the regression, education is only significant in re-election of directors when it is at the level of a completed university degree. And curiously, the coefficient for a university degree is a negative one (–.2280), suggesting that such education negatively affects re-election. Again, this is consistent with findings noted earlier in this chapter which suggested that decreased rates of incumbency corresponded to increased levels of education. In general, therefore, the coefficient for a completed university education may suggest that electoral processes in the co-operative sector work to the disadvantage of individuals with this level of education; it may well be that a higher level of education is perceived as a liability by electors. Indeed, that many of the credit union boards in smaller centres appear reluctant to place university graduates in management roles[9] might be seen as a reflection of a more pervasive wariness, in the co-operative sector, of individuals with university educations. At the same time, however, it is possible that those who are more highly educated are less inclined to seek re-election to their co-operatives' board of directors. It may well be that these individuals do not see the co-operative sector as an area which warrants or encourages their involvement. In either case, the sector is not able to benefit from their knowledge or their talents.

It would be unfair to suggest that a formal education is necessary for the successful performance of a director's duties, since nothing can replace the years of practical experience many directors bring to the administration of their co-operatives. If co-operatives are to remain competitive economically and alive philosophically, however, the importance of formal education cannot be overstated. This is not to say that a formal education is a prerequisite of ideological commitment; members' values take precedence here. But because the co-operative sector has a philosophical commitment to education, it is particularly important that it be at the fore in matters of educational technique and substance. This can be accomplished more easily and more effectively with a reliance on formally trained and educated individuals. Accordingly, whatever the reasons for a lower re-election rate among those directors with a university education, measures to encourage and ensure their participation in the co-operative sector may be quite worth while.

Directors' Involvement as Members of Co-operatives
The coefficient estimated for respondents' prior involvement as members of their co-operatives (–.0415) was significant at a level of less than 1 per cent. Of particular note, however, is the suggestion that consecutive terms served was related *negatively* to directors' experience as members. One might think that more experience as a member and, hence, more organizational familiarity would be electoral assets for prospective directors. In light of trends by political parties to select inexperienced and perhaps untainted individuals as their leaders, the existence of this phenomenon in the co-operative sector is not without precedent. But considered in conjunction with the education coefficients noted previously, the suggestion is that directors without higher formal levels of education *and* without much experience in the organization's membership are more prone to re-election. Because one might expect either education or experience to be a positive attribute in the electoral consideration of potential directors, this suggests a number of possibilities. It may indicate that electors value neither education nor experience as attributes for potential directors. Conversely, it may suggest that co-operative electors perceive a need and are willing to give newer members a chance to participate in their organization at meaningful levels. Another possibility is that individuals with higher levels of education or with more experience in these organizations lack the willingness to remain involved in the co-operative movement. If this is the case, the co-operative sector is unable to benefit from their experience and expertise. Clearly, however, looking at the length of time served as a co-operative member without considering the nature of that involvement does not permit an adequate assessment of candidates for board positions.

Directors' characterization of the nature or intensity of their involvement as members (as opposed to, simply, the length of time) may serve to clarify part of the reason for their electoral success. The coefficients arrived at for variables representing intensity of involvement suggest that prospects of re-election to directors' positions are positively related to the intensity of the respondent's involvement as a co-operative member. While the coefficient for medium involvement (.1280) was significant at approximately the 11 per cent level, the coefficient for high involvement (.2523) was significant at a level of less than 1 per cent. Accordingly, the figures suggest that intensity of involvement is more important to director re-election than simply the amount of time spent as a co-operative member which, as suggested earlier, appears to be negatively influential.

But while directors' own characterization of the intensity of their involvement suggests a positive relationship between intensity and re-election, other variables which might be considered indicative of involvement do not appear to be so related. The coefficients for committee involvement (.0511), for total number of directorships held at present (.1020), and for the number of electoral attempts at co-operative office (.0817) do not appear to be significant statistically.

Significant at a level of 1 per cent, however, was the coefficient estimated for any involvement at the board level in particular co-operatives by other members of the respondent's family (-.2191). The negative coefficient attributed to this variable seems to indicate that nepotism is not a significant factor in the attainment of board positions, or simply that such individuals may not seek re-election as often as others. Regardless, the coefficient suggests that the presence, at any time, of other family members on a co-operative's board of directors is less likely to lead to a director's re-election.

Directors' Political Involvement
The coefficients obtained for respondents' political activity (defined as an attempt to achieve political office) and their respective *t* values suggest that there is no clear link between such activity and consecutive terms served as a member of the board. As well, the coefficients and *t* values derived for these variables indicate that such success does not factor in director re-election. Neither political involvement nor political success appears to be an attribute influencing director incumbency in Saskatchewan co-operatives. While these variables do not account for respondents' grass-roots political involvement, the lack of a political relationship to director incumbency in co-operative organizations is interesting, particularly in contrast to the pervasive interrelationship between co-operative leaders of the 1940s and the Co-operative Commonwealth Federation (CCF) as revealed by S.M. Lipset.[10] One might expect vestiges of this sort of relationship to be reflected in the regression coefficients for organized political involvement, but they are not.

Directors' Beliefs re Co-operatives
The statements about co-operatives used in the regression were meant to assess directors' beliefs regarding the co-operative 'difference.' Directors were asked to indicate whether they believed co-operatives had responsibilities to the community different from other businesses, whether they were theoretically, and practically, different from private enterprise, and whether they were part of a social movement. Of these four statements, a statistically significant (at approximately the 3 per cent level) coefficient was received only for the one suggesting a practical difference between co-operatives and private enterprise (.0794). According to the regression results, individuals who believed more strongly in the practical difference of co-operatives were more apt to have served more consecutive terms as directors.

Directors' Beliefs re the Economy
Asking respondents to indicate their level of agreement with the two statements pertaining to the Canadian economy was part of an attempt to arrive at some sort of indicator of directors' ideological predispositions. These statements were included in the regression equation in an attempt to assess whether consecutive terms served was, in some way, a function of these predispositions. While the coefficient for the statement expressing the undesirability of government intervention in the economy was not significant statistically, the coefficient for that which attributed economic problems at least in part to government reinforcement of corporate power (.0666) was significant at the 6 per cent level. This is of particular interest given that the co-operative movement in Saskatchewan, in large part, began as a response to concerns of this nature. The coefficients suggest, therefore, that support for this ideological strain still exists among leaders within the co-operative sector and, furthermore, that these beliefs are a positive function of director re-election; it suggests that they are valued by co-operative members and leaders alike.

Conclusions

While this analysis has identified attributes and characteristics of co-operatives and of directors which correlate positively with consecutive terms served by directors, it is important that conclusions be considered in the context of the co-operative sector's democratic experience. Regression coefficients may support the possible existence of these relationships, but at the same time it is essential to consider what is known of democratic reality in co-operative circles. Of primary significance is the general lack of interest and concern for democratic matters displayed by most co-operative members and reflected in low rates of member participation at annual general meetings and in board elections. Additionally, as noted earlier, even the by-laws of some co-operatives might be considered as hindrances to democratic processes; in some cases, by-laws actually prevent the free dissemination of information about candidates for board positions that many consider essential to the democratic process.[11] That individuals with particular characteristics tend to enjoy a greater degree of electoral success in their co-operative might more likely be the result of their decision to seek election and re-election than it is the product of an informed electorate consciously selecting them on the basis of their qualities.

Cynicism aside, this is not meant to judge co-operative members harshly but, rather, to note that electoral processes in co-operatives, as well as in other segments of society, do little to ensure that electors are informed about candidates or the beliefs or principles to which they subscribe. This being the case, the regression has identified characteristics of individuals and co-operatives which appear to factor positively and negatively in director re-election (and some which do not appear to factor at all). It has not and cannot, however, explain *why* these relationships exist.

This account also has helped to illuminate electoral tendencies that have been the result of the co-operative sector's natural democratic processes, and that many would consider undesirable or philosophically incongruent with co-operative principles. In some cases the regression analysis has provided quantitative evidence supporting claims or criticisms of this nature. The apparent disjunction between education as a principle of co-operative philosophy and the relative scarcity of more highly educated directors in the sector is a case in point. Individual organizations in the sector may be well advised to adopt measures to encourage more participation by these individuals and others whose increased involvement may benefit the co-operative.

The low percentage of women directors in the sector, because it can be considered in conflict with the principle of member equality, is another anomaly; simply in terms of numbers, it appears women are not equitably represented on the boards of co-operative organizations. Clearly, however, this situation might reflect a variety of factors, such as the small number of women who actually run for board positions in particular co-operatives, or the electoral disadvantage women are at when they compete for office in most North American organizations. Incumbency rates and the regression analysis, however, suggest that women are at an electoral disadvantage in co-operative democratic processes. And if these results accurately reflect the number of women involved generally in the co-operative sector, this too may be considered undesirable. In any event, it would seem important that the situation be redressed through measures which promote and encourage women to participate or become more active in the sector.

This study also has illuminated electoral patterns for directors grouped according to a variety of personal and organizational characteristics. While incumbency rates for these groups may not be undesirable intrinsically, particular organizations in the sector may find them anomalous or counter-productive and wish to remedy them by revising by-laws and democratic practices. Co-operators may consciously wish to attract candidates for board positions who are, perhaps, more reflective demographically of themselves in terms of sex, age, education, and values. It may well be that particular values considered important by co-operators are not being reflected by their organizations' directors. If members are made more aware of the results and effects of the democratic processes of their co-operatives, they may wish to approach electoral issues more methodically or more thoughtfully in an effort to elect people to board positions who are more reflective of or attuned to accepted perceptions of the organization. As well, in some cases rates of incumbency among various groups of directors might be considered too high and hence undesirable since they may be perceived as conflicting with the concept and principle of grass-roots member control of co-operative organizations. Individual co-operatives or the sector as a whole may wish to redress these anomalies by scrutinizing and revising legislation, by-laws, and democratic practices with a view to making them more reflective of co-operative values.

Clearly, the existence of democratic structures is not sufficient proof that democratic behaviour and practices in any organization are congruent with their potential. An accurate assessment of democracy requires the consideration of electoral results in conjunction with value-laden philosophical objectives. The existence of some sort of democratic structure does not in itself legitimate attendant decision-making practices. Without the promotion of values and goals inherent in co-operative philosophy, the democratic potential of the co-operative sector will be seriously limited.

13 Collective and Individual Rights in Canada: A Legal Perspective on Co-operatives

This chapter begins with an argument designed to show that while the rights of individuals may be infringed by giving collective rights legal clout, recognition of collective rights is necessary for the protection of many socially important concerns. We then examine several court cases based on the Canadian Charter of Rights and Freedoms and involving collectively based, democratically controlled organizations and find that their power to pursue legitimate collective interests is undermined by what appear to be the ideological predispositions of the Canadian judiciary.

Introduction: Collective Rights in an Individualistic Society

In any society, the laws governing relationships among citizens reveal much about prevailing societal dynamics. Laws in modern western society thus reflect capitalism's philosophical bases, and the rights and freedoms accorded citizens in these societies are closely connected to liberal capitalist conceptions of human nature. Since capitalism is founded on a conception of the individual as being, among other things, competitive and acquisitive, legal protection of individuals' rights and freedoms is paramount.

By contrast, as Tom Campbell suggests, socialist critics of liberalism often contend that individual rights are important only 'to those who are seeking to protect their self-interest against the predations of others; they express the ground-rules of a type of society which consists of isolated or atomic individuals in perpetual conflict with each other in a struggle for wealth and domination ... The function of rights is to legitimize and regulate conflicts between such individuals.'[1] Richard Flatham notes that 'there is no doubt that the pursuit of individual interests and desires, objectives and purposes is at odds with, if not simply and directly destructive of, some of the kinds of relationships that proponents of community have valued. Justifications for the practice of individual rights are therefore inevitably arguments against some forms of community or at least arguments for limitations on communitarian relationships.'2

Accordingly, it seems clear that co-operatives and other organizations that justify their existence in terms of social or collectivist conceptions of human nature are at a fundamental disadvantage in a legal system founded on individualism. The legal structure that emphasizes the protection of individual interests in capitalist society has put 'proponents of community' on the defensive.

This emphasis on individual rights in western liberal society has its roots in classical English political philosophy. Isaiah Berlin noted that, for these liberal theorists, freedom essentially meant 'not being interfered with by others. The wider the area of non-interference the wider ... [the] freedom.'3 However, Hobbes and other early English liberal theorists quickly recognized that individual liberties could not be left unbridled since 'this would entail a state in which all men could boundlessly interfere with all other men; and this kind of "natural" freedom would lead to social chaos in which men's minimum needs would not be satisfied; or else the liberties of the weak would be suppressed by the strong.'4 Clearly, limitations on individual liberties were necessary for the sake of freedom itself, and for other more social values as well. A task of legislators, therefore, was to strike a balance between individual liberties and other values they wished to protect, such as justice, equality, and public order.

There is a huge gulf, however, between recognizing this as philosophical fact and coming to practical terms with it. Where the protection of the individual is paramount, the infringement of individual liberty is not taken lightly. For John Stuart Mill, for instance, virtually any law that curtailed individuals' free movement was anathema to the advancement of civilization as a whole. According to Mill, 'the danger which threatens human nature is not the excess, but the deficiency, of personal impulses and preferences.'5 For him, 'the only purpose for which power can be rightfully exercised over any member of a civilized community, against his will, is to prevent harm to others. His own good, either physical or moral, is not a sufficient warrant.'6 Mill and others of his tradition saw individual liberty as taking precedence over all other values and rights, since the progress of civilization itself hinged on it. 'Every plea for civil liberties and individual rights,' noted Berlin, 'every protest against exploitation and humiliation, against the encroachment of public authority, or the mass hypnosis of custom or organized propaganda, springs from this individualistic, and much disputed, conception of man.'[7] These are the foundations on which Berlin has suggested his concept of 'negative liberty' – that is, freedom *from* coercion – is based.

The idea of 'positive' liberty, in contrast, is premised on one's actualization as a conscious being; that is, freedom *to* act. Berlin suggests that this notion of liberty is reflected in the individual's desire for self-mastery and control over his or her own destiny.[8] While his description of positive liberty seems only a positive way of defining the 'negative' variety, Berlin argues that positive liberty is at the base of many modern authoritarian regimes.[9] He explains how the notion of positive liberty, while not necessarily a collective phenomenon, has been incorporated in the name of class, the nation, and other collective entities to infringe on the rights of individuals. His condemnation of freedom's positive variant is implicit: 'Pluralism, with the measure of negative liberty that it entails, seems ... a truer and more humane ideal than the goals of those who seek in the great, disciplined, authoritarian structures the ideal of "positive" self-mastery by classes, or peoples, or the whole of mankind.'[10]

Berlin's account of liberty does not bode well for organizations which find their *raison d'être* in collective action. Berlin's analysis might lead one to believe that collectively based organizations are premised on a positive emphasis of liberty and rights as he has described them. His arguments are similar to those of others who would give individual rights an entrenched veto power over more broadly based, collective rights. And their suggestion that collective interests are insidious and perhaps indiscriminately violate individual rights is often popularly, if misguidedly, accepted. These conclusions regarding freedom, however, flow largely from the narrowness of Berlin's definitions. For instance, while Berlin has stressed negative liberty as a guarantor of individual liberty, C.B. Macpherson has argued that 'negative liberty is no longer ... the shield of individuality: it has become the cloak for un-individualist, corporate, imperial, "free enterprise".'[11] Samuel Bowles and Herbert Gintis concur with Macpherson, arguing that 'both the liberal state and the capitalist economy have flourished by undermining sources of personal and traditional collective autonomy ... [Liberalism] has conspired with the imperatives of the capitalist economy to erode all collective bodies standing between the state and the individual save one: the capitalist corporation.'[12]

Indeed, Canadian legal practice bears evidence which, in principle, supports the contention that fair protection of the individual is *not* afforded where negative liberty is legally and politically paramount. Canadian courts, for instance, consider governments, corporations, and other organizations to be equal to individual citizens under the law.[13] Economic realities, however, ensure that those with the most resources at their disposal can make fuller use of the law and are more likely to tip the scales of justice in their favour. When economic discrepancies are ignored in these matters, in the name of negative liberty or because of the perceived undesirability of positive liberty (and hence the advocacy of non-interference by governments on behalf of those who are economically disadvantaged), individuals are put at a disadvantage in their legal relations with most governmental or corporate entities because of their generally less favourable economic positions. This is particularly interesting in view of Canadian legal traditions and constitutional vehicles such as the Charter of Rights and Freedoms which are seen as upholding the liberties of individual citizens.

Concerning the notion of positive liberty, William Connolly has noted that 'it is never in itself a sufficient argument against an idea to say that it can be misused. That is true of all important ideas.'[14] And it is clear that many of the 'positive' roles or projects that the modern state has undertaken have resulted in positive, progressive, and humane contributions to individual and social development. Anti-discrimination legislation and affirmative action programs are cases in point. While they make the 'freedom' of some individuals to practise discrimination illegal, these laws also promote the economic and social well-being and, indeed, the freedom of previously disadvantaged groups. The suggestion that such legislation is 'reverse discrimination' reflects a restrictive definition of liberty that ignores the existence of class or socially imposed economic impediments.

Macpherson has suggested a broader definition of liberty as 'the absence of humanly imposed impediments, and ... these impediments include not only coercion of one individual by another, and direct interference with individual activities by the state or society (beyond what is needed to secure each from invasion by others), but also lack of equal access to the means of life and the means of labour.'[15] He argues that 'the unequal access to the means of life and labour inherent in capitalism is, regardless of what particular social and economic theory is invoked, an impediment to the freedom of those with little or no access. It diminishes their negative liberty, since the dependence on others for a living, which deficiency of access creates, diminishes the area in which they cannot be pushed around ... We may conclude that a formulation of negative liberty which takes little or no account of class-imposed impediments, whether deliberate or unintentional, is not entirely adequate.'[16] In this vein, Bowles and Gintis have also argued that 'economic dependency no less than personal bondage is the antithesis of freedom.'[17]

Recognizing the social importance of such impediments requires us to confer legitimacy on some conception of collectively based rights, thereby reducing the priority given those of the individual. Macpherson suggests that if the pre-eminence of individual rights is reduced and more emphasis is placed on rights that protect against 'class imposed impediments' (deliberate or otherwise) which promote 'class-divided market' societies, the conflicts of values, which Berlin deems endemic, will diminish.[18] Macpherson argues, for instance, that many conflicts of values, which Berlin suggests are characteristic of humanity and modern society, stem particularly from class-divided market societies in which individual rights are paramount.[19]

Macpherson also takes issue with Berlin's argument that positive liberty, by nature, is oppressive. Macpherson suggests that, while perhaps a danger, authoritarianism is not inherent in positive liberty, but rather has its origins in the continued existence of class- imposed impediments.[20] Hence, the reduction of these impediments, through more emphasis on collective notions of rights, will extend liberty, even in the negative sense applauded by Berlin. Macpherson's comment on socialism is illustrative: 'Socialism ... (since it requires social, not individual, ownership of capital) removes from the arena of negative liberty the main individual activities celebrated as "free enterprise". But it increases the aggregate negative liberty, if the gain in liberty by those who had had doors closed to them more than offsets the loss of liberty by those (relatively few) who had been in a position to take full advantage of market freedoms.'[21]

It seems plausible to argue, then, that collective notions of legal rights may be invoked to enhance the rights and freedoms of individuals. Tom Campbell suggests that the law can be viewed as a positive vehicle for 'co-operative social behaviour' allowing 'the individual to make rational decisions about how to pursue his own interests, for sharing systems of rules makes possible new types of joint activities ... by ensuring [for instance] that numbers of people act in unison to achieve objectives which they could not acquire alone (such as paying taxes to support medical services).'[22] This is one of the premises on which the activities of organizations such as co-operatives, trade unions, and other collectively based entities are based.

Campbell illuminates one of the problems with which these organizations often are faced: 'Such a view of the function of law tends to give rise to an emphasis on duties or obligations, particularly positive or affirmative obligations, for these indicate what the individual is to contribute to the co-operative enterprise. Because the benefits of the system may be remote from the fulfillment of the individual obligations on which it depends, they may not obviously correlate with anyone's rights.'[23]

Difficulties arise regardless of whether an individual or a collective approach to the law is taken. Individual rights may be infringed when collective rights are stressed. But socially important concerns may be ignored and social fabric damaged if individual rights are given priority simply on the basis of their ideological pre-eminence. The case of trade unions is particularly illustrative, but their experience has lessons for co-operatives and other groups which define themselves in terms of collective interests and action. For these organizations, the power to realize social and economic gain for their members is founded on the legal recognition, legitimacy, and priority given collective rights. Without that recognition, these groups are ineffective and their goals unattainable.

The individual member of these organizations, however, may find his or her realm of 'freedom' reduced by such recognition should there be disagreement with decisions made and actions taken by the union. If the union acts in accordance with the wishes of a majority of its members, but contrary to the wishes of a particular member, individual representation is lost and the implication may be one of union paternalism, suggesting that individuals do not know their own interests. As Connolly has noted: 'the connative dispositions people have are themselves shaped by the concepts, beliefs, and roles they internalize from the society in which they are implicated. Thus slavery is a paradigm of unfreedom. And a slave who is socialized to accept his master's judgment that he is incapable of self-rule is not for that reason more free than a slave who wants to escape his master's rule.'[24]

An important and potentially dangerous dilemma is presented when the individual member does not know his or her own 'true' interests as a trade unionist and/or wishes to act against them. Connolly suggests that 'if the desires are not recognized in the idea of freedom, it will become definitionally possible to force people to act against their desires under the guise of increasing their real or true freedom. To push the actual desires of concrete individuals into the background of the idea of freedom, it is feared, will allow theorists and political elites to include as part of freedom the very forms of coercion and manipulation the idea is designated to expose.'[25]

The parallels to Berlin's concept of positive liberty and his fears of its ramifications are obvious. But if traditionally accepted notions of liberal individualism are relied on, objectives that may benefit the rest of the membership or society as a whole may be undermined.

This is not to suggest that collective organizations have a monopoly on truth and, therefore, a right to coerce dissidents into submission. Indeed, this would be repugnant and dangerous. Nor is it to suggest that collective rights always should be emphasized at the expense of individual rights. What needs to be recognized, however, is the legitimacy of collective rights and their essential role in the dynamics of modern society. Indeed, in recent Canadian experience, according to Cynthia Williams, there 'has been a shift of concern at the popular level from political and democratic rights to egalitarian and cultural rights ...

Closely related to this concern ... is the shift in emphasis from the rights of individuals to the rights of special groups ... [and the creation of] an environment in which individuals are highly conscious of their identity as members of particular groups and are encouraged to organize and lobby for their special interests.'[26] Williams has suggested that the Charter of Rights and Freedoms paved the way for Canada to become 'rights-ridden,' at least in part because of the recognition it may have allowed special interest groups. In her analysis, however, Williams links the legitimacy of rights to the political agendas of governments; she derogates collective interpretations of rights largely on the basis that they interfere with governmental prerogatives.[27] And in the context of modern Canadian society, these prerogatives are founded on the tenets of liberal individualism under which there is little danger or, rather, hope of recognizing the importance of collective rights.'[28]

According to Philip Resnick, the Charter is hardly responsible for the increased call for collective expressions of rights that Williams would have us believe are anathema to a free society. As well, it appears that Resnick would support the contentions of Macpherson and Bowles and Gintis that capitalist corporations and the market-place enjoy predominance in the interpretation of and protection afforded by rights in modern society. 'The Charter is ... being used as an ideological weapon in legitimizing, not the extension of democracy, but its diversion into narrowly juridical/legal channels ... Citizenship in the political sense, in the collective sense, in our day-to-day practice, has not been enhanced simply because of the Charter ... We may even have moved further into the realm of private liberty than before, one in which the market, rather than civil society and community, becomes the powerful determinant of citizen identity.'[29]

In addition to what may or may not be the increased social recognition of collective action by Canadians, the simple fact that various organizations are allowed legal status should obligate the courts to recognize the collective rights which define these groups and allow them effectiveness. But while, in recent years, it may have become socially acceptable and, in particular respects, recognized in law, the greater legal and public legitimacy given collective action is not always reflected in decisions made by the Canadian judiciary. Recent judicial decisions, in fact, suggest that quite the opposite has taken place.

While the courts have included the right to form a union as part of freedom of association, for instance, they have not included in it the right to bargain collectively or the right to strike.[30] Furthermore, in *Re Lavigne and Ontario Public Service Employees Union et al.*, the court upheld Lavigne's freedom of (non-)association not simply over collective rights normally allowed unions in regard to allocation of their resources, but implicitly over and above a decision presumably made by a democratic majority of union members.[31] Democratically sanctioned union activity was thwarted by the court's decision to uphold the individual rights of a non-union employee.

It might be argued that, because membership in co-operatives is voluntary, unlike in some trade unions, and because of co-operatives' strong democratic basis, their decisions and policy directions should be beyond reproach. Canadian courts, however, have ignored these realities and have been quite paternalistic in their regard for the democratic processes of co-operatives and credit unions. By-laws that had been democratically approved by members of co-operative organizations have been explicitly overridden or ignored in particular legal decisions. In *Civil Service Co-operative Credit Society Ltd.* v. *Ontario Credit Union League Ltd.*, for example, the court held that a by-law allowing League directors wide discretion in paying out withdrawing members was basically invalid because it contained no specific 'reference points or standards or proper conditions.'[32]

That the by-law had been democratically approved by at least two-thirds of votes cast by members of the League was of little consequence to Mr Justice Sirois. Furthermore, the by-law had been instituted as a measure by which members of the League could benefit *collectively*; it provided a fair system of pay-out to individual member organizations that wished to withdraw from the League while allowing for the League's organizational stability. In spite of a by-law intended for the collective protection of members of the League, however, the court's decision, in effect, was at the *expense* of this intent. Once again, recognition of the prerogatives and necessities of collective action was not forthcoming from the court.

Decisions of this nature should come as no surprise, given the Canadian political and legal experience. They illustrate the fundamental philosophical divergence between the liberal individualist tradition that has characterized Canadian society and the dynamics on which the efficacy of collectively based organizations rely.

The Collective Nature of Co-operation

It is no easy matter to assess the law's contribution to the balance between collective and individual rights in Canada. Through examples drawn from recent Supreme Court of Canada activity in the area of trade union law, and from recent co-operative law cases, however, the manner in which Canadian law balances collective and individual rights may be clarified. To the extent that the law reflects contemporary societal values, its clear tendency to place individual rights over collective rights poses problems for advocates and beneficiaries of collective action, including co-operatives. Also rendered problematic is the protection of individual rights through democratic collective action; individual freedom, in certain senses, and some individual rights, especially those of the poor and disenfranchised, can *only* be protected through collective action.[33]

Thus in some circumstances the practical prevention of effective collective action threatens the very existence of meaningful individual rights. Also, in the long term, a widespread erosion of interest in collective activity bodes ill for the health of the co-operative movement. Canadian law, reflecting Canadian social values, exhibits a growing tendency toward an ever greater supremacy of individual rights over collective rights as compared to pre-Charter days.[34] Accordingly, co-operators need to take measures to ensure that their *raison d'être* does not evaporate with changing social values and views.

Fair and Right in the Economic Context: Where Co-operatives Fit
Few would be prepared to admit that they believe in unfairness, yet the economies of western democracies work so as to create great wealth for some and great poverty and suffering for others. Milton Friedman argues that the only social responsibility of corporations is to make profits.[35] Co-operative principles, however, suggest an opposite approach. They envisage an economy in which economic activity is carried out for mutual benefit, and not primarily for the benefit of investors. As capital would not attract any speculative value, the gap between rich and poor would be expected to lessen (or at least there would not be gross inequalities which the present system generates) and the concerns of the poorest in society would be better addressed.

For the present debate, it is critical to have an appreciation of the underlying themes and philosophy on which co-operative principles are based. It is generally accepted that behind these principles is a vision of society in which people experience human, social, and economic dignity. This being the case, it can be argued that society is better off if organized in a way that promotes these dignities.

Dignity connotes worth and the opportunity for people to be free, in both a negative and a positive sense. It suggests an absence of servitude, allowing people to live their lives respecting others and having others respect them. As well, it suggests conditions under which worth, in terms of a person's being or self (human dignity), a person's interrelationship with his or her community and peers (social dignity), and material well-being (economic dignity) should be allowed to flourish. All of these might be encompassed by the phrase 'social justice.' Furthermore, implicit in these notions of dignity is that none of them should be obtained at the expense of another's dignity. While these phrases are imprecise, what is intended here is a representation of the concepts of dignity and social justice, not an account of Canadian co-operatives' practices towards their members or employees.[36]

To make the argument that co-operation is right, or at least preferable to competition, it will be necessary to state a number of practical assumptions or assertions that may be seen as contentious or overtly political. This cannot be avoided for, as will be argued, co-operation is unavoidably political.

Co-operation implies a dissatisfaction with free market institutions and a recognition that 'social justice cannot be realized through free market institutions premised on classical rights of liberal individualism as protected by the classical liberals' minimal state.' There is a need for 'state (and other collective) agencies to take an active role in economic affairs with a view to securing fair shares and fair opportunities for all citizens.' However, 'the civil rights and liberties proclaimed by classical liberalism are ... of fundamental importance to human beings, as moral persons, and ought to be qualified only so far as necessary to the securing of fair shares and fair opportunities.' [37]

The philosophy underlying co-operation has a good deal to say about equality. Indeed, the slogan 'Each for All, and All for Each' articulates a general appreciation of the need for people to work together to improve their lives. The rejection of competition as a means through which to order society constitutes a rejection of a prime vehicle for creating and maintaining inequality. However, there is no suggestion in these underlying ideas that complete equality is being sought, but rather that attempts should be made to strive for more (and more meaningful) equality. Fairness need not entail complete and simple equality.

There is much in the liberal notion of equality that is unconnected to equality. Our very concept of freedom of contract is based on stated notions of equality of bargaining power which, as indicated earlier in this discussion, are doubtful to say the least.[38] And unequal contractual relationships between workers and employers, and between consumers and sellers, are upheld regularly on this basis. We are also said to have equality of opportunity when accidents of birth, social class, family property and wealth, connections, and plain luck play critically important roles in how people's lives evolve.

Such liberal notions of equality undoubtedly will distract from fairness. And if equality is to mean anything to those who are exploited, it has to mean more and it has to offer more; it has to be real. In the search for meaningful alternatives and approaches, however, we must consider what options are realistically available.

Co-operation, as an economic model, is often referred to as a middle ground between socialism and capitalism. In Canada, co-operation's generally accepted premises would support such an assertion. Co-operators do not reject private property, nor even corporate private property. They seek a protected place in the market, not the dismantling of the market. They seek to maintain a good deal of what liberal democracies have to offer while attempting, through mutual action, to provide goods and services to their members. Co-operators seek to put capital to work for people rather than vice versa, and seek approaches to life which make people's needs pre-eminent. The overlap between the views of co-operators and those of the Catholic bishops is evident.[39] Neither seek a radical restructuring of society, but seek within the bounds of what is possible to inject more fairness and equality into people's lives and economic relationships.

The End of Collective Rights?

The law plays both an active and a passive role in society; it acts as a strong regulator of behaviour and it represents the mores of the time. This might suggest that those who make the law – legislators, administrators, and judges – pay continuous and careful attention to societal values. In reality, however, the process of law-making is much more haphazard. Nonetheless, the law still represents and reflects prevailing social values and views and, to that extent, it is a guiding force in society. An analysis of Canadian laws and legal decisions will give some indication of the relative value of collectivism and individualism in Canadian society, stemming from the respect that the law accords, and the protection it provides, collective and individual rights.

Perhaps the challenge for contemporary society is to balance the attention it pays to collective and individual rights to ensure the greatest amount of fairness and equality possible. The Charter of Rights and Freedoms, however, caused Canadian law to lurch towards individualism and the protection of individual rights. Whether this was the purpose of its drafters is debatable, but its effect is undeniable. And there is much that is unfortunate about such a move. As a case in point, it downplays the very important role collective rights can have in protecting individual rights, particularly those of disadvantaged members of society.

Labour and Co-operatives: Two Collective Movements on Parallel Paths?
Seen in the context of the matrix of collective and individual rights in a liberal democratic society, trade unions and co-operatives possess important similarities. They have similar historical roots as they were established to address the same sorts of oppression. They have common objectives– the betterment of the economic and social lives of their members. They have, of course, taken different routes to achieve these objectives, and there can be no

denying the unfortunate conflicts that have arisen between the labour and co-operative movements. Nonetheless, the similarities of purpose and structure recently led the Canadian Labour Congress to ask rhetorically whether the labour and co-operative movements were on parallel paths.[40] Accordingly, a review of the ways in which the law affects the balance between collective and individual rights in trade union activities may be instructive for co-operatives.

Trade Unions and the Charter of Rights and Freedoms
The erosion of collective rights and the enhancement of individual rights by Canadian courts in the area of trade union activity should be recognized as ominous by Canadian co-operators. Much of the impetus for this has come from the Charter. It should come as no surprise that Canadian judges have interpreted the Charter to place pre-eminent importance on individual rights. Nor should it be surprising that the judges, in general, seem unprepared to accept that some important individual rights (as provided for in the Charter and elsewhere) can only be espoused and protected through collective action.

In the main, the rights of employees vis-à-vis their employers can only be protected through strong and effective collective action. The same is true for farmers and consumers. But not everyone in society is aware of his or her weak bargaining position. Indeed, some have an aversion to recognizing their inability, individually, to best protect their interests. Some theorists have argued that this has been the product of a long and concerted effort on the part of establishment forces in Canada and elsewhere.[41] From another perspective, it can be said that this problem of interest recognition is closely related to the lack of a strong working-class identity and culture in Canada.[42] Those whose political views are not in a socialist or social democratic tradition generally do not espouse the importance of collective action. Classical liberals, now often referred to as conservatives, see strong, effective collective action, through such vehicles as trade unions and co-operatives, as dangerous to the interests they espouse. Consequently, such liberals and conservatives attempt to ensure that such collective action is discouraged, or at least not sanctioned. With very few exceptions, Canadian judges only grudgingly accept the legitimacy of collective activity.

Thus, it is almost natural that the rights and freedoms contained in the Charter should be seen as individual rights and freedoms and that they should be seen as enforceable by individuals *against* collectivities. One now expects that when collectivities such as trade unions are pitted against individuals who want to 'go it alone,' the individual rights will prevail. One can further expect that this will be true even when such individuals are clearly backed by self-interested groups whose power will increase as that of the collectivities with which they are in conflict decreases.[43]

The nature of the rights and freedoms contained in the Charter gives a very clear indication of what was important to its drafters. Economic rights are excluded while traditional political rights are included. Perhaps the concentration of rights can best be considered by attempting to understand the impact of the Charter on the lives of ordinary citizens. One may take as examples the freedoms and rights as they are articulated in the Charter. Is there really freedom of expression at work? Will an employee be protected if he or she makes derogatory remarks to his or her boss? What is more important to ordinary citizens, the right to freedom of expression in the wider political arena, a freedom which is unlikely to be at risk (except from over-reactions such as the invocation of the War Measures Act in 1970), or the right to adequate housing, education, nutrition, and work experience, which is actually denied hundreds of thousands of Canadians? What does it mean to say that there is freedom of expression when only the richest and most powerful in our society have the means to publish newspapers and operate radio and television stations? What does it mean when the Supreme Court of Canada decides that workers have the right to join trade unions but not the right to bargain collectively or to strike to protect their rights?[44]

There can be little doubt that the Charter is a liberal document, ill-suited to bringing about any significant redistribution of rights and freedoms in our society. It is designed and operates to leave the distribution of power in the same hands as it was before the Charter was proclaimed. If an ordinary citizen does not come into contact with the criminal law, the Charter will have little or no positive effect on his or her life. The grandiose claims and expectations of the Charter are, at best, but a smoke-screen for maintaining things as they have been and, at worst, a tool for an erosion of fragile rights and freedoms of ordinary citizens.[45]

Faced with legislation limiting their rights to bargain collectively and to strike, trade unions have sought protection in the Charter. The Supreme Court of Canada, however, has held that they have no such rights; the freedom of association does not include any freedom to carry out the objectives of the organization one is free to join. The purpose here is not to examine the relevant cases in detail, but rather to draw out indications of where the balance between collective and individual rights is heading in the Canadian context. Attitudes toward trade unions and co-operatives, for instance, are by no means uniform.

There are many for whom the collective action of co-operative activity is acceptable, even desirable, but who see trade union activity as undesirable or unacceptable. For these people, it is presumably the group whose interests are being pursued, rather than collective action itself, that is important. Indeed, political, legal, and social perceptions of rights in Canadian society tend to be quite issue-specific. Although it will be assumed here that this dichotomy is ultimately a false one, it will be taken into account in drawing appropriate conclusions for the co-operative movement.

Dissenting Trade Union Members and Their Remedies against Their Union
In *Re Lavigne and the Ontario Public Employees Union et al.*, Merve Lavigne did not approve of the union which represented him, the Ontario Public Service Employees Union (OPSEU), spending some of his dues to support the New Democratic Party, British coal miners, Polish Solidarity, and the Nicaraguan government. Mr Justice White of the Ontario High Court held[46] that the matter of the compulsory collection of union dues fell within the purview of the Charter because Lavigne's employer, a crown agency, agreed to a check-off clause in the collective agreement. In defining the freedom of association he argued that 'a right to freedom of association which did not include a right *not* to associate would not really ensure "freedom.'[47]

In *Lavigne* it was held that Lavigne's freedom of association was violated because, through the Rand formula, he was required to pay union dues even though he had declined to become a member of the union which represented him in negotiations and relations with his employer. This procedure forces payment of dues but not membership of the union in question. White J. wrote: 'It is not necessary for the collective agreement to require Mr. Lavigne to join the Union for there to be a forced association, it is the compelled combining of financial resources that has the effect of forcing Mr. Lavigne to associate with the Union.'[48] This is because 'while the purpose of the [check-off] clause is not to force association, the effect is to force non-members to combine their resources with members.'[49] White J. continued: 'if a government agent acts so as to force an individual to financially support a union when he opposes the union, its objects and its methods, then his freedom of association has been abridged.'[50]

However, Mr Lavigne's freedom of expression was not found to have been infringed by the compulsory dues check-off. It was considered that this freedom would be infringed only 'where the unwilling payor is placed in a position in which he appears to have endorsed the causes which have received his financial support.'[51]

Section 1 of the Charter would assist in the preservation of such traditional union rights that contravene section 2(b) and other sections setting out fundamental freedoms and rights, only to the extent that such rights and practices are 'reasonable limits *prescribed* by law as can be demonstrably justified in *a* free and democratic society.'[52] What this means in Canada surely can be subject to some dispute. In the present context, there are two particularly interesting aspects to section 1. Its wording, and especially the use of the term 'prescribed,' suggests that it would not be enough for legislation, or presumably the common law, to *permit* the practices pursued in the *Lavigne* case. For section 1 to be operative, it would be necessary for 'law' to require that the practices be pursued.[53] One can only conjecture the extent to which contemporary legislatures will 'prescribe' such things as compulsory dues check-off.

Another interesting aspect of section 1 is that such prescribed practices will be acceptable as reasonable limits if they are demonstrably justified, not in Canada per se, but rather in a free and democratic society. Presumably the use of this phrase encourages an assessment of what the international community would tolerate or require.[54] There is, of course, a range of free and democratic societies; the phrase is open to wide interpretation. Countries with quite different views of the appropriate balance between collective and individual rights fall within the definition, so this terminology could broaden the scope of inquiry. It is more likely to encourage uncertainty, or to be seen as meaning Canada.

Mr Justice White argued, however, that 'the use of compulsory dues for purposes other than collective bargaining and collective agreement administration cannot be justified in a free and democratic society.'[55] Clearly, however, some free and democratic societies would justify political use of compulsory dues. Accordingly, it appears that either Mr. Justice White is of the view that trade unions have too much power, or his political naiveté is such that he does not recognize that the only effective means of protecting some people's individual rights is through collective action. If the former interpretation is correct, co-operators have cause for general concern; if the latter is more accurate, they should be very worried for the health of their movement.

Rights to Strike and Bargain Collectively

On three recent occasions the Supreme Court of Canada has considered the scope of the enshrined freedom of association as it applies to trade union activity.[56] The arguments, in each case, are essentially the same, with a large majority of the court taking a restrictive approach to the matter.

The *Public Service Alliance of Canada* case involved the federal government's anti-inflation legislation. The act in question precluded negotiations on compensatory matters for federal public sector employees, replacing these with the '6 and 5' guidelines. It also took away the right to strike and the right to submit disputes to arbitration on both compensatory and non-compensatory matters. Thus the act significantly restricted the right to bargain collectively and federal public sector employees' right to strike.

The *Saskatchewan Dairy Workers* case involved an act passed by the Saskatchewan legislature after the dairy workers' unions announced rotating strikes and their employers responded with a lock-out. The act required the employees to continue working as they did before the dispute, prohibited lock-outs, and imposed compulsory arbitration on the parties if they could not settle their disagreement within fifteen days of the legislation being enacted. Again, there were severe restrictions placed on the right to bargain collectively and the right to strike.

Finally, the *Alberta Reference* case involved an assessment of the Alberta government's anti-inflation legislation. Three statutes prohibited strikes and imposed compulsory arbitration to resolve impasses in collective bargaining. This legislation affected a wide range of provincial public-sector employees.

Through the Convention Concerning Freedom of Association and the Right to Organize (Convention No. 87)[57] that Canada has ratified, the international community recognizes the right of trade unions to strike as 'one of the essential means available to all workers and their organizations for the promotion and protection of their economic and social interests.'[58] Mr Justice Cameron of the Saskatchewan Court of Appeal, writing in the *Saskatchewan Dairy Workers* case, considered that section 2(d) of the Charter, which sets out the parameters of freedom of association, should be interpreted in the context of these international values.[59]

The Supreme Court of Canada addressed this question, however, and resolved that the freedom of association did not include the right to strike. Thus, there is a freedom of association enshrined in the Charter, but not a right to act in association to further the aims and objectives of the association. If it had not been the Supreme Court of Canada that arrived at this conclusion, one might think it absurd. And when, in the context of trade union activity, the Supreme Court refuses to recognize that freedom of association includes the right to bargain collectively, the extent of the attack on collective action by and through trade unions becomes apparent.

The most comprehensive treatment of the majority approach is contained in the *Alberta Reference* case. Speaking for the majority, Mr Justice LeDain argued that, because of the wide range of associations covered by the freedom of association, it was necessary to consider the implications of extending freedom of association to the right to engage in activities on the ground that the activities were essential to give the association meaningful existence.[60] He argued that freedom of association, when applied in this narrow way to trade unions, still afforded a wide scope for protected activity, such as freedom of expression and freedom of conscience and religion.[61] Further, the majority of the court concurred that the freedom to work for the establishment of an association, to belong to an association, to maintain it, and to participate in its lawful activity, were all important.[62] The majority concentrated its attention on what it considered to be the main issue: not the importance of freedom of association, but whether a particular activity in pursuit of the association's objects is to be constitutionally protected. It did not see the right to strike and the right to bargain collectively as fundamental rights or freedoms. The majority claimed it was unwise, so far as these rights were concerned, to replace the legislature's judgment with that of the court.[63]

Mr Justice McIntyre concurred with separate reasons. While he argued that freedom of association recognizes that 'the attainment of individual goals, through the exercise of individual rights, is generally impossible without the aid and cooperation of others,'[64] that it 'promotes social goals,'[65] and that it 'plays an indispensable role ... in the functioning of democracy,'[66] he opined that freedom of association could not give individuals more rights than they could exercise as individuals.[67] He gave freedom of association a restrictive and individualistic interpretation, and in doing so relied on a good deal of American authority.[68] He expressed the view that freedom of association only protected collective activities that are constitutionally protected if engaged in by individuals.[69] He argued that 'individuals and organizations have no constitutional right to do in concert what is unlawful when done alone.'[70] As individuals did not have the right to strike, neither could an association. Consequently, freedom of association does not guarantee the right to strike.[71] The argument that individuals have the lawful right to refuse to work, he held, was not accurate[72] and not analogous because an 'employee who ceases work does not contemplate a return to work, while employees on strike always contemplate a return to work.'[73]

Finally, Mr Justice McIntyre noted that the overwhelming preoccupation of the Charter is with individual, political, and democratic rights with conspicuous inattention to economic and property rights. Accordingly, he argued that this spoke strongly against any implication of a constitutionally protected right to strike.[74]

Chief Justice Dickson and Madam Justice Wilson dissented. Speaking through Chief Justice Dickson, they argued that the purpose of the constitutional guarantee of association in section 2(d) of the Charter is a 'sine qua non of any free and democratic society, protecting individuals from the vulnerability of isolation and ensuring the potential of effective participation in society.'[75] They continued that section 2(d), at a minimum, guarantees the liberty of persons to be in association, to belong to an association, and that it must extend beyond a concern for associational status in order to give effective protection to the interests to which the constitutional guarantee is directed, and must protect the pursuit of the activities for which the association was formed.[76] They argued that freedom of association protected 'the freedom of individuals to interact with, support, and be supported by, their fellow humans in the varied activities in which they chose to engage.'[77] Further, they argued that the 'overarching consideration remains whether a legislative enactment or administrative action interferes with the freedom of persons to join and act with others in common pursuits. The legislative purpose which will render legislation invalid is the attempt to preclude associational conduct because of its concerted or associational nature.'[78]

Chief Justice Dickson and Madam Justice Wilson preferred the approach taken by the Ontario Divisional Court in the *Broadway Manor* case[79] and the Saskatchewan Court of Appeal in the *Dairy Workers'* case, arguing that freedom of association includes not only the freedom to form and join associations, but also the freedom to bargain collectively and to strike. They argued that 'the capacity to bargain collectively has long been recognized as one of the integral and primary functions of associations of working people ... collective bargaining remains vital to the capacity of individual employees to participate in ensuring equitable and humane working conditions.'[80] In addition, under the system of collective bargaining operative in Canada, 'effective constitutional protection of the associational interests of employees in the collective bargaining process also requires concomitant protection of their freedom to withdraw collectively their services, subject to section 1 of the *Charter*.'[81]

In considering the right to strike, Dickson C.J. and Wilson J. pointed out that the 'very nature of a strike, and its *raison d'être*, is to influence an employer by joint action which would be ineffective if it were carried out by an individual.'[82] As such, provisions which abridged the freedom of employees to strike infringed against section 2(d) of the Charter.[83] They also found the limits on freedom of association unjustifiable under section 1 of the Charter. The tests to be followed were laid down in *R. v. Oakes*.[84] The legislative objective must be 'sufficiently significant to warrant overriding a constitutionally guaranteed right; it must relate to social concerns which are pressing and substantial in a free and democratic society ... [and] the means chosen ... must be reasonable and demonstrably justified in a free and democratic society.'[85] Further, there must be a 'rational connection between the measures and the objective they are to serve,' they should 'impair as little as possible the right or freedom in question' and the 'deleterious effects of the measures must be justifiable in light of the objective which they are to serve.'[86]

Such were the competing arguments about the removal of the right to bargain collectively and the right to strike as presented by the Supreme Court of Canada. The judgments in the other two Supreme Court cases involving freedom of association under section 2(d) of the Charter were of a similar nature and add little to this discussion.

The Impact of Recent Canadian Co-operative Jurisprudence

A brief analysis of co-operative law cases before the Canadian courts can shed further light on this discussion. While this is not a very busy field in Canada, there has been some recent activity. For the purposes of the discussion here, the most relevant area of inquiry involves an individual dissenting (minority) member's relationship with the majority of members (with the co-operative itself).

Generally, there are legislative restrictions on the right of co-operatives to buy a terminating member's shares when the co-operative is insolvent or would become so by buying the shares.[87] Presumably, such provisions are designed to protect the interests of the collectivity in an effort to maintain a viable co-operative. A recent Prince Edward Island Court of Appeal case casts considerable doubt on the effectiveness of such provisions and, in the context of this discussion, appears to put the individual member's interests ahead of those of the collectivity. In a sense, this is ironic since co-operatives place a premium on collective action. Indeed, they recognize that for the range of purposes for which they exist, co-operative action is more meaningful than individual action. This is not to say, of course, that judges have the same appreciation of what is at stake.

In *Agro Co-operative Association Limited* v. *Cutcliffe*,[88] for instance, a former director and president of an insolvent co-operative used his line of credit to incur a debt to this association. In full knowledge that a by-law had been passed prohibiting the paying out of equity, he then claimed to be able to set off his equity against this line of credit obligation. Attention should be drawn to two facts in this case. First, while the co-operative had, by its by-laws, the power to transfer retained patronage dividends into share capital, it had not done so. Apart from one qualifying share, Cutcliffe's investment in Agro was in the form of retained patronage dividends and thus constituted a loan to the co-operative.[89] Second, the financial situation of Agro was sufficiently serious that it had entered into a financial support and management agreement with its wholesaler, Co-op Atlantic. Consequently, for the foreseeable future the investments held by members in Agro werc, to all intents and purposes, worthless.

In spite of the obvious intent of the by-law and statutory prohibition on equity pay-outs to protect the co-operative from becoming insolvent or worsening its insolvency, Cutcliffe was successful in his claim to set off his accrued patronage dividends against his outstanding debt, and was thus able to take his money out of Agro. In so doing, he clearly made the financial situation of the co-operative worse and damaged the interests of the remaining members. Further, to the extent that he had an interest in the continuation of the co-operative, Cutcliffe would have damaged his long-term interests through this conduct.[90]

One of the consequences of such a decision is to make Co-op Atlantic wary about the security of its financial arrangement with Agro. If its investment could be as easily eroded as Cutcliffe had shown, it would be less likely to maintain the support relationship. Every member and everyone beneficially affected by the presence of Agro in the market-place would thereby suffer. The actions of one member could precipitate undesirable consequences for all of the members, including the member in question. This case, and the approach taken by the court, illustrates the dangers of issues affecting co-operatives being decided by judges who do not appreciate either the importance or traditions of co-operatives and collective action, and graphically shows the dangers of so crudely giving precedence to individual interests over collective interests.

Harbin and McKane v. *Lloydminster Co-operative Association Ltd.*[91] is a recent case involving the relationship between the rights of the members in general meeting and the decision-making power of the board of directors. As is well known, and as was seen in chapter 3, it is difficult for shareholders of corporations and members of co-operatives who hold views not held by the majority to exert any influence. There are legal, pragmatic and economic reasons for the weakness of those with minority views; the majority rules.

This case involved a decision by the board of directors of a co-operative to close one of its branch stores because it was losing money. At the next annual general meeting of the co-operative, a motion to keep the store open was passed by the general membership.[92] At their first meeting after the annual meeting, however, the directors resolved to ignore this resolution and subsequently closed the store.

The court concluded that the common good was being served because closure of the store would have a positive impact on the surplus and, therefore, on patronage dividends payable to each of the members. Matched against this was the inconvenience caused to a few members – those who would no longer be able to shop at the closed store. The minority's claim that the conduct of the directors was 'oppressive or unfairly prejudicial to or ... unfairly disregard[ed] the interests of' the dissenting members was dismissed.[93]

While co-operatives espouse a participatory democratic model of governance, in actual practice the democratic processes in these organizations are quite elitist. Directors are elected to supervise the management of the co-operative, while members do not have management functions, except in limited, and generally extreme, circumstances. And if members are not satisfied with the performance of directors, their only remedy is to vote them out of office and replace them with others who will do their bidding. Directors are thereby permitted to ignore even a unanimous decision of the members in general meeting. This approach, and that taken by the court in the *Harbin and McKane* case, indicates that the law is of the view that the collective interests of the majority of members of the co-operative are better represented by the directors than by the majority of the members present and voting at a duly constituted general meeting. In itself, this presents an interesting perspective on the relationship between collective and individual rights in the operation of co-operatives.

Generally, corporation law and co-operative law operate on the basis of majority rule. At least in co-operatives, however, the law is prepared to permit elected officials to overrule and ignore decisions made by majorities. Judicially, an implicit assessment of what is best for the co-operative appears to be made on technocratic grounds, rather than on the foundations of participatory democracy that define these collective organizations. Courts traditionally have shunned any second-guessing of management decisions. An excerpt from the judgment is illustrative: 'In a democracy the will of the majority, subject to certain established rules, is what governs. However, the will of the majority of the [co-operative] was that of the board of directors until a contrary will was expressed. It is absurd to say that the will of 68 people could replace the mandate given the directors and become the will of the majority of the 10,000 members when the membership at large had no knowledge whatsoever of what the 68 proposed. Democracy does not function on the basis of ambush.'[94]

Another example of how the courts have viewed the relationship between the membership and the board of directors of a co-operative is provided by *Re Smythe et al. and Anderson et al.*[95] That case involved a dispute over how the co-operative should deal with a strike of its employees; 148 members of the co-operative petitioned the board of directors to call a special meeting as provided by the Co-operatives Act[96] so that the board could 'have the benefit of the members' directions regarding the handling of the negotiations and management of the ... Co-op during the strike and while the strike is still in progress.'[97] The board refused to call the meeting on the basis that it would be harmful to the negotiations, would not serve any purpose because some of the information requested by these members could not be obtained quickly and would be costly.[98] The members in question then sought a court order directing the meeting be called. The purpose of the meeting was set out and included discussing the conduct of the directors leading up to the strike, the effect of the strike, and the relationship between co-operative principles and labour relations.[99]

In his judgment refusing to order that the meeting take place, Mr Justice Hall pointed out that '[g]enerally speaking, the management of the affairs of the association is the function of the directors and cannot be exercised by the members.'[100] In discussing the function of the board of directors regarding labour relations and collective bargaining, Mr Justice Hall said the 'members cannot overrule or control the actions of the directors in this area ... the only remedy of the members, if they are dissatisfied with the manner in which the directors are managing the business is to remove them from office and elect new directors.'[101] He based his decision on the lack of impact such a meeting would have on the directors. He said: 'The applicants here do not request the special meeting for the purpose of transacting any business which they, as shareholders or members, are empowered to transact. The purpose amounts to an attempt to interfere with the management of the Association by the directors. No decision arrived at, nor any resolution passed at such a meeting could in any way bind the directors or compel them to alter their mode of direction and supervision of the business and property of the Association. The holding of the meeting would ... be a vain and useless thing.'[102]

Mr Justice Hall was concerned about two other things. First, he found nothing in the submissions to show that the conduct of the directors either had been detrimental to the co-operative or had caused any particular hardship to the members bringing the action. Second, while recognizing that the act only required one hundred members to call a meeting, he felt that the 'fact that only 200 members out of a total of over 28,000 have joined in the request cannot be disregarded.'[103] By contrast, in a similar situation in *Fraser Valley Credit Union* v. *Union of Bank Employees, Local 2100 et al.*,[104] a meeting was ordered.

At issue in the *Fraser Valley Credit Union* case was the means by which dissenting members could have a special resolution discussed at a general meeting. There was a strike at the credit union and disgruntled members wished to oust the majority of the board of directors and elect directors of their own choosing. The members in question wished to have a resolution discussed at the annual meeting. They sent the special resolution, the purpose of which was to change the by-laws of the credit union, to the board of directors. They also asked to have the resolution circulated to the membership as was required by statute for a valid by-law. The credit union's general manager refused to circulate the resolution; it was set out, however, in newspaper advertisements taken out by the dissenting members.

A court-ordered special meeting took place three days before the scheduled annual general meeting. At that special meeting, which was attended by 408 of the credit union's 22,000 members, resolutions were passed purporting to bring the labour dispute to an end by submitting the issues to arbitration, resolving not to lock out or lay off employees and selecting one of the members of the board, who was sympathetic to the cause of the dissenting members, as the arbitrator. Immediately after this meeting the board of directors resolved to ignore all of the resolutions and locked out the employees. At the annual general meeting, attended by approximately four hundred members, the dissenting members were successful in replacing the person chairing the meeting with someone who was more to their liking. They also ensured the passing of the resolution, which they had sought to have circulated, by the required two-thirds majority. The thrust of the resolution was to remove all of the directors and change the by-laws to permit an election of a new board at the meeting, rather than by mail-in ballot over a period of time. Nine directors were elected at the meeting.

Both the old and the new boards met. The old board commenced an action to declare the purported election void and to obtain an injunction prohibiting the new board from acting as directors and interfering with the business of the credit union. The new directors argued that they were the only lawful directors. In the middle of this the Credit Union Reserve Board appointed a trustee to administer the credit union.

The legal issue revolved around the validity of the by-law change. There were two elements to this. The by-law change had not been approved by the Superintendent of Credit Unions; this approval was required in order for any by-law change to be enforceable.[105] This, the court was not prepared to validate. The other difficulty was that such a resolution must be preceded by appropriate notice to be effective. As has been indicated, the reason why notice was not given was that the manager of the credit union refused to circulate it. The British Columbia Court of Appeal was concerned particularly with the need to protect the members and argued that nothing could be done to rectify the lack of notice and still protect the members' interests. It did not think, however, that the refusal to circulate notice of the proposed special resolution was a breach of the act.[106] The judges concluded that the resolution contemplated an immediate vote without the by-law change being approved by the Superintendent, and 'doubt[ed] that the board was obliged to circulate to the members a resolution which was so obviously and fundamentally defective.'[107]

Clearly, democratic decision-making cannot ignore questions of legal procedure. Had the credit union members awaited approval by the Superintendent before a new board was elected, the result may have been quite different. Under the circumstances, however, the election of the new board was declared invalid and the regular voting procedure ordered to take place.

The *Civil Service Co-operative Credit Society* case, as mentioned earlier, provides another example of the paternalism with which the Canadian judicial system has treated co-operatives. It is indicative, as well, of the tendency of the courts to impose the standards of liberal individualist society on organizations that have democratically chosen collective paths. For not only did Mr Justice Sirois ignore a democratically approved organizational by-law, but his decision was contrary to the spirit of co-operation and collective action on which these organizations are based.[108]

It is difficult to draw strong conclusions from these court decisions since they send sometimes conflicting messages about the philosophy of the legal framework with which co-operatives are faced. They illustrate, however, that the law, if anything, is an impediment to organizations that premise their activities on participatory forms of democracy. The decisions handed down by the courts indicate their willingness to ignore, or at least downplay, the democratic wishes of members who participate in these organizations and, instead, accept the primacy of boards of directors. That these organizations espouse, at least in theory, a democratic system that is oriented to member participation and control appears to be of little legal relevance. Furthermore, implicit in the theories of participatory democracy adopted by co-operatives is the notion that directors of these organization should be more closely accountable to their membership than directors of corporations are to their shareholders. In principle, however, the courts have set the foundation to undermine member control of Canadian co-operatives by imposing on them a framework for legal interpretation that is based on more elitist and capital-concerned forms of decision-making found in the corporate world.

Lessons for Co-operatives

This discussion poses a number of problems for co-operatives. At best, it illustrates that decisive forces in Canada have an increasing lack of interest in collective action. At worst, it suggests a hostility to such action. Regardless of how one accounts for the lack of a positive attitude toward collective action, co-operatives need to develop a long-term strategy to address it and communicate the benefits of collective action. Their neglect of wider political and social education strategies needs to be remedied.

What the Judges' Attitudes Tell Us
From a legal perspective, three points can be made. First, our discussion of the cases dealing with trade unions and their constitutionally guaranteed rights and of the cases dealing with co-operatives reveals a disturbing lack of support for collective action, as well as a lack of appreciation for the value of collective action in the pursuit of individual rights and freedoms. With the single exception of Madam Justice Wilson, the justices of the Supreme Court of Canada have given individual rights precedence over collective rights. Mr Justice McIntyre was particularly explicit on this point. While Chief Justice Dickson showed a greater appreciation for collective rights than the majority of his colleagues, he was not prepared to go as far as Madam Justice Wilson. He was prepared to rank inflation and harm to dairy farmers higher than fundamental freedoms to bargain collectively and the right to strike. The majority of the Supreme Court, however, found no such rights to be constitutionally guaranteed.

As the justices of the Supreme Court are appointed by the federal government, it can be assumed that they reflect the general values of the political party in power at the time of their appointment. As these appointees have responded in an overwhelmingly negative fashion to collective rights, it can be expected that this viewpoint would be shared by the political parties in question. With some isolated and notable exceptions, federal [109] and provincial governments[110] have not actively assisted co-operative movement development. Canadian governments generally see private enterprise, with its emphasis on individualism and competition, as the engine of economic development, and tend to reject or ignore co-operation, with its emphasis on collective action and working together.[111]

The discussion of the trade union cases in the Supreme Court of Canada is relevant here in one particular respect. It is clear that when those chosen by the government of Canada to interpret the constitution and the fundamental freedoms contained therein are faced with balancing collective and individual rights, they find in favour of the latter by an overwhelming majority. The decision in the *Lavigne* case is another clear illustration of the problems faced by advocates of the use of collective action to protect individual rights.

Co-operatives and co-operators should be very worried by the lack of sympathy for collective action at the highest levels of governmental and judicial decision-making in Canada. The co-operative movement will be further damaged if changes in attitudes at these highest levels are not forthcoming. The changes will not occur by themselves; they will require investment of greater resources and commitment than co-operatives have provided to date in this long-range educational process.

Intuitively one would suppose that the lack of interest in collective action identified in decisions of the Supreme Court of Canada is prevalent in the community at large. If co-operatives are to survive and thrive, it is essential that there be a favourable attitude toward collective action among the general population. To encourage a more receptive attitude to collective and thus co-operative activity, it will be necessary to develop much more sophisticated educational programs than have hitherto been available.

Our discussion of recent co-operative law cases further illustrates that few judges have experience with co-operative activity and law, and suggests a lack of appreciation on the part of judiciary for what lies at the root of co-operative activity. It also shows the essentially unco-operative character of co-operative law. Even though corporate and co-operative activities are predicated on different assessments of the respective value of collective and individual rights, the statutory and common law regimes under which they operate are essentially similar. Co-operative law is a virtual carbon copy of corporation law in spite of senior co-operators traditionally having been intimately involved in drafting co-operative statutes all across Canada. Consequently, part of the responsibility for the lack of a separate identity for co-operative law lies with the co-operative movement itself. This presents yet another educational challenge for the co-operative movement.

Conclusion

Clearly, the future of co-operatives in Canada requires that major challenges be addressed; the law and lawyers are important components of the success in meeting these challenges. There is a pressing need for more sympathetic treatment of collective interests and more sophisticated perspectives on the role of collective rights in making our society a better, fairer, and more co-operative place.

It is not an easy task to modify the traditional forces of liberal individualism that prevail in western society. Public recognition of the value and practical import of collective notions of rights will arise only from a more widespread understanding of the overarching importance to individuals of collective action by particular groups and organizations. Hence, the onus is on organizations such as co-operatives and trade unions to be aware of the ramifications of traditional legal premises and to present their cases for alternative points of legal reference.

When traditional bases of social, political, and legal thought are challenged, it is necessary to offer in their stead plausible, and in this case collective, alternatives to individualist approaches. Only in this way is it likely that collective rights will be awarded the judicial recognition that is their due.

PART FOUR

Co-operatives in the Economy

BRETT FAIRBAIRN

14 Big Capital, the Big State, and Co-operatives: Historical Perspectives

Co-operatives represent neither the private power of capital nor the collective power of the state. Their unique character as mutualist institutions of an open society allows them to find niches in the economy where neither of the other two forms of enterprise is meeting the perceived needs of a social group. This is particularly true in circumstances of economic development or technological change, where the groups affected may experience acute problems and have insufficient help from established business or government institutions. Where this happens, co-operatives give them a means to mobilize their own resources to deal with or bring about change. Co-operative movements have thrived where the economy was new or under pressure to change, where large numbers of people experienced similar socio-economic challenges, and where government and private initiatives were slow or inadequate.

Co-operatives do not precisely fit either of the two great economic ideologies of the twentieth century. Their de-emphasis of the rights of capital, expressed among other things in their characteristic attitudes concerning one shareholder/one vote, limited interest on capital; and distribution of 'profits' (surplus) in proportion to patronage distinguishes them from the usual capitalist model of a private company or corporation. Equally, their principles of local control and of autonomy from government (including compatibility with and commitment to private ownership) contradict the Soviet model of a centrally planned or 'state capitalist' economy. They are institutions of a market economy and pluralist society without individual control or domination by capital. It is important to observe that genuine co-operatives have existed within both kinds of settings, compromising with the profit motive in the

West and with government planning in the East, and yet representing in both environments a subtle or not-so-subtle form of dissent from the prevailing economic system.[1] This chapter considers the examples provided by the market economies and processes of technological change from which the first large co-operative movements emerged in Europe and North America. Its purpose is to identify in general terms historical patterns in the economic role of co-operatives, and in so doing to raise questions about their nature, function, and possible future development.

In philosophical terms, co-operatives have embodied neither theoretical collectivism nor theoretical individualism, but rather what might be called 'mutualism.' First, with regard to their differences from collectivism, co-operatives, in the form in which they spread historically, were unlike both ascribed forms of organization (guilds and communal structures in medieval society) and compulsory forms of organization (as in collectivized agriculture). It is fundamental to the modern idea of a co-operative that it is freely formed by independent individuals, and it normally competes in a market others may enter. While the earliest co-operative projects of the utopian sort did have a certain communal and collective focus (and, perhaps, even sometimes an authoritarian one), even they were intended to be formed on the basis of voluntary individual subscriptions, and since they were private projects, members could leave freely.[2] Nineteenth-century proposals for industrial production co-operatives might, it could be argued, have had a continuity with guild traditions; but they, like the agricultural communities, only ever amounted to a fringe movement. The successors to these utopian and production schemes, the consumer retail and credit co-operatives that spread into continent-wide movements, were fully creatures of a capitalist market economy, embracing (rather than attempting to escape) the necessity of functioning in an ostensibly free, liberal, monetary, and individualistic economic system.[3]

Indeed, co-operatives developed from some of the same principles embodied in the small-business economy of the early stages of European industrialization – thrift, self-help, autonomy from the state, the initiative of the population. In social-psychological terms as well as in economic function in local economies (concentrating the capital and mobilizing the initiative of the small), the co-operative sector's affinities to small business may well be greater than its affinities to any other segment of capitalist economies. Co-operative movements, however, developed later than small capitalist business, on behalf of different economic classes (labourers and peasants), and in response to particular kinds of economic problems that small business did not conveniently address. Unlike small business, they also stressed democratic decision-making and restrictions on capital investment and its privileges.

In their origins, then, modern co-operatives presume an open society in which individuals can make choices and commitments; but once formed, the essential point of a co-operative organization is emphasis on joint or common activity. This distinguishes them from individualist economic models. Collectively, members in a co-operative achieve an economy of scale or a market power in purchasing, manufacturing, or sales that they do not individually command. Unlike a joint-stock company, however, the co-operative is not controlled by its largest shareholders. Moreover, since a co-operative's owners are also users of its services and usually residents of the same community, there is a more intense connection between the firm and its owners than in the case of investors in most share companies. In referring to such a structure as mutualist we emphasize both its individualist origins as well as its participatory and egalitarian approach to common activity. This further distinguishes the co-operative from small business, in that the immediate purpose of co-operation is combination, not the economic independence of the individual.[4] The capacity to compete in big markets is what makes co-operation economically advantageous for members who would otherwise be too small to do so.

Co-operatives, therefore, to judge by their historical development, are neither fish nor fowl when it comes to the debates between big capital and big government. By adopting a comparative historical approach we can make some more definite observations about the necessary, and possible, relationships between co-operatives and the private economy, and between co-operatives and the state economy. Co-operative movements have existed in western industrialized countries for around a century and a half (in fact when co-operatives emerged some of these countries were still industrializing, a point to return to later). History therefore provides us with examples of co-operatives in many different economic, social, legal, and political settings. This range of particular experiences in many countries and many periods merits closer consideration.

One key to the economic interpretation of the formation of co-operatives is the historical observation that co-operatives have generally been reactive solutions to the problems posed by changing technology and markets. In the industrializing West the rise of co-operative movements in the nineteenth and twentieth centuries was directly parallel and an explicit reaction to the growing size of markets and competitors – a fundamental qualitative change in how the economy functioned and in how people perceived it.[5] Co-operatives were means of adaptation to a changed economy for people whose traditional patterns of production, marketing, or consumption were becoming unsatisfactory.

The earliest co-operative theorists were the utopian socialists of the early nineteenth century, who sought an answer to the fragmentation of urban and industrial society and specifically the decline of the independent artisan. Middle-class reformers such as Robert Owen and the followers of Charles Fourier sought a solution in removing impoverished labourers from the squalid conditions of the urban slums and transporting them to self-sufficient co-operative communities.

But the beginnings of significant mass co-operative movements lay in the 1840s, a decade which saw heightened social distress, the defeat of Chartism in Britain and the 1848 revolutions on the continent, and the birth of the Rochdale movement and other new co-operatives. The experience of the revolutions discredited (perhaps unjustly) socialist ideas of state-sponsored industrial production co-operatives such as those advocated by Louis Blanc in France.[6] While others who shared Blanc's ideas, notably Ferdinand Lassalle in Germany, sought to set up production co-operatives in the 1860s, these efforts were not successful. In Britain the distress of the 1840s helped stir Edward Vansittart Neale among the Christian Socialists to promote production co-operatives, but again with little success; in the end the Christian Socialists' greatest contribution was in heading and securing legal status for the consumer co-operative movement.[7] In the aftermath of the turmoils, ferment, and experiments of the 1840s, the successful new co-operative movements were the Rochdale consumer model in Britain and the Schulze-Delitzsch credit co-operatives in Germany, soon supplemented by the Raiffeisen model for agricultural credit unions.

What these newer models had in common was that they no longer sought to help the artisan or worker by removing him from the city, from his occupation, or from the competitive urban market, as the utopian communities had; and neither did they propose to revolutionize the workplace or the ownership of the means of production. Instead, with the savings made possible by membership in a consumer co-operative, or the credit provided by a credit union, and with the opportunities for education offered by both, the struggling individual labourer was to be able to improve his position in the market and in society, adapting to the new economic order rather than escaping it. Characteristically, it was in credit and retailing that co-operation blossomed, and not in schemes to create idealized self-sufficient communities or socially owned factories. Equally characteristically, it was the working poor of the industrial cities of northern England and of peasant farms in the Rhineland who adopted co-operation as their economic instrument, not the indigent poor of London or the landless rural labourers of eastern Europe. They did so largely after the middle of the nineteenth century, within the context of an emerging world industrial economy. Consumer and credit co-operatives were the means by which the marginal participants in the new economy (not the unviable losers) adapted to its requirements and enhanced their power and independence.

There was an especially close relation between co-operatives and technological adaptation in the agricultural sector. Agriculture, once the overwhelmingly dominant aspect of society, experienced in the course of industrialization and urbanization a steady erosion of its primacy and a series of fundamental technological challenges. This relationship between co-operatives and agricultural improvement began with Friedrich Wilhelm Raiffeisen. Schulze-Delitzsch's idea of credit co-operatives, which he initially applied to the needs of artisans in his own state of Saxony, was paralleled by Raiffeisen's associations for farmers in the Rhineland. In the 1850s and 1860s Raiffeisen organizations spread, forming the first nation-wide union of agricultural co-operatives in 1877.[8] From there co-operative rural credit spread, at first slowly, throughout central Europe, making inroads in Austria, and from the mid-1890s in Hungary and in the lands that were to become Czechoslovakia, Yugoslavia, and the other states of eastern and southeastern Europe. As with urban workers, credit unions in the country did not seek to create self-sufficient communities, or to revolutionize ownership. Instead they helped marginal peasant producers invest in new technology, modernize their operations, and so remain viable in the changing agricultural market – a market which, after 1870, saw falling grain prices, competition from the Americas, and pressure for improvement or rationalization. When, from the 1880s onward, Danish and Irish agricultural co-operation grew, it once again did not involve co-operative communities or production, but co-operative purchasing and marketing as services to help independent rural producers.[9]

Later, in the interwar period, land reform – one of the biggest social and economic issues in eastern Europe – was coupled with official sanction for nation-wide co-operative movements that were to support, integrate, and modernize the newly independent, small peasant producers.[10]

The experience of agriculture in the interior of North America was somewhat different; it was the new technology itself which opened up these lands, where no traditional agricultural system already existed. If anything, however, this only made the confrontation with big markets and big capital more explicit. The grain farmers who settled in the North American plains, selling to markets thousands of miles away and dependent on suppliers of equipment equally remote, found themselves utterly dependent on remote and monopolistic institutions of finance and transportation that moved their products.[11] Many discovered that the viability of the ideal of the small family farmer that had inspired them to emigrate in the first place was threatened by this dependence on concentrated capital. As one historian of American populism has put it, 'agrarian reformers attempted to overcome a concentrating system of finance capitalism that was rooted in Eastern commercial banks and which radiated outward through trunk-line railroad networks to link in a number of common purposes much of America's consolidating corporate community.' The aim of the 'cooperative crusade' was 'structural reform of the American economic system.'[12] It was the determination to do something about problems posed by concentration that led farmers to found their own political movements, their own elevator companies, and their own marketing organizations.[13] The purpose of this activity (as in continental European co-operatives of the same era) was to improve ordinary farmers' financial position. The function of the same activity, seen in broad economic-historical terms, was to help reconcile individual farmers' dreams of independence and ownership with the realities of huge market-places and complex systems of distribution and finance.

These examples illustrate the point that co-operativism in the industrializing countries of the nineteenth and early twentieth centuries was a characteristic response of the small to the big, and in particular of small workers and producers to big capital. But co-operatives were not merely reactions to the transformation of the economy; they were agents of that same transformation. Where most successful, they did not stop the process of increasing economic concentration and bigness, but rather furthered it in a certain sense while attempting to render it 'democratic' or 'popular.' Consumer co-operatives in Europe did not compete only with big chains and department stores; they also helped put independent shopkeepers out of business as part of the overall trend to bigger retail outlets and networks, and for that reason retail co-operatives earned shopkeepers' ire. To the declining shopkeeper, the retail co-operative, the department store, the mail-order shop, and the door-to-door salesman were all examples of the new 'unfair competition.'[14] In parts of North America this was no different; the success of the co-operative movement in Saskatchewan saw co-operators and small-town merchants engage in bitter fights.[15] Dairy co-operatives have also been agents of bigness, achieving virtual monopolies in selling their products in many countries or regions. The wheat pools that developed in the Canadian prairies in the 1920s became huge marketing, transportation, and supply organizations, overshadowing their private competitors in their regional markets.[16] Such co-operatives have never been, after all, successful reactions to bigness as such, but instead to the bigness of others, the bigness of remote and unresponsive institutions to be countered with the bigness of local and democratic ones, the bigness of centralization to be countered with the bigness of federation and participation.

Besides the linkage of co-operatives and development, especially in agriculture, there is another important observation to be made concerning the historical development of modern co-operative movements. Co-operatives, it is argued above, developed historically as reactions to bigness which functioned in the long term to help small participants in the economic system be more competitive with big ones. Typically this meant obtaining lower prices for the commodities their members purchased, or higher prices for those they produced, or both; and frequently it involved monopoly-busting to do so. Thus far the economic role of the co-operative can be interpreted purely in terms of price comparisons with local non-co-operative competitors. But there is more to it than that, at least for some of the kinds of co-operatives that grew to the status of movements. In many cases thriving co-operative movements were ones that took root in changing sectors of the economy where, for economic or attitudinal reasons, no adequate state or private institutions had evolved to meet a perceived need at the local level. That is, the comparative advantage of the co-operative organization, where this grew to the status of a movement, was not just quantitative (better prices for competitive services) but also qualitative (the co-operative frequently did something that would not otherwise have been done at all, such as providing services of a different kind or in a different place).

There are examples to illustrate this. The rural credit co-operatives of central Europe made credit available to peasants in the countryside at a time when most financial institutions were in the towns and cities. Moreover, they made loans to those who could never otherwise have obtained them, substituting intimate local knowledge of borrowers' character and reliability for regular banks' insistence on collateral. This was a feature of the Raiffeisen system in Germany, for example, that was praised not only by its members but by agriculturalists and government officials: through decentralized organization tightly integrated into local communities, the Raiffeisen banks successfully ran a business providing credit no normal credit institution would have provided. They could do so because the nature and degree of involvement of their membership provided an economic advantage over private or outside businesses.

The consumer co-operatives of the urban working classes in Britain and Germany in the nineteenth century permitted a group afflicted by deprivation, misery, and disenfranchisement to educate themselves, exercise their skills, build up their savings, and become part of a social community through organizations directed specifically toward their needs and interests. The democracy, training, and education found in the co-operative movement were not only a means to an economic end, but an end in themselves – and one not realizable through any other agency at the time.

The farmers' organizations of the North American plains derived their force from the need not only for better prices, but for better services: elevators and grain cars where and when the farmers wanted them, reliably honest weights and grades, organizational structures integrated into the needs and culture of local communities rather than arbitrary decisions by 'outsiders.' The consumer co-op and credit union movements that paralleled the farmers' movement brought retail and financial services into small towns that had few or no existing facilities of this kind; even today some relatively uneconomic stores or credit unions are kept going because they are the sole remaining commercial focal point for a small community. In all of these cases co-operatives served to break down barriers to services based on class, occupation, capital, or geography, and to meet perceived needs for institutions that could support and sustain a stable and integrated community.

There are several ways that these circumstances arose, circumstances in which the larger economy and government were unable or unwilling to respond to the needs of an economic group that was able, instead, to respond to those needs itself. First of all, it should by now be clear that one reason for co-operatives finding a niche in the economy has to do with remote, unresponsive, or monopolistic capital. As in the rural Rhineland, so in rural Saskatchewan farmers and bankers did not mix well. There was a barrier between the rural world of the one and the urban world of the other. The prairie wheat farmers' suppliers and creditors were in the cities of the east, while the co-operatives they created themselves were right at hand. In the case of urban workers, the gulf separating them from the owners of factories and stores was not a geographic but a social one. Seen in context, it is hardly surprising that the British consumer co-operative movement became an ally of the Labour party, or that by 1914 the German consumer co-operatives were largely affiliated to the Social Democratic party. In both cases a socialist co-operative movement acted parallel to a trade union movement to fight what were seen as hostile capitalist interests.

Many of the examples mentioned above also occurred in the political context created by governments dedicated in some degree to economic non-interventionism; that is, governments influenced by the sort of ideas that sprang out of nineteenth-century liberalism. Because of this, those who founded co-operative movements could not expect, or at least could not easily achieve, government intervention in response to their needs. Some of them in fact preferred governmental solutions to autonomous ones, but were forced to pursue the latter because of the government's differing regional or ideological commitments. This was true of many of the Canadian pool organizers of the 1920s, whose immediate impetus had come from their campaign to preserve farmers' grain monopoly as incorporated in the government's Wheat Board during the First World War. Farm movements, in Europe and America, looked in the late nineteenth and early twentieth centuries to tariff policy and currency reform as means for governments to solve all of their market problems at one stroke.[17] Meanwhile, as already noted, the majority of consumer co-operatives in Germany were fully integrated into that country's socialist movement by the early 1900s, a movement which strongly advocated social reform by the state. It is, however, true of the British tradition that most co-operators were dedicated to autonomous action and, like much of the rest of the middle and working classes, had taken free trade and opposition to state intervention to heart. A substantial part of the Canadian co-operative movement retained this anti-statist heritage.[18] Nevertheless, at least in some cases, co-operatives arose partly because governments would not do the things potential co-operators wanted them to, rather than because the potential co-operators disliked governments.

Indeed, in some cases where governments were supportive of the co-operative movement, co-operatives were eager to accept assistance. The province of Saskatchewan, which developed one of the most powerful co-operative sectors in Canada, was noteworthy for the degree of government support extended to co-operatives in terms of leadership, advice, and legislation. W. Waldron, who was acting commissioner of the Co-operation and Markets Branch of the Saskatchewan Department of Agriculture, formed a close friendship with George Keen, the head of the Co-operative Union of Canada, in the 1920s. Waldron, his department, and his successor, B.N. Arnason, were integrally involved in improving co-operative legislation, in developing the Co-operative League of Saskatchewan, and in promoting the Saskatchewan Co-operative Wholesale Society founded in 1928. Since both Waldron, as a British co-operator, and Keen, as a leader in the consumer co-operative movement, were vitally interested in consumer co-operation, this leadership may help explain why Saskatchewan's co-operative wholesale developed as a major success. Diversifying and amalgamating with a petroleum co-operative and with the other provincial wholesales of western Canada over the period from 1944 to 1971, it became the headquarters for co-operative wholesaling in western Canada. The self-help motive in co-operation means retaining autonomous control, not, obviously, spurning the aid of governments or of other co-operatives.

Such aid has generally been more readily forthcoming for agricultural co-operatives than for others; the political significance attached to agriculture has ensured this. The bailing-out and reorganization of the Canadian wheat pools when they collapsed in 1931 is evidence of the state's interest in agricultural co-operation. But in other times and places that interest has been taken too far for some co-operators' liking. The German co-operative movement, with its nineteenth-century liberal heritage, was deeply divided in the 1890s when state governments decided, owing to the perceived agricultural crisis, to subsidize agricultural co-operatives by providing them with cheap credit from state-funded banks. The 'purest' of the co-operative federations, the liberal Schulze-Delitzsch federation, refused government money out of a deep fear of state control and an aversion to public funding. Yet it is worth noting that rival co-operative federations arose and eagerly accepted state funds, growing to become bigger and more powerful than the Schulze Delitzsch co-operatives that preferred financial independence. While they did, as their critics predicted, encounter some difficulties with regard to autonomy from the state, it is apparent that many co-operators were not averse to indirect subsidization by government.[19] We must be careful, then, in saying that co-operatives are opposed to state intervention; what they are consistently opposed to is state control.

It was in the context of an economic threat or challenge to adapt, and where capital and government did not provide obvious solutions, that producers or consumers created co-operatives to cope with new needs or, indeed, with crisis. An important part of the Danish co-operative movement, to quote a crisis example, owes its origins to a virtual embargo on live pigs enforced by the German government in 1887, using health regulations. By banding together to form co-operative bacon factories, which within three years of the embargo had spread to every region of Denmark, the Danish pig farmers were able to redirect their industry in a short time from the sale of live animals to Germany toward the sale of bacon to Britain. The strong Danish dairy co-operative system also developed as a means of reorienting agricultural production toward more profitable intensive farming in the face of falling prices for grain. The co-operative movement in this example, which became one of the model co-operative movements in the world, served in functional terms to save farmers from ruin by the speedy reorientation of their processing and marketing. In response (it should be noted) to adverse big government intervention (foreign protectionism), Danish co-operatives served as agents for restructuring the industry and allowed their members to adapt to the changed circumstances.[20] The example of Ireland is perhaps even better known in the Anglo-Saxon world, for at the end of the nineteenth century the Irish co-operative movement helped address that country's long-term crisis in agriculture and modernize its technology. Where neither government nor private enterprise seemed ready to address a structural problem quickly enough, co-operatives could do so.[21]

Co-operative movements thrived where the economy was new or under strong pressure to change, where large numbers of people experienced similar challenges, and where government and private initiatives were slow or inadequate. They were able to mobilize small participants in the economic process to adjust, in a comparatively simple and flexible way, to a situation that might otherwise have required a thoroughgoing economic restructuring and concentration. They found their economic niche where change occurred and other types of institutions were leaving the needs of large and cohesive groups unsatisfied. This seems on the surface to support the self-avowed historical role of co-operatives as a 'progressive' one, as agents of change, of adaptation, and of improvement. But co-operatives have served to prop up declining economic sectors as well as to mobilize new ones. Shopkeepers' and some peasants' co-operatives in the European experience served more to stave off inevitable decline, or to mitigate it, than to usher in modernization; and their politics, reflecting this, were sometimes of the radical-conservative sort.[22]

Still, by and large the advocates of co-operative innovation were also the advocates of technological innovation, promoting improved methods, sharing information, developing and providing technical resources, and promoting general education. The relevant point may be that these activities were more effective in stable or growing sectors of the economy than in those suffering decline, for the people who became involved in founding and leading co-operative movements were normally the innovative and the economic survivors, rather than the marginalized or those confined to declining sectors. Shopkeepers' co-operatives in Europe preserved for policy reasons an economic system that was in decline, as did some of the nationalistic rural co-operative movements, but these tended to remain small in numbers and weak in organization. By contrast, in Danish agriculture the co-operative movement was obviously wedded to rapid improvement and modernization. Likewise working-class consumer co-operatives took the offensive in an expanding urban retail market. The latter movement became, in some of the more industrialized countries of western Europe, more innovative, more dynamic, and larger than the agricultural movement. To judge by such examples, co-operatives did not arise solely in growing or modernizing sub-sectors of the economy, but they did spread much better and have a much greater impact in such sectors. This ought not to be surprising, since one would expect economic and attitudinal limitations to co-operation among producers or consumers who are hamstrung, set against each other, and forced to adopt a defensive mentality by longterm economic trends adverse to them.

This relationship of co-operatives to economic adaptation has other implications when viewed as a process of response to the strengths and weaknesses of a particular economic system. In a sentence, co-operative movements that achieved a large scale have tended to supplement the predominant (state or private) economic system and to compensate for its shortcomings. This is natural enough, since in a society disposed toward capitalism or toward central planning, co-operatives will take root and spread where the dominant economic institutions are weaker or less adequate. In this sense as well, it is not surprising to see that farmers and the urban working classes have been the nuclei of the largest co-operative movements, since the integration of these groups into modern industrial economies has been among the most vexing problems of nineteenth- and twentieth-century societies. Agriculture, in relative terms the loser in the process of industrialization, is still debt-, subsidy-, and crisis-ridden (or is perceived to be so) in many capitalist countries; and if capitalism has failed to answer the question of how best to organize agriculture in a modern industrial economy, Soviet-style central planning has so far done worse. Similarly, meeting the needs of the new mass urban consumer market was beyond the immediate abilities of the nineteenth-century small shopkeeping trade, so co-operatives (alongside new chain stores, department stores, and door-to-door salesmen) did it instead. Rather than undermining or replacing other systems of economic organization, co-operatives, to judge by historical examples, have helped do what the others could not, and so complemented or mitigated the negative aspects of the prevailing economic system.

The above discussion seeks to understand the development of co-operatives by relating it to the large-scale transformation of economies in the last century and a half. One of the main points is that co-operatives have not been universal phenomena, but have existed in specific times, specific places, and specific combinations of circumstances. Their roles can only be fully understood when their relation to their own times is understood. Since our society and economy continue to change, however, it may be taken almost for granted that co-operatives will not be the same today or in the future as they were at any one time in the past. Does past experience supply any indications of what might be expected in the 1990s and beyond? One way to approach this question is by analogy: perhaps we may assume that co-operatives will bear a similar sort of relationship to the society of the future to that which they bore to the societies of the past.

The great modern wave of co-operativism developed from the middle of the nineteenth century to the middle of the twentieth. The boundaries are somewhat arbitrary, yet this period encompasses the origins of modern co-operative principles, the formation of most of the large co-operative movements, and their growth to become imposing and influential structures. This wave of co-operation was concerned with the chief economic development of its time: the emergence of a concentrated industrial economy. Co-operatives' usual solution to centralized bigness was federated bigness in purchasing, marketing, and credit, to make groups of smaller producers or consumers competitive with large organizations.

It is now fashionable in some circles, however, to argue that both bigness and industrialism are in decline. Western societies are held to be entering a post-industrial phase, in which the huge, inflexible organizations of heavy industries that were once the dynamos of the economy are to be superseded by flexible structures such as those held to be characteristic of the services and electronics industries. As part of this trend the service sector is expanding, and an 'information economy' is thought by many to be emerging, which will place high value on specialized knowledge and communications.

Such trends ought, in a way, to be in co-operatives' favour, for co-operatives have always been concentrated in distribution, marketing, and services, rather than in production; and they have always had the image of responsiveness to their members and of adaptability. But in starting small and fighting to grow they have also become preoccupied with volume, size, and market power, so that the democratic flexibility of the movement has often been de-emphasized in the name of strength and efficiency. People may become more interested in their local co-operative's service and relevance to their specific, particular needs, less interested in the size and impressiveness of co-operative 'centrals' and 'systems,' or in their generic and standardized high-volume products and services. And there may be pressure on co-operatives to use their membership base more effectively, to involve it more actively at the local level in decisions, in order to keep ahead of changing demands. Co-operatives have a built-in 'information advantage,' in that their customers are their owners – but this advantage must be organized and mobilized by getting people talking and involved. One lesson, then, of possible economic changes may be that co-operatives will need to become more aggressive about education to capture new and more committed members, and about organization of internal democracy, if they wish to turn the possible trend towards smallness and flexibility to their own advantage.

If the perceived present trends continue, then new co-operatives may also be of new kinds. Just as earlier co-operatives responded to the fundamental changes and challenges of their eras, finding ways to humanize bigness and reconcile small producers and consumers with big markets, so one would expect new co-operatives to develop best where they serve an analogous function, coping this time with the trend to smallness and flexibility. If consumer co-operation and agricultural pooling had built-in ideas of expansion to achieve economies of scale, perhaps new co-operatives will be those that reject such ideas and concentrate on limited scale, narrowly defined interests and memberships, and maximum responsiveness. One would expect to see successful new co-operatives, as in earlier periods, in parts of the economy challenged by change, and perhaps where government and private initiatives are slow or inadequate owing to remoteness or social/attitudinal barriers.

Many co-operatives of the mid-nineteenth to mid-twentieth centuries were based on agriculture or the working classes. Yet western societies, where not overwhelmingly urban already, continue to urbanize, decreasing the role of agriculture in the population and in the economy; at the same time, we are told, the urban working population identifies itself largely as middle-class and lacks the sense of separateness and disadvantage that inspired the early working-class co-operative movements of Europe. New co-operatives will not function in the nearly homogeneous communities of farmers or labourers where they were once created, but in a heterogeneous and more urban environment where occupation may not be the pre-eminent factor in people's assessment of their place in society and their needs. To follow such trends, co-operatives might have to represent economic units based not on occupational category (all farmers, all consumers) but on special groupings defined by narrower economic interests, by status, by life-style, by non-job-related interests. Society is becoming more, not less, complex, and accordingly we should not expect broad and categoric co-operative movements to develop in the future as they did in the past. If new co-operatives spread sufficiently to justify being called a new movement, we would expect, arguing from historical experience, that they would now be small and urban, oriented toward issues such as housing and health, day care and recreation, special consumer interests and special workplace aspirations. Co-operatives have never been concerned solely with prices, yet in future we might expect some of them to be even less so, as they find greater justification in humanizing the urban environment and the workplace.

Production or worker co-operatives, whether in agriculture, industry, or services, have been repeatedly advocated but rarely implemented in the western industrialized nations. The utopian communities of Owen and Fourier, the social workshops of Blanc and Lassalle, have been dead ends.[23] The large co-operative movements were in the areas of retailing and credit, organized by consumers of these services, and in agricultural marketing, organized by independent farmer-producers. It is conceivable that the limitation of largescale co-operation to these sectors of the economy is due to the internal logic of co-operative endeavour; but it seems more likely that the crucial barrier to co-operative production has been the historical circumstances that required immense amounts of capital to set up viable agricultural or industrial enterprises. If small-scale enterprise is more viable, or if aid from governments or established co-operatives were forthcoming, then the conditions that in the past militated against co-operative production might be altered. Indeed, worker co-operatives may have some advantages in light of current discussion of employee morale as a factor in productivity, and the corresponding advocacy of Japanese style 'quality circles,' German-style 'co-determination,' and employee share-ownership plans (ESOPs). If prevailing wisdom should come to emphasize the need to give workers a voice and a share in their companies, then workers' co-operatives will be much less isolated from the mainstream of business thought than in the past.

Finally, our understanding of the role of the co-operatives in the past has international implications. The apparently deep and abiding association between co-operatives and the popular experience of economic change implies a special role for co-operatives in developing economies.[24] Just as the co-operative movement emerged in Europe during Europe's industrialization, and in North America as the industrial economy was organized in new regions, so we would expect co-operatives to play an important role in developing countries today – as, indeed, they do, often as a conscious element of governments' economic strategies. Of all the areas where we would expect to see new co-operative movements, this would be (to judge by history) one of the biggest. But one major circumstance is different for many countries industrializing today: their industrialization is forced, a policy undertaken in knowledge of the past and attempting to pick and choose from the existing precedents. It is more important than ever, therefore, that we know and understand what co-operatives are and what they do, what conditions favour them and what do not, if their position in such development strategies is to be assessed correctly.

LOU HAMMOND KETILSON

15 Management in Co-operatives: Examining the Marketing Competitiveness of Consumer Co-operatives

In co-operative organizations the concept of autonomous, local control through democratic decision-making processes has shaped and influenced the design of the organization to the extent that organizational structure, evolving from organizational philosophy, appears to have determined strategy selection. In western Canadian consumer co-operatives, the predetermined structure and strategy is inconsistent with that found in the industry. This chapter presents a theoretical explanation for the development of this phenomenon, and raises questions regarding the impact of such inconsistencies on the future survival and success of consumer co-operative organizations.

Consumer co-operatives in western Canada evolved as a response to inequities in the market-place, as did many other types of co-operative organizations. Individuals, encouraged by the success of other co-operatives, identified this form of economic organization as a means for providing economic and social benefits to consumers. From their inception in the early 1900s, grass-roots involvement was central to consumer co-operatives' success, with the autonomy of the independent retails a highly valued commodity. Because members controlled decision-making at the local level, the organizations were responsive to their needs and provided services not previously delivered by privately owned organizations. The decentralized, federated system, with its emphasis on local ownership and control, was the strength of the consumer co-operative movement in western Canada.[1]

A briefer version of this chapter appeared in the Bayley and Parnell, eds., *Yearbook of Co-operative Enterprise 1988*.

During the 1960s and 1970s the retailing industry changed dramatically, with a move away from small independents to large, wholesaler-owned, centrally controlled concerns. Consumer co-operatives went through a period of expansion during this buoyant economic period, keeping pace with the large national firms. However, in the early 1980s, with a downturn in the economy, market-place competition became severe. Centralization of services and decision-making became the order of the day. The consumer co-operatives, though larger in size, continued to adhere to a decentralized, loosely federated system. Consequently, they are now caught between the need to centralize in order to retain their competitiveness within the retailing industry, and the demands of retail members wishing to retain an autonomous network more sensitive to local member needs.

Such conflicting demands have required consumer co-operatives to forgo some of the flexibility available to privately owned firms. Within private industry the generally accepted position regarding strategy selection and implementation in organizational settings is that strategies are chosen first and the structure of the organization is subsequently altered to implement the chosen strategy.[2] The factors contributing to the identification of a preferred strategy are rooted in the environment, primarily the structure of the industry within which the organization competes.

Those who adhere to this position accept that the primary determinants of market performance[3] are identified as being industry-wide elements of structure, the characteristics of the strategic group in which the organization competes, and the organization's position within its strategic group. All of these variables are structural factors considered to be relatively stable and difficult to overcome. Internal factors such as the organization's ability to implement the chosen strategy are considered to be less important in determining market performance.

In co-operative organizations, however, organizational structure has historically been linked to co-operative principles. Because of the nature of the ownership relationship between Federated Co-operatives, the co-operative wholesaler, and the Co-operative Retailing System, the wholesaler has not been able to follow the strategic decision-making patterns evolving within private industry. The concept of autonomous, local control through democratic decision-making processes has shaped and influenced the design of these organizations to the point that it would appear that organizational structure, evolving from organizational philosophy, determines strategy selection. The subsequent strategies chosen must mesh with given structural limitations if co-operative integrity is to be maintained.

Consequently, the consumer co-operatives in western Canada are faced with a particular dilemma. Their organizational structure, as prescribed by philosophy, is inconsistent with that demanded by their respective industry. However, member loyalty, stemming from grass-roots organizing and locally based control systems, has built, and to a limited extent continues to sustain the consumer co-operative system. The challenge to contemporary consumer co-operative leaders is to convert this cornerstone of the 'co-operative difference' into strategies that will provide the needed edge in the market.

Issues Affecting the Management of Co-operatives

The dual nature of co-operative organizations' objectives – to address both the economic and social needs of the membership – has been identified as contributing to what one author has called the 'co-operative dilemma.'[4] Researchers examining the nature of management and decision-making within co-operatives consider this 'duality of purpose' to be a major confounding factor.[5] The co-operative, like any other business enterprise, must operate efficiently to survive, but, it has to attach a great deal more significance to the successful attainment of social ends.

Shaviro argues that duality is not exclusive to co-operative institutions, and suggests that a social conscience is shared by co-operatives and private firms alike.[6] This criticism is justified, but it is generally assumed that in the long run private enterprise will subordinate value concerns when they interfere with profitability.[7] It has been argued that 'a business that defined "right" and "wrong" in terms that would satisfy a well developed contemporary conscience could not survive. No company can be expected to serve the social interest unless its self interest is also served, either by the expectation of profit or by the avoidance of punishment.'[8]

A factor which further complicates the management process is the centrality of the concepts of democracy and participation in co-operative organizations. Historically, co-operatives were considered to be a major vehicle of democracy. They offered political, economic, and social participation to the nineteenth-century industrial working class before this right was included in the definition of citizenship for that class. As such, co-operatives played a major role in educating their members in the democratic process and in preparing individuals for participation in a national political democracy.[9] One member, one vote continues to symbolize the democratic principles underlying co-operative organizations. While the importance of this education process for political participation has generally diminished, the co-operative organization remains an institution in which the possibility for participation in the decision-making process exists more than in privately owned enterprises.

Briscoe argues that the organizational structures initially put into place to facilitate participatory decision-making have themselves become reified.[10] He suggests that in the early days of its development the institutional form of democracy was instrumental in effecting certain changes and improvements, such as providing access to participation in the economic system to those who might not otherwise have had access. However, he suggests that currently the democratic structure has taken on *institutional* value without possessing *instrumental* value in terms of business operation.[11] He concludes that democracy is valued for its moral superiority and, as an institutional value, 'resists change and exerts normative restrictions on business activities – burdens not borne by the co-op's competitors.'[12]

The necessity of having to juggle the membership's right of access to participation in organizational decision-making[13] with the imperatives of efficient business operation has contributed to the development of rather elaborate mechanisms for member participation.[14] As a result the various organizational *structures* currently in place in co-operatives, and the *processes* established for facilitating participation, have evolved from the initially instrumental and now possibly institutional value placed on the ideal of democratic models for participation.

The goal-setting and decision-making processes are key variables affecting structure within co-operative organizations. The democratic nature of co-operatives is reflected in these two processes and serves to increase their complexity.

Goal-setting
Rational models of organization consider goal-setting to be the responsibility of the primary decision-makers in the organization – the owner in smaller corporations and senior management in larger corporations. This rather limited understanding of goals as static elements established by individuals in the organization may be applicable to corporations or co-operatives in their earliest stages of development, where decision-making and control are linked to one omnipotent position of authority; but it cannot continue to be applicable as the organization grows and its task environment becomes more complex.

A natural system model recognizes that 'domain consensus,'[15] or the claims recognized by those agents in the environment able to provide necessary support to the organization, defines the set of expectations about what the organization will or will not do, and thus effectively defines operational goals. Accepting this perspective leads one to conclude that the ideological goals of co-operatives (mission statements or official goals, as Perrow defines them)[16] will often be undermined by agencies in the external environment whose operative goals are inconsistent with the official goals of the focal organization, but who control resources essential to that organization.

Goals are not static but evolve, reflecting the influence of a variety of interest groups[17] and the power of the dominating elite.[18] By identifying the groups in control of resources central to the focal organization, we can trace the evolution of operative goals throughout its history. For example, consumer co-operatives were dominated in the early years by the members who contributed financial resources and legitimation to the co-operative as a social and economic institution. Power over decision-making and goal-setting rested with the board of directors, who acted as trustees for the membership. As the consumer co-operatives grew in size and complexity, reliance for financial resources shifted from the members to financial institutions, and to suppliers of goods and technical services. The membership's power over decision-making and goal-setting diminished as board decisions began to reflect the desires of these external agents. Organizations that drew financial resources from retained earnings tended to remove decision-making even further from the membership by allowing management to assume that role. This consequence also reflects the importance currently attributed to managerial task areas. As co-operatives have grown in size and complexity, it has become more difficult for a lay board to possess the technical and administrative skills necessary for making decisions. Increasingly management has been allowed to assume this role, and the distinction between elected and paid officials' responsibilities has thereby been blurred.[19]

Further developments in the study of goals have expanded the concept of external dependency[20] to include a broader range of stakeholders who influence the process of setting goals.[21] Perrow[22] set the stage for this perspective by identifying a variety of goal categories, delineated by external (societal, output, and investor goals) and internal (system, product characteristics, and derived goals) reference points. Examples in each of these categories contribute further to understanding the behaviour of co-operative organizations.

Societal goals are expressed in terms of the function co-operatives perform for society. Consensus regarding the co-operative organization's societal goals has not yet been reached. Co-operatives are considered by some to be agents for social change capable of undertaking the complete reformation of society; some view co-operation as an aid to specific occupational groups or classes; others see the movement as a corrective to abuses apparent in the existing society;[23] still others see co-operatives acting to improve the competitive performance of the total economic system.[24]

Goals as *output* can be identified by asking the question, 'Who benefits?' Originally, and for most co-operators now, the answer was the members, who are also the owners. Adding to the complexity of the situation, we find that the member/owners of most co-operatives are also the clients or consumers. In terms of the idealized conception of co-operatives' purpose (that of social change agent), society in general also benefits, thereby also having an influence over goal-setting.

The *traditional investor* goal, return on investment, is the goal most often cited as the primary directive for privately owned corporations, and is often advocated as the normative directive for co-operative organizations. However, capital is not the only item of value invested in co-operatives. Labour and legitimation are also contributed and thereby occupy a position which commands response from goal-setters. As a result, maximization of profit may be a necessary but not sufficient characterization of the goals of a co-operative organization.

System goals, as demonstrative of internal referents, include such variables as size, growth, market share, and, ultimately, survival. Increasingly, these goals are being established by top management, with input from boards of directors. A long-standing debate in the co-operative community has centred on the issue of size versus democratic participation in decision-making.[25] One school of thought advocates increased size as a means for achieving economies of scale and competitive power within the market-place, while another school advocates 'small is beautiful,' and the democratic process for participation in decision-making as the co-operative *raison d'être*.

Product goals, as a subset of system goals, can be useful as a means of comparing co-operative organizations to similar privately owned corporations. For example, the product and service policies of consumer co-operatives as compared to other supermarket chains or independents can be used to identify how the 'co-operative difference' is interpreted in terms of quality of goods, disclosure of information, or additional services.

Finally, *derived* goals, defined as such because 'the ability to pursue them is derived from the existence and behaviour of the organization but is not considered essential to its conduct,'[26] may be considered to be the social goals of the organization. It is generally assumed that co-operatives have a greater obligation to their membership, to their employees, and to society in general than do privately owned organizations. Co-operatives pioneered the social audit as a means for measuring achievement of social responsibility goals. However, they are not alone in this approach, as other corporations have recognized the need to measure performance on the basis of corporate citizenship, as well as profitability or size.

According to Perrow, the latter two goal categories underscore the characterization of organizations as 'coalitions or sets of interacting interest groups,' rather than as integrated entities.[27] The ultimate conclusion to be drawn is that, unlike the picture of goal-setting and behaviour posited by the rational model, not all behaviour in the organization is completely integrated or functionally indispensable, contributing to the achievement of an ultimate goal. The organization pursues a variety of goals, some of which may be in competition with each other. Consequently, to understand what may be perceived as seemingly erratic or non-rational behaviour by co-operatives, a stakeholder perspective regarding goal-setting and decision-making must be adopted.[28]

Decision-making

Traditional conceptions of the decision-making process also used a rational model, assuming that authority over decision-making rested with the owners or, as the organization increased in size, with the representatives of the owners, the board of directors and management. It was also assumed that these representatives made decisions with the best interests of the owners in mind. It soon became apparent, however, that as ownership and control were effectively separated, the degree to which this was true depended on the degree to which the self-interest of those in control ran parallel to the owners' interests, and, if this was different, the degree to which there were checks on the use of that power.[29]

In theory, then, the 'powers of control,' or the power to exercise virtually all the rights of ownership, should rest with the board of directors in a co-operative organization, as the trustees of the members/owners.[30] In reality, however, these powers of control are more likely to rest with senior management officials. What the directors decide to do in the end will be determined by what those who hold this power choose to do. If the powers of control rest with top management, and that in turn is oriented toward an agent in the external environment other than the membership, it is unlikely that the needs of the members will be given top priority in decision-making. Indeed, the rather tenuous nature of the organization as a discrete entity is underscored when the discretion of the organization is challenged, and other elements in the task environment assume control over its activities.[31]

Those on the other side of the debate regarding the power and role of boards of directors contend that the board really does exercise ultimate control through its ability to terminate senior executives, and 'that, other things being equal, the board controls at the internal organizational level.'[32] Mazzolini endorses this position by suggesting that 'managing the structural context'[33] is the key to influencing decision-making.

It appears that this is also the position taken by senior managers with regard to members' control over decision-making in the larger co-operative organizations in Saskatchewan.[34] By being able to elect the board, which in turn should be able to fire senior management if it is dissatisfied with their decision-making, it is assumed that the membership is effectively participating in the decision-making process. This definition of participation, however, is far removed from the democratic process which many envision when they speak of members 'owning and controlling' their co-operative organizations. However, Ellerman suggests that members in co-operatives have effectively given up ownership rights to the board and management by hiring out their capital to the co-operative, thereby reducing their claim to control over decision-making.[35] Laidlaw argues that the effect of the elected board system has been to weaken the democratic process rather than to strengthen it.[36] He suggests that 'attendance at meetings has generally fallen off to the point where it is often hard to get a quorum together, in the main because the members are leaving everything by way of planning and decision-making to the board.'[37] Cotterill, in contrast, argues that democratic decision-making is enhanced by a growth in the size of the organization through a broadening of the membership base and a stabilization of the decision-making process.[38] His 1978 survey of small mid-western American food co-operatives indicated that decision-making in the smallest (less than $250,000 annual sales) of them tended to be quite erratic, sometimes done by 'town meeting,' sometimes by staff, and sometimes by one person. The decision-making in larger co-operatives was done by elected boards of directors and management, with a regular use of the general membership meeting. He concluded that the threat of undemocratic control was therefore greater in the smaller than in the larger co-operatives.

The point that must be underscored following the presentation of these diverse views about the way decisions are made within co-operatives is that, whatever model is accepted, the multiplicity of interests that a co-operative serves must be recognized. I would argue that the most appropriate model of decision-making in co-operatives, as well as in many other kinds of organizations, is a processual one incorporating the effects of interest groups or stakeholders both inside and outside the organization.[39]

The stakeholder approach to planning and decision-making, which is currently viewed with favour in some parts of the co-operative system, holds promise for incorporating the needs of a co-operative's many interest groups. An integral premise of the stakeholder approach is that decision-making with regard to policies or strategies becomes much more complicated because there can be no assumed consensus about the nature of the problem under consideration. Indeed, the only consensus is that there is disagreement as to what the central problem is. And, just as there is disagreement as to the nature of the problem, so there is also a range of solutions. In defining the problem, one must adopt the perspective of the various stakeholders who influence the organization. If we apply this perspective to co-operative organizations, we find that the ultimate decision-makers, be they management, the board, or the general membership, must attempt to incorporate the problem definition and solution alternatives of a wide range of stakeholders. One cannot assume that the decision-making process within co-operative organizations is a simple matter, completely controlled by any one individual or group of decision-makers.

The Structure of Co-operatives in Canada

Issues relating to member control over goal-setting and decision-making do not arise only at the intra-organizational level of first-tier co-operatives. Co-operative merger and growth is an extremely contentious issue affecting relationships between first-, second-, and third-tier co-operatives.[40] From the perspective of the membership, growth of the organization through merger with others is viewed as negative in that it dilutes membership control. Mergers result in shifts in decision-making from local to central organizations, and conflicts may result between management at different levels, as well as within the membership. An associated cost from the perspective of the membership is the increased probability that management will dominate in decision-making.[41]

Marketing co-operatives in Canada, and indeed in many other countries,[42] adopted a highly centralized structure in the early stages of development. The major marketing co-operatives are almost all under the single-unit system.[43] Research has shown that, within the agricultural industry, highly centralized organizations 'capable of directing and, on occasion, coercing their members'[44] are necessary, the relationship between organizational structure and market performance having been shown to be significant. The loss of local autonomy has become an accepted fact. LeVay argues that the organization may still retain its co-operative form, but it loses its co-operative character. She suggests, however, that this is necessary for organizational survival: 'much as this departure from co-operative principles may be decried by purists it may be the key to the attainment of efficiency equal to that of the non-co-operative firm.'[45] The centralized structure enables decision-makers to have a large measure of control over the local co-operatives. The mechanisms that allow local members to participate in organizational decision-making are based primarily on a representative, rather than participatory, model.

The Credit Union System, although modelled on a federated structure, still possesses unitary characteristics for inclusive decision-making.[46] The legitimacy of controlling the actions of the autonomous credit unions at the local level rests in the legislation enacted in each province.[47] In accordance with the Saskatchewan legislation, a credit union is required to meet the 'standards of sound business practice' prescribed by the Credit Union Deposit Guarantee Corporation. If it fails to meet these standards, and does not respond to suggestions by the corporation as to how it might, then it is subject to being under supervision until its business status improves, or it successfully merges with another credit union.[48]

Consumer co-operatives, however, differ from marketing co-operatives and credit unions in their decision-making and control structures. The typical pattern of formation of first- and second-tier consumer co-operatives involved organization of independent retails at a local level, who then pooled resources to purchase a wholesaler. The retails own the wholesaler and formally control its decision-making through their representatives on the board of directors. As a result, consumer co-operatives in Canada have neither the legitimacy of ownership nor legislation to fall back on when external forces prescribe a centralized structure. Indeed, between the wholesaler and the independent retails there is not likely to be even a formalized contract controlling the reciprocal behaviours of the channel members. There has been a particular reluctance to merge in this sector despite the potential efficiencies gained, because members of the federated organization fear the threat to their local autonomy.

The issue of merger and growth becomes particularly critical as it applies to the consumer co-operatives operating within the food retailing industry. The development of vertical marketing systems has been a major trend in the past twenty to thirty years. As compared to conventional, individualistic channel structures, the newer integrated systems provide substantial scale economies and co-ordination in distribution. This eliminates duplication of marketing efforts and results in the provision of any given marketing activity at the most advantageous position in the system.[49] Another outgrowth of this phenomenon has been the advent of the superstore, a combination store offering wide ranges of food and non-food items at competitive prices.[50]

Despite competition from the leaders in the food retailing industry, consumer co-operatives in Canada have maintained a loosely amalgamated, federated structure. In other countries the need to centralize has been recognized, although the central bodies are still struggling with the issue of providing for participation in decision-making within a highly centralized structure.[51]

In a 1968 interim report of the Committee on Structure of Consumer Co-operatives sponsored by the Co-operative Union of Canada, a similar recommendation regarding centralization was made for Canada's consumer co-operatives: 'The committee believes that the chief structural weakness to be corrected as quickly as possible is the wholesale-retail relationship and that these two levels should be made a single-unit system. The idea of numerous independent local units under a wholesale should be replaced by that of an integrated organization with direct membership for the individual consumer. This, in brief, means that, ideally, there will be just five consumer co-operatives in Canada, perhaps four.'[52]

The restructuring of consumer co-operatives in Canada has, however, generally been resisted by the membership. The irony of this recommended move toward centralization is that consumer co-operatives are seen to act as a control factor for abuses arising from concentration within the food retailing industry.[53] Kristjanson noted that, although the consumer co-operative was not in a position to pursue an 'all-out struggle for power with the chain stores,' it was able to improve the performance of the industry by carefully selecting the abuses to be targeted and the techniques for doing so such that retaliation was difficult.[54] The examples he cites include the appointment of a consumer consultant to aid the public in making rational consumption decisions.

Mather found that in larger communities the presence of consumer co-operatives results in lower food prices, while in smaller communities they facilitate a wider price and product quality range.[55]

Despite their ability to act as a countervailing power within the industry, consumer co-operatives are not a significant factor in the grand scheme of things.[56] However, Cotterill suggests that increasing market concentration in local food markets is once again opening the door for growth of consumer co-operatives. It is again ironic that Cotterill argues that federation, consolidation, and vertical integration are required if consumer co-operatives are to survive.[57]

It would appear that consumer co-operatives are faced with a dilemma because their organizational structure, as prescribed by philosophy, is inconsistent with that prescribed by their industrial sector. Leaders in the co-operative movement have recognized and grappled with this structural limitation for some time now. Dealing with the issues surrounding the need of the wholesaler to control the independent retails has been a significant problem faced by members of consumer co-operatives, not only in Canada, but in the United States, Britain, and Sweden. As mentioned previously, the marketing co-operatives and financial co-operatives, such as the credit unions, have resolved this need for centralized decision-making in ways consistent with their industry and their member needs. While marketing and financial co-operatives have been able to make needed adjustments in this area, consumer co-operatives continue to seek solutions regarding the necessary changes to be made. One might well ask why this is so. The following is a tentative explanation.

The Relationship between Philosophy, Structure, and Strategy

Historically, the market performance of co-operative organizations has been quite effective[58] when the strategies required by its structure have been complementary to the strategies demanded by the industry's structure.[59] However, as industries have changed, many co-operatives have found that their strategic options are out of sync with those demanded by the evolving industry. To remain competitive, co-operative organizations have had to choose between two alternatives. The organization could choose to implement an innovative strategy fitting the characteristics of the organization's structure, and possibly force a change in the industry's structure (that is, if the organization has enough power within its strategic group to be able to do so); or the organization could choose a strategy in conflict with existing organizational structure but consistent with the industry's given structure. Both of these alternatives have been chosen by co-operative organizations with varying results. The situation of Federated Co-operatives Limited (FCL) and its associated independent retail outlets provides an example of the results of choosing the latter alternative.

FCL was formed as a result of the desire of the independent retails to own their own wholesaling concern. The retails of the western provinces initiated this move in the mid 1920s to ensure supplies and management advice, to accumulate funds for manufacturing, and to provide a voice for the consumer movement.[60] The consumer co-operatives flourished during the 1930s, forming the Consumers' Co-operative Refinery and the Saskatchewan and Manitoba Trading Associations in 1934, and eventually consolidating producer and consumer interests in the Saskatchewan Wholesale Society (SWS). In the 1940s the SWS bought a coal mine and a lumber mill, began to manufacture feed, and finally merged with Consumers' Co-operative Refineries in the mid 1950s to form Saskatchewan Federated Co-operatives, and eventually Federated Co-operatives Limited.

Since the establishment of the wholesale society by the independent retails, the co-operatives have struggled to define an appropriate relationship. This has also been a continuing problem for the United Co-operatives of Ontario, Coop Fédérée du Québec and Co-op Atlantic, three other major Canadian co-operative wholesalers.[61] Various attempts at a branch model,[62] which would provide the control required by the wholesaler within the context of the retailing industry, have been made but none have succeeded. As Vern Leland, the president of FCL, states, 'despite the buying power of FCL ... the structure of the retail co-operative system does not permit head–to-head competition with superstores ... retail co-operatives are forced by their very nature to work around these giant retailers.'[63]

The very nature of co-operatives to which Leland refers is the democratic system of decision-making that allows for participation in decision-making at the wholesale level by the retail co-operative membership, and autonomous, local control by the retails. It would appear, in this example, that co-operative philosophy clearly has an influence over structure and process, and acts to constrain strategy. This observation is also consistent with other research findings regarding consumer co-operatives.[64]

One model of organizational culture explains the nature of the relationship between philosophy and structure in the following way:

The cultural and socio-structural systems of the organization are in a complex relationship, mutually supportive in 'normal' circumstances but fraught with great potential for tension and stress whenever the organization is subjected to sudden pressures for change ... the cultural and socio-structural systems should have developed concommitantly and harmoniously, the former bestowing legitimacy upon the latter, and in turn receiving support and reinforcement from it. However, abrupt, discontinuous changes in its relevant environment, or slow, cumulative environmental changes that have gone undetected by the organization and suddenly burst upon it may easily disrupt this relationship. The requirements of adaptation may be accommodated by changes in the formal socio-structural system that may not be, and could not be, immediately translated into the cultural system, thus bringing these systems to a state of dissonance and dissynchronization.[65]

Consumer co-operatives in western Canada would now appear to be struggling to align organizational strategic behaviour with necessary industry strategies. This phenomenon may arise from the dilemma created by conflict between two control systems, the internal democratic control by the membership consistent with co-operative philosophy, and the external control originating in the dependent relationship with the environment.[66]

Because of the ideological basis of economic co-operation, members have a right to participate in organizational decision-making. The various organizational structures currently in place in co-operatives, such as the boards of directors, and the processes established for facilitating participation in decision-making (annual meetings, resolutions) have evolved from the institutional value placed on democratic models for participation. Democratic ideals have become a part of the culture of co-operative organizations.

The relationship between the wholesaler and the independent retail, however, is fraught with tension. This tension is created by the juxtaposition of the principle of co-operation between co-operatives and the expectation of autonomous, local control by the retails (the internal democratic control), with the necessity of relying on the power provided by association with the wholesaler (and conversely the retailer) and the need for control by the wholesaler within the distribution process (external control linked to dependency).

Conflict within a channel of distribution is not atypical. However, that it is a channel system with co-operatives as members compounds the conflict and complicates matters further.

Consumer co-operatives have used a variety of strategies to satisfy the demands of co-operative philosophy, while allowing for survival within the industry. The retails have surrendered to the wholesaler the legitimacy to exercise discretion in certain areas, such as the training of managers and the development of market strategy. However, conflict arises when the two parties to the arrangement have different expectations regarding what constitutes the 'zone of indifference.'[67] This is most obvious when the wholesaler appears to be interfering in matters that should (from the perspective of local members) be controlled by local decision-makers. Exactly what is under the sole discretion of local decision-makers is a central issue, which is confounded even more because most managers receive their training from FCL and may tend to place their loyalties there. The co-operative boards, however, tend to hold a local orientation, and to believe that they are in control of decision-making as it affects their local co-operative. The legitimacy of local control over decision-making is provided by co-operative philosophy, thereby creating countervailing power within the system, and presenting a dilemma for FCL managers regarding the nature of strategies deemed appropriate for maintaining co-operative integrity.[68]

The tension created by attempting to adhere to co-operative values while operating a business is not found at the wholesaler level only. Managers and the members of co-operative boards struggle with these issues at the local level as well. The problems are magnified because most managers receive their business training in environments not particularly supportive of co-operative values. This perception of co-operative values as being incompatible with business success in turn has an impact on the strategies chosen by the decision-makers.[69] Conflict arises when the members feel that co-operative values should direct business actions.

This situation raises questions that apply not only to consumer co-operatives, but to other types of co-operative organizations as well. How does an organization such as a co-operative survive and succeed when the strategies demanded by the industry conflict with strategies complementary to existing organizational structures? What kinds of strategies are chosen? What happens to organizational structure? How is conflict handled? What are the trade-offs and what impact do these have on the organization and its members?

Conclusion

These questions are not easily answered. Centralization will continue to be a preferred alternative from the perspective of the wholesaler, while the retails will continue to demand autonomy and control over local decision-making. The reality of the situation, however, is that what has evolved in western Canada is a dichotomized strategy on the part of the wholesaler. At the formal level, it would appear that retails are involved in making decisions.[70] At the informal level, disparities in power determine the strategic actions taken. Despite this, the wholesaling organization is not in a position to define strategy unilaterally and alter organizational structure to implement it. Co-operative philosophy continues to intervene.

The ultimate dilemma the wholesaler and the retails face derives from the need to strengthen the Co-operative Retailing System's position within the retailing industry. A move toward even greater centralization of decision-making and control, although apparently necessary from the point of view of survival within the industry, will not encourage the grass-roots involvement imperative for member loyalty. The strategy of increasing member loyalty and attracting a younger membership may be just as important a factor in co-operative survival as centralized operations are seen to be. As a consequence, it is likely that the unavoidable conflicts between the business imperatives and democratic values inherent in co-operative enterprise will continue for the foreseeable future.

MURRAY FULTON

16 Co-operatives in Oligopolistic Industries

Competition between a small number of co-operatives and profit-maximizing firms is a feature of many of the markets in which the larger Canadian co-operatives operate. The question raised in this chapter concerns the impact that co-operatives may have in such oligopolistic markets. The theoretical analysis suggests that co-operatives can improve the well-being of their members and the overall efficiency of these markets. However, there are a number of reasons why co-operatives may not behave in this manner. These include an inadequate knowledge of the impact they can exert on a market and the proper incentives for the managers to operate the co-operative in a manner that will achieve these results. It is suggested that member and board education is one way of alleviating such problems.

Co-operatives are many things: a place where members can exert their democratic power; a place where services can be provided that would otherwise not be; and a place where local control can replace centralized or international control. As well, the co-operative is often a major force in an economy or industry. For instance, six out of the top ten agricultural firms in Canada in 1986 in terms of sales were co-operatives, while of the top ten conglomerates in Canada in 1986, Federated Co-operatives ranked seventh.[1] In specific markets the importance of co-operatives is even more pronounced. As an example, dairy co-operatives in Quebec and on the prairies handle 80 to 90 per cent of the milk produced by farmers, while in many small prairie towns, the local co-operative or credit union is the only alternative to profit-maximizing grocery/hardware stores or banks.

While not all co-operatives compete with profit-maximizing firms, such competition characterizes many larger Canadian co-operatives. For example, local consumer co-operatives compete with the likes of Supervalu and Safeway in the retail grocery market, or with Esso, Shell, and Petro-Canada in the local gasoline market; the three prairie wheat pools and United Grain Growers compete with Pioneer and Cargill in the grain handling market; and Western Co-operative Fertilizers Ltd. competes with Esso, Cominco, and Sherrit Gordon in the western Canadian fertilizer market. Indeed, these co-operatives were often formed to provide competition to the existing profit-maximizing firms in the market. For instance, the grain handling co-operatives on the prairies were established by farmers who felt that the monopolistic practices of the 'line' elevator companies were having a detrimental effect on their farming practices.[2]

In economic terminology, the examples listed above all share one characteristic: the markets in which the co-operatives operate are oligopolistic in nature. That is, the markets are characterized by a small number of firms, each of which has a sufficient portion of the market to exert market power, for example, by raising prices or restricting output to some degree. The question that immediately arises is how the existence of a co-operative in such markets affects the well-being of both the co-operative members and society as a whole. Are co-operatives effective in offsetting some of the market power exercised by oligopolistic firms, that is, are co-operatives likely to make the industry more competitive?

The purpose of this chapter is to investigate the impact of a co-operative on a market that is oligopolistic in nature. The analysis begins with an examination of economic theory, which suggests that co-operatives, acting in the best interests of their members, can be expected to improve the efficiency of the markets in which they operate. The chapter then asks whether co-operatives act in the manner presumed by theory. While a complete answer to this question would involve the study of many co-operatives, some insight into the question can be obtained by examining a specific co-operative. This chapter studies Western Co-operative Fertilizers Ltd., which operated in the western Canadian fertilizer market, and concludes that this co-operative does not appear to have acted in a way predicted by theory. A discussion of some of the reasons why the co-operative did not behave as prescribed concludes the chapter.

Co-operative Behaviour and Economic Theory

The theoretical literature on co-operatives suggests that if the co-operative is the only firm in the industry it may be able to have a beneficial impact on an industry, making it more competitive and efficient.[3] What about an

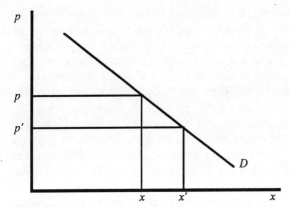

Figure 1. Demand curve for a good or service

oligopolistic market? Can a co-operative improve the efficiency of this type of industry? What kind of behaviour should a co-operative follow to fulfill its responsibilities to its members?

To answer these questions, we must begin by looking at co-operative members, since it is presumed that the co-operative is in place to further their goals. Consider, for example, a consumer co-operative.[4] Members of this co-operative have a demand for whatever good or service the co-operative was formed to provide. In the case of grain handling co-operatives, the demand is for grain handling and transportation services. For consumers, the demand is for grocery and hardware products, while for farmers requiring farm inputs, the demand is for fertilizer and agricultural chemicals. This demand can be represented graphically by plotting the quantities the members would like to purchase against each of the prices they might be faced with. For instance, Figure 1 indicates that at price p, co-operative members would demand a quantity x, while at a lower price p', the members would demand a larger quantity x'.

As consumers of the product, co-operative members would like to obtain as much of the good as they can at as low a price as possible; in the extreme they would like to pay nothing for the product or service. Using the notion of 'consumer surplus,' which is defined as the area under the demand curve and above the price that is being paid,[5] the notion is that consumers would like to maximize the level of consumer surplus, i.e., set a price that is as low as possible.

Members of a co-operative wear two hats: one as a consumer, the other as an owner. If it costs something to produce or supply the product to the members, then selling the good or service at a zero price (which maximizes consumer surplus) will result in a loss to the members as owners of the co-operative. Indeed, as owners, the members would like to see the largest profits possible. Since each co-operative member has two personae, owner and consumer, the strategy that makes each as well off as he or she can be is one that balances off the objectives of the two personae. Thus, the co-operative should attempt to maximize the sum of consumer surplus plus profits.[6]

Following traditional economic analysis, this measure of the well-being of co-operative members will be maximized if the co-operative equates marginal benefit with marginal cost. The marginal cost is nothing but the additional cost of producing or supplying another unit of the good or service. The marginal benefit, however, is the change in the area under the demand curve that results when output is changed by one unit. Since the latter is nothing more than the price of the output, the welfare-maximizing output level is one where price is equated with marginal cost. In other words, given the members' demand curve, the welfare-maximizing point is determined by equating the demand curve with the marginal cost of producing the good.[7]

Figure 2 illustrates the type of cost curves faced by firms in the fertilizer industry. As Bayri, Rosaasen, and Furtan argue, the cost curves have the property that average cost is flat over a wide range of output.[8] Given the members' demand curve, D, the co-operative would therefore set a price of p (which equals marginal cost, MC) and sell a quantity x_c. At this price, profits are zero, since price equals average cost (AC).[9] A lower price than this would, of course, increase consumer surplus but would necessarily decrease profits by a greater amount. For instance, if the co-operative charged a price of p', consumer surplus would increase by the area $pacp'$, but profits would now be negative and equal to $pbcp'$ – co-operative members would have lost the area abc. A higher price would increase profits, but would also decrease consumer surplus, again by a greater amount. As an example, a price of p'' would reduce consumer surplus by an amount equal to $p''dap$, while profits would now be positive and equal to $p''dep$. Members would therefore lose the area dea. The only price-quantity point that maximizes the sum of profits and consumer surplus, that is, maximizes the benefit of being a consumer and an owner at the same time, is that which equates demand to marginal cost.

The behaviour undertaken by the co-operative can be expected to be quite different from that undertaken by a profit-maximizing firm. In the profit-maximizing firm, the owners are solely that, and they will only be interested in maximizing the level of profits they can obtain from the sale of the good. As Figure 2 illustrates, raising price above a level p will increase profits. If there is only one profit-maximizing firm operating in the industry (a monopoly),

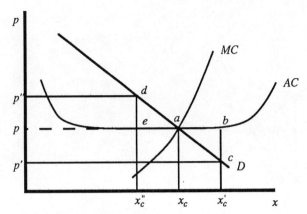

Figure 2. Pricing and output behaviour for a co-operative

then price and output will be set so that marginal revenue equals marginal cost (Figure 3). At a price of p_m and a level of output x_m, profits of the profit-maximizing monopolist will equal $p_m abc$. Notice that, at this level, consumer surplus has decreased by an amount $p_m adc$ as compared to the situation that would result were the co-operative the only firm in the industry.

In most markets in the economy, however, a single firm does not have complete monopoly power. Instead, the norm is a small number of firms who compete with each other, but realize that they are sufficiently large to have an impact on the market in which they operate. In such a situation it would be expected that the competition between the firms would reduce the price below the monopoly level, as each of them attempts to increase sales and capture a bit more market share.

It would also be expected that the price would not be driven down to the level where zero profits are being made, for this is likely to happen only in the perfectly competitive case where there are a large number of firms, each very small. In such a situation, none of the firms believe they can have any effect on price in the market if they increase their production. As a result, each increases production in an attempt to increase profits. The result of all firms doing this is that total production increases and price falls until the point where zero profits are being made (i.e., $p = AC$).

If there are only a small number of firms in the industry, however, it is unlikely that firms will compete to the extent that they will drive profits down to zero. Each firm knows that if it increases production, it can increase its market share. If price were to remain the same, such behaviour would lead to increased profits for the firm. But each firm also knows that since it has a

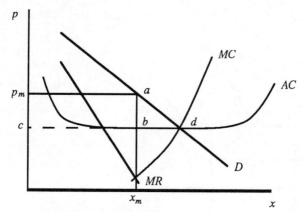

Figure 3. Pricing and output behaviour for a profit-maximizing monopolist

significant portion of the market, increasing output will lower price. The result is that in an oligopolistic industry firms do not expand production to the extent they would if they were in a competitive market. This behaviour keeps price up, with the result that larger profits are earned. Note that while price is unlikely to be as high as in a monopoly case, it will almost certainly be higher than in the competitive case.

What happens, however, if profit-maximizing firms are not the only firms in the industry, but instead are competing with a co-operative? To analyse this situation, it is necessary to review the behaviour of the co-operative. Given the members' demand curve, D, the co-operative will produce a level of output x_c and will sell this output at a price p (Figure 2). The profit-maximizing firms will be forced to sell their output at this same price, since if they do not, they can expect to lose customers and sales to the co-operative. Assuming that the co-operatives and the profit-maximizing firms have similar cost structures, a price of p will mean that neither type of firm will make any excess profits, since price equals marginal cost (MC) equals average cost (AC).

Suppose, however, that the co-operative is operating a small, high-cost plant. What will be the impact of this? From the discussion above, recall that the price set by the co-operative becomes the market price for all firms in the market. The lowest price that the co-operative can establish is given by its minimum average cost, since if price is less than this, the co-operative will be incurring a loss. Thus, if the minimum average cost of the co-operative is less than the oligopoly price established by the profit-maximizing firms, the market price can be expected to fall to this lower level. If this price is greater than the average cost of the profit-maximizing firms, then they can be expected to earn excess profits.

Thus, the presence of a co-operative can lower the market price below the oligopoly price, but only if the cost structure of the co-operative allows it to break even at this new price. This, of course, raises the question of whether it will pay a co-operative with a high-cost plant to invest in its facilities to make them more productive, thereby lowering the average cost of production and thus the price in the market. A natural extension of this question is whether a co-operative will enter an industry in which it does not already have a presence.

The answer to the question of whether a co-operative can be expected to invest in lower-cost facilities depends on the price in the market prior to the new investment. Suppose, as in Figure 4, that the co-operative has cost curves AC and MC. With members' demand curve, D, the price the co-operative will establish is p. The co-operative members' welfare at this price is given by the area above the price line pa and below the demand curve D. It is known that if the co-operative invests in new facilities (given by the shift in the cost curves to MC' and AC'), the price will fall to a level p'. At this price, co-operative members will be earning consumer surplus equal to the area above the price line $p'b$ and below the demand curve D. Thus, the effect of the co-operative investment is to increase members' welfare by the area $pabp'$.

It is obvious from the above that if the area $pabp'$ is greater than the cost of upgrading their facilities, the co-operative members will go ahead with their investment.[10] Since economic theory assumes that the average cost curve embodies a normal rate of return, the capital cost of building a new fertilizer plant will be covered in the average cost curve AC'. Thus, as long as the area $pabp'$ is greater than any unusual costs associated with starting a new plant, it should pay the co-operative to upgrade its facilities to the most efficient degree possible.

The impact of a co-operative entering an industry in which it is not already present can be analysed in a similar fashion. Suppose, as in Figure 4, that the profit-maximizing firms operating in the industry establish an oligopoly price of p. Entry by the co-operative with an up-to-date plant will result in the price falling to p'. The gain in welfare experienced by the co-operative members will be equal to the area $pabp'$. If this area is greater than the cost of entering the industry, then the members of the co-operative will find it profitable to have the co-operative enter.

It is clear from the above discussion that the degree to which price will be reduced influences whether or not the co-operative will want either to upgrade its facilities or enter the industry. This suggests that if the profit-maximizing

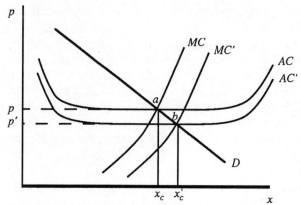

Figure 4. Pricing and output behaviour for a co-operative with a high-cost plant

firms in the industry wish to deter the co-operative from entering or upgrading, they can do so by establishing a price that is low enough to make such decisions unprofitable. Such behaviour on the part of the profit-maximizing firms, however, means that the market price is lowered, with the result that the members of the co-operative are able to benefit from the lower price, even without any action on the part of the co-operative.

In conclusion, the existence, or the threat of existence, of a co-operative in an oligopolistic industry should make the industry more competitive. The reason is that the co-operative is not solely interested in maximizing profits. If the co-operative members were interested only in the benefits they received from the co-operative as owners, then it would be expected that they would behave much like profit-maximizing firms, raising price above marginal cost and average cost and making some level of excess profits. However, since the co-operative members are also interested in the benefits they receive as consumers of the good or service being provided, they will not wish to see price raised in order to earn greater profits. Rather, they will want to see price lowered in order to obtain a greater level of consumer surplus. The result is a greater benefit for consumers, whether they are members of the co-operative or not, and an improvement in the efficiency of the particular market being examined.

The Reality of Co-operative Behaviour

The theoretical model developed above suggests that the existence of co-operatives in an industry should result in pricing and output behaviour that is closer to the perfectly competitive model than it is to the monopoly or oligopolistic models. How well does this theory correspond to the manner in which co-operatives actually operate?

To develop a complete answer to this question, it would of course be necessary to examine empirically and in depth all the industries in which co-operatives operate. While this is not feasible, it is interesting to note that at least one firm owned by co-operatives does not appear to have behaved according to the theory outlined above. An analysis of the industry in which this co-operative operated, while not transferable to other industries, may point out some reasons why it can be expected that co-operatives may not give rise to a more competitive environment.

Western Co-operative Fertilizers Ltd. (WCFL) operated in the western Canadian fertilizer industry from 1964 until it was closed in the summer of 1987.[11] Other firms in this industry include Cominco, Sherritt Gordon, Simplot, and Imperial Oil. WCFL is jointly owned by Federated Co-operatives Ltd., Saskatchewan Wheat Pool, Alberta Wheat Pool, and Manitoba Pool Elevators as a subsidiary of these co-operative organizations. As a result, WCFL was not owned directly by the co-operative members, no doubt a factor in the behaviour it exhibited.

Bayri, Rosaasen, and Furtan argue that the western Canadian fertilizer industry is not competitive. Although there has been a rapid increase in the amount of fertilizer used in recent years, no new firms have entered the industry since Simplot and Imperial Oil began production in 1967 and 1969, respectively. The lack of entry into the industry, along with the small number of firms, suggests that the existing firms in the industry may be restricting entry. Bayri, Rosaasen, and Furtan concluded that the existing firms in the industry have followed a limit pricing strategy which raises price above the competitive level and allows them to earn above-normal profits.[12]

Unlike what co-operative economic theory suggests, co-operatives have not been lining up to enter the industry or to upgrade their facilities. No new firms have entered the industry since 1969 and while co-operatives have had a presence in the industry, WCFL did not increase its capacity substantially over the years and, when it closed, was operating two plants that were among the smallest three in the industry.[13] This suggests WCFL had not been following the type of behaviour the theoretical model suggests.

One answer to why WCFL may have adopted behaviour inconsistent with co-operative theory reflects the distinction that was made between a co-operative and a profit-maximizing firm. While a profit-maximizing firm is interested in maximizing profits, the co-operative should have as its goal the maximization of profits plus consumer surplus. Although this latter goal is an easy objective to give to a firm in a theoretical setting, it is much more difficult to translate into practice. For instance, it is relatively simple for co-operative members, directors, and managers to forecast what profits will be from a new store or a different pricing strategy; however, it is much more difficult to conceptualize and measure the consumer surplus part of the co-operative goal. Thus, to the extent that full knowledge concerning the impact on members of investment or output decisions is unavailable, it might be expected that the co-operative would make decisions based on the traditional measure of profits. This, in turn, would make the co-operative behave less like an organization designed to maximize member welfare.

Related to this is the possibility that co-operative members and managers may not be fully aware of the differences between their firm and profit-maximizing firms. For instance, while co-operative economic theory has been discussed for over forty years, the academic emphasis placed on this form of enterprise has been far less than that placed on the profit-maximizing firm. Although there is a body of literature on co-operative pricing and output, it is scattered through various journals and is not available in any coherent form. Few textbooks have ever been written describing the problem facing co-operatives, although virtually every introductory economics text describes profit-maximizing firms and their problems. Thus, it may not be surprising that co-operative managers tend to adopt the thinking and decision-making skills of their profit-maximizing firm counterparts. It is likely that co-operative managers are steeped in a sort of corporate culture, the spread of which has been reinforced lately by the 'requirement' that managers be hired from business schools, and thus less able to deviate from the norm of profit maximization.

Members as well as managers may not be fully aware of the difference between their co-operative organization and profit-maximizing enterprises in the community. Recall that members have to think both as consumers and owners, and to give equal weight to the concerns of both. Without formal education regarding this distinction, members might also fall into the trap of using the intuition they have garnered from observing profit-maximizing institutions. Clearly, then, co-operative education for members, directors, and managers may be crucial in allowing co-operatives to play the role to which they are so ideally suited.

The behaviour of WCFL described above may also be the result of a principal-agent problem – a consequence of the bureaucracy of co-operatives and the incentive structure that is in place. (see chapter 1 for a discussion of the principal-agent problem). Of course, this bureaucracy is present in profit-maximizing firms, but, it may be that in co-operatives the effect is of much more consequence.

As Monson and Downs point out, the directors and managers of a profit-maximizing corporation are unlikely to have goals that are in complete agreement with those of the owners. For instance, the well-being of the managers (promotions, pay raises) may be better served by relatively conservative strategies that do not subject the firm to risks, but also do not maximize profits. As well, managers and directors can be expected to withhold information to the management levels above them if transmitting such information would injure their employment or chances of promotion.[14]

The same developments are also likely to occur in co-operatives. As in profit-maximizing companies, the typical co-operative manager will be interested more in his or her own personal goals than in the objectives of the members who own the co-operative. In fact, since it is likely that decisions to promote managers are made on the basis of how well the co-operative has operated financially, the managers are more likely to be interested in maximizing profit than in improving the welfare of the members. This is especially likely to be true when the enterprise is a subsidiary of a co-operative or group of co-operatives. In such instances the enterprise may be looked on more as a source of funds than as a vehicle for promoting member welfare.

In addition, the managers might be expected to withhold information to the members and the board of directors if such information suggested that the co-operative should become involved in an undertaking that would appear to be poor 'business.' Withholding information and failing to carry out fully the decisions that are made, which is a corollary to such behaviour, are likely to erode the power of the board of directors to have policies which it prefers carried out.

Indeed, the board of directors may actually be incapable of developing a policy that is independent of the beliefs and objectives of the managers. Owing to a lack of board and member education, the board may not have the information necessary to suggest alternative objectives and actions to the managers, relying instead on the views put forward by the managers. This, of course, reduces the chance that the owner and consumer interests of the members will both be represented. As well, since the information required by the board to set policy is provided by the management, selective provision of such information can greatly influence the direction the board takes.

The conclusion is that it would be surprising if co-operatives behaved in the manner suggested by theory. Indeed, if co-operatives act consistently at all, the most likely behaviour is something akin to profit maximization, not member welfare maximization.

Summary and Conclusions

The purpose of this paper was to examine the impact of co-operatives on oligopolistic industries. The theoretical analysis carried out suggests that a co-operative entering an industry can be expected to improve the industry's efficiency. In particular, the existence or threat of existence of a co-operative can be expected to drive the price down to the competitive level. This result derives from co-operative members being interested in at least two things from their co-operative: profits and consumer surplus. Thus, while profit-maximizing firms will wish to keep price from falling to the competitive level so that profits can be sustained, co-operatives will be interested in seeing it reduced so that their members can benefit from the lower prices.

While such behaviour by the co-operative would result in the greatest welfare for the members, there are a number of reasons to believe that such behaviour may not actually occur. First, the information required to maximize profits plus consumer surplus is difficult to obtain and conceptualize, making behaviour consistent with the maximization of this goal much more unlikely. Second, little work has been done on the economics of co-operatives relative to the profit-maximizing firm. Research is thus needed to establish the theoretical basis on which co-operatives should be making their decisions. Third, the conclusions of bureaucratic theories of decision-making suggest that even if members and their board are aware of the proper thing for co-operatives to do, the managers may not have the proper incentives to carry out their wishes. In fact, since the managers' personal goals are much more closely linked to the profitability of the co-operative than to members' welfare, it is to be expected that the co-operative would follow a path that more closely resembles profit maximization.

The analysis also suggests that for co-operatives to perform the role of improving the economic efficiency of markets and maximizing the welfare of their members, they may have to become much more active in a number of areas. Of primary importance appears to be member education, since members must be aware, not only that the co-operative can be used to make them better off, but of the proper way for it to do so. Closely related is the question of board education. Board members must be able to develop policies and have knowledge of the manner in which bureaucratic institutions work and the implications this has for achieving co-operative goals. In particular, they require the expertise and power to challenge the management and to demand that it carry out the policies that have been laid down. To aid the board in this task, the co-operative must also ensure that the goals and incentive structure developed for management in some way reflect the objectives of the members. Under such a system, the managers, acting in their own self-interest, will better contribute to the achievement of the members' goals.

DAVID LAYCOCK

17 Level and Style of Government Intervention in Co-operative Business Activity

This chapter has very specific and limited objectives: to characterize and provide some examples of the formal relationships between co-operatives and governments in Canada, so as to add some empirical depth to the theoretical and historical account of co-operative–government relations in chapter 10. The analysis focuses on federal and provincial powers over co-operative activity, co-operatives' autonomy from state control, and low levels of both the co-operative businesses' integration into policy-making processes and state aid to co-operatives.

Several features characterize formal relationships between co-operatives and governments in Canada:

1 division of responsibility for co-operative enabling and regulatory legislation between the federal and provincial governments, with provincial paramountcy in most matters of regulation and administration for most co-operatives;
2 considerable autonomy of co-operatives from control or direction by state agencies;
3 formal recognition of the distinctiveness of co-operatives relative to the private sector, but unsystematic integration of co-operative organizations into the economic policy-making processes of governments;
4 a low level of state financial support or promotion of co-operative economic development projects, relative to that provided to the private sector.

In this chapter I will address each of these points. Taken together with chapter 10, this information clarifies how relationships between co-operatives and Canadian governments fit together in a distinctive pattern.

Federal and Provincial Jurisdiction over Co-operatives

The division of jurisdictional responsibility for co-operative businesses between federal and provincial governments is based on the constitutional division of powers between these two orders of government in the Canadian federal system. In most ways, this division is merely an extension of constitutional principles pertaining to the private business sector. Each province is responsible for legislation governing incorporation of provincial co-operative businesses. Although in theory this leaves room for variation, the legislation has been quite uniform across the ten provinces since the Second World War.

In all cases, the stated intention of enabling and regulatory legislation for co-operatives is the same as the equivalent legislation for private sector firms. Such legislation is to provide a legal environment within which this form of business enterprise may achieve its socially legitimate objectives. The principal elements of provincial distinctiveness in the area of co-operative legislation reflect the greater incidence and economic force of co-operatives in different regions. For example, some provinces have dealt specifically with worker co-operatives in their Co-operatives Act,[1] or have gone so far as to enact separate legislation for specific co-operatives, as in the case of the Saskatchewan Wheat Pool.

The other way in which provincial governments differ in their treatment of co-operatives is also largely a function of the strength of co-operatives in the provincial economy. This is in the area of government organization for the purpose of co-operative regulation, administration, and in some cases, business development. From 1944 to 1 April 1987 Saskatchewan had a separate Department of Co-operation and Co-operative Development. Manitoba's Department of Co-operative Development was established in 1969, threatened briefly in 1977 by the Lyon government, was active from 1984 to 1987 in promoting co-operative development, and was eliminated by the new Conservative government in 1988. Québec had a large co-operative development and administration section within the Department of Industry and Commerce from 1976 to 1985; following the Liberal victory in 1985, the Direction des coopératives was first cut back, then deprived of its assistant deputy minister – and hence intra-departmental clout – in 1988.

The other seven provinces provide anything from a dozen knowledgeable and efficient employees working in a department of consumer and corporate affairs or agriculture, to several isolated bureaucrats concerned exclusively with registration and inspection of co-operatives. Regulation of financial co-operatives is more complicated than that of non-financial co-operatives, because of the existence of separate and rather complicated credit union legislation in most provinces. This regulation is undertaken by separate staffs, sometimes in separate departments, in those provinces with more extensive credit union systems.

The federal government has formal responsibility for regulation of approximately ten co-operative businesses: those for whom most business is inter-regional.[2] This is not to say that changes made to the federal Co-operatives' Act are of minor significance. Because this legislation directly affects some of the largest second-tier co-operatives, and indirectly affects the provincially located co-operative member businesses in these inter-provincial organizations, the federal legislation specific to co-operatives is important.

It can easily be argued, however, that federal tax legislation is of greater business significance to virtually all co-operatives than the federal Co-operatives Act. By providing co-operatives with the same kinds of investment tax incentives as the private sector, or by removing the special tax treatment of patronage dividends, the federal government could positively or negatively affect the performance of co-operatives in crucial ways. Canadian co-operatives have struggled to receive fair treatment in federal tax legislation since their inception, and will likely do so for the foreseeable future.[3]

Autonomy from the State

Canadian co-operatives have traditionally insisted on as much autonomy from state control as the private sector, if not more. This insistence has its roots in several things: a suspicion of the state as an agent of compulsory action (as opposed to voluntary, collective self-help); concern about the close links between powerful private economic interests and particular governments; and a commitment to political neutrality, which would be endangered if close links were forged between co-operative leaders and officials in the government departments and dominant political forces of particular regimes.[4]

For their part, Canadian governments have generally been quite happy to refrain from actions that could cumulatively lead to dependence of co-operative development on public finances and state initiatives. To a large degree, this is due to a long-standing view among government policy-makers that the private sector should be the engine of economic growth, and that if co-operatives wish to participate in economic development they must take the initiative themselves. It is true that many Canadian regulations affecting the operation of co-operative business do express a degree of paternalism, in many cases involving less 'self-regulation' than equivalent private sector firms are allowed.[5] But this paternalism cannot reasonably be portrayed as state control, at least not when compared to what is practised in many non-European or non–North American countries.

Formal Involvement of Co-operatives in Public Policy Development

One of the easiest ways to gain a perspective on the nature of formal relationships between Canadian governments and co-operatives is to ask how co-operatives are involved in federal and provincial public policy development.The answer, put simply, is unsystematically for the co-operative sector as a whole, but with increasing impact in some sectors of provincial economies where co-operatives have a significant market share.

Canadian co-operative organizations participate unsystematically in government policy-making processes for several reasons. There is no tradition of corporatist or ongoing comprehensive involvement by peak organizations of businesses, producers, or employees in formal policy development and implementation processes in Canada.[6] The exceptions to this rule do sometimes include co-operatives, especially where they are beneficiaries of agricultural product marketing boards.[7] But co-operatives are in these relatively advantageous positions by virtue of their size and importance as economic organizations, not by virtue of the state's recognition of the value of the co-operative organizational form. Co-operative participation in policy-making processes is also unsystematic because diverse interests and organizations in the co-operative business scene have great difficulty reaching a consensus on many specific policy issues. If the federal and provincial governments realize this, as they apparently do, they have few good reasons to invite co-operative organizations (as opposed to individual co-operative businesses) to consult on issues that are more easily dealt with inside the more specific policy communities related to the major economic departments, regulatory agencies, and central agencies of government.

Some provincial governments – especially those whose economies have a large co-operative presence – are more inclined to consult co-operatives as a group. But, even in these cases, co-operatives are not consulted in proportion to their regional economic clout. The most recent and distressing evidence of this is to be found in Saskatchewan, where the Progressive Conservatives' elimination of a forty-year-old co-operative department indicates how much importance the government gives to the 'co-operative sector,' in a province where four of the ten largest businesses are co-operatives.

The low level of government canvassing of co-operatives' opinions is partly a function of co-operatives' own wishes. Their interpretation of the co-operative principle of political neutrality has made them particularly cautious about interaction with government bureaucrats or elected officials, on matters which are not specific to the immediate business interests of their memberships. If co-operative leaders and officials become less cautious about these things, and emphasize their desire to comment on a broader range of public policy issues, government officials are more likely to invite co-operative officials to participate meaningfully in the policy development process.

One sign that this process has begun is a series of federal-provincial meetings among government ministers and senior bureaucrats responsible for government dealings with co-operatives since the fall of 1985. Elected officials and senior managers from the major Canadian co-operative organizations have also participated in these meetings, initially to focus on how participating governments and co-operatives could co-ordinate efforts to achieve some aspects of the co-operative system's stated development agenda. This process has been regularized to some extent with the creation of the federal Co-operative Secretariat.

The ability of a nine-person secretariat to improve the profile of co-operative concerns in the cabinet, central agencies, and senior levels of the federal bureaucracy is by no means assured. Some of this burden may be borne by an Interdepartmental Co-operatives Committee, also announced by the Honourable Charles Mayer on 5 May 1987. This committee has senior bureaucratic representation from fifteen federal departments and agencies, and should provide the secretariat with sufficient liaison capacity to act as more than an ad hoc device for informing federal departments about co-operatives' concerns. A similar value may also be demonstrated eventually for the Co-operative Advisory group, chosen by the minister responsible for liaison with co-operatives to provide 'sector' input into the secretariat's activities.

We can get some indication of present co-operative involvement in policy development and implementation (or, alternatively, government 'intervention' in the affairs of co-operative business) by listing the major federal government departments and agencies with which co-operatives and/or co-operatives' organizations (such as the Canadian Co-operative Association) have direct and ongoing contact. These major departments are Agriculture, Finance, Fisheries and Oceans, Revenue Canada (Taxation), Atlantic Canada Opportunities Agency and the Western Diversification Office, National Health and Welfare, Employment and Immigration, Energy, Mines and Resources, and Transport.

Only in Agriculture was there ever a formally distinct section in the department dealing exclusively with co-operatives. From 1976 to 1987 the Co-operatives Unit's several employees were charged with generating statistical information regarding economic performance of all reporting, non-financial co-operatives in Canada. They also acted as a contact point for co-operatives to other federal government departments, liaised with agricultural co-operatives for Agriculture Canada, assisted co-operative involvement in international trade, and occasionally briefed senior government personnel on Canadian co-operatives. Their limited personnel and resources meant they had great difficulty doing any of these jobs as well as they wished or co-operatives required. The creation of the Co-operative Secretariat has removed their interdepartmental co-ordination and contact responsibilities.

The only other federal department that has staff permanently assigned to working with co-operatives specifically is Fisheries and Oceans. Selected personnel in the departments responsible for regional economic development, Finance, Energy, Mines and Resources, and Employment and Immigration have recently become somewhat familiar with co-operatives' distinctive character, needs, and development potential, but are by no means able or expected to devote most of their time to such matters.

At the sub-sectoral level of federal government agencies, crown corporations, and commissions, the major Canadian co-operatives are relatively well represented, and well received by government. The Canadian Co-operative Credit Society and the Desjardins Confederation of caisses populaires in Québec, the two peak organizations for Canadian credit unions, closely monitor and often participate in the activities of the Canada Deposit Insurance Corporation. The Bank of Canada, the Export Development Corporation, and the Farm Credit Corporation of Canada are also regularly listened to by these national credit union organizations, and sometimes by provincial credit union centrals' officials directly.

Other federal agencies in which co-operatives receive regular hearings are the Canadian Grain Commission, the Canadian Dairy Commission, the Canadian Wheat Board, the Federal Business Development Bank, the Canadian Transport Commission, and the Canadian Mortgage and Housing Corporation, which provides subsidized and guaranteed mortgages for co-operative housing in Canada. All of these bodies have staff, and sometimes even directors (especially in the case of the Grain Commission, the Dairy Commission, and the Wheat Board), who are well acquainted with Canadian co-operatives' roles in relevant economic sectors. Finally, the Canadian International Development Agency works closely with Canadian co-operatives through the Canadian Co-operative Association (the Co-operative Union of Canada, prior to September 1987) and the Desjardins system to facilitate aid to third-world co-operative development projects.

There are many formal and ongoing ties between the national government and co-operative organizations in Canada. These are of great importance to the co-operatives concerned, just as their equivalents are to private sector firms and organizations. But while the input of private sector firms and organizations into government policy-making is crucial to the eventual shape and direction of overall economic policy in Canada, the same cannot be said of co-operatives' inputs into the policy process. It is unlikely that this will change significantly as co-operatives become slightly more formally integrated into policy development exercises in major government departments. Traditional private sector concerns will continue to be given the lion's share of attention by federal governments, which assume that the private sector is the principal and most socially legitimate source of economic growth in the Canadian economy. However, greater policy participation by Canadian co-operatives would at least ensure that fewer aspects of government policy would be unconsciously or otherwise detrimental to the interests of the Canadian co-operative system and its members.

State Assistance for Co-operative Economic Development

Canadian co-operatives have only recently received substantial sums of development assistance funding from the federal and provincial governments. Both outstanding examples of this have occurred in the field of energy development. Co-Enerco (1982) is a joint-venture energy exploration and development company established by the federal government and a consortium of Canadian co-operatives. The Nu-Grade Heavy Oil Upgrader (1986) in Saskatchewan involves large loan guarantees by the federal and provincial governments, equity participation by the Saskatchewan government and Federated Co-operatives Limited, and an eventual investment of over $700 million. Most other direct subsidies to co-operatives from federal and provincial governments have been on a much smaller scale, and on an ad hoc basis until very recently.

Between 1984 and 1987 provincial government departments in Quebec and Manitoba were uncharacteristically aggressive in promoting new forms of co-operative enterprise – in particular, worker co-operatives – through well-designed programs. But even in these provinces such promotional activities absorb only a small fraction of the government money and effort available to encourage development by private enterprise. At the federal level, one can count on two hands the number of co-operative development projects or existing firms subsidized by more than $1 million since 1980.

Some of the reason for this disproportionately low level of government financial assistance to Canadian co-operatives lies in their proud independence. They have traditionally insisted that so long as co-operatives are not prevented from competing in their respective markets on even terms, they can look after their development needs by themselves. The 1984 report of the National Task Force on Co-operative Development, *A Co-operative Development Strategy for Canada*, signalled a decisive change in this attitude among major Canadian co-operatives. The report argued that the federal government had a responsibility to share the financial burden of co-operative development with the co-operative system, in the areas of co-operative education, promotion of worker, housing, health care, and fishing co-operatives, and to provide for tax-deductible investments in co-operative capital formation arrangements.

It is too early to say how much of this responsibility the federal government wishes to share with the major co-operatives, or would wish to share if they did not believe that the federal deficit was too large. If co-operatives can present enough evidence that co-operative enterprise is one of several effective vehicles for achieving the government's policy objectives, especially cost-effective job creation and regional development, they should receive more financial assistance for their development agenda than they have in the past. Such increased assistance carries the potential of reduced autonomy from the policy objectives of the federal government. Canadian co-operatives should examine the record of state–co-operative relationships in other countries to see whether certain negative features of such a scenario can be avoided.

Notes

Full citation of these references is found in the bibliography.

Chapter 1. Introduction

1   In 1987 co-operatives and credit unions in Canada had over 10 million members, and assets of approximately 73 billion dollars. See Canadian Co-operative Association, *Co-operatives Canada '88*.

2   See Monson and Downs, 'A Theory of Large Managerial Firms,' 221-36, for a non-technical application of this theory.

3   The literature on principal-agent problems (as well as the closely related question of property rights) is large. See, for instance: Ross, 'The Economic Theory of Agency: The Principals Problem,' 134-9; Furubotn and Pejovich, 'Property Rights and Economic Theory: A Review of Recent Literature,' 1137-62; Fama, 'Agency Problems and the Theory of the Firm,' 288-307; Jensen and Meckling, 'Theory of the Firm: Managerial Behaviour, Agency Costs, and Ownership Structure,' 305-60; and the references contained therein.

4   See Offe, *Disorganized Capitalism*, chap. 7. While it cannot be mapped directly on to the case of co-operatives, Offe's account suggests how different organized interests within the market – including co-operatives – possess significantly different relations to the biases, internal logics of power, and overarching social goals of the capitalist market.

5   The idea that there are two logics inherent in co-operative organizations is an important theme of the French literature on co-operatives. See Viénney, *Socio-économie des organisations coopératives*. Discussion of issues similar to those in

the principal-agent problem is found in Desroche, *Le Project coopératif.*

6 See Offe, *Disorganized Capitalism,* and Olson, *The Logic of Collective Action,* chap. 6.

7 For the best illustrations and theoretical account of this, see Coleman, *Business and Politics.*

8 Offe, *Disorganized Capitalism.*

Chapter 2. Co-operative Institutions

1 The Third [Owenite] Co-operative Congress in London in 1832 already proposed model rules for the British co-operative movement. Almost as soon as the Rochdale Society of Equitable Pioneers was founded in 1844 it became the model, for the British, and then for the world co-operative movement, and to this day the International Co-operative Alliance refers to its principles as 'the Rochdale principles.' Nevertheless, debate about what constitutes the Rochdale principles began within the first generation of that co-operative's founding and has continued; the reader may refer to Lambert, *Studies in the Social Philosophy of Co-operation.*

2 'Report of I.C.A. Commission on Cooperative Principles,' in *Report of the Twenty-Third Congress at Vienna,* 154-215. The commission of 1963-6 was charged with modernizing and updating the work of the previous commission of 1934-7.

3 Watkins, *Co-operative Principles,* 6-13. Ian MacPherson, *Each for All: A History of the Co-operative Movement in English Canada,* 1-7, also argues that the co-operative movement as a whole cannot be grasped by dissecting internal procedures of its individual member organizations. What made co-operatives a movement was something more than rules.

4 When they have needed to have large central organizations, co-operatives have normally come together in federations, sometimes referred to as second- or third-tier co-operatives. That is, the locals own the central, rather than vice versa. Such organizations as the North American, Sapiro-style marketing pools were an exception to the general rule of decentralization established by consumer and credit co-operatives – and they were criticized for this, among other things, at the time of their formation. See MacPherson, *Each for All,* 97, and Fairbairn, *From Prairie Roots,* 81. More recently other co-operatives in several countries have adopted a centralized structure to deal with competitive pressure, and in doing so some have ceased in law to be co-operatives.

5 There is no single recent work on the history of the co-operative movement world-wide – the closest in English is Digby's short *The World Co-operative Movement;* Fay's *Co-operation at Home and Abroad* provides a wealth of

contemporary and historical information. The four-part historical division used here is equivalent to Viénney's division by social-economic function, *Socio-économie des organisations coopératives*, I 20-1.

6 In their original statutes the Pioneers specified that the purpose of this accumulation of capital was the founding of a self-sufficient co-operative community of the sort advocated since the 1820s by Robert Owen, but in time this evolutionary purpose was abandoned by the British co-operative movement. On the place of Rochdale in British co-operation see, among others, Bonner, *British Co-operation*, chaps. 1-4.

7 Extensive literature exists on the German socialist labour movement in the nineteenth and twentieth centuries. In English, see Grebing, *The History of the German Labour Movement*; Lidtke, *The Alternative Culture*.

8 For two analyses of the European co-operatives, fifty years apart, see the relevant parts of *Report of the Inquiry on Cooperative Enterprise in Europe* (1937) and Nader Task Force on European Cooperatives, *Making Change? Learning from Europe's Consumer Cooperatives* (1986). On the United States, see Knapp, *The Rise of American Co-operative Enterprise*; and on Canada see MacPherson, *Each for All*, as well as, for consumer co-operatives in western Canada, Fairbairn, *Building a Dream*.

9 MacPherson, *Each for All*, 124; Fairbairn, *Building a Dream*, 19-23.

10 A general history of the credit union movement, concentrating on the United States, is provided by Moody and Fite, *The Credit Union Movement*. For wealth of detail on the European credit banks there is nothing in English to match Wolff, *People's Banks*, an old classic by an influential advocate of credit co-operation, and Tucker, *The Evolution of People's Banks*. Schulze consolidated his theory and practice in *Vorschuß- und Credit-Vereine als Volksbanken*; Raiffeisen published his in *Die Darlehnskassen-Vereine*.

11 Earle, *The Italian Cooperative Movement*, 14-15.

12 On the Quebec co-operative movement and its nationalist basis, see Martel, 'Émergence du mouvement coopératif agricole au Québec,' 13-39.

13 Digby, *Agricultural Co-operation in the Commonwealth*, provides a short survey of agricultural co-operative development in more than a dozen countries and regions of the world. On the relationship between late nineteenth- and early twentieth-century agricultural co-operatives and what would now be called diffusion of technology, see Tracy, *Agriculture in Western Europe,* esp. 112-14.

14 The Raiffeisen credit associations also functioned as purchasing and marketing societies. On Denmark, see Smith-Gordon and O'Brien, *Co-operation in Denmark*. On Ireland, see Smith-Gordon and Staples, *Rural Reconstruction in Ireland*. There are a few biographies of Sir Horace Plunkett, who led in creating the Irish co-operative movement; the most recent is West, *Horace Plunkett*.

15 Joint Stock Companies Act, 7 & 8 Vict., c. 110.
16 Cole, *A Century of Co-operation*, 116-18.
17 Friendly Societies Act, 33 Geo. III, c. 54, s. 2, s. 3, and s. 16.
18 Amendment to Friendly Societies Act, 4 & 5 Will. IV, c. 40.
19 Amendment to Friendly Societies Act, 9 & 10 Vict., c. 27. See Cole, *A Century of Co-operation*, 118.
20 Ibid.; Industrial and Provident Societies Act, 15 & 16 Vict., c. 31.
21 Ibid., s. 2, s. 8, and s. 7 respectively.
22 Ibid., s. 11; Cole, *A Century of Co-operation*, 120.
23 The Joint Stock Companies Act, 19 & 20 Vict., c. 47, ss. 3, 28, 30, 31; and the Industrial and Provident Societies Act, 25 & 26 Vict., c. 86, ss. 3, 20, 10, 12, 11, 17. While companies could pursue 'any lawful purpose,' co-operatives could pursue any lawful purpose *except* mining, quarrying, or banking (s. 3 in each case), 16.
24 [1897] A.C. 22.
25 See, for example, *Kelly* v. *Electrical Construction Co.* (1908), 16 O.L.R. 232 (Ont. H. Ct.). On the roles of boards, members, and management in co-operatives, see chaps. 3 and 13 in this volume.
26 S.O. 1865, c. 22, ss. 11, 15.
27 Co-operatives Associations Act, S.M. 1887, c. 12; S.S. 1913, c. 62.
28 S.S. 1950, c. 66; S.S 1983, c. C-37.1.
29 For crown corporations, see, Rees, 'A Positive Theory of Public Enterprises,' in Marchand, Pestieau, and Tulkens, eds., *The Performance of Public Enterprises*, 170-92. The most explicit statement of this view for co-operatives is found in Helmberger and Hoos, 'Cooperative Enterprise and Organization Theory,' 279. An analysis of this perspective, as well as an overview of literature on the economics of the agricultural co-operative is found in Staatz, 'Recent Developments in the Theory of Agricultural Cooperation,' 74-95. One of this article's themes is the question of the appropriate way to model the co-operative – as a firm, or as some other type of organization. This same theme runs through this section.
30 Enke, 'Consumer Cooperatives and Economic Efficiency,' 148-55; Taylor, 'The Taxation of Co-operatives,' 13-23.
31 Leibenstein, 'Allocative Efficiency vs. "X-Efficiency",' 392-415.
32 Coté, 'Effects of Ownership Structure on Efficiency.'
33 In the British case, see Jones, 'The Productivity of Worker Directors and Financial Participation by Employees in the Firm.'
34 Monson and Downs, 'A Theory of Large Managerial Firms,' 221-36. Chapter 3 provides a further discussion of this topic.
35 Chapter 16 discusses some of the consequences of this member-management relationship.

36   Staatz, 'Agriculture Cooperation,' and the same for the following paragraph.
37   Sexton, 'The Formation of Cooperatives,' 214-25; Staatz, 'The Cooperative as a
     Coalition,' 1084-9. Chapter 7 provides a further discussion of this topic.
38   The role of contracts in the firm was first raised by Coase in 'The Nature of the
     Firm,' 386-405. See Staatz, 'Agriculture Cooperation,' for a review of
     applications of Coase's work to agricultural co-operatives.
39   For examples of the first three approaches, see respectively, Melnyk, *The Search
     for Community*; LeVay, 'Agricultural Co-operative Theory: A Review,' 1-43; and
     MacPherson, *Each for All*.
40   Morgan, 'Paradigms, Metaphors, and Puzzle Solving,' 605-22.
41   Burns and Stalker, 'Mechanistic and Organic Systems,' in *The Management of
     Innovation*.
42   Thompson, *Organizations in Action;* Mitroff, *Stakeholders of the Organizational
     Mind*.
43   Taylor, 'Strategic Planning – Which Style Do You Need?' 51-62, on 'reactive' and
     'preactive' planning; Ackoff, *A Concept of Corporate Planning;* George A.
     Steiner, *Top Management Planning*.
44   Morgan, 'Paradigms,' 609.
45   For example, the 'organism' metaphor described in Burns and Stalker,
     'Mechanistic and Organic Systems'; Cyert and March, *A Behavioral Theory of the
     Firm*.
46   Ackoff, *Creating the Corporate Future,* 30.
47   Pfeffer and Salancik, *The External Control of Organizations*.
48   Ackoff, *Creating the Corporate Future*; Mason and Mitroff, *Challenging Strategic
     Planning Assumptions*; Trist, 'Action Research and Adaptive Planning.'
49   Taylor, 'Strategic Planning.'
50   Berle and Means, *The Modern Corporation and Private Property*.
51   See, for example, Cole and Postgate, *The Common People*, for the British case,
     and MacPherson, *Each for All*, for the Canadian case.
52   See Ostergaard and Halsey, *Power in Co-operatives*.
53   See Cole, *Century of Co-operation*.
54   See Palmer, *Working-Class Experience*.
55   See MacPherson, *Each for All*, and Laycock, *Populism and Democratic Thought
     in the Canadian Prairies*.
56   Ostergaard and Halsey, *Power in Co-operatives*; and MacPherson, 'The CCF and
     the Co-operative Movement in the Douglas Years,' in Brennan, ed., *Building the
     Co-operative Commonwealth*. The former make this point more tellingly than
     the latter.
57   See Bailey, *Encouraging Democracy in Consumer and Producer Co-operatives*,
     and Holland, *A Preliminary Report on Member Education in Canadian Co-*

operatives. Much more research is needed on this subject, to address a problem that has reached virtually crisis proportions – by the standards of traditional co-operative democracy – in most major Canadian co-operatives.

58 See Holland, *Member Education.*
59 See Axworthy, *Co-operatives and Their Employees*; and Wetzel and Gallagher, 'A Conceptual Analysis of Labour Relations in Co-operatives,' 517-40.
60 See Laycock, *Co-operative–Government Relations in Canada.*
61 See Laycock, 'The Politics of Canadian Co-operative Development Strategy,' for a discussion of this general issue in theoretical terms and reference to the new federal Co-operative Secretariat.

Chapter 3. Myth and Reality in Co-operative Organizations

1 Coase, 'The Nature of the Firm,' 393. See Fama and Jensen, 'Separation of Ownership and Control,' 377.
2 See, for example, the Co-operatives Act, S.S. 1983, c. C-37.1.
3 For a discussion of 'elite' and 'participatory' democratic theory and practice, see Macpherson, *The Life and Times of Liberal Democracy.*
4 Ish, *The Law of Canadian Co-operatives*, 104-27.
5 Mace, *Directors: Myth and Reality*; Mace, 'Directors: Myth and Reality – Ten Years Later,' 293; Eisenberg, *The Structure of the Corporation.*
6 See, for example, Canada Business Corporations Act, R.S.C. 1985, c. C-44, s. 122 [hereinafter C.B.C.A.]; Co-operatives Act, s. 94.
7 [1925] Ch. 407 at 428.
8 Ibid., 429
9 [1911] 1 Ch. 425 at 437.
10 Bishop, 'Sitting Ducks and Decoy Ducks,' 1078-9.
11 See, for example, C.B.C.A., s. 124.
12 Parsons, 'The Director's Duty of Good Faith,' 395.
13 *Report of the Ontario Select Committee on Company Law*, 53.
14 See Beck, Getz, Iacobucci, and Johnston, *Business Associations Casebook*, 216.
15 See, for example, *Walker* v. *Wimborne* (1976), 50 A.L.J.R. 446 (H.C. of A.).
16 See, for example, *Boardman* v. *Phipps*, [1967] 2 A.C. 46 (H.L.); *Regal (Hastings) Ltd.* v. *Gulliver* [1967] 2 A.C. 134 (H.L.).
17 See *infra.*
18 (1973), 33 D.L.R. (3d) 288 (B.C.S.C.).
19 [1966] S.C.R. 673.
20 Directors follow the statutory procedures to declare their interests in the matter under discussion and refrain from participating in the debate and vote at the Board of Directors' meetings. See e.g., C.B.C.A. s. 120; Co-operatives Act, s. 95.

21 [1956] 1 Ch. 565.
22 Referred to by Templeman J. in *Daniels* v. *Daniels* [1978] 2 W.L.R. 73, at 80 (Ch.).
23 298 F. 614 (S.D.N.Y., 1924).
24 Ibid., 616-17.
25 Ish, *Law of Canadian Co-operatives*, 81-3.
26 In most contemporary statutes this refers to a two-thirds majority, while some acts still refer to a three-quarters majority.
27 See e.g., C.B.C.A., s. 137; Co-operatives Act, s.113.
28 See e.g., C.B.C.A., s. 143; Co-operatives Act, s.106.
29 (1970), 11 D.L.R. (3d) 503 (Sask. C.A.).
30 Ibid., at 507.
31 Ibid., at 508.
32 (1983), 149 D.L.R. (3d) 130 (B.C.C.A.).
33 See, e.g., C.B.C.A., s. 239; Co-operatives Act, s. 189.
34 See e.g., C.B.C.A., s. 241; Co-operatives Act, s. 190.
35 (1984), 33 Sask. R. 41 (Q.B.).
36 Ibid., at 46.
37 Berle and Means, *The Modern Corporation and Private Property*.
38 See Mace, *Directors*.
39 See Axworthy, *Co-operatives and Their Employees*.

Chapter 4. Social Bases of Co-operation

1 Digby, *The World Co-operative Movement*, 12. There are, however, those who argue that co-operatives are part of a tradition going back to pre-modern times; chap. 14 in this volume, which considers co-operatives in their economic context, also considers these ideas.
2 See the contributions in Crossick and Haupt, eds., *Shopkeepers and Master Artisans in Nineteenth-Century Europe*. On the general changes in economic structure and ideology, see Polanyi, *The Great Transformation*.
3 On Owen, see Harrison, *Robert Owen and the Owenites in Britain and America*. On Fourier, see Beecher, *Charles Fourier: The Visionary and His World*. On the Utopians in general, see Manuel and Manuel, *Utopian Thought in the Western World*.
4 Bonner, *British Co-operation. The History, Principles, and Organisation of the British Co-operative Movement*, 9.
5 Garnett, *Co-operation and the Owenite Socialist Communities in Britain*, describes the patriarchal and authoritarian structure of the communities. Their dependence on a few sponsors proved fatal in some cases: one of the most

successful, the Ralahine community in County Clare, Ireland, failed because its wealthy patron gambled away the estate on which it was located (118-19).

6   Ibid., 110-14; quotation, 123 (on Ralahine).

7   On the historical significance of Rochdale within the British co-operative movement, see Bonner, *British Co-operation*, 41-86; on its significance as a theoretical model and system, see Lambert, *Studies in the Social Philosophy of Co-operation*, 61-108.

8   Sheehan, *German Liberalism in the Nineteenth Century*, 90-94; Aldenhoff, *Schulze-Delitzsch*, 77-106.

9   On the German co-operative movement, see Faust, *Geschichte der Genossenschaftsbewegung*; on Schulze, 193-234; on Raiffeisen, 323-67. Note that, as Faust correctly observes and contrary to what older English-language sources say, Raiffeisen founded no co-operatives before 1862; his earlier organizations were charities rather than co-operatives, lacking the essential co-operative feature of democratic ownership and control by users.

10 Earle, *The Italian Cooperative Movement*, 15.

11 Hasselmann, *Consumers' Co-operation in Germany*, 5. The italics are Hasselmann's. I quote this short book because it is in English; Hasselmann's *Geschichte der deutschen Konsumgenossenschaften*, at 740 pages, is considerably more exhaustive.

12 Hasselmann, *Consumers' Co-operation*, 8; Faust *Geschichte*.

13 The political aspects of this change are discussed more fully in chap. 9. Not all urban, working-class consumer co-operatives in Germany were socialist; Catholic co-operatives based in western Germany soon split away to form their own grouping.

14 On the 'dangerous poor,' see Jones, *Outcast London: A Study in the Relationship between Classes in Victorian Society*.

15 See Smith-Gordon and O'Brien, *Co-operation in Denmark*; on the Danish consumer movement, see Otto Riis, 'Danish Consumer Co-operation,' 139-42. On Ireland, Trevor West, *Horace Plunkett*, 25, 28-9.

16 On German shopkeepers and their co-operatives, see Gellately, *The Politics of Economic Despair*, 65-74. On the changes affecting the German lower middle class, artisans and shopkeepers, see Blackbourn, 'Between Resignation and Volatility,' in Crossick and Haupt, eds., *Shopkeepers and Master Artisans*, 35-61.

17 Wood, *A History of Farmers' Movements in Canada*; Fowke, *The National Policy and the Wheat Economy*; Fairbairn, *From Prairie Roots: The Remarkable Story of Saskatchewan Wheat Pool*; Nesbitt, *Tides in the West: A Wheat Pool Story*. On the way in which American farmers' grievances developed out of their experiences with dependence on monopolistic business interests, see Goodwyn, *Democratic Promise*.

18 Based on archival sources cited in Fairbairn, 'The Politics of Sectional Revolt.'
19 Turner, *Case Studies of Consumers' Cooperatives*, esp. 26-8.
20 MacPherson, *Each for All,* 103-4 and 113-15.

Chapter 5. Democracy and Co-operative Practice

1   An important expression of this belief can be found in the report of the 1984
    National Task Force on Co-operative Development, *A Co-operative Development
    Strategy for Canada.* See also Laidlaw, *Co-operatives in the Year 2000.*
2   See Macpherson, *Democratic Theory*, chaps. 2 and 3, and *The Rise and Fall of
    Economic Justice and Other Essays,* 79ff.
3   Barber, *Strong Democracy,* 155 and 232ff.
4   For an outline of most of these lines of criticism, see Pennock, *Democratic
    Political Theory*, and Held, *Models of Democracy*, chap. 8. For reviews of the
    range of major debates in contemporary democratic theory, see Duncan, ed.,
    Democratic Theory and Practice; Macpherson, *The Life and Times of Liberal
    Democracy*; and Dahl, *Dilemmas of Pluralist Democracy.*
5   Wolfe, 'Inauthentic Democracy,' 60.
6   This may be almost as much a function of the atomizing and anti-rational
    character of the technological medium used by television as it is the actual
    content of television programming. For a compelling argument to this effect, see
    Postman, *Amusing Ourselves to Death.*
7   This expression was coined by Macpherson in his analysis of the political
    thought of seventeenth-century English liberalism, *The Political Theory of
    Possessive Individualism*, but is still appropriate as a general description of the
    civic orientation developed in the political cultures of western capitalist societies.
8   The 1984 National Task Force on Co-operative Development Report recognizes
    this, albeit in rather elliptical fashion (Report, 5-6, 26, 59, and 120-2).
9   Such initiatives within the Canadian co-operative system seem to have been
    undertaken recently largely by the credit unions, notably VanCity Credit Union in
    Vancouver and Ontario Credit Union Central, both involved in community
    economic development projects, the caisses populaires Desjardins system in
    Quebec, with promotion of worker co-operatives and other local co-operative
    development, and the Community Development Fund in Nova Scotia, co-
    sponsored by co-operatives, trade unions, and churches.
10 For a fuller discussion of both the interpretation of and problems with the
    Canadian co-operative doctrine of political neutrality, see chap. 11, this volume,
    and Laycock, *Co-operative–Government Relations in Canada,* esp. chap. 5.
11 This is argued or demonstrated in a variety of recent works. See, among others,
    Levin and Jackall, eds., *Worker Co-operatives in America*; Co-operative Union of

Canada, *A Co-operative Development Strategy for Canada*, 69-74; Henk and Logan, *Mondragon: An Economic Analysis*; Gutierrez-Johnson, 'Compensation, Equity, and Industrial Democracy in the Mondragon Cooperatives,' 267; Gutierrez-Johnson and Whyte, 'The Mondragon System of Worker Production Cooperatives', 18-30; Rothschild and Whitt, *The Cooperative Workplace*; and Axworthy, *Co-operatives and Their Employees.*

12 See Ekelund, *The Property of the Common.*

13 Perhaps the most obvious case in point here is the strikes by the grain handlers at the major export terminals for prairie co-operators' wheat.

14 See the range of publications that have emerged from the 1977 'Quality of Life' study by York University's Institute for Social Research.

15 Taylor, 'Legitimation, Identity and Alienation in Late Twentieth Century Canada,' in *Constitutionalism, Citizenship and Identity in Canada*, Cairns and Williams eds., 198. See also Macpherson, *Economic Justice*, 39.

16 This is the finding of a number of recent surveys done by several Canadian governments and major co-operative enterprises, and by Douglas Holland of the Canadian Co-operative Association.

17 Macpherson, *Economic Justice*, 98-9.

18 Far from being an exclusively Canadian phenomenon, this has been much in evidence in Britain and the United States over the past decade, and has been both responsible for and reinforced by the success of Ronald Reagan and Margaret Thatcher. For a nice theoretical overview of this, see Held, *Models of Democracy*, chaps. 8 and 9.

19 The classic statement of this can be found in Crozier, Huntington, and Watunuki. For critical assessments of the 'ungovernability thesis', see Held, *Models of Democracy*, chaps. 8 and 9, Macpherson, *Economic Justice*, chap. 10, and Offe, '"Ungovernability": the Renaissance of Conservative Theories of Crisis,' in Keane, ed., *Contradictions of the Welfare State.*

20 For revealing theoretical accounts of the relative strengths of these rights, see Bowles and Gintis, *Democracy and Capitalism.*

21 In *Retrieving Democracy*, 5, Green contends that 'the development of the welfare state has not been accompanied by any efforts to get people thinking of their social being as a realm of more co-operation and participation than of competition and withdrawal into the life of privatized consumption.' His American experience seems to have coloured his perspective excessively, but it is true that his contention points to a major failing of the social democratic left's response to the rise and success of the new right over the past decade. For some suggestive argument along these lines, see Held and Keane, 'Socialism and the Limits of State Action,' in Curran, ed., *The Future of the Left.*

22 See Whitaker, 'Images of the State in Canada,' in Panitch, ed., *The Canadian State*, and Horowitz, 'Conservatism, Liberalism and Socialism in Canada,' 143-71.

23 This conclusion is easily arrived at by reviewing a decade of Gallup polls, or the more sophisticated election surveys of the past two decades, as reported and analysed in H. Clarke et al., *Absent Mandate*.

24 To some extent, this is recognized by the Report of the Task Force on Co-operative Development, 2 and 3.

25 Wolfe, in 'Inauthentic Democracy,' explores the conflict between democratic values and orientations, on the one hand, and an overriding concern with economic expansion, on the other.

26 The Report of the Task Force on Co-operative Development provided some evidence that these opportunities were recognized by at least some co-operative leaders in Canada.

27 This point is made very effectively by Bowles and Gintis, *Democracy and Capitalism*. More generally, see chaps. 2, 6, and 7 in Macpherson, *Economic Justice*, esp. 84, where he argues that human rights will be taken seriously only if they are treated and presented as individual property rights: 'We have made property so central to our society that any thing and any rights that are not property are apt to take second place ... given our present scale of values, it is only if the human right to a full life is seen as a property right that it will stand much chance of general realization.'

28 Ekelund, *Property of the Common*, presents an extended and intriguing argument along these lines.

29 For a compelling argument to this effect, see Dahl, *A Preface to Economic Democracy*.

30 Barber, *Strong Democracy,* hints at some of the problematic dimensions of this relationship within modern liberal societies in the following: 'The dialectic between participation and community is not easily institutionalized. Individual civic activity (participation) and the public association formed through civic activity (the community) call up two strikingly different worlds. The former is the world of autonomy, individualism, and agency; the latter is the world of sociability, community, and interaction. The world views of individualism and communalism remain at odds; and institutions that can facilitate the search for common ends without sabotaging the individuality of the searchers, and that can acknowledge pluralism and conflict as starting points of the political process without abdicating the quest for common ends, may be much more difficult to come by than a pretty paragraph about the dialectical interplay between individual participation and community.'

Chapter 6. Canadian Co-operatives and Public Education

1 Craig and Carden, *Co-operatives in Canada: Focus for the 1990s.*
2 Opinion Research Index, *Financial Institutions Survey.*
3 Co-operative Future Directions Project, *Patterns and Trends.*
4 Creelman, personal interview, January 1987.
5 Giroux, 'The Politics of Schooling and Culture.'
6 Henry, *Culture against Man*, 83.
7 Slavin, 'Learning Together.'
8 Henry, *In Suburban Classrooms*, 83.
9 Campbell, *On Being Number One*, 146.
10 Henry, *Culture against Man*, 83.
11 Campbell, *On Being Number One*, 146.
12 Gallup poll, *Star Phœnix*, 24 October 1977.
13 Johnson, Marvyama, Johnson, Nelson, and Skon, *The Effects of Co-operative, Competitive, and Individualistic Goal Structures on Achievement.*
14 Ibid., 1.
15 Kohn, 'How to Succeed without Even Vying,' 42.
16 Cornoy and Levin, *Schooling and Work in the Democratic State.*
17 Kohn, 'How to Succeed without Even Vying,' 44.
18 Graves and Graves, 'Co-operative Learning – Problems and Promise,' 8.
19 Kohn, 'How to Succeed without Even Vying.'
20 National Task Force on Co-operative Development, *A Co-operative Development Strategy for Canada.*
21 Holland, 'Preliminary Report on Member Education Research.'
22 Phillips, personal interview, March 1986.
23 The Co-operative Resource Materials project, administered by the Co-operative College of Canada and sponsored by Canadian co-operatives, has initiated a nation-wide process to make materials concerning co-operation and co-operatives available to classroom teachers at both the elementary and secondary levels.

Chapter 7. Individual and Collective Interests in Co-operatives

1 In western Canadian agriculture, where co-operatives have traditionally been strong, farm size is becoming much more diverse, as evidenced by the increasing variance of this measure of farm structure. For instance, in Manitoba the ratio of the standard deviation in farm size to the average farm size has increased from 0.67 in 1921 to 0.93 in 1981. In Saskatchewan this ratio increased from 0.46 in 1921 to 0.76 in 1981. Over this same period the ratio in Alberta increased from 0.57 in 1921 to 1.00 in 1981.

2 Zusman, 'Group Choice in an Agricultural Marketing Co-operative,' 221.
3 The impossibility of such a method was first demonstrated by Kenneth Arrow and has come to be known as the Arrow impossibility theorem. See Arrow, *Social Choice and Individual Values*; and Mueller, *Public Choice*, for a discussion.
4 A discussion of the above points and an analysis of the effect of member diversity when decisions are made by majority rule is found in Zusman, 'Group Choice.'
5 For an application of co-operative games to co-operatives, see, Sexton, 'The Formation of Cooperatives: A Game Theoretic Approach,' 214-25; Staatz, 'The Cooperative as a Coalition,' 1084-9.
6 Sexton, 'Formation of Co-operatives.'
7 See Hardin, *Collective Action*.
8 The numbers in Figure 1 are arbitrary in the sense that they can be altered in several ways to produce the 'compete' result among players. To obtain this result, the pay-offs for each player must follow the same pattern. For X, the ranking must be (compete, co-operate) > (co-operate, co-operate) > (compete, compete) > (co-operate, compete).
9 As quoted in Hardin, *Collective Action*, 1.
10 The implications of the *N*-player Prisoners' Dilemma for provision of collective goods such as political lobbying, environmental control, and market collusion is examined in Olson, *The Logic of Collective Action*.
11 Hardin, *Collective Action*, 3.
12 Axelrod, *The Evolution of Co-operation*.
13 Runge, 'Institutions and the Free Rider,' 154-81.

Chapter 8. Marketing Member Commitment

1 Leiss, Kline, and Jhally, *Social Communication in Advertising*, 11.
2 Leiss et al. associate the writings of H. Marcuse with the Marxist perspective on the function of advertising (the creation of false needs) and those of J. K. Galbraith and W.C. Mills with the neo-liberal view (the use of unscrupulous ways to appeal to existing needs).
3 Which includes promotional activities such as the sponsorship of an athletic team by an organization, personal selling, and advertising.
4 Levitt, 'Marketing Myopia,' 45-56.
5 Kotler, *Marketing for Nonprofit Organizations*.
6 Engel and Blackwell, *Consumer Behavior*.
7 Kotler and McDougall, *Principles of Marketing*.
8 It has been argued that one's concept of the nature of marketing is a function of the perspective from which the phenomenon is viewed. Three perspectives have been identified and characterized as:

The Distribution System Perspective: marketing is seen as a system of distributing institutions performing economic functions required to move products from points of production to points of consumption. All those institutions involved in the distribution of goods within society are included within the boundaries of marketing, and the focus is on the nature of the functions being performed by the distribution system, as well as on structure, performance, and inter-relationships within the distribution system.

The Organizational System Perspective: this perspective sets the boundaries of marketing at those 'publics' which have a 'potential impact on there source converting efficiency of the organization.' Marketing is viewed exclusively as a generic technology which can be employed by any organization, business, or non-business, in order to elicit desired responses from its publics. Research activities are devoted primarily to the evaluation and refinement of this technology. This is currently the most popular view of marketing.

The Social System Perspective: from this perspective, marketing is viewed as an integral and inherent part of society – a fundamental societal process required for the smooth and effective functioning of a social system. The focus of the marketing discipline from this point of view is on the determinants, structure, and performance of the process which evolves to facilitate the exchanges required among the interdependent producing and consuming units in a social system. A perspective such as this demands a very broad definition of the boundaries of marketing. It requires the student of marketing to think beyond the organization to its place within a specific distribution system, and to examine all marketing institutions executing exchanges throughout the social system. It facilitates a comprehensive 'social viewpoint' on marketing which accepts the need for social responsibility on the part of marketers. Because the organization cannot be studied in isolation from the rest of the social system, the marketer is required to contemplate the consequences of an organization's actions on the rest of society. Sweeney, 'Marketing: Technology or Social Process?' 3-10.

9   Kotler, *Marketing for Nonprofit Organizations.*
10 The definition most widely accepted for social marketing is 'the design, implementation, and control of programs calculated to influence the acceptibility of social ideas and involving considerations of product planning, pricing, communication, distribution, and marketing research.' Kotler and Zaltman, 'Social Marketing,' 3-12.
11 Lazniak, Lusch, and Murphy, 'Social Marketing: Its Ethical Dimensions,' 29-36.
12 For a more detailed discussion of this topic, see Fox and Kotler, 'Marketing of Social Causes,' 24-33.
13 For a discussion, see Lazniak, Lusch, and Murphy, 'Social Marketing.'
14 Fox and Kotler, 'Marketing of Social Causes.'

15 Kotler, 'A Generic Concept of Marketing,' 46-54.
16 The notion of publics is central to this broadened concept. The acceptance of this notion forces the organization to focus on all groups or organizations which have some impact on the functioning of the organization. Kotler identifies three input publics: suppliers, employees, and supporters; two ouput publics: agents and consumers; and four sanctioning publics: government, competitors, special publics, and the general public. The publics concept holds many similarities to the stakeholders concept found in the strategic planning literature.
17 Kotler and Levy, 'Broadening the Concept of Marketing,' 15.
18 Thompson and Jones, Jr., 'Economic Appraisal of Co-operative Enterprise in the United States,' 386.
19 Bakken and Schaars, *The Economics of Co-operative Marketing.*
20 Ibid.
21 LeVay, 'Agricultural Co-operative Theory,' 1-43.
22 Levay citing Pigou, *Economics of Welfare.*
23 Burley, *The Consumers' Co-operative as a Distributive Agency,* 7.
24 Ibid.
25 Ibid., 136.
26 This would appear to be an early recognition of what came to be defined as the 'marketing concept' in the 1950s.
27 Boisvert, 'Le Marketing dans la Perspective Co-operative,' in La Flame et al., eds., *La Gestion Moderne des Co-opératives.* He considered these to be analogous to a private sector model and a social marketing model.
28 Collard, *Altruism and Economy*; Weisbrod, *The Voluntary Non-profit Sector.*
29 Takas, 'Societal Marketing,' 3.
30 Burley, *Consumers' Co-operative,* is representative of these approaches.
31 Ibid., 140.
32 For a more detailed examination of this issue, see Ketilson, 'Towards a Co-operative Marketing Management Approach,' 1-17.
33 Dinu, 'Member Participation in Co-operatives through Marketing.'
34 For a detailed discussion of the CU FIC, refer to their planning document, published in 1987 by Saskatchewan Credit Union Central.
35 Laczniak, Lusch, and Murphy, 'Social Marketing,' 29.
36 Ibid., 32.
37 The author would consider many co-operatives to fall within the latter category.
38 Pettigrew, 'Examining Change in the Long-Term Context of Culture and Politics,' in Pennings and Associates, eds., *Organizational Strategy and Change.*
39 Prakish Sethi, 'Institutional/Image Advertising and Idea/Issue Advertising as Marketing Tools,' 68-78.
40 Foxall, 'Social Marketing of Agricultural Co-operation in Britain,' 1-12.

Chapter 9. Co-operatives as Politics

1 Bonner, *British Co-operation*, 29-30.
2 See Lambert, *Studies in the Social Philosophy of Co-operation*, 86.
3 Neutrality was, however, along with cash trading and promotion of education, considered a subsidiary principle to the four main principles of open and voluntary membership, democratic control, limited interest on capital, and dividends on transactions. The next committee on co-operative principles in 1963-6 subsumed the idea of neutrality under the idea of open and voluntary membership, stating only that membership should be 'available without artificial restriction or any social, political, racial or religious discriminations.' For a brief overview, see the recent book by Watkins, *Co-operative Principles Today and Tomorrow*, 5-8.
4 Bonner, *British Co-operation*, 187-94.
5 On the Tory reaction against Owen by the 1840s, see Garnett, *Co-operation and the Owenite Socialist Communities in Britain*, 171-83.
6 Bonner, *British Co-operation*, 41-59.
7 Hasselmann, *Consumers' Co-operation in Germany*, 5.
8 Saul, *Staat, Industrie und Arbeiterbewegung im Kaiserreich*, 19. See also Grebing, *Arbeiterbewegung: Sozialer Protest und kollektive Interessenvertretun*, 104.
9 Two English-language histories of the SPD in this period are Lidtke, *The Alternative Culture,* and Guttsman, *The German Social Democratic Party*.
10 See Grebing, *History of the German Labour Movement*, 70-1.
11 The Fabians in Britain found in the idea of the Co-operative Commonwealth a bridge between co-operation and Labour socialism; see Woolf, ed., *Fabian Essays on Co-operation*, and Sidney and Beatrice Webb, *The Consumers' Co-operative Movement*. On the Co-operative Commonwealth idea in Canada, which had direct inspiration from British Fabian socialism, see Brennan, ed., *Building the Co-operative Commonwealth*. On the equivalent French idea, see Poisson, *The Co-operative Republic*.
12 See, for example, Hesselbach, *Public, Trade Union and Cooperative Enterprise in Germany*.
13 See Sheehan, *German Liberalism in the Nineteenth Century*, 90-4, on the significance of Schulze-Delitzsch's ideas in the liberal movement. See Aldenhoff for a biography of Schulze-Delitzsch.
14 Concerning the attitudes of the German lower middle class, see Blackbourn, 'Between Resignation and Volatility,' in *Shopkeepers and Master Artisans,* Crossick and Heinz-Gerhard Haupt, eds., 35-61; and the same author's 'Class and Politics in Wilhelmine Germany,' esp. 245-7 on the split between working-class and lower-middle-class co-operatives. The research on *Mittelstandspolitik* (lower-

middle-class policy) in Germany is extensive; one reference is Winkler, *Mittelstand, Demokratie und Nationalsozialismus.*

15 On the German Agrarian League and its conservative ideology, see Puhle, *Agrarische Interessenpolitik und preußischer Konservatismus.* The Catholic peasants' leagues also turned to protectionist demands.

16 On the conflict between agriculture and industry in Germany see Barkin, *The Controversy over German Industrialization.* On the relationship between social change and conservative agrarian populism, see Puhle, *Politische Agrarbewegungen in kapitalistischen Industriegesellschaften* – perhaps an overdrawn case.

17 Miller, *A Conservative Looks at Cooperatives,* 43, 9, 62, and 49 for the four quotations. These are based on Miller's speeches and publications during 1960-3.

18 Zeldin, *France 1848-1945,* esp. the sections Ambition and Love, 131-97 (on the peasantry); and Politics and Anger, 64-102 (on political ideas in general), 276-318 (on solidarism), and 361-423 (on socialism).

19 A good account by a contemporary can be found in Wood, *A History of Farmers' Movements in Canada,* 329-64. Canadian farmers were inspired by American examples such as that of the Nonpartisan League; on this see Morlan, *Political Prairie Fire;* on the American farm movements more generally, see the works by Danbom, McConnell, Goodwyn, Hofstadter, and Pollack, listed in the bibliography. See also Parsons et al., 'The Role of Co-operatives in the Development of the Movement Culture of Populism,' 866-85.

20 See Lipset, *Agrarian Socialism.*

21 Fairbairn, *Building a Dream,* 103-5.

22 Haynes, 'Farm Coops and the Election of Hubert Humphrey to the Senate,' 201-11.

23 For an account of co-operatives' attempts to represent their interests within the framework of interest group–government relations in Canada, see Laycock, *Co-operative–Government Relations in Canada.*

Chapter 10. Co-operation and Government

1 See esp. Thorburn, *Interest Groups in the Canadian Federal System.*

2 Recent cases include the establishment of a Honda assembly plant in Alliston, Ontario, instead of a Quebec location, and the awarding of a federal contract for fighter plane maintenance to a Quebec rather than a Manitoba-based firm. This tactic has often proved useful in agricultural policy as well. See Skogstad, *The Politics of Agricultural Policy Making in Canada.*

3 See Stevenson, *Unfulfilled Union;* and Panitch, 'The Role and Nature of the Canadian State,' in *The Canadian State.*

4 Responsive and sympathetic legislation regarding co-operative grain marketing in Saskatchewan and caisses populaire development in Quebec are excellent examples of this.

5 There was, after all, no federal Co-operatives Act until 1970, and significant direct financial support for co-operative economic development was entirely absent until 1982. On the Co-operatives Act, see Ish, *The Law of Canadian Co-operatives*; on the 1982 case of Co-Enerco, see Laycock, *Co-operative–Government Relations in Canada*. One could argue that the establishment of the Canadian Wheat Board was as good as direct financial support to the prairie wheat pools, but it is stretching the point to claim that the federal government initiated this in 1935 primarily to assist co-operative enterprise per se, as opposed to prairie farmers and the Canadian export trade.

6 The following section is an abridged version of a discussion in Laycock, *Co-operative–Government Relations in Canada*, chap. 1.

7 For a contemporary expression of this, see Laidlaw, *Co-operatives in the Year 2000*. Laidlaw remarks that 'if one were asked to identify the greatest danger looming before the co-operative movement in most parts of the world, it would be adverse relations with all-powerful governments' (12).

8 Pross, *Group Politics and Public Policy*, 3. The reader is advised to consult several other recent studies of pressure group politics in Canada to obtain a subtler and more systematic account of pressure groups. The most important are Coleman, 'Analysing the Associative Action of Business'; Coleman, 'Canadian Business and the State,' in Banting, ed., *State and Economic Interests*; Thorburn, *Interest Groups*; and Stanbury, *Business-Government Relations*.

9 Provincial medical and legal associations' control over licensing and discipline of their members provides good examples of this latter activity. For a general account of these functions and their importance to public policy development in Canada, see Pross, *Group Politics*, chap. 4.

10 Stigler, 'The Theory of Economic Regulation,' 3-21; Posner, 'Theories of Economic Regulation,' 213-36.

11 Coleman, 'Associative Action of Business.'

12 Ibid., 417.

13 Salisbury, 'Interest Representation,' 64-76.

14 Skogstad, *Agricultural Policy Making*.

15 Coleman, 'Associative Action of Business.'

16 Salisbury, 'Interest Representation,' argues that membership groups (pressure groups) are not the only players involved in political action in the United States, but rather that institutions – corporations, firms, universitites, etc. – are playing an increasingly important role.

17 The CCA was officially initiated in September 1987, after over one year of

negotiations between the CUC's member organizations and the Co-operative College of Canada over the ways in which the CCA would be funded by, and provide educational, organizational, lobbying, international development, and other services to, the member organizations.

18 First-tier co-operatives operate at the community level with a broad individual member base. Second-tier co-operatives operate at a central provincial or regional level, and provide services to and for first-tier co-operatives, who comprise their membership. Third-tier co-operatives operate at a national level, and provide services for the 'centrals' and beyond to the first-tier co-operatives. In what follows, the term CCA will be used to represent the current organization, as well as its predecessor, the CUC.

19 On the unrepresentative character of the large Canadian private sector peak associations, see Coleman, 'Canadian Business and the State,' 282-3.

20 The argument outlined here is elaborated in Laycock, *Co-operative–Government Relations in Canada*, and 'The Politics of Co-operative Development Strategy.'

21 Mayer, cited in CUC News Service, 15 May 1987, 1.

22 National Task Force on Co-operative Development, *A Co-operative Development Strategy for Canada*, 110.

23 Several of the more striking of these are for federal financial 'solutions' to the problems of capital formation in co-operatives, through Co-op Registered Savings Plans, the problems of financing development and education for worker co-operatives, and the problems of co-operative export development.

24 These projects were Co-Enerco in 1982 and the NuGrade Heavy Oil Upgrader in 1986.

25 Over the past five years United Co-operatives of Ontario, United Maritime Fishermen, and Co-operative Implements Ltd. have all been rescued by federal loans and/or loan guarantees.

26 National Task Force, 2-3.

27 Sullivan, *Co-operation in Canada:* Lane and Harman, *Co-operative Organizations in Eastern Canada.*

28 An exception is found in Laycock, *Co-operative–Government Relations.*

29 Côté and Vézina, 'L'organisation des marchés dans l'industrie laitière au Québec,' 39-60.

30 Forbes, *Institutions and Influence in Canadian Farm and Food Policy*, 58; Coleman, 'Canadian Business and the State.'

31 For a balanced and insighful account of the different winners and losers in the outcome of the Crow debate, see Skogstad, *Agricultural Policy Making.*

32 Coleman, 'Associative Action of Business.'

33 Ibid.; Wilson, 'Snapshot of the family,' in *Western Producer*, 29 January 1987.

34 Forbes, *Farm and Food Policy.*

35 Coleman, 'Associative Action of Business.'
36 Ibid.
37 For an interesting discussion of this, see Anderson, 'Political Design and the Representation of Interests,' in *Trends towards Corporatist Intermediation*, ed. Schmitter and Lehmbruch. For some discussion of the obstacles to representative economic democracy, especially as it applies to co-operatives, see Laycock, 'Representative Economic Democracy and the Problem of Policy Influence.'

Chapter 11. Political Neutrality and the Problem of Interest Representation

1   For one of the most stimulating theoretical discussions of these questions, see Pitkin, *The Concept of Representation.*
2   For a useful discussion of this process within organizations, see Offe, 'Two Logics of Collective Action,' in Keane, eds., *Disorganized Capitalism,* 170-220.
3   See Pitkin, *Representation.*
4   This latter element is what Pitkin refers to as the 'substantive' dimension of representation, which is the minimum condition of an actively democratic representation; ibid., 141-2.
5   Bachrach and Baratz, 'The Two Faces of Power,' 942-52.
6   See Coleman, 'Associative Action of Business,' 413-33.
7   See Macpherson, *Democracy in Alberta*, chap. 7.
8   See Goodwyn, *Democratic Promise.*
9   For an interpretation of political neutrality in the British Co-operative movement, see Cole, *A Century of Co-operation*, and Bonner, *British Co-operation.*
10 For an excellent account of this, see MacPherson, 'The Co-operative Union of Canada and Politics,' 152-74.
11 Keen was general secretary of the CUC from 1909 to 1947; Good was CUC president from 1921 to 1944.
12 Quoted in Good, *Farmer Citizen*, 253.
13 Keen's contempt for the traditional world of party competition is nicely represented in an excerpt from a 1926 editorial in the *Canadian Co-operator*, 'Co-operation and Politics,' provided in Good, *Farmer Citizen*, 257.
14 MacPherson, 'Co-operative Union,' 152-74.
15 The abstract attractiveness of these principles, and as their ultimate irrelevance in the Canadian political context, are both revealed (the latter unknowingly) in Good, *Farmer Citizen*, esp. 163-98.
16 MacPherson, 'Co-operative Union,' 173.
17 See Good's insistence on the gap in the democratic strategy and logic of the Regina Manifesto, in *Farmer Citizen*, 207-8.

18 It should be noted in passing, however, that one could argue that the same factors at work in this failure are responsible for the limited economic and cultural impact of co-operatives in Canadian society. Co-operative movement politicization at an early stage might have eventually strengthened the hand of the CCF when they appeared to be on the verge of a national breakthrough in the early 1940s. This contention deserves considerably more argument than we can allow it here.

19 Competitive here is understood as having a good chance of forming either or both of the national or several large provinces' governments at any given time.

20 For a discussion of the Canadian party system which focuses on this fact and its implications, see Brodie and Jenson, *Crisis, Challenge and Change.*

21 Cole, *Century of Co-operation,* 269.

22 Ibid., chap. 19; 'Politics and the Co-operative Movement,' *Society for Co-operative Studies Bulletin,* April 1979, articles by Graham, Wise, Clarke, and Gallacher; and Barou, ed., *The Co-operative Movement in Labour Britain,* chaps. 10 and 12.

23 Cole, *Century of Co-operation,* 315-16.

24 Society for Co-operative Studies, 19.

25 Cole, *Century of Co-operation,* 317-19.

26 Ibid., 319.

27 Ibid., 331.

28 See Society for Co-operative Studies, and essays by Watkins, Barou, Warswick, and Bailey in Barou, ed., *Co-operative Movement.*

29 See Society for Co-operative Studies, esp. essays by Wise, Graham, and Clarke.

30 For an extended account of the rationale for continuing the alliance with Labour, via a Co-operative party, see the recent pamphlet by the Co-operative Union, *Opportunities for Co-operative Politics.*

31 Hirschman, *Exit, Voice and Loyalty.*

32 See his critique of the Regina Manifesto along these lines in Good, *Farmer Citizen.*

33 See Laycock, *Co-operatives–Government Relations,* 38-43 and 81-90. The pattern continued in the Canadian Co-operative Association and Canadian Co-operative Credit Society's 'On the Doorstep' campaign of 1988, which leaders conceded had virtually no impact, in what was admittedly close to a single-issue campaign; with the exception of Co-op Atlantic, major co-operative associations took no official position on the free trade issue.

34 While this is hard to document, it was the impression acquired by the author during interviews for *Co-operative–Government Relations.*

35 MacPherson, *Co-operative Union,* 174.

36 See Co-operative Union, *The Role and Effectiveness of the Co-operative Party,*

14-15, for an argument that lobbying by Labour/Co-op MPs is far more effective than lobbying by paid lobbyists.

37 For a case study of an ongoing instance of this, see Laycock, 'Co-operatives, Governments.'

38 For a discussion of these costs and perceptions, see Laycock, 'Representative Economic Democracy.'

Chapter 12. Election of Directors in Saskatchewan Co-operatives

1 Linden and Norman, *Democracy and Efficiency*, 11-12.

2 Information regarding the survey, including methodology, questions posed and results, may be obtained by contacting the Centre for the Study of Co-operatives, University of Saskatchewan, Saskatoon, Saskatchewan.

3 The categories of co-operatives are straightforward. The agricultural co-operatives category includes: a) farms, b) farmers' markets, c) pasture and grazing, d) seed cleaning, and e) others. The day care category includes pre-school co-operatives. Recreational co-operatives include: a) community halls, b) curling clubs, c) resorts, d) senior citizens' centres, and e) others. Included in the 'other' category are: a) funeral, b) snow plough, c) firefighter, d) cable television, e) insurance, f) additional co-operatives from the main listings to which the respondent also belonged, and g) others. Credit Union Central is included in the credit union category. Federated Co-operatives Limited is included in the retail category.

4 Michels, *Political Parties*, 365.

5 Still, *Voter Equality in Electoral Systems*, i.

6 Laidlaw, 'Speaking of Co-ops,' 5.

7 Lipset, *Agrarian Socialism*, 224.

8 Respondents from recreational co-operatives frequently commented that they accepted board positions because no one else wanted them.

9 According to Randy Dove, manager, employment services at Saskatchewan Credit Union Central, 'Many local boards appear to believe that university graduates are a threat to the status quo of their credit union and ultimately the membership.' See Bionda, 'Succession: Managing the Future,' 6.

10 See Lipset, *Agrarian Socialism*, esp. chap. 9. He noted, for instance, 'that most cooperative leaders have held some post in the CCF party' (224), and 'that the social and economic characteristics of cooperative leaders differ from those of the general rural population in the same way as do those of CCF officials' (228).

11 By-law 5.02(e) of the Saskatoon Credit Union, for instance, reads as follows: 'Nominees are to provide a brief personal biography, which will be made available to voting members during election week. Nominees will not campaign in public or through the media.'

Chapter 13. Collective and Individual Rights in Canada

1 Campbell, *The Left and Rights*, 83-4.
2 Flathman, *The Practice of Rights*, 184-5.
3 Berlin, ' Two Concepts of Liberty,' in *Four Essays on Liberty*, 123.
4 Ibid.
5 Mill, *On Liberty*, 125.
6 Ibid., 68.
7 Berlin, 'Two Concepts,' 128.
8 Ibid., 131.
9 Ibid.
10 Ibid., 172.
11 Macpherson, ' Berlin's Division of Liberty' in *Democratic Theory*, 116.
12 Bowles and Gintis, *Democracy and Capitalism*, 177.
13 Glasbeek, 'Workers of the World Avoid the Charter of Rights,' 14.
14 Connolly, *The Terms of Political Discourse*, 144.
15 Macpherson, 'Berlin's Division of Liberty,' 96.
16 Ibid., 101.
17 Bowles and Gintis, *Democracy and Capitalism*, 177.
18 Macpherson, 'Berlin's Division of Liberty,' 112.
19 Ibid., 113.
20 Ibid., 114-15.
21 Ibid., 103.
22 Campbell, *The Left and Rights*, 47.
23 Ibid.
24 Connolly, *Political Discourse*, 148.
25 Ibid.
26 Williams, 'The Changing Nature of Citizen Rights,' in Cairns and Williams, eds., *Constitutionalism, Citizenship and Society in Canada*, 124-5.
27 Ibid., 127-8.
28 It might be argued, for instance, that the acceptance of the demands of womens' and native groups, for their collective protection under the Canadian Charter of Rights and Freedoms, is less an indication of the recognition given collective rights than of the political need of government to gain popular support for constitutional entrenchment of the document by appeasing the legitimate claims of particular societal groups. Indeed, the lack of continued progress on issues of concern to these groups might be considered further indication of the hollowness of the actual constitutional recognition given collective rights under the Charter.
29 Resnick, 'State and Civil Society,' 398.
30 See *In the Matter of a Reference from Alberta*, S.C.C. 1987, No. 19234;

P.S.A.C. v. *Canada*, S.C.C. 1987, No. 18942, and *R.W.D.S.U.* v. *Saskatchewan*, S.C.C. 1987, No. 19430.

31 *Re Lavigne and Ontario Public Service Employees Union et al.*, (1986), 55 O.R. (2d) 449 (H.C.). In January 1989 the Ontario Court of Appeal overturned this lower court ruling. A focal point for the decision, however, was that 'union dues and their use are private, internal matters not covered by the Charter – which, the court said, applies only to government activities' (Lorne Slotnick, 'Use of union dues for political causes does not violate Charter, court rules,' *Globe and Mail*, 31 January 1989, A1). Questions of individual and collective rights appeared to be of little importance in the court's decision.

32 *Civil Service Co-operative Credit Society Ltd.* v. *Ontario Credit Union League Ltd.*, No. 18687/84, 176 (S. Ct. Ont.).

33 Campbell, *The Left and Rights*.

34 Constitution Act, 1982, Part I, ss. 1-34, enacted by the Canada Act 1982 (U.K.), c. 11.

35 Friedman, *Capitalism and Freedom*, 133.

36 There is very often a large gap between theory and practice. See Axworthy, *Co-operatives and Their Employees*.

37 These three assertions from MacCormick, *Legal Right and Social Democracy*, 1, are three-quarters of his definition of social democracy, and reflect our idea of what co-operation is designed and equipped to address.

38 Glasbeek, 'Workers of the World.'

39 For a selection of their views on the moral criteria for business activity, see Baum and Cameron, eds., *Ethics and Economics*.

40 Canadian Labour Congress, *The Labour Movement and the Co-operative Movement*.

41 See, for instance, Palmer, *Working-Class Experience*, 190-5.

42 In the liberal political philosophy that reflects the power structure of Canadian society, as Gad Horowitz notes, the 'political process is seen not so much as one in which *groups* with differing interests confront one another and arrive a compromise, but as a process in which individuals *suppress* their group interests' (*Canadian Labour in Politics*, 239).

43 E.g., the National Citizens' Coalition's role in funding the *Lavigne* case. See discussion later in this chapter.

44 See the discussion later in the chapter.

45 See Berger, *Fragile Freedoms and Dissent in Canada*.

46 For the purposes of this paper we can leave aside some issues raised in this and other cases, including the question of whether public service unions, but not unions of workers in private business, are subject to the Charter.

47 *Re Lavigne*, 495 (emphasis added). The British Columbia Supreme Court in

Bhindi v. *B.C. Projectionists* (1985), 63 B.C.L.R. 352 (S.C.) held that statutory provisions permitting or enabling closed shops may violate the Charter. Section 1 of the Charter should be expected to save such provisions, but recent past history of the Charter in trade union cases may make this more doubtful. See also Fichaud, 'Analysis of the Charter and Its Application to Labour Law,' 416.

48 *Re Lavigne*, 497.
49 Ibid., 498. See *R.* v. *Big M Drug Mart* [1985] 1 S.C.R. 295.
50 *Re Lavigne*, 508.
51 *Ibid.*, 507.
52 Canada Act, s. 1 (emphasis added).
53 *Black's Law Dictionary*, 5th ed., 1064, defines 'prescribe' as: 'To lay down authoritatively as a guide, direction, or rule; to impose as a peremptory order; to dictate; to point; to direct; to give as a guide, direction, or rule of action; to give law. To direct; define; mark out.'
54 See Dickson C.J. in *In the Matter of a Reference from Alberta*.
55 *Re Lavigne*, 516-17.
56 See *Reference from Alberta, P.S.A.C.* v. *Canada*, and *R.W.D.S.U.* v. *Saskatchewan*.
57 67 U.N.T.S. 18, 1948, was ratified by Canada in 1972 and came into force on 23 March 1972.
58 See the discussion in *Re Service Employees International Union and Broadway Manor Nursing Home et al.* (1985), 13 D.L.R. (4d) 220 (Alta. C.A.), per O'Leary J.
59 *R.W.D.S.U.* v. *Saskatchewan* [1985] 5 W.W.R. 97, 140 (Sask. C.A.).
60 See *Reference from Alberta, P.S.A.C.* v. *Canada*, and *R.W.D.S.U.* v. *Saskatchewan*, 2 (judgment of LeDain J.)
61 *In the Matter of a Reference from Alberta*, S.C.C. 1987, No. 19234, *P.S.A.C.* v. *Canada*, S.C.C. 1987, No. 18942, 3.
62 Ibid.
63 Ibid.
64 Ibid., 5 (judgment of McIntyre J.)
65 Ibid., 6.
66 Ibid.
67 Ibid., 7.
68 Ibid., 5-10.
69 Ibid., 18.
70 Ibid.
71 Ibid., 20.
72 Referring to the judgment of Belzil J.A. in the Alberta Court of Appeal decision in this case, in which there was a discussion of the remedies available for breach

of contract. Neither of the judges could have looked at the definition of 'lawful' in *Black's Law Dictionary*, 5th ed., 797.

73 *In the Matter of a Reference from Alberta*, S.C.C. 1987, No. 19234, *P.S.A.C.* v. *Canada*, S.C.C. 1987, No. 18942, 23. See also, Dickson C.J., 46 (judgment of Dickson C.J.), *In the Matter of a Reference from Alberta*, S.C.C. 1987, No. 19234, *P.S.A.C.* v. *Canada*, S.C.C. 1987, No. 18942, 3. Cf. Dickson C.J. 23 quoting Bayda C.J.S. in the Saskatchewan Court of Appeal decision in the *Dairy Workers'* case (judgment of Dickson C.J.).

74 *In the Matter of a Reference from Alberta*, S.C.C. 1987, No. 19234, *P.S.A.C.* v. *Canada*, S.C.C. 1987, No. 18942, 23-4.

75 Ibid., 11.

76 Ibid., 40.

77 Ibid., 43.

78 Ibid., 45.

79 *Re Service Employees' International Union, Local 204 and Broadway Manor Nursing Home.*

80 *In the Matter of a Reference from Alberta*, S.C.C. 1987, No. 19234, *P.S.A.C.* v. *Canada*, S.C.C. 1987, No. 18942, 46.

81 Ibid., 48.

82 Ibid., 49.

83 Ibid., 50.

84 [1986] 1 S.C.R. 103.

85 *In the Matter of a Reference from Alberta*, S.C.C. 1987, No. 19234, *P.S.A.C.* v. *Canada*, S.C.C. 1987, No. 18942, 51.

86 Ibid.

87 See, e.g., S.S. 1983, c. C-37.1, s. 37(3).

88 (1984), 46 Nfld. & P.E.I. Rep. 111 (P.E.I.C.A.).

89 Retained patronage dividends which had not been converted into share capital were seen by the court as a loan and subject to set-off. The dividends were credited to a share capital account in Cutcliffe's name, but share certificates were never issued.

90 He may have wanted to continue trading with the co-operative and/or it may have been in his interests for the co-operative to have played a moderating role in the prevailing market. Either would have constituted a benefit to Cutcliffe.

91 (1984), 33 Sask. R. 41 (Q.B.).

92 The meeting attracted 202 members from a total membership of over 11,000; 68 voted in favour of the motion, 21 voted against, and 113 abstained.

93 See S.S. 1983, c. C-37.1, s. 37(3), s. 190.

94 (1984), 33 Sask. R. 41 (Q.B.), 46.

95 (1970), 11 D.L.R. (3d) 503 (Sask C.A.)

96 R.S.S. 1965, c. 246, s. 57 which provided that the board 'shall call' a meeting

when requisitioned to do so by one hundred members or 10 per cent of the membership, whichever is the lesser.

97 Quoted in the judgment of Hall J.A., (1970), 11 D.L.R. (3d) 503 (Sask C.A.), 505.
98 Ibid.
99 Ibid., 507-8.
100 11 D.L.R. (3d) 503 (Sask C.A.)
101 Ibid., 507.
102 Ibid., 507-8.
103 Ibid., 508.
104 (1983), 149 D.L.R. (3d) 130 (B.C.C.A.).
105 Credit Union Act, R.S.B.C. 1979, c.79, s. 98.
106 11 D.L.R. (3d) 503 (Sask C.A.), 138.
107 Ibid.
108 For a more detailed discussion of this case, see C.S. Axworthy, ' The Uniqueness of Credit Unions,' 283-321.
109 Co-Enerco; the Co-op Upgrader and the National Task Force on Co-operative Development are three notable federal exceptions; see David Laycock, *Co-operative-Government Relations*.
110 Provincially, Quebec under the Parti Québécois government, Saskatchewan under successive NDP governments, and Manitoba under the recent NDP government are also exceptions.
111 Witness, for example, the recent dismantling of the Saskatchewan Department of Co-operation and Co-operative Development, and the downgrading of Quebec's Direction des coopératives.

Chapter 14. Big Capital, the Big State, and Co-operatives

1 Kitching discusses this in terms of the economic 'populism' of the critics of western European industrialization in the early nineteenth century and 'neo-populism' in the Soviet Union and the third world in the twentieth. He sees co-operative movements in each case as part of the economic dissent from bigness (see *Development and Underdevelopment in Historical Perspective*, esp. 29-30 and 41-2). On the tension between the co-operatives and state planning in eastern Europe, see Balawyder, ed., *Cooperative Movements in Eastern Europe*.
2 A good overview of the confused goals, grandiose projects, methods, and eventual failure of the Owenite settlement movement within Britain can be gleaned from Garnett, *Co-operation and the Owenite Socialist Communities in Britain*.
3 The characteristics noted here are in contrast to pre-industrial economies characterized by guild or communal regulation, ascribed status, subsistence-

oriented activity by the bulk of the population, and relatively less use of currency and of marketing for cash. In some traditions it is fashionable to argue that 'co-operation' is based upon preiindustrial roots; Gierke, in *Das deutsche Genossenschaftsrecht,* provided 629 pages on the legal history of 'co-operatives' before the year 1525. Following Gierke, Antony Black takes a similar view in *Guilds and Civil Society in European Political Thought,* chaps. 15 and 18. Black's view of guilds is ahistorical.

4   Of course, co-operation was seen as a means to *personal* independence; its distinctive appeal was its claim that in the long term it could reconcile the need for economic concentration with the ideal of personal dignity and responsibility for every individual.

5   Polanyi, in *The Great Transformation,* presents the revolution in economics and ideas that went together with the rise of the market economy in nineteenth-century Europe.

6   Blanc advocated *ateliers sociaux* (social workshops) in his *Organisation du travail* of 1839. Yet the 'national workshops' created by the revolutionary government in France, of which Blanc was a member, were not in fact co-operatives but rather a state-owned network of make-work institutions. This was largely due to the orthodox attitudes of Blanc's partners in government concerning property rights and authority. The workshops were suppressed in June 1848, provoking a bloody uprising. While his proposals had not in fact ever been attempted, Blanc was nevertheless discredited.

7   See Backstrom, *Christian Socialism and Co-operation in Victorian England: Edward Vansittart Neale and the Co-operative Movement.*

8   The Raiffeisen co-operatives were more than just credit associations; characteristically they were multi-purpose co-operatives and emphasized moral improvement and education. These and certain organizational differences led to a bitter and lasting *Systemstreit* between the Schulze-Delitzsch and Raiffeisen federations. On the German co-operative movement, see Faust, *Geschichte der Genossenschaftsbewegung* (on Schulze, 193-234; on Raiffeisen, 323-67). Note that, contrary to what older English-language sources say, Raiffeisen founded no co-operatives before 1862; his earlier organizations were charitable.

9   See Tracy, *Agriculture in Western Europe,* 19-40, 106-16.

10 Some idea of the growth and spread of central and eastern European co-operative movements from the 1890s to the 1930s can be gained from Morgan, ed., *Agricultural Systems of Middle Europe.* This volume consists mostly of the official, governmental version of the story. See also Held, ed., *The Modernization of Agriculture.*

11 The standard (and still essential) analysis for Canada is V.C. Fowke, *The National Policy and the Wheat Economy.*

12 Goodwyn, *Democratic Promise*, xviii, and the same for the following.

13 It is interesting to consider whether these developments followed any particular sequence; whether, for example, it was generally true that agrarian movements started first as interest groups or political groups attempting to influence policy, and turned to direct formation of local co-operatives only as grander measures failed, and finally to attempts to form large-scale marketing co-operatives when the strength of the co-operative movement permitted it. Such a sequence of development would apply to several regions of North America.

14 For revealing insights into the demands of politicized shopkeepers and their opposition to consumer co-ops and department stores alike, see Crossick and Haupt, eds., *Shopkeepers and Master Artisans in Nineteenth-Century Europe*, esp. the contributions by Crossick on Britain and Blackbourn on Germany; and Gellately, *The Politics of Economic Despair,* esp. 123ff.

15 For example, see Lipset, *Agrarian Socialism*, 182-5, on the opposition of merchants to the Co-operative Commonwealth Federation; the merchants tended toward Social Credit, while the CCF was dominated by leaders also active in co-operatives.

16 The most recent Saskatchewan Pool history is Fairbairn, *From Prairie Roots*. On the Alberta Pool, see Nesbitt, *Tides in the West*. Another Canadian prairie marketing organization, the United Grain Growers, has co-operative origins; see Colquette, *The First Fifty Years.*

17 Canovan, *Populism*, comments upon the persistent currency obsessions of populists.

18 On the diversity of opinion about relations with the government in the Canadian movement, see Ian MacPherson, *Each for All*, esp. 186-9; Laycock, *Co-operative–Government Relations in Canada;* and Laycock, *Populism and Democratic Thought.*

19 The acceptance or non-acceptance of state aid was part of a deeper political split among the Schulze-Delitzsch, Raiffeisen, and Haas federations. See Faust, *Geschichte* (1977), and Fairbairn, 'The Politics of Sectional Revolt, Farmers and Capital in Germany, 1890-1903,' paper delivered to the Western Canadian Studies Conference in Saskatoon, October 1987.

20 See Tracy, *Agriculture in Western Europe*, 116, 119. For illustrations of the contemporary impact of the Danish success, see Smith-Gordon and O'Brien, *Co-operation in Denmark*, and Haggard, *Rural Denmark and Its Lessons.*

21 For a favourable contemporary view, see Smith-Gordon and Staples, *Rural Reconstruction in Ireland.*

22 See Gellately, *Economic Despair*, on the politics of German shopkeepers' co-operatives.

23 Workers' co-operatives on a large scale were set up in Spain following the

accession of the Popular Front government in 1936, but it is impossible to know how they would have developed because the loyalists lost the civil war to Franco. One source for this subject is Dolgoff, ed., *The Anarchist Collectives.*

24 The literature on co-operatives in third world economic development is substantial, and complicated by the overlap between co-operative and collectivist solutions. For an overview of many countries with an anthropological slant see Nash, Dandler, and Hopkins, eds., *Popular Participation in Social Change: Cooperatives, Collectives and Nationalized Industry.* For theory and practice, see Benecke, *Cooperation and Development*; Enriquez, ed., *Cooperatives in Third World Development.*

Chapter 15. Management in Co-operatives

1 The retails of the western provinces joined together to form their own wholesaling concern in the mid-1920s. Each member retail holds an equity position in the wholesale, Federated Co-operatives Limited, and has access to participation in decision-making through a representational system.

2 This generally accepted position is based on a rational model of organization, the organization as *machine.* In this traditional view, it is assumed that the organization is a closed system in search of certainty and determinateness. All components and actions are chosen specifically for their contribution toward a goal, and the structures implemented are chosen to attain maximum efficiency. Alternatively, the organization can be viewed as an open system, an *organism*, subject to influence from the environment. Goals are established not by a single decision-making group within a hierarchical system, but rather through coalition behaviour, with operational goals determined by domain consensus in the task environment. A third metaphor depicts the organization as a *system*, within other systems, made up of coalitions of interest groups, both inside and outside the focal organization. As a result, the organization is likely to pursue a variety of goals that may be in direct conflict with each other. For a discussion of the three metaphors outlined, refer to Burns and Stalker, *The Management of Innovation*, and Ackoff, *A Concept of Corporate Planning.*

3 The use of this term is consistent with its use in the business policy literature, and applies primarily to the economic performance or financial success of the organization within the market-place. See, for example, Porter, *Competitive Advantage Creating and Sustaining Superior Performance.*

4 Kreitner,'The Theory of Economic Co-operation, U.S. New Generation Food Co-ops, and the Co-operative Dilemma.'

5 Laidlaw, 'Co-operatives in the Canadian Environment'; Ostergaard and Halsey, *Power in Co-operatives.*

6   Shaviro, 'A Critique of Consumer Cooperation,' 29-42.
7   A corporation is required by law to ensure that the profitability of the
     organization is given priority.
8   Briscoe, 'Traders and Idealists,' 113, quoting A.Z. Carr.
9   Ostergaard and Halsey, *Power in Co-operatives*.
10   Briscoe, 'Traders and Idealists.'
11   Briscoe cites Wheelis, *Quest for Identity*, 73. He defines institutional values as
     being those associated with myth, mores, and status within society. These values
     claim absolute status and immunity to change, as they are seen to be in accord
     with the dominant institutional directive. Instrumental values are related to
     relative adequacy of function for an implied or specified function.
12   Briscoe, 'Traders and Idealists,' 110. Briscoe found in his study that many
     managers and directors of co-operatives perceived co-op values to be incompatible
     with business success. Co-operatives whose managers held this view suffered
     from what he termed the 'frozen co-op syndrome' and failed to formulate long-term
     goals and strategies to enable them to move out of this situation. The more
     successful co-operatives had managers who had found a way to transcend this
     dilemma and were able to embody co-operative values in their business
     operations.
13   Despite having the right of access to participation in decision-making, not all
     members will exercise that right. Recent research indicates that only a very small
     percentage of members could be considered to be active in this process. See
     Alexander Laidlaw, *Co-operatives in the Year 2000*.
14   One such example is the Saskatchewan Wheat Pool which holds a two-week-long
     annual meeting where 145 delegates from across the province discuss and debate
     resolutions directed toward setting policy for the organization's board of directors.
     This system of representative democracy is often criticized by co-operators who
     support the participative democracy found in town meetings. The appropriate
     nature of democracy for co-operatives is a much-debated issue among co-operative
     enthusiasts.
15   Thompson, *Organizations in Action*.
16   Perrow, 'The Analysis of Goals in Complex Organizations,' 854-966.
17   Pfeffer and Salancik, *The External Control of Organizations*.
18   Perrow, 'Organizational Goals,' 305-11.
19   Ostergaard and Halsey, *Power in Co-operatives*.
20   Pfeffer and Salancik, *Control of Organizations*.
21   Ackoff, *Corporate Failure*; Mason and Mitroff, *Challenging Strategic Planning
     Assumptions*; Mitroff, *Stakeholders of the Organizational Mind*.
22   Perrow, 'Goals in Comples Organizations.'
23   Macpherson, *Each for All*.

24 Nourse, 'The Place of the Co-operative in Our National Economy.'
25 Craig, 'Achieving Economic Effectiveness, Efficiency and Democracy in Organizations'; Laidlaw, 'Co-operatives.'
26 Perrow, 'Goals in Complex Organizations,' 308.
27 Ibid., 309.
28 Mason and Mitroff, *Strategic Planning*.
29 Berle and Means, *The Modern Corporation and Private Property*.
30 Mace, *Directors: Myth and Reality*.
31 Pfeffer and Salancik, *Control of Organizations*, define the boundaries of an organization on the basis of where the discretion of one organization ends and that of another takes over. Thus, an organization can be viewed as a separate, autonomous entity to the extent that it controls discretion over decision-making. The point at which this discretion ends and the discretion of another takes over is the boundary of that organization. Co-operatives have a rather amorphous quality because of their close (sometimes highly dependent) relationship with other co-operative organizations within the system. For example, the relationship between the wholesaler, Federated Co-operatives Limited, and the retail co-operatives it supplies is interlocking because of the provision of technical services and advice, the hiring and training of management staff, and until recently, its role as guarantor of loans. In return, this relationship provides FCL with a great deal of control over the retail organizations and a guaranteed distribution system for its products.
32 Mizruchi, 'Who Controls Them?' 427.
33 Mazzolini, 'How Strategic Decisions Are Made,' 93.
34 Chilomo, 'Management Planning Systems with Particular Emphasis on Co-operative Organizations.'
35 Ellerman, 'The Employment Relation, Property Rights and Organizational Democracy,' in Crouch and Heller, eds., *Organizational Democracy and Political Processes*.
36 Laidlaw, *Co-operatives in the Year 2000*.
37 Ibid., 1.
38 Cotterill, 'Marketing and Organizational Strategies for Retail Co-operatives,' in Cotterill, ed., *Consumer Food Cooperatives*.
39 See for example March and Simon, *Organizations*; Mazzolini, 'Strategic Decisions'; Pettigrew, 'Examining Change,' in Pennings and Associates, eds., *Organizational Strategy and Change*.
40 Canadian co-operatives are, as are many others around the world, divided into three levels or tiers. First-tier co-operatives operate at the community level with a broad individual member base. Second-tier co-operatives operate at a central provincial or regional level, and provide services to and for first-tier co-operatives,

who comprise their membership. Third-tier co-operatives operate at a national level, and provide services for the centrals and beyond to their first-tier co-operatives and their members.

41 LeVay, 'Agricultural Co-operative Theory'; Ostergaard and Halsey, *Power in Co-operatives*.
42 Foxall, 'Co-operative Marketing in European Agriculture,' 42-57.
43 Co-operative Union of Canada, 'The Structure of Consumer Co-operatives in Canada.'
44 Foxall, 'Co-operative Marketing,' 42.
45 LeVay, 'Agricultural Co-operative Theory,' 31.
46 Warren, 'The Interorganizational Field a Focus for Investigation,' 396-419.
47 Credit Union Act, 1985, c. C-45.1, s.257(1).
48 DeGrass, 'Under Supervision: Burden or Benefit?' 6.
49 Kaynak and Cavusgil, 'The Evolution of Food Retailing Systems,' 249-69.
50 Canadian Grocer, 'CFBA Convention,' 6.
51 Briscoe 'Traders and Idealists'; Arnott, 'When the Co-operating Faltered,' 88-92.
52 Co-operative Union of Canada, 10.
53 This was one of several key arguments made by the Co-operative Union of Canada in their 1975 submission to the National Royal Commission on Corporate Concentration.
54 Kristjanson, 'The Effect of Growth Problems of Consumer Co-operatives,' 191.
55 Mather, 'Consumer Co-operatives in the Grocery Retailing Industry.'
56 A recent American study shows that just 50 of 20,000 food firms today control nearly two-thirds of food manufacturing assets, up from 42 per cent in 1962. Co-operatives do not play a major role in the concentrated manufacturing end of the marketing channel. Torgerson, 'The Changing Nature of Economic Power and Co-operatives,' 2.
57 Cotterill, 'Co-operative Wholesaling Systems'; Hall and Hall, 'The Potential for Growth of Consumer Co-operatives: A Comparison with Producer Co-operatives,' 23-45.
58 Effective in terms of maintaining a strong presence in the market-place. For example, the Saskatchewan Wheat Pool and Federated Co-operatives Limited rank 1 and 2 respectively in terms of sales volume within Saskatchewan. *Saskatchewan Business*, August 1984.
59 Ostergaard and Halsey *Power in Co-operatives*; Arnott, 'When the Co-operating Faltered,'; Foxall, 'Co-operative Marketing.'
60 Co-operative Future Directions Project, *Patterns and Trends of Canadian Co-operative Development*.
61 Ibid.
62 The branch model suggests that the independent co-operative retail would be

treated as a branch of a central organization, rather than acting as an autonomous co-operative. This model was experimented with in New Brunswick in the early 1920s, and in the western provinces as a part of the Westland Experiment in the early 1970s. This model has never been well received by members of the local co-operatives.

63 Bionda, 'The Problem Urban Retail Co-ops Battle Grocery Giants,' 27.
64 Brown, 'Organizational Ideology, Structure, Process and Participation,' and 'Democracy in Organizations,' 313-34.
65 Allaire and Firsirotu, 'Theories of Organizational Culture,' 215.
66 Pfeffer and Salancik, *Control of Organizations.*
67 Pondy, 'Organizational Conflict,' 296-320.
68 Bionda, 'The Problem.'
69 Briscoe 'Traders and Idealists.'
70 Formal goals as used in this context should be understood in a manner consistent with Perrow's 'official goals,' and informal goals consistent with Perrow's 'operative' goals.

Chapter 16. Co-operatives in Oligopolistic Industries

1 *The Financial Post 500.*
2 Fowke, *The National Policy and the Wheat Economy,* esp. chap. 7.
3 Enke, 'Consumer Cooperatives and Economic Efficiency,' 148-55; Taylor, 'The Taxation of Co-operatives,' 13-23.
4 The following discussion examines consumer co-operatives. A similar analysis with similar conclusions can be undertaken for producer co-operatives.
5 Just, Hueth, and Schmitz, *Applied Welfare Economics and Public Policy.*
6 Enke, 'Consumer Cooperatives.'
7 Ibid.
8 Bayri, Rosaasen, and Furtan, 'Limit Pricing in the Nitrogen Fertilizer Market.'
9 As Sexton points out, setting price equal to minimum average cost generates a stable solution in the sense that no member or group of members will have an incentive to leave the co-operative. If the members' demand curve cuts marginal cost to the left of the output where average cost becomes flat, it benefits existing members of the co-operative to attract new members, thereby shifting the demand curve so that it intersects the average cost curve at its minimum. If the members' demand curve cuts the marginal cost to the right of the output where average cost ceases to be flat, it benefits the remaining members if some members leave the co-operative, thereby shifting the demand curve inward. The members that leave are also be better off if they are able to join another co-operative which is pricing its output at a price p. Sexton, 'The Formation of Cooperatives,' 214-25.

10   Since the gain the members experience is not a one-time thing, but can be expected to occur over many years (i.e., in the absence of the co-operative entering, the price would have continued at a level), the actual condition that must be satisfied for co-operative entry is that the discounted sum of the area *padc* over the expected life of the plant must be greater than any costs incurred in entering the industry. See Sexton and Sexton for a full discussion of the conditions under which a co-operative can be expected to enter an oligopolistic industry. The material in the paragraphs following is taken from Sexton and Sexton, 'Co-operatives as Entrants,' 581-95.

11   Saskatchewan Wheat Pool, *Annual Report*.

12   Bayri, Rosaasen, and Furtan, 'Limit Pricing.' For some empirical evidence on this question, see Fulton, 'Co-operatives in Oligopolistic Industries.'

13   Blue, Johnson and Associates, 'Strategic Issues Surrounding a Nitrogen Plant in Saskatchewan.'

14   Monson and Downs, 'A Theory of Large Managerial Firms,' 221-36.

Chapter 17. Level and Style of Government Intervention in Co-operative Business Activity

1   This is currently true in Quebec and Saskatchewan, and will likely soon be the case in Ontario.

2   The legal requirements for federal incorporation are somewhat vague, but the costs of such incorporation are sufficiently small that all major co-operatives doing inter-provincial trade are federally incorporated. See Ish, *The Law of Canadian Co-operatives*, chap. 1.

3   For an illuminating study of this tax question, taken as a symptomatic case study of Canadian co-operatives' historical treatment by public policy-makers, see Holland, *The Co-operative Movement and Taxation*. See also Ish, *Canadian Co-operatives*, chap. 7.

4   For historical and contemporary accounts of these 'autonomist' orientations, see MacPherson, *Each for All*; Laycock, *Prairie Populists and the Idea of Co-operation, 1910-1945*; and Laycock, *Co-operative–Government Relations in Canada*.

5   See Holland, 'Legislation for Co-operative Corporations.'

6   See, among others, Coleman, 'Canadian Business and the State,' and Pross, *Group Politics and Public Policy*.

7   See Blais, *A Political Sociology of Aid to Industry*, and Coleman and Jacek, 'The Roles and Activities of Business Interest Associations in Canada.'

Bibliography

Aaker, David A. 1984. *Strategic Market Management: An Overview*. New York: John Wiley and Sons

Ackoff, Russell L. 1970. *A Concept of Corporate Planning*. New York: John Wiley and Sons

– 1981. *Creating the Corporate Future, Plan or Be Planned For*. New York: John Wiley and Sons

Adie, Robert, and Paul Thomas. 1982. *Canadian Public Administration*. Toronto: Prentice-Hall

Aldenhoff, Rita. 1984. *Schulze-Delitzsch: Ein Beitrag zur Geschichte des Liberalismus zwischen Revolution und Reichsgründung*. Baden-Baden: Nomos

Allaire, Yvan, and Mihaela E. Firsirotu. 1984. 'Theories of Organizational Culture.' *Organization Studies* 5/3: 193-226

American Law Institute. 1982. *Principles of Corporate Governance and Structure: Restatement and Recommendations*. Tentative Draft No. 1. Philadelphia: ALI

Anderson, C. 1979. 'Political Design and the Representation of Interests.' In *Trends Towards Corporatist Intermediation*, ed. P. Schmitter and G. Lehmbruch, 271-98. Beverly Hills: Sage Publications

Apland, L. 1987. *Election of Directors in Saskatchewan Co-operatives: Processes and Results*. Saskatoon: Centre for the Study of Co-operatives

Arnott, Deborah. 1983. 'When the Co-operating Faltered.' *Management Today,* October: 88-92

Arrow, K. 1951. *Social Choice and Individual Values*. New Haven: Yale University Press

Axelrod, Robert. 1984. *The Evolution of Cooperation*. New York: Basic Books, Inc.

Axworthy, C.S. 1986a. 'Corporation Law as if Some People Mattered.' *University of Toronto Law Journal* 36: 404-7
– 1986b. *Co-operatives and Their Employees: Towards a Harmonious Relationship.* Saskatoon: Centre for the Study of Co-operatives
– 1987–8. 'The Uniqueness of Credit Unions.' *Banking and Finance Law Review* 2: 283-321
Bachrach, Peter, and Morton Baratz. 1962. 'The Two Faces of Power.' *American Political Science Review* 56 (November): 942-52
Backstrom, Philip N. 1974. *Christian Socialism and Co-operation in Victorian England: Edward Vansittart Neale and the Co-operative Movement.* London: Croom Helm
Bailey, Stuart. 1986. *Encouraging Democracy in Consumer and Producer Co-operatives.* Saskatoon: Centre for the Study of Co-operatives
Bakken, Henry H., and Marvin A. Schaars. 1937. *The Economics of Co-operative Marketing.* New York: McGraw-Hill
Balawyder, Aloysius, ed. 1980. *Cooperative Movements in Eastern Europe.* London: Macmillan
Barber, Benjamin. 1984. *Strong Democracy: Participatory Politics for a New Age.* Berkeley: University of California Press
Barkin, Kenneth. 1970. *The Controversy over German Industrialization, 1890-1902.* Chicago and London: University of Chicago Press
Barou, N., ed. 1948. *The Co-operative Movement in Labour Britain.* London: Victor Gollancz
Baum, G., and D. Cameron. 1984. *Ethics and Economics.* Toronto: Lorimer
Bayley, J. Elise, and Edgar Parnell, eds. 1988. *Yearbook of Co-operative Enterprise 1988.* Oxford: Plunkett Foundation for Co-operative Studies
Bayri, T., K.A. Rosaasen, and W.H. Furtan. 1986. 'Limit Pricing in the Nitrogen Fertilizer Market: An Application to the Saskatchewan Market.' Selected Paper presented at the AAEA annual meeting, Reno, Nevada
Beck, S.M., L. Getz, F. Iacobucci, and D.L. Johnston. 1979. *Business Associations Casebook.* Toronto: De Boo
Beecher, Jonathan. 1986. *Charles Fourier: The Visionary and His World.* Berkeley: University of California Press
Benecke, Dieter W. 1972. *Cooperation and Development.* Mainz: v. Hase and Koehler
Berger, T.R. 1981. *Fragile Freedoms and Dissent in Canada.* Toronto: Clarke, Irwin
Berle, A.A. 1932. 'For Whom Corporate Managers Are Trustees: A Note.' *Harvard Law Review* 45: 1365
Berle, A.A., and G.C. Means. 1932. *The Modern Corporation and Private Property.* New York: Commerce Clearing House

- 1968. *The Modern Corporation and Private Property*, rev. ed. New York: Harcourt, Brace & World
Berlin, Isaiah. 1979. *Four Essays on Liberty*. Oxford: Oxford University Press
Bionda, R. 1986. 'The Problem – Urban Retail Co-ops Battle Grocery Giants.' *Credit Union Way*, September: 26-7
- 1987. 'Succession: Managing in the Future.' *Credit Union Way* 40 (April): 6-7
Bishop, J.W. 1968. 'Sitting Ducks and Decoy Ducks: New Trends in Indemnification of Corporate Directors and Officers.' *Yale Law Journal* 77: 1078-9
Black, Antony. 1984. *Guilds and Civil Society in European Political Thought from the Twelfth Century to the Present*. London: Methuen
Blackbourn, David. 1976. 'Class and Politics in Wilhelmine Germany: The Center Party and the Social Democrats in Württemberg.' *Central European History* 9/3 (September): 220-49
- 1984. 'Between Resignation and Volatility: The German Petite Bourgeoisie in the Nineteenth Century.' In *Shopkeepers and Master Artisans in Nineteenth Century Europe*, ed. Geoffrey Crossick and Heinz-Gerhard Haupt, 35-61. London and New York: Methuen
Blais, André. 1985. *A Political Sociology of Aid to Industry*. Toronto: University of Toronto Press
Blanc, Louis. 1850. *Organisation du travail*, 9th ed. Paris: Au bureau du Nouveau monde
Blue, Johnson and Associates. 1985. 'Strategic Issues Surrounding a Nitrogen Plant in Saskatchewan.' Unpublished report, Saskatchewan Department of Economic Development and Trade, Regina
Boisvert, Jacques. 1981. 'Le Marketing dans la perspective co-operative.' In *La Gestion Moderne des Co-opératives*, ed. Marcel LaFlame et al. Montreal: Gaetan Morin et Associes Ltée.
Bonner, Arnold. 1961. *British Co-operation: The History, Principles, and Organisation of the British Co-operative Movement*. Manchester: Co-operative Union
Bowles, Samuel, and Herbert Gintis. 1986. *Democracy and Capitalism: Property, Community and the Contradictions of Modern Social Thought*. New York: Basic Books
Braybrooke, David, and C.E. Linblom. 1963. *A Strategy of Decision: Policy Evaluation as a Social Process*. New York: Free Press
Brennan, J.W., ed. 1985. *Building the Co-operative Commonwealth: Essays on the Democratic Socialist Tradition in Canada*. Regina: Canadian Plains Research Centre
Briscoe, Robert. 1971. 'Traders and Idealists, a Study of the Dilemmas of Consumer Co-operatives.' PhD diss., Harvard University, Cambridge, Mass.
Brodie, Janine, and Jane Jenson. 1980. *Crisis, Challenge and Change: Party and Class in Canada*. Toronto: Methuen

Brown, Leslie H. 1983. 'Organizational Ideology, Structure, Process and Participation: Twin City Food Co-operatives.' PhD diss., University of Minnesota, Minneapolis
- 1985. 'Democracy in Organizations: Membership Participation and Organizational Characteristics in U.S. Retail Food Co-operatives.' *Organization Studies* 6/4: 313-34.
Burley, Orin E. 1939. *The Consumers' Co-operative as a Distributive Agency.* Manchester: McGraw-Hill
Burns, T., and G.M. Stalker. 1961. *The Management of Innovation.* London: Tavistock Publications
Burrell, G., and G. Morgan. 1979. *Sociological Paradigms and Organizational Analysis.* London: Heinemann
Cairns, Alan, and Cynthia Williams, eds. 1985. *Constitutionalism, Citizenship and Society in Canada.* Volume 33 of the Special Research Studies for the Royal Commission on Economic Union and Development Prospects for Canada. Toronto: University of Toronto Press
Campbell, D.N. 1977. 'On Being Number One: Competition in Education.' *Phi Delta Kappan* 56/2: 143-6
Campbell, Tom. 1983. *The Left and Rights.* London: Routledge and Kegan Paul
Canadian Co-operative Association. 1988. *Co-operatives Canada '88.* Ottawa: Canadian Co-operative Association
Canadian Grocer. 1986. 'CFBA Convention – Mix and Market Decide Power Retailers,' August: 6
Canadian Labour Congress. 1986. *The Labour Movement and the Co-operative Movement: Parallel Paths?* Ottawa: Canadian Labour Congress
Canovan, Margaret. 1981. *Populism.* New York and London: Harcourt Brace Jovanovich
Chilomo, Philip P. 1985. 'Management Planning Systems with Particular Emphasis on Co-operative Organizations.' Paper presented at the Canadian Association for Co-operative Studies, 31 May, Montreal
Clarke, Harold, et al. 1984. *Absent Mandate: The Politics of Discontent in Canada.* Toronto: Gage
Coase, R.H. 1937. 'The Nature of the Firm.' *Economica* 4 (November): 386-405
Cochrane, D. 1987. 'Letters to the Editor.' *Saskatchewan Teachers' Federation Bulletin,* January: 16, 4
Cohen M., J.G. March, and J.P. Olsen. 1972. 'A Garbage Can Model of Organizational Choice.' *Administrative Science Quarterly* 17: 1-25
Cole, G.D.H. 1920. *Social Theory.* London: Allen and Unwin
- 1944. *A Century of Co-operation.* London: George Allen and Unwin
Cole, G.D.H., and Raymond Postgate. 1938. *The Common People, 1746-1938.* London: Methuen
Coleman, W.D. 1985. 'Analysing the Associative Action of Business: Policy Advocacy and Policy Participation.' *Canadian Public Administration* 28/3: 413-33

– 1986. 'Canadian Business and the State.' In *The State and Economic Interests*, ed. K. Banting, 245-89. Volume 32 of the Special Research Studies for the Royal Commission on the Economic Union and Development Prospects for Canada. Toronto: University of Toronto Press

– 1988. *Business and Politics: A Study of Collective Action*. Montreal: McGill-Queen's University Press

Coleman, W.D., and H.J. Jacek. 1983. 'The Roles and Activities of Business Interest Associations in Canada.' *Canadian Journal of Political Science* 16/2 (June): 257-80

Collard, David. 1978. *Altruism and Economy, Study in Non-selfish Economics*. Oxford: Martin Robertson Company Limited

Colquette, R.D. 1957. *The First Fifty Years: A History of United Grain Growers Limited*. Winnipeg: The Public Press

Connolly, William E. 1983. *The Terms of Political Discourse,* 2nd ed. Princeton: Princeton University Press

Co-operative Future Directions Project. 1982. *Patterns and Trends*. Downsview: Co-operative College of Canada

Co-operative Party. 1987. *Opportunities for Co-operative Politics*. London: Co-operative Party, November, 170-220

Co-operative Union. 1979. *The Role and Effectiveness of the Co-operative Party*. Manchester: Co-operative Union

Co-operative Union of Canada. 1968. 'The Structure of Consumer Co-operatives in Canada.' Interim Report of the Committee on Structure of Consumer Co-operatives. Ottawa

– 1985. *Co-operatives Canada 1985*. Ottawa

Cornoy, M., and H.M. Levin. 1985. *Schooling and Work in the Democratic State*. Menlo Park: Stanford University Press

Côté, D.O. 1986. 'Effects of Ownership Structure on Efficiency: The Case of Electric Utilities.' Paper presented to the Canadian Economic Association, Winnipeg, 29-31 May

Côté, D.O., and M. Vézina. 1986. L'organisation des marchés dans l'industrie laitière au Québec. *Coopératives et développment, revue du CIRIEC* 18/2: 39-60

Cotterill, Ronald. 1978. 'Declining Competition in Food Retailing: An Opportunity for Consumer Food Cooperatives?' *Journal of Consumer Affairs* 122/2 (Winter): 250-65

– 1982a. 'Cooperative Wholesaling Systems.' In *Consumer Food Cooperatives*, ed. Ronald Cotterill, 139-174. Danville, Ill.: The Interstate Printers and Publishers

– 1982b. 'Marketing and Organizational Strategies for Retail Cooperatives.' In *Consumer Food Cooperatives*, ed. Ronald Cotterill, 77-118. Danville, Ill.: The Interstate Printers and Publishers

Craig, J.G. 1971. 'Internal Participation or External Power? A Dilemma for Voluntary Organizations.' PhD diss., University of Washington, Seattle

– 1977a. *Co-operative Thought and Practice.* Saskatoon: Co-operative College of Canada

– 1977b. 'Achieving Economic Effectiveness, Efficiency and Democracy in Organizations.' Paper presented at the Conference on Co-operative Thought and Practice, Economic Efficiency and Democratic Control, Saskatoon

Craig, J.G., and F. Carden. 1986. *Co-operatives in Canada: Focus for the 1990s.* Co-operative College of Canada Working Papers, vol. 4, no. 153

Crossick, Geoffrey, and Heinz-Gerhard Haupt, eds. 1984. *Shopkeepers and Master Artisans in Nineteenth-Century Europe.* London and New York: Methuen

Crozier, Michael, Samuel Huntington, and Joji Watunuki, eds. 1975. *The Crisis of Democracy: Report on the Governability of Democracies to the Trilateral Commission.* New York: New York University Press

Cyert, Richard, and James G. March. 1963. *A Behavioral Theory of the Firm.* Englewood Cliffs, NJ: Prentice-Hall

Dahl, Robert. 1982. *Dilemmas of Pluralist Democracy.* New Haven: Yale University Press

– 1985. *A Preface to Economic Democracy.* Berkeley: University of California Press

Danbom, David B. 1979. *The Resisted Revolution: Urban America and the Industrialization of Agriculture, 1900-1930.* Ames, Iowa: Iowa State University Press

DeGrass, Jan. 1987. 'Under Supervision: Burden or Benefit?' *Enterprise,* January: 6

Desroche, Henri. 1976. *Le Project coopératif.* Paris: Editions Ouvrieres

Dickerson, R.W.W., J.L. Howard, and L. Getz. 1971. *Proposals for a New Business Corporations Law for Canada.* Ottawa: Information Canada

Digby, Margaret. 1960. *The World Co-operative Movement.* London: Hutchinson and Company

Dinu, William. 1981. 'Member Participation in Co-operatives through Marketing.' A major paper submitted to the Faculty of Environmental Studies in partial fulfilment of the degree of Master in Environmental Studies, York University

Dodd, E.M. 1932. 'For Whom Are Corporate Managers Trustees?' *Harvard Law Review* 45: 1145

Doern, G. Bruce, and Richard Phidd. 1983. *Canadian Public Policy: Ideas, Structure, Process.* Toronto: Methuen

Dolgoff, Sam, ed. 1974. *The Anarchist Collectives: Workers' Self-management in the Spanish Revolution, 1936-1939.* Montreal: Black Rose Books

Duncan, Graeme, ed. 1983. *Democratic Theory and Practice.* Cambridge: Cambridge University Press

Earle, John. 1986. *The Italian Cooperative Movement: A Portrait of the Lega Nazionale delle Cooperative e Mutue.* London: Allen and Unwin

Eisenberg, M.A. 1976. *The Structure of the Corporation.* Boston: Little Brown

Ekelund, Finn Aage. 1987. *The Property of the Common: Justifying Co-operative Activity*. Saskatoon: Centre for the Study of Co-operatives

Ellerman, David P. 1983. 'The Employment Relation, Property Rights and Organizational Democracy.' In *Organizational Democracy and Political Processes*, ed. C. Crouch and F. Heller, 265-78. New York: John Wiley and Sons

Emery, F.E., and E.L. Trist. 1965. 'The Causal Texture of Organizational Environments.' *Human Relations* 18: 245-62

Engel, J., and R. Blackwell. 1982. *Consumer Behavior*. New York: The Dryden Press

Enke, Stephen. 1945. 'Consumer Cooperatives and Economic Efficiency.' *American Economic Review* 35: 148-55

Enriquez, Charles G., ed. 1986. *Cooperatives in Third World Development. Workshops on Basic Issues and Case Studies*. Antigonish, NS: Coady International Institute, St Francis Xavier University

Evan, William M. 1960. 'The Organization-Set: Toward a Theory of Interorganizational Relations.' In *Approaches to Organizational Design*, ed. J.D. Thompson, 173-91. Pittsburgh: University of Pittsburgh Press

Fairbairn, Brett. 1987. 'The Politics of Sectional Revolt: Farmers and Capital in Germany 1892-1903.' Paper presented to the Western Canadian Studies Conference in Saskatoon, October

− 1989. *Building a Dream: The Co-operative Retailing System in Western Canada, 1928-1988*. Saskatoon: Western Producer Prairie Books

Fairbairn, Garry L. 1984. *From Prairie Roots: The Remarkable Story of Saskatchewan Wheat Pool*. Saskatoon: Western Producer Prairie Books

Fama, E. 1980. 'Agency Problems and the Theory of the Firm.' *Journal of Political Economy* 88: 288-307

Fama, E., and M. Jensen. 1983. 'Separation of Ownership and Control.' *Journal of Law & Economics* 26: 375

Faust, Helmut. 1977. *Geschichte der Genossenschaftsbewegung. Ursprung und Aufbruch der Genossenschaftsbewegung in England, Frankreich und Deutschland sowie ihre weitere Entwicklung im deutschen Sprachraum*, 3rd ed. Frankfurt am Main: Fritz Knapp

Fay, C.R. 1908. *Co-operation at Home and Abroad*. New York: Macmillan; London: King

Fichaud, Joel. 1984. 'Analysis of the Charter and Its Application to Labour Law.' *Dalhousie Law Journal* 8: 402-34

Financial Post. 1987. *The Financial Post 500*. Toronto: Maclean Hunter Limited

Flathman, Richard. 1976. *The Practice of Rights*. Cambridge: Cambridge University Press

Forbes, J.D. 1985. *Institutions and Influence in Canadian Farm and Food Policy*.

Toronto: The Institute of Public Administration of Canada

Fowke, V.C. 1957. *The National Policy and the Wheat Economy*. Toronto: University of Toronto Press

Fox, Karen, and Philip Kotler. 1980. 'The Marketing of Social Causes: The First Ten Years.' *Journal of Marketing* 44 (Fall): 24-33

Foxall, Gordon. 1977. 'Social Marketing of Agricultural Co-operation in Britain: An Exploration.' *Agricultural Administration* 4: 1-12

– 1984. 'Co-operative Marketing in European Agriculture: Organizational Structure and Market Performance.' *International Marketing Review,* Spring/Summer: 42-57

Friedman, M. 1962. *Capitalism and Freedom*. Chicago: University of Chicago Press

Fulton, M. 1989. 'Co-operatives in Oligopolistic Industries: The Western Canadian Fertilizer Industry.' *American Journal of Cooperation* 4: 1-19

Furubotn, E., and S. Pejovich. 1972. 'Property Rights and Economic Theory: A Review of Recent Literature.' *Journal of Economic Literature* 10: 1137-62

Garnett, R.G. 1972. *Co-operation and the Owenite Socialist Communities in Britain, 1825-1845*. Manchester: Manchester University Press

Gellately, Robert. 1974. *The Politics of Economic Despair: Shopkeepers and German Politics 1890-1914*. London and Beverly Hills: Sage

Gierke, Otto von. 1868-81. *Das deutsche Genossenschaftsrecht*, 3 vols. Berlin

Giroux, H. 1986. 'The Politics of Schooling and Culture.' *Orbit Magazine* 17/4 (December)

Glasbeek, Harry 1987. 'Workers of the World Avoid the Charter of Rights.' *Canadian Dimension* 21/2 (April)

Good, W.C. 1958. *Farmer Citizen: My Fifty Years in the Canadian Farmers' Movement*. Toronto: Ryerson Press

Goodwyn, Lawrence. 1976. *Democratic Promise. The Populist Moment in America*. New York: Oxford University Press

Graves, N., and T. Graves. 1986. 'Co-operative Learning – Problems and Promise.' *International Association for the Study of Co-operation in Education Newsletter,* December

Grebing, Helga. 1969. *The History of the German Labour Movement: A Survey*, trans. E. Körner. London: Wolff

– 1985. *Arbeiterbewegung. Sozialer Protest und kollektive Interessenvertretung bis 1914*. Munich: Deutscher Taschenbuch Verlag

Green, Philip. 1985. *Retrieving Democracy: In Search of Civic Equality*. Totowa, NJ: Rowman and Allenheld

Gutierrez-Johnson, Ana, 1978. 'Compensation, Equity, and Industrial Democracy in the Mondragon Cooperatives,' *Economic Analysis and Workers' Management* 12: 267-81

Gutierrez-Johnson, Ana, and William Foote Whyte. 1977. 'The Mondragon System of

Worker Production Cooperatives,' *Industrial and Labor Relations Review* 31/1 (October): 18-30

Guttsman, W.L. 1981. *The German Social Democratic Party 1875-1933*. London: George Allen and Unwin

Haggard, H. Rider. 1911. *Rural Denmark and Its Lessons*. New York: Longmans, Green and Company

Hall, B.F., and L.L. Hall. 1982. 'The Potential for Growth of Consumer Co-operatives: A Comparison with Producer Co-operatives.' *The Journal of Consumer Affairs* 16/1 (Summer): 23-45

Hall, Richard H. 1982. *Organizations, Structure and Process*, 3rd ed. Englewood Cliffs, NJ: Prentice-Hall

Hammond Ketilson, Lou. 1986. 'Towards a Co-operative Marketing Management Approach.' *Co-operative College of Canada Working Papers* 4/2: 1-17

Hardin, Russell. 1982. *Collective Action*. Washington, DC: Resources for the Future

Harrison, J.F.C. 1969. *Robert Owen and the Owenites in Britain and America*. London: Routledge and Kegan Paul

Hasselmann, Erwin. 1961. *Consumers' Co-operation in Germany*, 3rd ed. Hamburg: Verlagsgesellschaft Deutscher Konsumgenossenschaften

– 1971. *Geschichte der deutschen Konsumgenossenschaften*. Frankfurt am Main: Fritz Knapp

Haynes, John Earle. 1983. 'Farm Coops and the Election of Hubert Humphrey to the Senate.' *Agricultural History* 57/2: 201-11

Held, David, 1987. *Models of Democracy*. Palo Alto: Stanford University Press

Held, David, and John Keane. 1984. 'Socialism and the Limits of State Action.' In *The Future of the Left*, ed. John Curran, 170-81. Cambridge: Polity Press

Held, Joseph, ed. 1985. *The Modernization of Agriculture: Rural Transformation in Hungary, 1848-1975*. New York: Columbia University Press

Helmberger, P., and S. Hoos. 1962. 'Cooperative Enterprise and Organization Theory.' *Journal of Farm Economics* 44/2 (May): 275-90

Henk, Thomas, and Chris Logan. 1982. *Mondragon: An Economic Analysis*. London: Goerge Allen and Unwin

Henry, J. 1965. *Culture against Man*. New York: Random House

– 1969. *In Suburban Classrooms. Radical Student Reform*. New York: Simon and Schuster

Hesselbach, Peter. 1976. *Public, Trade Union and Cooperative Enterprise in Germany: The Commonwealth Idea*. London: Cass

Hirschman, A.O. 1970. *Exit, Voice and Loyalty: Responses to Decline in Firms, Organizations, and States*. Cambridge: Harvard University Press

Hofstadter, Richard. 1955. *The Age of Reform: From Bryan to FDR*. New York: Knopf

Holland, D. 1980. 'Legislation for Co-operative Corporations: Ontario and Canada.'
    Unpublished paper for seminar in Law of Corporate Management, Osgoode Hall Law
    School, April
– 1981. 'The Co-operative Movement and Taxation: A Case Study in Canadian Public
    Policy.' Master's thesis, York University, Toronto
– 1986. 'Preliminary Report on Member Education Research.' Saskatoon: Co-operative
    College of Canada
Horowitz, Gad. 1966. 'Conservatism, Liberalism and Socialism in Canada: An
    Interpretation.' *Canadian Journal of Economics and Political Science* 32/2: 143-71
– 1968. *Canadian Labour in Politics*. Toronto: University of Toronto Press
Howard, John L. 1982. *Corporate Law in the 80's – An Overview*. Law Society of
    Upper Canada Special Lectures, Don Mills: De Boo
International Co-operative Alliance Commission on Cooperative Principles. 1966.
    'Report of I.C.A. Commission on Cooperative Principles.' In *Report of the Twenty-
    Third Congress at Vienna, 5th to 8th September, 1966*: 154-215
Ish, D. 1981. *The Law of Canadian Co-operatives*. Toronto: Carswell
Jensen, M., and W. Meckling. 1976. 'Theory of the Firm: Managerial Behaviour,
    Agency Costs, and Ownership Structure.' *The Journal of Financial Economics* 3: 305-
    60
Johnson, D.W., et al. 1981. 'The Effects of Co-operative, Competitive, and
    Individualistic Goal Structures on Achievement: A Meta-Analysis.' *Psychological
    Bulletin* 8/9: 47-62
Jones, D.C. 1987. 'The Productivity of Worker Directors and Financial Participation by
    Employees in the Firm: The Case of British Retail Cooperatives.' *Industrial and
    Labor Relations Review* 41(October):79-92.
Just, R.E., D.L. Hueth, and Andrew Schmitz. 1982. *Applied Welfare Economics and
    Public Policy*. Englewood Cliffs, NJ: Prentice-Hall
Katz, D., and R.L. Kahn. 1966. *The Social Psychology of Organizations*. New York:
    John Wiley and Sons
Kaynak, Erdener, and S. Tamer Cavusgil. 1982. 'The Evolution of Food Retailing
    Systems: Contrasting the Experience of Developed and Developing Countries.'
    Journal of the Academy of Marketing Science 10/2 (Summer): 249-69
Kitching, Gavin. 1982. *Development and Underdevelopment in Historical Perspective*.
    London and New York: Methuen
Knapp, Joseph G. 1969 and 1973. *The Rise of American Co-operative Enterprise*, 2
    vols. Danville, Ill.: Interstate
Kohn, A. 1986. 'How to Succeed without Even Vying.' *Psychology Today* 20/9
    (September): 22-9

Kornberg, Alan, et al. 1979. *Citizen Politicians – Canada: Party Officials in a Democratic State*. Durham: Duke University Press

Kotler, Philip. 1972. 'A Generic Concept of Marketing.' *Journal of Marketing* 36 (April): 46-54

– 1982. *Marketing for Nonprofit Organizations*. Englewood Cliffs, NJ: Prentice-Hall

Kotler, Philip, and S.J. Levy. 1969. 'Broadening the Concept of Marketing.' *Journal of Marketing* 33 (January): 15

Kotler, Philip, and G. McDougall. 1983. *Principles of Marketing*. Toronto: Prentice-Hall Canada, Inc.

Kotler, Philip, and Gerald Zaltman. 1971. 'Social Marketing: An Approach to Planned Social Change.' *Journal of Marketing* 35 (July): 3-12

Kreitner, P.C. 1978. 'The Theory of Economic Co-operation, U.S. New Generation Food Co-ops, and the Co-operative Dilemma.' PhD diss., University of Michigan, Ann Arbor

Kristjanson, L.F. 1963. 'The Effect of Growth Problems of Consumer Co-operatives on Their Potential to Control Abuses of Economic Power – A Case Study.' PhD diss., University of Wisconsin, Madison

Laidlaw, A.F. 1976. 'Speaking of Co-ops: Democratic Control (1).' *The Maritime Co-operator,* October: 5

– 1977. 'Co-operatives in the Canadian Environment.' Paper presented at the Conference on Co-operative Thought and Practise, Economic Efficiency and Democratic Control, Saskatoon

– 1981. *Co-operatives in the Year 2000*: London: International Co-operative Alliance

Lambert, Paul. 1963. *Studies in the Social Philosophy of Co-operation,* trans. Joseph Létargez. Manchester, Chicago, and Brussels: Co-operative Union

Lane, S.H., and L. Harman. 1986. 'Co-operative Organizations in Eastern Canada.' Working paper. Guelph: School of Agricultural Economics, University of Guelph

– 1988-9. 'The Politics of Co-operative Development Strategy in English Canada.' *Coopératives et développment, revue du CIRIEC* 20/2: 91-120

Laycock, D. 1985. *Prairie Populists and the Idea of Co-operation, 1910-1945*. Saskatoon: Centre for the Study of Co-operatives

– 1986-7. 'Co-operatives, Governments and the Challenge of Worker Co-operative Development in Canada.' *Coopératives et développement, revue du CIRIEC* 18/2: 93-128

– 1987a. *Co-operative–Government Relations in Canada: Lobbying, Public Policy Development, and the Changing Co-operative System*. Saskatoon: Centre for the Study of Co-operatives

– 1987b. 'The Politics of Canadian Co-operative Development Strategy.' Paper

presented at the International Conference on State–Co-operative Relations, Université de Sherbrooke, 2 June
– 1988. 'Representative Economic Democracy and the Problem of Policy Influence: The Case of Canadian Co-operatives.' Paper presented at the Annual Meetings of the Canadian Political Science Association, University of Windsor, 9 June
– 1990. *Populism and Democratic Thought in the Canadian Prairies.* Toronto: University of Toronto Press
Lazniak, G., R. Lusch, and P. Murphy. 1979. 'Social Marketing: Its Ethical Dimensions.' *Journal of Marketing* 43 (Spring): 29-36
Leibenstein, H. 1966. 'Allocative Efficiency vs. "X-Efficiency".' *American Economic Review* 56/3 (June): 392-415
Leiss, W., S. Kline, and S. Jhally. 1986. *Social Communication in Advertising.* New York: Methuen
LeVay, Clare. 1984. 'Agricultural Co-operative Theory: A Review.' *Journal of Farm Economics* 35 (January): 1-43
Levin, Henry, and Robert Jackall, eds. 1984. *Worker Co-operatives in America.* Berkeley: University of California Press
Levitt, T. 1960. 'Marketing Myopia.' *Harvard Business Review,* July-August: 45-56
Lidtke, Vernon L. 1985. *The Alternative Culture: Socialist Labor in Imperial Germany.* New York and Oxford: Oxford University Press
Linden, Ä., and R. Norman. 1975. 'Democracy and Efficiency.' Paper presented at Research Officers Group Meeting in Scion on behalf of Cooperative Union and Wholesale Society, Stockholm, Sweden
Lipset, S.M. 1950. *Agrarian Socialism.* Berkeley: University of California Press
– 1968. *Agrarian Socialism: The Cooperative Commonwealth Federation in Saskatchewan – A Study in Political Sociology.* Garden City: Doubleday
– 1971. *Agrarian Socialism: The Cooperative Commonwealth Federation in Saskatchewan: A Study in Political Sociology,* rev. ed. Berkeley and London: University of California Press
Luck, David J. 1969. 'Broadening the Concept of Marketing – Too Far.' *Journal of Marketing* 33 (July): 53-63
MacCormick, N. 1982. *Legal Right and Social Democracy.* Oxford: Clarendon Press
Mace, M.L. 1971. *Directors: Myth and Reality.* Cambridge, Mass.: Harvard University Press
– 1979. 'Directors: Myth and Reality – Ten Years Later.' *Rutgers Law Review* 32: 293
Macpherson, C.B. 1953. *Democracy in Alberta.* Toronto: University of Toronto Press
– 1963. *The Political Theory of Possessive Individualism.* London: Oxford University Press
– 1973. *Democratic Theory: Essays in Retrieval.* Oxford: Oxford University Press

- 1977. *The Life and Times of Liberal Democracy*. London: Oxford University Press
- 1978. *Property: Mainstream and Critical Positions*. Toronto: University of Toronto Press
- 1985. *The Rise and Fall of Economic Justice and Other Essays*. London: Oxford University Press

MacPherson, Ian. 1973. 'The Co-operative Union of Canada and Politics, 1909-31.' *Canadian Historical Review* 54/2: 152-74
- 1979. *Each for All: A History of the Co-operative Movement in English Canada, 1900-1945*. Toronto: Macmillan
- 1984. *Building and Protecting the Co-operative Movement: A Brief History of the Co-operative Union of Canada*. Ottawa: Co-operative Union of Canada
- 1985. 'The CCF and the Co-operative Movement in the Douglas Years: An Uneasy Alliance.' In *Building the Co-operative Commonwealth: Essays on the Democratic Socialist Tradition in Canada*, ed. J.W. Brennan, 181-203. Regina: Canadian Plains Research Centre

Manuel, Frank, and Fritzie P. Manuel. 1979. *Utopian Thought in the Western World*. Cambridge, Mass.: The Belknap Press of Harvard University Press

March, James G., and Herbert Simon. 1958. *Organizations*. New York: John Wiley and Sons

Martel, Jean-Louis. 1986-7. 'Émergence du mouvement coopératif agricole au Québec: d'un mouvement populaire à une politique de développement.' *Coopératives et développement revue du CIRIEC* 18/1: 13-39

Mason, R. 1982. *Participatory and Workplace Democracy*. Carbondale: Southern Illinois University Press

Mason, Richard O., and Ian Mitroff. 1981. *Challenging Strategic Planning Assumptions*. New York: John Wiley and Sons

Mather, L.L. 1968. 'Consumer Co-operatives in the Grocery Retailing Industry.' PhD diss., University of Wisconsin, Madison

Mazzolini, Renato. 1981. 'How Strategic Decisions Are Made.' *Long Range Planning* 14/3 (June): 83-90

McConnell, Grant. 1953. *The Decline of Agrarian Democracy*. Berkeley: University of California Press

Melnyk, George. 1985. *The Search for Community. From Utopia to a Co-operative Society*. Montreal: Black Rose Books

Michels, R. 1962. *Political Parties: A Sociological Study of the Oligarchical Tendencies of Modern Democracy*, trans. E. Paul and C. Paul. New York: The Free Press

Miles, Raymond E., and Charles C. Snow. 1978. *Organizational Strategy, Structure, and Process*. New York: McGraw-Hill

Mill, John Stuart. 1980. *On Liberty*. Harmondsworth: Penguin

Miller, Raymond. 1964. *A Conservative Looks at Cooperatives*. Athens, Ohio: Ohio University Press

Mitroff, Ian I. 1983. *Stakeholders of the Organizational Mind*. San Francisco: Jossey-Bass

Mizruchi, Mark. S. 1983. 'Who Controls Whom? An Examination of the Relation between Management and Boards of Directors in Large American Corporations.' *Academy of Management Review* 8/3: 426-35

Monson, J.R., Jr., and A. Downs. 1965. 'A Theory of Large Managerial Firms.' *Journal of Political Economy* 73: 221-36

Moody, J. Carroll, and Gilbert C. Fite. 1984. *The Credit Union Movement. Origins and Development 1850 to 1980*. Dubuque, Iowa: Kendall/Hunt

Morgan, Gareth. 1980. 'Paradigms, Metaphors, and Puzzle Solving in Organization Theory.' *Administrative Science Quarterly* 25/4 (December): 605-22

Morgan, O.S., ed. 1933. *Agricultural Systems of Middle Europe. A Symposium*. New York: Macmillan

Morlan, Robert L. 1955. *Political Prairie Fire. The Nonpartisan League, 1915-1922*. Minneapolis: University of Minnesota Press

Mueller, D.C. 1979. *Public Choice*. Cambridge: Cambridge University Press

Nash, June, Jorge Dandler, and Nicholas S. Hopkins, eds. 1976. *Popular Participation in Social Change: Cooperatives, Collectives and Nationalized Industry*. The Hague and Paris: Mouton

National Task Force on Co-operative Development. 1984. *A Co-operative Development Strategy for Canada*. Ottawa: Co-operative Union of Canada

Nesbitt, Leonard D. n.d. *Tides in the West: A Wheat Pool Story*. Saskatoon: Modern Press

Nourse, E.G. 1957. 'The Place of the Co-operative in Our National Economy.' *American Cooperation, 1942-45*. Washington, DC: American Institute of Cooperation

Offe, Claus. 1984. '"Ungovernability": The Renaissance of Conservative Theories of Crisis.' In *Contradictions of the Welfare State: Essays by Claus Offe*, ed. John Keane, 65-88. Cambridge: MIT Press

– 1985. 'Two Logics of Collective Action.' In *Disorganized Capitalism: Contempory Transformations of Work and Politics*, ed. John Keane, 170-220. Cambridge: MIT Press

Olson, Mancur. 1971. *The Logic of Collective Action: Public Goods and the Theory of Groups*. Cambridge: Harvard University Press

Ostergaard, G.N., and A.H. Halsey. 1965. *Power in Co-operatives: A Study of Democratic Control in British Retail Societies*. Oxford: Blackwell

Palmer, Bryan. 1983. *Working-Class Experience: The Rise and Reconstitution of Canadian Labour, 1800-1980*. Toronto: Butterworths

Panitch, L. 1984. 'The Role and Nature of the Canadian State.' In *The Canadian State: Political Power and Political Economy*, ed. Panitch, 3-27. Toronto: University of Toronto Press

Parsons, R.W. 1965-7. 'The Director's Duty of Good Faith.' *Melbourne University Law Review* 5: 395

Parsons, Stanley B., et al. 1983. 'The Role of Co-operatives in the Development of the Movement Culture of Populism.' *Journal of American History* 69/4: 866-85

Pateman, C. 1970. *Participation and Democratic Theory*. Cambridge: Cambridge University Press

Pennock, J.R. 1979. *Democratic Political Theory*. Princeton: Princeton University Press

Perlin, George, ed. 1988. *Canadian Political Leadership*. Toronto: Prentice-Hall

Perrow, Charles. 1961. 'The Analysis of Goals in Complex Organizations.' *American Sociological Review* 26/6 (December): 854-966

– 1968. 'Organizational Goals.' In *International Encyclopedia of Social Science*, ed. David E. Sills, 305-11. New York: Macmillan

Pettigrew, Andrew. 1985. 'Examining Change in the Long-Term Context of Culture and Politics.' In *Organizational Strategy and Change*, ed. Johannes M. Pennings and Associates, 269-318. San Francisco: Jossey-Bass Publishers

Pfeffer, Jeffrey. 1981. *Power in Organizations*. Cambridge: Ballinger Publishing Company

Pfeffer, Jeffrey, and Gerald R. Salancik. 1978. *The External Control of Organizations: A Resource Dependence Perspective*. New York: Harper and Row

Pitkin, Hannah F. 1967. *The Concept of Representation*. Berkeley: University of California Press

Poisson, Ernest. 1925. *The Co-operative Republic*, trans. W.P. Watkins. Manchester: Co-operative Union

Polanyi, Karl. 1957. *The Great Transformation: The Political and Economic Origins of Our Time*. Boston: Beacon Press

Pollack, Norman. 1962. *The Populist Response to Industrial America: Midwestern Populist Thought*. Cambridge, Mass.: Harvard University Press

Pondy, Louis R. 1967-8. 'Organizational Conflict: Concepts and Models.' *Administrative Science Quarterly* 12: 296-320

Porter, M.E. 1980. *Competitive Strategy Techniques for Analyzing Industries and Competitors*. New York: Free Press

– 1985. *Competitive Advantage Creating and Sustaining Superior Performance*. New York: Free Press

Posner, R.A. 1974. 'Theories of Economic Regulation.' *Bell Journal of Economics and Management Science* 5 (Autumn): 213-36

Postman, Neil. 1986. *Amusing Ourselves to Death: Public Discourse in the Age of Show Business*. New York: Penguin

Pross, A.P. 1986. *Group Politics and Public Policy*. Toronto: Oxford University Press

Puhle, Hans-Jürgen. 1966. *Agrarische Interessenpolitik und preußischer Konservatismus im wilhelminischen Reich 1893-1914. Ein Beitrag zur Analyse des Nationalismus in Deutschland am Beispiel des Bundes der Landwirte und der Deutsch-Konservativen Partei*. Hanover: Verlag für Literatur und Zeitgeschehen

– 1975. *Politische Agrarbewegungen in kapitalistischen Industriegesellschaften. Deutschland, USA und Frankreich im 20. Jahrhundert*. Göttingen: Vandenhoeck and Ruprecht

Raiffeisen, Friedrich Wilhelm. 1887. *Die Darlehnskassen-Vereine*, 5th ed. Neuwied: Verlag der Raiffeisendruckerei

Ralph Nader Task Force on European Cooperatives. 1985. *Making Change? Learning from Europe's Consumer Cooperatives*. Washington, DC: Center for Study of Responsive Law

Rees, R. 1984. 'A Positive Theory of Public Enterprises.' In *The Performance of Public Enterprises: Normative, Positive and Empirical Issues*, ed. M. Marchand, P. Pestieau, and H. Tulkens, 170-92. Amsterdam: North Holland

Report of the Inquiry on Cooperative Enterprise in Europe. 1937. Washington, DC: United States Government Printing Office

Report of the Ontario Select Committee on Company Law. 1967. Toronto

Resnick, Philip. 1987. 'State and Civil Society: The Limits of a Royal Commission.' *Canadian Journal of Political Science* 20/2 (June): 379-401

Riis, Otto. 1966. 'Danish Consumer Co-operation 1866-1966.' *Review of International Co-operation* 59/3 (May): 139-42

Ross, S.A. 1973. 'The Economic Theory of Agency: The Principals Problem.' *American Economic Review* 62: 134-9

Rothschild, Joyce, and J. Allen Whitt. 1986. *The Cooperative Workplace*. Cambridge: Cambridge University Press

Rousseau, Jean-Jacques. 1974. *The Social Contract and Discourses*, ed. and trans. by G.D.H. Cole. London: J.M. Dent and Sons

Runge, Carlisle Ford. 1984. 'Institutions and the Free Rider: The Assurance Problem in Collective Action.' *The Journal of Politics* 46: 154-81

Salisbury, R.H. 1984. 'Interest Representation: The Dominance of Institutions.' *American Political Science Review* 78: 64-76

Sanger, M. 1986. *Economic Education Funded by the Private Sector*. Toronto: Ontario Institute for Studies in Education

Saskatchewan Wheat Pool. 1987. *Annual Report*. Regina

Saul, Klaus. 1974. *Staat, Industrie und Arbeiterbewegung im Kaiserreich. Zur Innen-und Außenpolitik des wilhelminischen Deutschland 1903-1914*. Düsseldorf: Bertelsman Universitätsverlag

Schermerhorn, John R., Jr. 1975. 'Determinants of Interorganizational Cooperation.' *Academy of Management Journal* 18: 846-56

Schulze-Delitzsch [Hermann von]. 1876. *Vorschuß- und Credit-Vereine als Volksbanken. Praktische Anweisung zu deren Einrichtung und Gründung*, 5th ed. Leipzig

Sethi, S. Prakash. 1979. 'Institutional/Image Advertising and Idea/Issue Advertising as Marketing Tools: Some Public Policy Issues.' *Journal of Marketing* 43 (January): 68-78

Sexton, R.J. 1986. 'The Formation of Cooperatives: A Game Theoretic Approach with Implications for Cooperative Finance, Decision Making and Stability.' *American Journal of Agricultural Economics* 68: 214-25

Sexton, R.J., and T.A. Sexton. 1987. 'Co-operatives as Entrants.' *Rand Journal of Economics* 18 (Winter): 581-95

Shaviro, Sol. 1982. 'A Critique of Consumer Cooperation: "Cheap Cheese" or the Heavenly Kingdom as the Issue that Divides Practical Cooperators from Utopians.' *American Journal of Economics and Sociology* 41/1 (January): 29-42

Sheehan, James J. 1982. *German Liberalism in the Nineteenth Century*. London: Methuen

Skogstad, G. 1987. *The Politics of Agricultural Policy Making in Canada*. Toronto: University of Toronto Press

Slavin, R. 1986. 'Learning Together.' *American Educator* 10/2 (Summer): 6-13

Smith-Gordon, Lionel, and Cruise O'Brien. 1919. *Co-operation in Denmark*. Manchester: Co-operative Union

Smith-Gordon, Lionel, and L.C. Staples. 1919. *Rural Reconstruction in Ireland. A Record of Co-operative Organization*. New Haven: Yale University Press

Society for Co-operative Studies. 1979. *Society for Co-operative Studies Bulletin: Politics and the Co-operative Movement*. April

Staatz, J.M. 1983. 'The Cooperative as a Coalition: A Game-Theoretic Approach.' *American Journal of Agricultural Economics* 65: 1084-9

– 1987. 'Recent Developments in the Theory of Agricultural Cooperation.' *Journal of Agricultural Cooperation* 2: 74-95

Stanbury, R. 1986. *Business-Government Relations in Canada*. Toronto: Methuen

Stedman Jones, Gareth. 1984. *Outcast London: A Study in the Relationship between Classes in Victorian Society*, rev. Peregrine ed. with new preface. Harmondsworth: Penguin

Steiner, George A. 1969. *Top Management Planning*. New York: Macmillan

Stevenson, G. 1982. *Unfilled Union: Canadian Federalism and National Unity*, rev. ed. Toronto: Gage

Stigler, G.J. 1971. 'The Theory of Economic Regulation.' *Bell Journal of Economics and Management Science* 2 (Spring): 3-21

Still, J.W. 1977. 'Voter Equality in Electoral Systems.' Doctoral diss., Department of Political Science, Yale University

Sullivan, J.M. 1983. *Co-operation in Canada 1983*. Ottawa: Agriculture Canada, Co-operative Section, Marketing and Economics Branch

Sweeney, D.J. 1972. 'Marketing: Technology or Social Process?' *Journal of Marketing* 36 (October): 3-10

Takas, Andrew. 1974. 'Societal Marketing: A Businessman's Perspective.' *Journal of Marketing* 38: 2-7

Taylor, Bernard. 1984. 'Strategic Planning – Which Style Do You Need?' *Long Range Planning* 17/3 (June): 51-62

Taylor, Charles. 1985. 'Legitimation, Identity and Alienation in Late Twentieth Century Canada.' In *Constitutionalism, Citizenship and Society in Canada* (Volume 33, Research Studies for the Royal Commission on the Economic Union and Development Prospects for Canada), ed. Alan Cairns and Cynthia Williams, 185-229. Toronto: University of Toronto Press

Taylor, R.A. 1971. 'The Taxation of Cooperatives: Some Economic Implications.' *Canadian Journal of Agricultural Economics* 19: 13-23

Thompson, J.C., and H.B. Jones, Jr. 1980-1. 'Economic Appraisal of Co-operative Enterprise in the United States: Principles and Issues.' *Agricultural Administration* 8: 385-400

Thompson, James D. 1967. *Organizations in Action*. New York: McGraw-Hill

Thorburn, Hugh T. 1985. *Interest Groups in the Canadian Federal System*. Volume 69, Special Research Studies for the Royal Commission on the Economic Union and Development Prospects for Canada. Toronto: University of Toronto Press

Torgerson, Randall R. 1980. 'The Changing Nature of Economic Power and Cooperatives.' *Farmer Co-operatives,* August: 2

Tracy, Michael. 1982. *Agriculture in Western Europe. Challenge and Response 1880-1980*, 2nd ed. London: Jonathan Cape

Trist, Eric. 1974. 'Action Research and Adaptive Planning.' Keynote address to the twenty-first anniversary conference of the School of Community and Regional Planning, University of British Columbia

Tucker, D.S. 1922. *The Evolution of People's Banks*. New York and London: Columbia University

Tucker, Robert C., ed. 1978. *The Marx-Engels Reader*, 2nd ed. New York: W.W. Norton and Company

Turner, H. Haines. 1941. *Case Studies of Consumers' Cooperatives: Successful Cooperatives Started by Finnish Groups in the United States Studied in Relation to Their Social and Economic Environment*, reprinted 1968. New York: AMS Press

Vanek, Jan. 1972. *The Economics of Workers' Management*. London: George Allen and Unwin

Vanek, Jaroslav. 1968. *Industrial Democracy: The Sociology of Participation*. London: Constable

– 1970. *The General Theory of Labor-Management*. Ithaca: Cornell University Press

– 1977. *The Labor-Managed Economy*. Ithaca: Cornell University Press

Viénney, Claude. 1980. *Socio-économie des organisations coopératives*, 2 vols. Paris: Coopérative d'Information et d'Édition Mutualiste (CIEM)

Warren, Roland L. 1967-8. 'The Interorganizational Field as a Focus for Investigation.' *Administrative Science Quarterly* 12: 396-419

Watkins, W.P. 1986. *Co-operative Principles Today and Tomorrow*. Manchester: Holyoake Books / Co-operative Union

Webb, Sidney, and Beatrice Webb. 1921. *The Consumers' Co-operative Movement*. London and New York: Longmans, Green and Company

Weiner, J.L. 1964. 'The Berle-Dodd Dialogue on the Concept of the Corporation.' *Columbia Law Review* 64: 1459-67

Weisbrod, Burton A. 1977. *The Voluntary Non-profit Sector*. Lexington: Lexington Books

West, Trevor. 1986. *Horace Plunkett: Co-operation and Politics, an Irish Biography*. Gerrards Cross, Bucks.: Colin Smythe

Wetzel, Kurt W., and Daniel G. Gallagher. 1987. 'A Conceptual Analysis of Labour Relations in Co-operatives.' *Economic and Industrial Democracy* 8: 517-40

Whitaker, Reginald. 1977. 'Images of the State in Canada.' In *The Canadian State: Political Economy and Political Power*, ed. Leo Panitch, 28-68. Toronto: University of Toronto Press

Wilson, B. 1987. 'Snapshot of the Family.' In 'Special Report: Farm Voices.' *The Western Producer*, 29 January

Winkler, Heinrich August. 1972. *Mittelstand, Demokratie und Nationalsozialismus: Die politische Entwicklung von Handwerk und Kleinhandel in der Weimarer Republik*. Cologne: Kiepenheuer and Witsch

Witte, John F. 1980. *Democracy, Authority, and Alienation in Work*. Chicago: University of Chicago Press

Wolfe, Alan. 1986. 'Inauthentic Democracy: A Critique of Public Life in Modern Liberal Society.' *Studies in Political Economy* 21 (Autumn): 57-81

Wolff, Henry S. 1910. *People's Banks*, 3rd ed. London: P.S. King

Wood, Louis Aubrey. 1924. *A History of Farmers' Movements in Canada: The Origins and Development of Agrarian Protest 1872-1924*, reprinted 1975. Toronto: University of Toronto Press

Woolf, Leonard, ed. 1923. *Fabian Essays on Co-operation*. London: Fabian Society

Zeldin, Theodore. 1979. *France 1848-1945*. Oxford: Oxford University Press

Zusman, Pinhas. 1982. 'Group Choice in an Agricultural Marketing Co-operative.' *Canadian Journal of Economics* 15: 220-34

Contributors

Lars Apland is Research Associate/Consultant with the Canadian Co-operative Association, and was formerly a research officer with the Centre for the Study of Co-operatives (1985-8). His interests include the application of political theory to co-operatives and the role played by health care co-operatives in providing health care services. He has co-ordinated a number of research projects, including surveys of the members and directors of Saskatchewan co-operatives, and the compilation of statistics on co-operatives across Canada.

Christopher S. Axworthy has published widely in the areas of contract, business association, consumer, commercial, and co-operative law, and about co-operatives and worker co-operatives generally. He has been a professor at the universities of New Brunswick, Dalhousie, and Saskatchewan, and was the first director of the Centre for the Study of Co-operatives. Since 1988 he has been the Member of Parliament for Saskatoon–Clark's Crossing.

Brett Fairbairn is a historian and a member of the Centre for the Study of Co-operatives at the University of Saskatchewan. His interests include the history of co-operatives and of populist, agrarian, and democratic reform movements in Germany, Canada, and elsewhere. He is the author of *Building a Dream: The Co-operative Retailing System in Western Canada, 1928-1988* (Western Producer Prairie Books, 1989).

Murray Fulton is an Associate Professor in the Department of Agricultural Economics and is a member of the Centre for the Study of Co-operatives at the

344 Contributors

University of Saskatchewan. His interests include the economics of co-operatives, agricultural policy, and industrial organization. Murray is a co-author of a study for the Economic Council of Canada entitled *Canadian Agricultural Policy and Prairie Agriculture* (Minister of Supply and Services, 1989).

Lou Hammond Ketilson is an Assistant Professor of Management and Marketing in the College of Commerce, and a member of the Centre for the Study of Co-operatives, University of Saskatchewan. Her research interests include effectiveness evaluation within systems of organizations, organizational decision-making, development of business strategy, and the practice of management in democratically structured organizations. She is author of *Enhancing the Service Potential of Preventive Health Care Organizations: A Marketing Audit Approach* (Health and Welfare Canada, 1987).

K.J. (Skip) Kutz is a faculty member in the Saskatchewan Urban Native Teacher Education Program at the University of Saskatchewan, and was formerly the Director of Programs, Co-operative College of Canada. He was a founding member and president of the Co-operative Housing Association of Saskatchewan, and a member of the Member Relations Committee of the Saskatoon Co-operative Association. He is currently doing research on the privatization of post-secondary education in Saskatchewan.

David Laycock is Assistant Professor and Canada Research Fellow, Department of Political Science, Simon Fraser University and was a former Research Associate with the Centre for the Studies of Co-operatives (1985-9). His research areas include Canadian political ideas, democratic theory, worker co-operatives and the politics of business-government relations in Canada. He is the author of *Co-operative–Government Relations in Canada* (Centre for the Study of Co-operatives, 1987), *Populism and Democratic Thought in the Canadian Prairies, 1910 to 1945* (University of Toronto Press, 1990), and 'Representative Economic Democracy and the Problem of Policy Influence: The Case of Canadian Co-operatives' (*Canadian Journal of Political Science*, 22:4 [December 1989]).

The Centre for the Study of Co-operatives at the University of Saskatchewan was established in 1982 through an agreement between the Saskatchewan co-operative sector (represented by Saskatchewan Wheat Pool, Federated Co-operatives Limited, Credit Union Central, and the Co-operative College of Canada), the provincial Department of Co-operatives and Co-operative

Development, and the University of Saskatchewan. The centre came into being as a result of a recognition by the signatories that it would be beneficial to have the academic community focus on contemporary issues facing co-operatives. The specific objectives of the centre include the establishment of a program of study in co-operatives at the undergraduate and graduate level, the undertaking of research of interest and relevance to co-operatives and credit unions, and the publication and dissemination of the results of this research. For further information, please write: Centre for the Study of Co-operatives, University of Saskatchewan, Saskatoon, Canada S7N 0W0.